Bloomsbury Keys
Quotations

Edited by

Fran Alexander

BLOOMSBURY

First published by Bloomsbury Publishing Limited,
2 Soho Square, London W1V 5DE.
Copyright © 1994 by Bloomsbury Publishing Limited.

British Library Cataloguing in Publication Data. A CIP
record for this book is available from the British Library
ISBN 0 7475 1884 X

Compiled and prepared for typesetting by
Market House Books Ltd, Aylesbury.

Printed in Great Britain by
HarperCollins Manufacturing, Glasgow.

Introduction

This book is a collection of over 4500 quotations selected for their succinctness, aptness and wit. The quotations have been classified into about 600 thematic headings. These are major topics, such as LIFE, DEATH, LOVE, WAR, etc. The themes are arranged in alphabetical order.

Under each thematic heading, the quotations are listed in alphabetical order by author. The source of the quotations is given, together with any explanatory note that may be required.

The thematic arrangement is ideal for seeking an apt quotation about a particular topic. It also produces an interesting and amusing collection through which to browse.

In addition, the book can be used to locate known or half-remembered quotations. There are two indexes. There is an index based on *key words* in the quotations, directing the user to the theme under which the quotation appears. The numbers in the index are the quotation numbers, which indicate where the quotation appears within a theme. There is also a *name index* that provides references to quotations by given authors. Again the reference is to the theme and the quotation number.

F.A., 1994

Contents

A

ABSENCE

Out of sight, out of mind.
Proverb

Absence makes the heart grow fonder,
Isle of Beauty, Fare thee well!
Thomas Haynes Bayly: Isle of Beauty

Absence is to love what wind is to fire; it extinguishes the small, it inflames the great.
Bussy-Rabutin: Histoire amoureuse des Gaules

We seek him here, we seek him there,
Those Frenchies seek him everywhere.
Is he in heaven? – Is he in hell?
That damned elusive Pimpernel?
Baroness Orczy: The Scarlet Pimpernel, Ch. 12

ABSTINENCE

See also alcohol, sex, smoking

Teetallers lack the sympathy and generosity of men that drink.
W. H. Davies: Shorter Lyrics of the 20th Century, Introduction

If you resolve to give up smoking, drinking and loving, you don't actually live longer; it just seems longer.
Clement Freud: The Observer, 27 Dec 1964

Mr Mercaptan went on to preach a brilliant sermon on that melancholy sexual perversion known as continence.
Aldous Huxley: Antic Hay, Ch. 18

4 My experience through life has convinced me that, while moderation and temperance in all things are commendable and beneficial, abstinence from spirituous liquors is the best safeguard of morals and health.
Robert E. Lee: Letter, 9 Dec 1869

5 The people who are regarded as moral luminaries are those who forego ordinary pleasures themselves and find compensation in interfering with the pleasures of others.
Bertrand Russell: Sceptical Essays

ACCIDENTS

See also chance, misfortune

1 ACCIDENT n. An inevitable occurrence due to the action of immutable natural laws.
Ambrose Bierce: The Devil's Dictionary

2 The Act of God designation on all insurance policies; which means, roughly, that you cannot be insured for the accidents that are most likely to happen to you.
Alan Coren: The Lady from Stalingrad Mansions, 'A Short History of Insurance'

3 Accidents will occur in the best-regulated families.
Charles Dickens: David Copperfield, Ch. 28

4 Here's another fine mess you've gotten me into.
Oliver Hardy: Catchphrase; said to Stan Laurel

5 O Diamond! Diamond! thou little knowest the mischief done!
Isaac Newton: Said to a dog that set fire to some papers, representing several years' work, by knocking over a candle. Wensley-Dale...a Poem (Thomas Maude)

world hath lived better than I have done, to achieve that I have done.
Thomas Malory: Morte d'Arthur, Bk. XVII, Ch. 16

8 To achieve great things we must live as though we were never going to die.
Marquis de Vauvenargues: Réflexions et maximes

ACHIEVEMENT

See also effort, success

1 Every man who is high up likes to feel that he has done it himself; and the wife smiles, and lets it go at that. It's our only joke. Every woman knows that.
J. M. Barrie: Peter Pan

2 Be not afraid of growing slowly, be afraid only of standing still.
Chinese proverb

3 Our greatest glory is not in never falling, but in rising every time we fall.
Confucius: Analects

4 One never notices what has been done; one can only see what remains to be done.
Marie Curie: Letter to her brother, 18 Mar 1894

5 We never do anything well till we cease to think about the manner of doing it.
William Hazlitt: On Prejudice

6 Well, we knocked the bastard off!
Edmund Hillary: On first climbing Mount Everest (with Tenzing Norgay), 29 May 1953. Nothing Venture, Nothing Win

7 For, as I suppose, no man in this

ACTING

See also actors, cinema, theatre

1 Theatre director: a person engaged by the management to conceal the fact that the players cannot act.
James Agate: Attrib.

2 It's not whether you really cry. It's whether the audience thinks you are crying.
Ingrid Bergman: Halliwell's Filmgoer's and Video Viewer's Companion

3 Acting is the expression of a neurotic impulse. It's a bum's life. Quitting acting, that's the sign of maturity.
Marlon Brando: Halliwell's Filmgoer's and Video Viewer's Companion

4 For the theatre one needs long arms; it is better to have them too long than too short. An *artiste* with short arms can never, never make a fine gesture.
Sarah Bernhardt: Memories of My Life, Ch. 6

5 Just know your lines and don't bump into the furniture.
Noël Coward: Attrib.

6 It is easier to get an actor to be

cowboy than to get a cowboy to be an actor.
John Ford: Attrib.

7 Blank face is fine. The computer works faster than the brain, don't forget. The art of acting is not to act. Once you show them more, what you show them, in fact, is bad acting.
Anthony Hopkins: Knave, Nov 1980

8 The art of acting consists in keeping people from coughing.
Ralph Richardson: The Observer

9 Speak the speech, I pray you, as I pronounced it to you, trippingly on the tongue; but if you mouth it, as many of your players do, I had as lief the town-crier spoke my lines.
William Shakespeare: Hamlet, III:2

ACTION

1 Easier said than done.
Proverb

2 Let's meet, and either do, or die.
Francis Beaumont: The Island Princess, II:2

3 He who desires but acts not, breeds pestilence.
William Blake: The Marriage of Heaven and Hell, 'Proverbs of Hell'

Liberty's in every blow!
Let us do or die!
Robert Burns: Scots, Wha Hae

Deliberation is the work of many men. Action, of one alone.
Charles de Gaulle: War Memoirs, Vol. 2

No action is in itself good or

bad, but only such according to convention.
W. Somerset Maugham: A Writer's Notebook

7 If to do were as easy as to know what were good to do, chapels had been churches, and poor men's cottages princes' palaces.
William Shakespeare: The Merchant of Venice, I:2

8 So many worlds, so much to do, So little done, such things to be.
Alfred, Lord Tennyson: In Memoriam A.H.H., LXXIII

ACTORS

See also cinema, plays, theatre

1 An actor's a guy who, if you ain't talking about him, ain't listening.
Marlon Brando: The Observer, 'Sayings of the Year', Jan 1956

2 An actor is something less than a man, while an actress is something more than a woman.
Richard Burton: Halliwell's Filmgoer's and Video Viewer's Companion

3 Actors should be treated like cattle.
Alfred Hitchcock: Said in clarification of a remark attributed to him, 'Actors are like cattle'. Quote, Unquote (N. Rees)

4 They didn't act like people and they didn't act like actors. It's hard to explain. They acted more like they knew they were celebrities and all. I mean they were good, but they were *too* good.
J. D. Salinger: The Catcher in the Rye, Ch. 17

ADMIRATION

ADMIRATION

See also love, praise, respect

1 Here's looking at you, kid.
Humphrey Bogart: Casablanca

2 A fool always finds a greater fool to admire him.
Nicolas Boileau: L'Art poétique, I

3 I do think better of womankind than to suppose they care whether Mister John Keats five feet high likes them or not.
John Keats: Letter to Benjamin Bailey, 18 July 1818

4 Many a man has been a wonder to the world, whose wife and valet have seen nothing in him that was even remarkable. Few men have been admired by their servants.
Michel de Montaigne: Essais, III

5 Not to admire, is all the art I know
To make men happy, and to keep them so.
Alexander Pope: Imitations of Horace, 'To Mr. Murray'

ADULTERY

See also marriage, sex

1 What men call gallantry, and gods adultery,
Is much more common where the climate's sultry.
Lord Byron: Don Juan, I

2 Sara could commit adultery at one end and weep for her sins at the other, and enjoy both operations at once.
Joyce Cary: The Horse's Mouth, Ch. 8

3 I say I don't sleep with married men, but what I mean is that I don't sleep with happily married men.
Britt Ekland: Attrib.

4 You know, of course, that the Tasmanians, who never committed adultery, are now extinct.
W. Somerset Maugham: The Bread-Winner

5 Madame, you must really be more careful. Suppose it had been someone else who found you like this.
Duc de Richelieu: Discovering his wife with her lover. The Book of Lists (D. Wallechinsky)

6 With all my heart. Whose wife shall it be?
John Horne Tooke: Replying to the suggestion that he take a wife. Attrib.

ADVERTISING

1 Any publicity is good publicity.
Proverb

2 It pays to advertise.
Anonymous: Already current by c. 1912 when Cole Porter used it as the title of an early song.

3 Advertising is the most fun you can have with your clothes on.
Jerry Della Femina: From those wonderful folks who gave you Pearl Harbor

4 Half the money I spend on advertising is wasted, and the trouble is I don't know which half.
Viscount Leverhulme: Confessions of an Advertising Man (D. Ogilvy)

5

ADVICE

1 A good scare is worth more than good advice.
Proverb

2 Advice is seldom welcome; and those who want it the most always like it the least.
Earl of Chesterfield: Letter to his son, 29 Jan 1748

3 One gives nothing so freely as advice.
Duc de la Rochefoucauld: Maximes, 110

4 Don't tell your friends their social faults, they will cure the fault and never forgive you.
Logan Pearsall Smith: Afterthoughts

5 No one wants advice – only corroboration.
John Steinbeck: Attrib.

AFTERLIFE

See also death, heaven

1 We have no reliable guarantee that the afterlife will be any less exasperating than this one, have we?
Noël Coward: Blithe Spirit, I

2 We sometimes congratulate ourselves at the moment of waking from a troubled dream; it may be so the moment after death.
Nathaniel Hawthorne: American Notebooks

3 Work and pray, live on hay, You'll get pie in the sky when you die.
Joe Hill: The Preacher and the Slave

4 My doctrine is: Live that thou mayest desire to live again – that is thy duty – for in any case thou wilt live again!
Friedrich Nietzsche: Eternal Recurrence

5 After your death you will be what you were before your birth.
Arthur Schopenhauer: Parerga and Paralipomena

6 The dread of something after death –
The undiscover'd country, from whose bourn
No traveller returns.
William Shakespeare: Hamlet, III:1

AGE

See also longevity, old age, youth

1 Never too late to learn.
Proverb

2 Years ago we discovered the exact point, the dead center of middle age. It occurs when you are too young to take up golf and too old to rush up to the net.
Franklin P. Adams: Nods and Becks

3 All evil comes from the old. They grow fat on ideas and young men die of them.
Jean Anouilh: Catch as Catch Can

4 I think your whole life shows in your face and you should be proud of that.
Lauren Bacall: Remark, Mar 1988

5 Age will not be defied.
Francis Bacon: Essays, 'Of Regiment of Health'

6 You grew old first not in your own eyes, but in other people's

eyes; then, slowly, you agreed with their opinion of you.
Julian Barnes: Staring at the Sun

7 What is an adult? A child blown up by age.
Simone de Beauvoir: La Femme rompue

8 If thou hast gathered nothing in thy youth, how canst thou find any thing in thine age?
Bible: Ecclesiasticus: 25:3

9 And all the days of Methuselah were nine hundred sixty and nine years: and he died.
Bible: Genesis: 5:27

10 Therefore I summon age
To grant youth's heritage.
Robert Browning: Rabbi ben Ezra, XIII

11 There's many a good tune played on an old fiddle.
Samuel Butler: The Way of All Flesh, Ch. 6

12 A lady of a 'certain age', which means
Certainly aged.
Lord Byron: Don Juan, VI

13 A man is as old as he's feeling,
A woman as old as she looks.
Mortimer Collins: The Unknown Quantity

14 Youth is a blunder; manhood a struggle; old age a regret.
Benjamin Disraeli: Coningsby, Bk. III, Ch. 1

15 Ah, but I was so much older then
I'm younger than that now.
Bob Dylan: My Back Pages

16 The years between fifty and seventy are the hardest. You are always being asked to do things,

and you are not yet decrepit enough to turn them down.
T. S. Eliot: Time, 23 Oct 1950

17 According to the doctors, I'm only suffering from a light form of premature baldness.
Federico Fellini: After spending four days in a clinic in Rome. Variety, 1986

18 At twenty years of age, the will reigns; at thirty, the wit; and at forty, the judgement.
Benjamin Franklin: Poor Richard's Almanack

19 A diplomat is a man who always remembers a woman's birthday but never remembers her age.
Robert Frost: Attrib.

20 Middle age is when your age starts to show around the middle.
Bob Hope

21 Whenever a man's friends begin to compliment him about looking young, he may be sure that they think he is growing old.
Washington Irving: Bracebridge Hall, 'Bachelors'

22 It is sobering to consider that when Mozart was my age he had already been dead for a year.
Tom Lehrer

23 Will you still need me, will you still feed me
When I'm sixty-four?
John Lennon: When I'm Sixty-Four (with Paul McCartney)

24 The four stages of man are infancy, childhood, adolescence and obsolescence.
Art Linkletter: A Child's Garden of Misinformation, 8

25 A man is only as old as the woman he feels.

Groucho Marx: Attrib.

26 I am old enough to be – in fact am – your mother.

A. A. Milne: Belinda

27 How soon hath Time, the subtle thief of youth,
Stolen on his wing my three-and-twentieth year!

John Milton: Sonnet: 'On Being Arrived at the Age of Twenty-three'

28 Do you think my mind is maturing late,
Or simply rotted early?

Ogden Nash: Lines on Facing Forty

29 At 50, everyone has the face he deserves.

George Orwell: Last words in his manuscript notebook, 17 Apr 1949.

30 Life Begins At Forty.

W. B. Pitkin: Book title

31 One of the pleasures of middle age is to *find out* that one WAS right, and that one was much righter than one knew at say 17 or 23.

Ezra Pound: ABC of Reading, Ch. 1

32 Inexperience is what makes a young man do what an older man says is impossible.

Herbert V. Prochnow: Satuday Evening Post, 4 Dec 1948

33 The young man who has not wept is a savage, and the old man who will not laugh is a fool.

George Santayana: Dialogues in Limbo, Ch. 3

34 Crabbed age and youth cannot live together:
Youth is full of pleasure, age is full of care;
Youth like summer morn, age like winter weather;
Youth like summer brave, age like winter bare.

William Shakespeare: The Passionate Pilgrim, XII

35 All that the young can do for the old is to shock them and keep them up to date.

George Bernard Shaw: Fanny's First Play

36 Men come of age at sixty, women at fifteen.

James Stephens: The Observer, 'Sayings of the Week', 1 Oct 1944

37 The British loathe the middle-aged and I await rediscovery at 65, when one is too old to be in anyone's way.

Roy Strong: Remark, Jan 1988

38 From birth to age eighteen, a girl needs good parents. From eighteen to thirty-five, she needs good looks. From thirty-five to fifty-five, she needs a good personality. From fifty-five on, she needs good cash.

Sophie Tucker: Attrib.

39 No woman should ever be quite accurate about her age. It looks so calculating.

Oscar Wilde: The Importance of Being Earnest, III

40 The older one grows the more one likes indecency.

Virginia Woolf: Monday or Tuesday

41 Wine comes in at the mouth
And love comes in at the eye;

That's all we shall know for
truth
Before we grow old and die.
W. B. Yeats: A Drinking Song

AGREEMENT

1 I am always of the opinion with
the learned, if they speak first.
William Congreve: Incognita

2 We seldom attribute common
sense except to those who agree
with us.
*Duc de la Rochefoucauld:
Maximes, 347*

3 Ah! don't say you agree with
me. When people agree with me
I always feel that I must be
wrong.
*Oscar Wilde: The Critic as Artist,
Pt. 2*

ALCOHOL

See also drinks, drunkenness

1 A cask of wine works more miracles than a church full of saints.
Proverb

2 There's many a slip 'twixt the
cup and the lip.
Proverb

3 First the man takes a drink,
then the drink takes a drink,
then the drink takes the man.
Proverb

4 I feel no pain, dear mother, now
But oh, I am so dry!
O take me to a brewery
And leave me there to die.
Anonymous: Shanty

5 Woe unto them that rise up early in the morning, that they may
follow strong drink; that continue until night, till wine inflame
them!
Bible: Isaiah: 5:11

6 Drink no longer water, but use a
little wine for thy stomach's sake
and thine often infirmities.
Bible: I Timothy: 5:23

7 There's nought, no doubt, so
much the spirit calms
As rum and true religion.
Lord Byron

8 So was hir joly whistle wel y-wet.
*Geoffrey Chaucer: The
Canterbury Tales, 'The Reve's
Tale'*

9 I must point out that my rule of
life prescribed as an absolutely
sacred rite smoking cigars and
also the drinking of alcohol before, after, and if need be during
all meals and in the intervals between them.
*Winston Churchill: Said during a
lunch with the Arab leader Ibn
Saud, when he heard that the
king's religion forbade smoking
and alcohol. The Second World
War*

10 Apart from cheese and tulips,
the main product of the country
is advocaat, a drink made from
lawyers.
*Alan Coren: Referring to Holland.
The Sanity Inspector, 'All You
Need to Know about Europe'*

11 Then trust me, there's nothing
like drinking
So pleasant on this side the
grave;
It keeps the unhappy from
thinking,
And makes e'en the valiant more
brave.
Charles Dibdin: Nothing like Grog

12 A good gulp of hot whisky at bedtime – it's not very scientific, but it helps.
Alexander Fleming: When asked about a cure for colds. News summary, 22 Mar 1954

13 Best while you have it use your breath,
There is no drinking after death.
John Fletcher: With Jonson and others. The Bloody Brother, II:2

14 Let schoolmasters puzzle their brain,
With grammar, and nonsense, and learning,
Good liquor, I stoutly maintain,
Gives genius a better discerning.
Oliver Goldsmith: She Stoops to Conquer, I

15 Who could have foretold, from the structure of the brain, that wine could derange its functions?
Hippocrates

16 Our country has deliberately undertaken a great social and economic experiment, noble in motive and far-reaching in purpose.
Herbert Hoover: Referring to Prohibition. Letter to W.H. Borah, 28 Feb 1928

17 Malt does more than Milton can
To justify God's ways to man.
A. E. Housman: A Shropshire Lad, 'The Welsh Marches'

18 O for a beaker full of the warm South,
Full of the true, the blushful Hippocrene,
With beaded bubbles winking at the brim,
And purple-stained mouth.
John Keats: Ode to a Nightingale

19 Even though a number of people have tried, no one has yet found a way to drink for a living.
Jean Kerr: Poor Richard

20 I'm so holy that when I touch wine, it turns into water.
Aga Khan III: Defending drinking alcohol. Who's Really Who (Compton Miller)

21 If we heard it said of Orientals that they habitually drank a liquor which went to their heads, deprived them of reason and made them vomit, we should say: 'How very barbarous!'
Jean de La Bruyère: Les Caractères

22 I've made it a rule never to drink by daylight and never to refuse a drink after dark.
H. L. Mencken: New York Post, 18 Sept 1945

23 Candy
Is dandy
But liquor
Is quicker.
Ogden Nash: Hard Lines, 'Reflection on Ice-Breaking'

24 In vino veritas.
Truth comes out in wine.
Pliny the Elder: Natural History, XIV

25 A good general rule is to state that the bouquet is better than the taste, and vice versa.
Stephen Potter: One-Upmanship, Ch. 14

26 People may say what they like about the decay of Christianity; the religious system that pro-

duced green Chartreuse can
never really die.
*Saki: Reginald on Christmas
Presents*

27 It provokes the desire, but it
takes away the performance.
Therefore much drink may be
said to be an equivocator with
lechery.
*William Shakespeare: Macbeth,
II:3*

28 MACDUFF. What three things
does drink especially provoke?
PORTER. Marry, sir, nose-
painting, sleep, and urine.
*William Shakespeare: Macbeth,
II:3*

29 Alcohol is a very necessary article…It enables Parliament to
do things at eleven at night that
no sane person would do at
eleven in the morning.
*George Bernard Shaw: Major
Barbara, II*

30 Well, then, my stomach must
just digest in its waistcoat.
*Richard Brinsley Sheridan: On
being warned that his drinking
would destroy the coat of his
stomach. The Fine Art of Political
Wit (L. Harris)*

31 Fifteen men on the dead man's
chest
Yo-ho-ho, and a bottle of rum!
Drink and the devil had done for
the rest –
Yo-ho-ho, and a bottle of rum!
*Robert Louis Stevenson: Treasure
Island, Ch. 1*

32 An alcoholic is someone you
don't like who drinks as much as
you do.
Dylan Thomas: Attrib.

33 I hadn't the heart to touch my

breakfast. I told Jeeves to drink
it himself.
P. G. Wodehouse: My Man Jeeves

34 I must get out of these wet
clothes and into a dry Martini.
*Alexander Woollcott: Reader's
Digest*

AMBITION

See also desire

1 He who rides a tiger is afraid to
dismount.
Proverb

2 Per ardua ad astra.
Through endeavour to the stars.
*Anonymous: motto of the Royal
Air Force.*

3 Ah, but a man's reach should
exceed his grasp,
Or what's a heaven for?
*Robert Browning: Andrea del
Sarto*

4 You seem to have no real purpose in life and won't realize at
the age of twenty-two that for a
man life means work, and hard
work if you mean to succeed.
*Jennie Jerome Churchill: Letter to
her son Winston Churchill, 26 Feb
1897. Jennie (Ralph G. Martin),
Vol. II*

5 If thy heart fails thee, climb not
at all.
*Elizabeth I: Written on a window
in reply to Walter RALEIGH's line.
Worthies of England (Fuller),
Vol. I*

6 Hitch your wagon to a star.
*Ralph Waldo Emerson: Society
and Solitude, 'Civilization'*

7 With a suitcase full of clothes
and underwear in my hand and
an indomitable will in my heart,

I set out for Vienna…I too hope to become 'something'.
Adolf Hitler: Mein Kampf

8 I am going to build the kind of nation that President Roosevelt hoped for, President Truman worked for and President Kennedy died for.
Lyndon B. Johnson: The Sunday Times, 27 Dec 1964

9 If you would hit the mark, you must aim a little above it;
Every arrow that flies feels the attraction of earth.
Henry Wadsworth Longfellow: Elegiac Verse

10 Ambition is the grand enemy of all peace.
John Cowper Powys: The Meaning of Culture

11 Fain would I climb, yet fear I to fall.
Walter Raleigh: Written on a window pane. For the reply see ELIZABETH I. Attrib.

12 Ambition should be made of sterner stuff.
William Shakespeare: Julius Caesar, III:2

13 I have no spur
To prick the sides of my intent, but only
Vaulting ambition, which o'er-leaps itself,
And falls on th' other.
William Shakespeare: Macbeth, I:7

14 And he that strives to touch the stars,
Oft stumbles at a straw.
Edmund Spenser: The Shepherd's Calendar, 'July'

15 There is always room at the top.
Daniel Webster: When advised not to become a lawyer because the profession was overcrowded. Attrib.

ANGER

1 The man who gets angry at the right things and with the right people, and in the right way and at the right time and for the right length of time, is commended.
Aristotle: Nicomachean Ethics, Bk. IV

2 When they heard these things, they were cut to the heart, and they gnashed on him with their teeth.
Bible: Acts: 7:54

3 Never go to bed mad. Stay up and fight.
Phyllis Diller: Phyllis Diller's Housekeeping Hints

4 Anger is one of the sinews of the soul.
Thomas Fuller: The Holy State and the Profane State

5 Spleen can subsist on any kind of food.
William Hazlitt: On Wit and Humour

6 Anger supplies the arms.
Virgil: Aeneid, Bk. I

ANIMALS

See also cats, dogs, horses

1 There was a young lady of Riga,
Who went for a ride on a tiger;
They returned from the ride
With the lady inside,
And a smile on the face of the tiger.
Anonymous

2 The fox knows many things – the hedgehog one *big* one.
Archilochus: Attrib.

3 And God said, Let the earth bring forth the living creature after his kind, cattle, and creeping thing, and beast of the earth after his kind: and it was so.
Bible: Genesis: 1:24

4 Tiger! Tiger! burning bright
In the forests of the night,
What immortal hand or eye
Could frame thy fearful symmetry?
William Blake: Songs of Experience, 'The Tiger'

5 Rats!
They fought the dogs and killed the cats,
And bit the babies in the cradles.
Robert Browning: The Pied Piper of Hamelin

6 Wee, sleekit, cow'rin', tim'rous beastie,
O what a panic's in thy breastie!
Robert Burns: To a Mouse

7 Whenever you observe an animal closely, you feel as if a human being sitting inside were making fun of you.
Elias Canetti: The Human Province

8 The devil's walking parody
On all four-footed things.
G. K. Chesterton: The Donkey

9 Animals are such agreeable friends – they ask no questions, they pass no criticisms.
George Eliot: Scenes of Clerical Life, 'Mr Gilfil's Love Story', Ch. 7

10 Dogs, like horses, are quadrupeds. That is to say, they have four rupeds, one at each corner, on which they walk.
Frank Muir: You Can't Have Your Kayak and Heat It (Frank Muir and Denis Norden), 'Ta-ra-ra-boom-de-ay!'

11 The cow is of the bovine ilk;
One end is moo, the other, milk.
Ogden Nash: The Cow

12 There are two things for which animals are to be envied: they know nothing of future evils, or of what people say about them.
Voltaire: Letter, 1739

13 Let dogs delight to bark and bite,
For God hath made them so;
Let bears and lions growl and fight,
For 'tis their nature too.
Isaac Watts: Divine Songs for Children, 'Against Quarrelling'

APOLOGIES

See also regret

1 Very sorry can't come. Lie follows by post.
Charles Beresford: Reply, by telegram, to a dinner invitation issued at short notice by Edward, Prince of Wales. The World of Fashion 1837–1922 (R. Nevill), Ch. 5

2 Love means never having to say you're sorry.
Erich Segal: Love Story

3 When a man holds you round the throat, I don't think he has come to apologise.
Ayrton Senna: Referring to Nigel Mansell after a collision in the 1987 Belgian Grand Prix

4 Mr. Speaker, I said the honor-

able member was a liar it is true and I am sorry for it. The honourable member may place the punctuation where he pleases.

Richard Brinsley Sheridan: On being asked to apologize for calling a fellow MP a liar. Attrib.

It is a good rule in life never to apologize. The right sort of people do not want apologies, and the wrong sort take a mean advantage of them.

P. G. Wodehouse: The Man Upstairs and Other Stories

APPEARANCE

See also beauty, clothes, cosmetics

Fine feathers make fine birds.
Proverb

A homely face and no figure have aided many women heavenward.
Minna Antrim: Naked Truth and Veiled Allusions

She never had the looks to lose so she never lost them.
Angela Carter: Wise Children

Mirrors should think longer before they reflect.
Jean Cocteau: The Sunday Times, 20 Oct 1963

It's nothing to be born ugly. Sensibly, the ugly woman comes to terms with her ugliness and exploits it as a grace of nature.
Colette: Journey for Myself

I am so changed that my oldest creditors would hardly know me.
Henry Stephen Fox: Remark after an illness. Letter from Byron to John Murray, 8 May 1817

There is a great difference between painting a face and not washing it.
Thomas Fuller: Church History, Bk. VII

8 We tolerate shapes in human beings that would horrify us if we saw them in a horse.
Dean Inge: Attrib.

9 That white horse you see in the park could be a zebra synchronized with the railings.
Ann Jellicoe: The Knack, III

10 The Lord prefers common-looking people. That is why he makes so many of them.
Abraham Lincoln: Our President (James Morgan), Ch. 6

11 I eat like a vulture. Unfortunately the resemblance doesn't end there.
Groucho Marx: Attrib.

12 All I say is, nobody has any business to go around looking like a horse and behaving as if it were all right. You don't catch horses going around looking like people, do you?
Dorothy Parker: Horsie

13 Had Cleopatra's nose been shorter, the whole face of the world would have changed.
Blaise Pascal: Pensées, II

14 Your face, my thane, is as a book where men
May read strange matters. To beguile the time,
Look like the time; bear welcome in your eye,
Your hand, your tongue: look like the innocent flower,
But be the serpent under't.
William Shakespeare: Macbeth, I:5

15 Why not be oneself? That is the

whole secret of a successful appearance. If one is a greyhound why try to look like a Pekinese?
Edith Sitwell: Why I Look As I Do

16 Grief has turned her hair.
Oscar Wilde: Referring to the fact that a recently bereaved lady friend had dyed her hair blonde. Attrib.

APPEARANCES

See also deception, hypocrisy

1 All that glitters is not gold.
Proverb

2 Appearances are deceptive.
Proverb

3 Never judge from appearances.
Proverb

4 Things are not always what they seem.
Proverb

5 You can't tell a book by its cover.
Proverb

6 The lamb that belonged to the sheep whose skin the wolf was wearing began to follow the wolf in the sheep's clothing.
Aesop: Fables, 'The Wolf in Sheep's Clothing'

7 No-wher so bisy a man as he ther nas,
And yet he semed bisier than he was.
Geoffrey Chaucer: Referring to the lawyer. The Canterbury Tales, Prologue

8 Keep up appearances; there lies the test
The world will give thee credit for the rest.
Charles Churchill: Night

9 Appearances are not held to be

a clue to the truth. But we seem to have no other.
Ivy Compton-Burnett: Manservant and Maidservant

10 Mirrors are the windows of the devil, overlooking nothing but a landscape of lies!
Leon Garfield: The Prisoners of September, Ch. 2

11 Strip the phoney tinsel off Hollywood and you'll find the real tinsel underneath.
Oscar Levant: Attrib.

12 Ugliness is a point of view: an ulcer is wonderful to a pathologist.
Austin O'Malley

13 Things are entirely what they appear to be and *behind them*… there is nothing.
Jean-Paul Sartre: Nausea

14 Through tatter'd clothes small vices do appear;
Robes and furr'd gowns hide all.
William Shakespeare: King Lear, IV:6

15 And thus I clothe my naked villany
With odd old ends stol'n forth of holy writ,
And seem a saint when most I play the devil.
William Shakespeare: Richard III, I:3

16 So may the outward shows be least themselves:
The world is still deceived with ornament.
William Shakespeare: The Merchant of Venice, III:2

17 It is only shallow people who do not judge by appearances.
Oscar Wilde: The Picture of Dorian Gray, Ch. 2

ARCHITECTURE

See also houses, stately homes

1 Sir Christopher Wren
Said, 'I am going to dine with
some men.
If anybody calls
Say I am designing St Paul's.'
*Edmund Clerihew Bentley:
Biography for Beginners*

2 Like a carbuncle on the face of
an old and valued friend.
*Charles, Prince of Wales: Referring
to a proposed modern extension to
the National Gallery. Speech,
1986*

3 A modern, harmonic and lively
architecture is the visible sign of
an authentic democracy.
*Walter Gropius: The Observer,
'Sayings of the Week', 8 Dec 1968*

4 Sculpture to me is like poetry,
and architecture like prose.
*Maya Lin: The Observer,
'Sayings of the Week', 14 May
1994*

5 When you think of some of the
high flats around us, it can hardly be an accident that they are as
near as one can get to an archi-
tectural representation of a filing
cabinet.
*Jimmy Reid: In his address as new
Rector of Glasgow University. The
Observer, 'Sayings of the Week',
30 Apr 1972*

6 No person who is not a great
sculptor or painter can be an architect. If he is not a sculptor or
painter, he can only be a *builder.*
*John Ruskin: Lectures on
Architecture and Painting*

7 Architecture in general is frozen
music.
*Friedrich von Schelling:
Philosophie der Kunst*

8 When we mean to build,
We first survey the plot, then
draw the model.
*William Shakespeare: Henry IV,
Part Two, I:3*

9 How simple-minded of the Germans to imagine that we British
could be cowed by the destruction of our ancient monuments!
As though any havoc of the German bombs could possibly equal
the things we have done ourselves!
*Osbert Sitwell: The Collected
Essays, Journalism and Letters of
George Orwell, Vol. III*

10 Architecture has its political
use; publick buildings being the
ornament of a country; it estab-
lishes a nation, draws people
and commerce; makes the people love their native country,
which passion is the original of
all great actions in a common-
wealth.
Christopher Wren: Parentalia

ARGUMENTS

1 It takes two to make a quarrel.
Proverb

2 There is only one way under
high heaven to get the best of an
argument – and that is to avoid
it.
*Dale Carnegie: Dale Carnegie's
Scrapbook*

3 It takes in reality only one to
make a quarrel. It is useless for
the sheep to pass resolutions in
favour of vegetarianism while

the wolf remains of a different opinion.
Dean Inge: Outspoken Essays

4 Though a quarrel in the streets is a thing to be hated, the energies displayed in it are fine; the commonest man shows a grace in his quarrel.
John Keats: Letter

5 Quarrels would not last so long if the fault were on only one side.
Duc de la Rochefoucauld: Maximes, 496

6 The most savage controversies are those about matters as to which there is no good evidence either way.
Bertrand Russell: Unpopular Essays

ARISTOCRACY

See also class, nobility, stately homes

1 One has often wondered whether upon the whole earth there is anything so unintelligent, so unapt to perceive how the world is really going, as an ordinary young Englishman of our upper class.
Matthew Arnold: Culture and Anarchy, Ch. 2

2 Like many of the upper class He liked the sound of broken glass.
Hilaire Belloc: New Cautionary Tales, 'About John'

3 The nobility of England, my lord, would have snored through the Sermon on the Mount.
Robert Bolt: A Man for All Seasons

4 Democracy means government by the uneducated, while aristocracy means government by the badly educated.
G. K. Chesterton: New York Times, 1 Feb 1931

5 If human beings could be propagated by cutting, like apple trees, aristocracy would be biologically sound.
J. B. S. Haldane: The Inequality of Man, title essay

6 There are no credentials. They do not even need a medical certificate. They need not be sound either in body or mind. They only require a certificate of birth – just to prove that they are first of the litter. You would not choose a spaniel on these principles.
David Lloyd George: Budget Speech, 1909

7 An aristocracy in a republic is like a chicken whose head has been cut off: it may run about in a lively way, but in fact it is dead.
Nancy Mitford: Noblesse Oblige

8 He is without strict doubt a Hoorah Henry, and he is generally figured as nothing but a lob as far as doing anything useful in this world is concerned.
Damon Runyon: Short Takes, 'Tight Shoes'

9 Kind hearts are more than coronets,
And simple faith than Norman blood.
Alfred, Lord Tennyson: Lady Clara Vere de Vere, VI

10 Unlike the male codfish which, suddenly finding itself the parent of three million five hundred

thousand little codfish, cheerfully resolves to love them all, the British aristocracy is apt to look with a somewhat jaundiced eye on its younger sons.

P. G. Wodehouse: Wodehouse at Work to the End (Richard Usborne), Ch. 5

ARMY

See also officers, soldiers, war

1 An army is a nation within a nation; it is one of the vices of our age.

Alfred de Vigny: Servitude et grandeur militaire, 1

2 I have got an infamous army, very weak and ill-equipped, and a very inexperienced staff.

Duke of Wellington: Written at the beginning of the Waterloo campaign. Letter to Lord Stewart, 8 May 1815

3 The army ages men sooner than the law and philosophy; it exposes them more freely to germs, which undermine and destroy, and it shelters them more completely from thought, which stimulates and preserves.

H. G. Wells: Bealby, Pt. VIII, Ch. 1

ARROGANCE

See also conceit, egotism, pride

1 The need to be right – the sign of a vulgar mind.

Albert Camus: Notebooks, 1935–42

2 He was like a cock who thought the sun had risen to hear him crow.

George Eliot: Adam Bede

3 Well, not bad, but there are decidedly too many of them, and they are not very well arranged. I would have done it differently.

James Whistler: His reply when asked if he agreed that the stars were especially beautiful one night. Attrib.

4 All men think all men mortal, but themselves.

Edward Young: Night Thoughts

ART

See also painting

1 The object of art is to give life a shape.

Jean Anouilh: The Rehearsal

2 The lower one's vitality, the more sensitive one is to great art.

Max Beerbohm: Seven Men, 'Enoch Soames'

3 Art is the only thing that can go on mattering once it has stopped hurting.

Elizabeth Bowen: The Heat of the Day, Ch. 16

4 Art is not a pastime, but a priesthood.

Jean Cocteau: New York Times

5 Art for art's sake.

Victor Cousin: Lecture, Sorbonne, 1818

6 Art is vice, you don't marry it legitimately, you ravish it!

Edgar Degas: Degas by himself (ed. R. Kendall)

7 Art is a jealous mistress.

Ralph Waldo Emerson: Conduct of Life, 'Wealth'

8 Art has to move you and design

does not, unless it's a good design for a bus.
David Hockney: Remark, Oct 1988

9 In free society art is not a weapon…Artists are not engineers of the soul.
John Fitzgerald Kennedy: Address at Dedication of the Robert Frost Library, 26 Oct 1963

10 But the Devil whoops, as he whooped of old:
'It's clever, but is it art?'
Rudyard Kipling: The Conundrum of the Workshops

11 You're not meant to understand – they're bloody works of art.
Sonia Lawson: The Observer, 6 June 1993

12 In England, pop art and fine art stand resolutely back to back.
Colin MacInnes: England, Half English, 'Pop Songs and Teenagers'

13 Art is not a mirror to reflect the world, but a hammer with which to shape it.
Vladimir Mayakovsky: The Guardian, 11 Dec 1974

14 All art deals with the absurd and aims at the simple. Good art speaks truth, indeed is truth, perhaps the only truth.
Iris Murdoch: The Black Prince, 'Bradley Pearson's Foreword'

15 When I was their age, I could draw like Raphael, but it took me a lifetime to learn to draw like them.

Pablo Picasso: Visiting an exhibition of drawings by children.
Picasso: His Life and Work (Ronald Penrose)

16 Life without industry is guilt, and industry without art is brutality.
John Ruskin: Lectures on Art, 3, 'The Relation of Art to Morals', 23 Feb 1870

17 Skill without imagination is craftsmanship and gives us many useful objects such as wickerwork picnic baskets. Imagination without skill gives us modern art.
Tom Stoppard: Artist Descending a Staircase

18 What a delightful thing this perspective is!
Paolo Uccello: Men of Art (T. Craven)

19 Any authentic work of art must start an argument between the artist and his audience.
Rebecca West: The Court and the Castle, Pt. I, Ch. 1

20 Art is the imposing of a pattern on experience, and our aesthetic enjoyment is recognition of the pattern.
A. N. Whitehead: Dialogues, 228

21 All Art is quite useless.
Oscar Wilde: The Picture of Dorian Gray, Preface

ARTISTS

See also painting, poets

1 Poets and painters are outside the class system, or rather they constitute a special class of their own, like the circus people and the gipsies.

Gerald Brenan: Thoughts in a Dry Season, 'Writing'

2 Beware of the artist who's an intellectual also. The artist who doesn't fit.
F. Scott Fitzgerald: This Side of Paradise, Bk. II, Ch. 5

3 An amateur is an artist who supports himself with outside jobs which enable him to paint. A professional is someone whose wife works to enable him to paint.
Ben Shahn: Attrib.

4 What is an artist? For every thousand people there's nine hundred doing the work, ninety doing well, nine doing good, and one lucky bastard who's the artist.
Tom Stoppard: Travesties, I

5 An artist is someone who produces things that people don't need to have but that he – for *some* reason – thinks it would be a good idea to give them.
Andy Warhol: From A to B and Back Again, 'Atmosphere'

ASSASSINATION

See also killing, murder

1 Assassination has never changed the history of the world.
Benjamin Disraeli: Speech, House of Commons, 1 May 1865

2 My fellow citizens, the President is dead, but the Government lives and God Omnipotent reigns.
James A. Garfield: Speech following the assassination of Lincoln.

3 Will no one rid me of this turbulent priest?
Henry II: Referring to Thomas Becket, Archbishop of Canterbury; four of Henry's household knights took these words literally, hurried to Canterbury, and killed Becket in the cathedral (Dec 1170). Attrib.

4 A piece of each of us died at that moment.
Michael J. Mansfield: Referring to the assassination (22 Nov 1963) of President Kennedy. Speech, Senate, 24 Nov 1963

5 Assassination is the extreme form of censorship.
George Bernard Shaw: The Shewing-Up of Blanco Posnet, 'The Limits of Toleration'

ATHEISM

See also God, religion

1 An atheist is one point beyond the devil.
Proverb

2 God never wrought miracle to convince atheism, because his ordinary works convince it.
Francis Bacon: Essays, 'Of Atheism'

3 Wandering in a vast forest at night, I have only a faint light to guide me. A stranger appears and says to me: 'My friend, you should blow out your candle in order to find your way more clearly.' This stranger is a theologian.
Denis Diderot: Addition aux pensées philosophiques

4 An atheist is a man who has no invisible means of support.
Harry Emerson Fosdick: Attrib.

5 He was an embittered atheist (the sort of atheist who does not so much disbelieve in God as personally dislike Him).
George Orwell: Down and Out in Paris and London, Ch. 30

6 It has been said that the highest praise of God consists in the denial of Him by the atheist, who finds creation so perfect that he can dispense with a creator.
Marcel Proust: A la recherche du temps perdu: Le Côté de Guermantes

7 By night an atheist half believes a God.
Edward Young: Night Thoughts

AUTHORITARIANISM

See also tyranny

1 *Roma locuta est; causa finita est.*
Rome has spoken; the case is concluded.
St Augustine of Hippo: Sermons, Bk. I

2 And the Lord said unto Moses, Come up to me into the mount, and be there: and I will give thee tables of stone, and a law, and commandments which I have written; that thou mayest teach them.
Bible: Exodus: 24:12

3 Dictators ride to and fro upon tigers which they dare not dismount. And the tigers are getting hungry.
Winston Churchill: While England Slept

4 I will have this done, so I order it done; let my will replace reasoned judgement.
Juvenal: Satires, VI

5 Big Brother is watching you.
George Orwell: Nineteen Eighty-Four

6 I don't mind how much my ministers talk – as long as they do what I say.
Margaret Thatcher: The Times, 1987

B

BABIES

See also birth, children

1 There is no finer investment for any community than putting milk into babies.
Winston Churchill: Radio broadcast, 21 Mar 1943

2 Infants do not cry without some legitimate cause.
Ferrarius: The Advancement of Child Health (A. V. Neale)

3 Other people's babies –
That's my life!
Mother to dozens,
And nobody's wife.
A. P. Herbert: A Book of Ballads, 'Other People's Babies'

4 A loud noise at one end and no sense of responsibility at the other.
Ronald Knox: Attrib.

5 We all of us wanted babies – but did we want children?
Eda J. Leshan: How to Survive Children (Katharine Whitehorn)

BEAUTY

See also appearance

1 A wife is sought for her virtue, concubine for her beauty.
Chinese proverb

2 A good face is a letter of recommendation.
Proverb

3 Beauty is only skin-deep.
Proverb

4 Small is beautiful.
Proverb

5 There is no excellent beauty that hath not some strangeness in the proportion.
Francis Bacon: Essays, 'Of Beauty'

6 Exuberance is Beauty.
William Blake: The Marriage of Heaven and Hell, 'Proverbs of Hell'

7 She walks in beauty, like the night
Of cloudless climes and starry skies;
And all that's best of dark and bright
Meet in her aspect and her eyes.
Lord Byron: She Walks in Beauty

8 There is nothing ugly; *I never saw an ugly thing in my life:* for let the form of an object be what it may, – light, shade, and perspective will always make it beautiful.
John Constable: Letter to John Fisher, 23 Oct 1821

9 There is nothing so lovely as to be beautiful. Beauty is a gift of God and we should cherish it as such.
Marie de Sévigné: Letters of Madame de Sévigné to her daughters and friends

10 Love built on beauty, soon as beauty, dies.
John Donne: Elegies, 2, 'The Anagram'

11 Beauty is a social necessity.
James Goldsmith: The Times, 10 June 1994

12 Beauty in things exists in the mind which contemplates them.

David Hume: Essays, 'Of Tragedy'

13 Beauty is altogether in the eye of the beholder.

Margaret Wolfe Hungerford: Also attributed to the US soldier and writer Lew Wallace (1827–1905). Molly Bawn

14 A thing of beauty is a joy for ever:

Its loveliness increases; it will never

Pass into nothingness; but still will keep

A bower quiet for us, and a sleep

Full of sweet dreams, and health, and quiet breathing.

John Keats: Endymion, I

15 'Beauty is truth, truth beauty,'
– that is all

Ye know on earth, and all ye need to know.

John Keats: Ode on a Grecian Urn

16 Was this the face that launch'd a thousand ships

And burnt the topless towers of Ilium?

Sweet Helen, make me immortal with a kiss.

Christopher Marlowe: Doctor Faustus, V:1

17 Beauty stands

In the admiration only of weak minds

Led captive.

John Milton: Paradise Regained, Bk. II

18 There are no ugly women, only lazy ones.

Helena Rubinstein: My Life for Beauty, Pt. I, Ch. 1

19 Remember that the most beautiful things in the world are the most useless, peacocks and lilies for instance.

John Ruskin: The Stones of Venice, Vol. I, Ch. 2

20 Health is beauty, and the most perfect health is the most perfect beauty.

William Shenstone: Essays on Men and Manners, 'On Taste'

21 All changed, changed utterly:
A terrible beauty is born.

W. B. Yeats: Easter 1916

BED

See also sleep

1 Early to bed and early to rise, makes a man healthy, wealthy and wise.

Proverb

2 The cool kindliness of sheets, that soon

Smooth away trouble; and the rough male kiss of blankets.

Rupert Brooke: The Great Lover

3 Believe me, you have to get up early if you want to get out of bed.

Groucho Marx: The Cocoanuts

4 And so to bed.

Samuel Pepys: Diary, 6 May 1660 and passim

5 Early to rise and early to bed makes a male healthy and wealthy and dead.

James Thurber: Fables for Our Time, 'The Shrike and the Chipmunks'

BEGINNING

1 A journey of a thousand leagues begins with a single step.

Chinese proverb

BETRAYAL

...m small beginnings come
great things.
Proverb

3 No task is a long one but the
task on which one dare not start.
It becomes a nightmare.
*Charles Baudelaire: My Heart
Laid Bare*

4 The distance doesn't matter; it
is only the first step that is difficult.
*Marquise du Deffand: Referring to
the legend of St Denis, who carried
his severed head for six miles after
his execution. Letter to d'Alembert,
7 July 1763*

5 In my beginning is my end.
*T. S. Eliot: Four Quartets, 'East
Coker'*

6 From today and from this place
there begins a new epoch in the
history of the world.
*Goethe: On witnessing the victory
of the French at the battle of Valmy.
The Story of Civilization (W.
Durant), Vol. II*

7 We stand today on the edge of a
new frontier.
*John Fitzgerald Kennedy: Said on
his nomination as presidential
candidate. Speech, Democratic
Party Convention, 15 July 1960*

8 Are you sitting comfortably?
Then I'll begin.
*Julia S. Lang: Introduction to the
story in Listen with Mother.*

BELIEF

See also faith, religion

1 Believe nothing of what you
hear, and only half of what you
see.
Proverb

2 Seeing is believing.
Proverb

3 Vain are the thousand creeds
That move men's hearts: un-
utterably vain;
Worthless as wither'd weeds.
Emily Brontë: Last Lines

4 If Jesus Christ were to come today, people would not even cru-
cify him. They would ask him to
dinner, and hear what he had to
say, and make fun of it.
*Thomas Carlyle: Carlyle at his
Zenith (D. A. Wilson)*

5 Action will furnish belief, – but
will that belief be the true one?
This is the point, you know.
*Arthur Hugh Clough: Amours de
voyage, V*

6 The true believer is in a high degree protected against the danger of certain neurotic afflic-
tions; by accepting the universal
neurosis he is spared the task of
forming a personal neurosis.
*Sigmund Freud: The Future of an
Illusion, Ch. 8*

7 I believe because it is impossible.
*Tertullian: The usual misquotation
of 'It is certain because it is
impossible.' De Carne Christi, V*

8 If there were a verb meaning 'to
believe falsely', it would not
have any significant first person,
present indicative.
*Ludwig Wittgenstein: A Certain
World (W. H. Auden)*

BETRAYAL

See also treason

1 And he answered and said, He
that dippeth his hand with me in

BIRTH

the dish, the same shall betray me.
Bible: Matthew: 26:23

2 Just for a handful of silver he left us,
Just for a riband to stick in his coat.
Robert Browning: The Lost Leader

3 It is all right to rat, but you can't re-rat.
Winston Churchill: Attrib.

4 I hate the idea of causes, and if I had to choose between betraying my country and betraying my friend, I hope I should have the guts to betray my country.
E. M. Forster: Two Cheers for Democracy, 'What I Believe'

5 He…felt towards those whom he had deserted that peculiar malignity which has, in all ages, been characteristic of apostates.
Lord Macaulay: History of England, Vol. I, Ch. 1

6 I let down my friends, I let down my country. I let down our system of government.
Richard Milhous Nixon: The Observer, 'Sayings of the Week', 8 May 1977

7 *Et tu, Brute?*
You too, Brutus?
William Shakespeare: Said by Julius Caesar. Julius Caesar, III:1

BIRTH

See also babies, life and death

1 For man's greatest crime is to have been born.
Pedro Calderón de la Barca: La Vida es Sueño, I

2 The history of man for the nine months preceding his birth

would, probably, be far more interesting and contain events of greater moment than all the three-score and ten years that follow it.
Samuel Taylor Coleridge: Miscellanies, Aesthetic and Literary

3 If men had to have babies they would only ever have one each.
Diana, Princess of Wales: The Observer, 'Sayings of the Week', 29 July 1984

4 MACBETH. I bear a charmed life, which must not yield
To one of woman born.
MACDUFF. Despair thy charm;
And let the angel whom thou still hast serv'd
Tell thee Macduff was from his mother's womb
Untimely ripp'd.
William Shakespeare: Macbeth, V:8

5 Our birth is but a sleep and a forgetting.
William Wordsworth: Ode: Intimations of Immortality

BLESSING

See also prayer

1 I see the moon,
And the moon sees me;
God bless the moon,
And God bless me.
Anonymous: Gammer Gurton's Garland

2 'God bless us every one!' said Tiny Tim, the last of all.
Charles Dickens: A Christmas Carol

BLINDNESS

See also disability

A nod is as good as a wink to a blind horse.
Proverb

Men are blind in their own cause.
Proverb

My eyes are dim
I cannot see
I have not brought my specs with me.
Anonymous: The Quartermaster's Stores

How reconcile this world of fact with the bright world of my imagining? My darkness has been filled with the light of intelligence, and behold, the outer day-light world was stumbling and groping in social blindness.
Helen Keller: The Cry for Justice (ed. Upton Sinclair)

Ask for this great deliverer now, and find him
Eyeless in Gaza at the mill with slaves.
John Milton: Samson Agonistes

I have only one eye: I have a right to be blind sometimes: I really do not see the signal.
Lord Nelson: Remark, Battle of Copenhagen, 2 Apr 1801; Nelson ignored Admiral Parker's order to disengage by placing his telescope to his blind eye; an hour later, he was victorious. Life of Nelson Ch. 7 (Robert Southey)

He clapped the glass to his sightless eye,
And 'I'm damned if I see it', he said.
Henry John Newbolt: Referring to Lord Nelson at the Battle of Copenhagen. Admirals All

BOATS

See also navy, sea

1 As idle as a painted ship
Upon a painted ocean.
Samuel Taylor Coleridge: The Rime of the Ancient Mariner, I

2 For you dream you are crossing the Channel, and tossing about in a steamer from Harwich
Which is something between a large bathing machine and a very small second-class carriage.
W. S. Gilbert: Iolanthe, II

3 There is nothing – absolutely nothing – half so much worth doing as simply messing about in boats.
Kenneth Grahame: The Wind in the Willows, Ch. 1

4 The little ships, the unforgotten Homeric catalogue of *Mary Jane* and *Peggy IV*, of *Folkestone Belle*, *Boy Billy*, and *Ethel Maud*, of *Lady Haig* and *Skylark*…the little ships of England brought the Army home.
Philip Guedalla: Referring to the evacuation of Dunkirk. Mr. Churchill

5 I'd like to get you
On a slow boat to China.
Frank Loesser: Slow Boat to China

6 Quinquireme of Nineveh from distant Ophir
Rowing home to haven in sunny Palestine,
With a cargo of ivory,
And apes and peacocks,

Sandalwood, cedarwood, and
sweet white wine.
John Masefield: Cargoes

BOOKS

See also fiction, literature, novels,
reading

1 Books and friends should be few
but good.
Proverb

2 Some books are undeservedly
forgotten; none are undeservedly remembered.
*W. H. Auden: The Dyer's Hand,
'Reading'*

3 Some books are to be tasted,
others to be swallowed, and
some few to be chewed and di-
gested.
*Francis Bacon: Essays, 'Of
Studies'*

4 When I am dead, I hope it may
be said:
'His sins were scarlet, but his
books were read.'
*Hilaire Belloc: Epigrams, 'On His
Books'*

5 And further, by these, my son,
be admonished: of making many
books there is no end; and much
study is a weariness of the flesh.
Bible: Ecclesiastes 12:12

6 'Tis pleasant, sure, to see one's
name in print;
A book's a book, although
there's nothing in't.
*Lord Byron: English Bards and
Scotch Reviewers*

7 A good book is the purest
essence of a human soul.
*Thomas Carlyle: Speech made in
support of the London Library.
Carlyle and the London Library
(F. Harrison)*

8 A best-seller was a book which
somehow sold well simply be-
cause it was selling well.
*Daniel J. Boorstin: The Image,
'From Shapes to Shadows:
Dissolving Forms'*

9 Books cannot always please,
however good;
Minds are not ever craving for
their food.
*George Crabbe: The Borough,
'Schools'*

10 A book is not harmless merely
because no one is consciously
offended by it.
T. S. Eliot: Religion and Literature

11 Books are made not like children but like pyramids…and
they're just as useless! and they
stay in the desert!…Jackals piss
at their foot and the bourgeois
climb up on them.
*Gustave Flaubert: Letter to Ernest
Feydeau, 1857*

12 Learning hath gained most by
those books by which the print-
ers have lost.
*Thomas Fuller: The Holy State
and the Profane State*

13 Few books today are forgiv-
able.
*R. D. Laing: The Politics of
Experience, Introduction*

14 Borrowers of books – those
mutilators of collections, spoil-
ers of the symmetry of shelves,
and creators of odd volumes.
*Charles Lamb: Essays of Elia,
'The Two Races of Men'*

15 Get stewed:

Books are a load of crap.
Philip Larkin: A Study of Reading Habits

16 Never judge a cover by its book.
Fran Lebowitz: Metropolitan Life

17 Who kills a man kills a reasonable creature, God's image; but he who destroys a good book, kills reason itself, kills the image of God, as it were in the eye.
John Milton: Areopagitica

18 An anthology is like all the plums and orange peel picked out of a cake.
Walter Raleigh: Letter to Mrs Robert Bridges, 15 Jan 1915

19 We all know that books burn — yet we have the greater knowledge that books cannot be killed by fire. People die, but books never die....In this war, we know, books are weapons.
Franklin D. Roosevelt: Message to American Booksellers Association, 23 Apr 1942

20 If a book is worth reading, it is worth buying.
John Ruskin: Sesame and Lilies, 'Of Kings' Treasuries'

21 A best-seller is the gilded tomb of a mediocre talent.
Logan Pearsall Smith: Afterthoughts, 'Art and Letters'

22 Books are good enough in their own way, but they are a mighty bloodless substitute for life.
Robert Louis Stevenson: Virginibus Puerisque

23 There is no such thing as a moral or an immoral book. Books are well written, or badly written.
Oscar Wilde: The Picture of Dorian Gray, Preface

BOREDOM

1 Nothing happens, nobody comes, nobody goes, it's awful!
Samuel Beckett: Waiting for Godot, I

2 I wanted to be bored to death, as good a way to go as any.
Peter De Vries: Comfort me with Apples, Ch. 17

3 You ought not to be ashamed of being bored. What you ought to be ashamed of is being boring.
Lord Hailsham: The Observer, 'Sayings of the Week', 12 Oct 1975

4 Symmetry is tedious, and tedium is the very basis of mourning. Despair yawns.
Victor Hugo: Les Misérables, Vol. II, Bk. IV, Ch. 1

5 The effect of boredom on a large scale in history is underestimated. It is a main cause of revolutions, and would soon bring to an end all the static Utopias and the farmyard civilization of the Fabians.
Dean Inge: The End of an Age, Ch. 6

6 When you're bored with yourself, marry and be bored with someone else.
David Pryce-Jones: Owls and Satyrs

BORES

1 BORE, n. A person who talks when you wish him to listen.

Ambrose Bierce: The Devil's Dictionary

2 Society is now one polish'd
horde,
Form'd of two mighty tribes, the
Bores and Bored.
Lord Byron: Don Juan, XIII

3 He is not only a bore but he
bores for England.
*Malcolm Muggeridge: Referring to
Sir Anthony Eden, Conservative
prime minister (1955–57). In
Newstatesman (E. Hyams),
'Boring for England'*

4 A healthy male adult bore consumes each year one and a half
times his own weight in other
people's patience.
*John Updike: Assorted Prose,
'Confessions of a Wild Bore'*

BORROWING

1 Be not made a beggar by ban-
queting upon borrowing, when
thou hast nothing in thy purse:
for thou shalt lie in wait for thine
own life, and be talked on.
Bible: Ecclesiasticus 18:33

2 The human species, according
to the best theory I can form of
it, is composed of two distinct
races, the men who borrow, and
the men who lend.
*Charles Lamb: Essays of Elia, The
Two Races of Men*

3 Neither a borrower nor a lender
be;
For loan oft loses both itself and
friend,
And borrowing dulls the edge of
husbandry.
This above all: to thine own self
be true,

And it must follow, as the night
the day,
Thou canst not then be false to
any man.
William Shakespeare: Hamlet, 1:3

4 Let us all be happy, and live
within our means, even if we
have to borrer the money to do it
with.
*Artemus Ward: Science and
Natural History*

BREVITY

1 You lose.
*Calvin Coolidge: When a lady at a
dinner told him that someone had
bet her that she would not get more
than two words out of him. Attrib.*

2 I strive to be brief, and I become
obscure.
Horace: Ars Poetica

3 ?
*Victor Hugo: The entire contents of
a telegram sent to his publishers
asking how Les Misérables was
selling; the reply was '!' The
Literary Life (R. Hendrickson).*

4 Brevity is the soul of lingerie.
*Dorothy Parker: While Rome
Burns (Alexander Woollcott)*

5 Trust the man who hesitates in
his speech and is quick and
steady in action, but beware of
long arguments and long beards.
*George Santayana: Soliloquies in
England, 'The British Character'*

6 Brevity is the soul of wit.
*William Shakespeare: Hamlet,
II:2*

BUREAUCRACY

1 A committee is a cul-de-sac

down which ideas are lured and then quietly strangled.
Barnett Cocks: New Scientist, 1973

2 Whatever was required to be done, the Circumlocution Office was beforehand with all the public departments in the art of perceiving – HOW NOT TO DO IT.
Charles Dickens: Little Dorrit, Bk. I, Ch. 10

3 A difficulty for every solution.
Herbert Samuel: Referring to the Civil Service. Attrib.

BUSINESS

See also capitalism

1 Today's sales should be better than yesterday's – and worse than tomorrow's.
Anonymous

2 You ask me what it is I do. Well actually, you know,
I'm partly a liaison man and partly P.R.O.
Essentially I integrate the current export drive
And basically I'm viable from ten o'clock till five.
John Betjeman: Executive

3 Pile it high, sell it cheap.
Jack Cohen: Business motto

4 The business of America is business.
Calvin Coolidge: Speech, Washington, 17 Jan 1925

5 A business that makes nothing but money is a poor kind of business.
Henry Ford: Interview

6 No nation was ever ruined by trade.
Benjamin Franklin: Essays, 'Thoughts on Commercial Subjects'

7 Remember that time is money.
Benjamin Franklin: Advice to a Young Tradesman

8 There's no such thing as a free lunch.
Milton Friedman: Used before Friedman but popularized by him.

9 If you pay peanuts, you get monkeys.
James Goldsmith: Attrib.

10 When you are skinning your customers, you should leave some skin on to grow so that you can skin them again.
Nikita Khrushchev: Said to British businessmen. The Observer, 'Sayings of the Week', 28 May 1961

11 He is the only man who is for ever apologizing for his occupation.
H. L. Mencken: Referring to the businessman. Prejudices, 'Types of Men'

12 He's a businessman. I'll make him an offer he can't refuse.
Mario Puzo: The Godfather

13 A friendship founded on business is better than a business founded on friendship.
John D. Rockefeller

14 The customer is always right.
H. Gordon Selfridge: Slogan adopted at his shops

15 The big print giveth and the fine print taketh away.
J. Fulton Sheen: Referring to his contract for a television appearance. Attrib.

16 People of the same trade sel-

dom meet together but the conversation ends in a conspiracy against the public, or in some diversion to raise prices.

Adam Smith: The Wealth of Nations

17 All business sagacity reduces itself in the last analysis to a judicious use of sabotage.

Thorstein Bunde Veblen: The Nature of Peace

18 The best sun we have is made of Newcastle coal.

Horace Walpole: Letter to Montagu, 15 June 1768

19 If Max gets to Heaven he won't last long. He will be chucked out for trying to pull off a merger between Heaven and Hell...after having secured a controlling interest in key subsidiary companies in both places, of course.

H. G. Wells: Referring to Lord Beaverbrook. Beaverbrook (A. J. P. Taylor)

20 The trouble with the profit system has always been that it was highly unprofitable to most people.

Elwyn Brooks White: Attrib.

C

CAPITALISM

See also business

1 Capitalism is the exploitation of man by man. Communism is the complete opposite.
Anonymous

2 What mean ye that ye beat my people to pieces, and grind the faces of the poor? saith the Lord God of hosts.
Bible: Isaiah: 3:15

3 Property has its duties as well as its rights.
Thomas Drummond: Letter to the Earl of Donoughmore, 22 May 1838

4 If I had to give a definition of capitalism I would say: the process whereby American girls turn into American women.
Christopher Hampton: Savages, Sc. 16

5 Militarism…is one of the chief bulwarks of capitalism, and the day that militarism is undermined, capitalism will fail.
Helen Keller: The Story of My Life

6 Under capitalism we have a state in the proper sense of the word, that is, a special machine for the suppression of one class by another.
Lenin: The State and Revolution, Ch. 5

7 Not every problem someone has with his girlfriend is necessarily due to the capitalist mode of production.
Herbert Marcuse: The Listener

8 Capitalist production begets, with the inexorability of a law of nature, its own negation.
Karl Marx: Das Kapital, Ch. 15

9 Man is the only creature that consumes without producing.
George Orwell: Animal Farm, Ch. 1

10 Property is theft.
Pierre Joseph Proudhon: Qu'est-ce que la Propriété?, Ch. 1

11 Property is organised robbery.
George Bernard Shaw: Major Barbara, Preface

12 The public be damned. I am working for my stockholders.
William Henry Vanderbilt: Refusing to speak to a reporter, who was seeking to find out his views on behalf of the public.

CATS

1 The Naming of Cats is a difficult matter,
It isn't just one of your holiday games.
T. S. Eliot: The Naming of Cats

2 If a fish is the movement of water embodied, given shape, then cat is a diagram and pattern of subtle air.
Doris Lessing: Particularly Cats, Ch. 2

3 When I play with my cat, who knows whether she is not amusing herself with me more than I with her?
Michel de Montaigne: Essais, II

4 If a dog jumps onto your lap it is because he is fond of you; but if

a cat does the same thing it is because your lap is warmer.
A. N. Whitehead: Dialogues

CAUTION

See also prudence

1 Better be safe than sorry.
Proverb

2 Don't put all your eggs in one basket.
Proverb

3 He that fights and runs away, may live to fight another day.
Proverb

4 Look before you leap.
Proverb

5 Chi Wen Tzu always thought three times before taking action. Twice would have been quite enough.
Confucius: Analects

6 The only way to be absolutely safe is never to try anything for the first time.
Magnus Pyke: BBC radio programme

CENSORSHIP

See also prudery

1 More to the point, would you allow your gamekeeper to read it?
Anonymous: Referring to 'Lady Chatterley's Lover' by D.H. Lawrence.

2 To defend society from sex is no one's business. To defend it from officiousness is the duty of everyone who values freedom – or sex.
Brigid Brophy: The Observer, 'Sayings of the Week', 9 Aug 1970

3 Whenever books are burned men also in the end are burned.
Heinrich Heine: Almansor

The author of the Satanic Verses book, which is against Islam, the Prophet and the Koran, and all those involved in its publication who were aware of its content, are sentenced to death. I ask all Moslems to execute them wherever they find them.
Ayatolla Ruholla Khomeini: Speech, 14 Feb 1989

5 I call upon the intellectual community in this country and abroad to stand up for freedom of the imagination, an issue much larger than my book or indeed my life.
Salman Rushdie: Press statement, 14 Feb 1989

6 Censorship is more depraving and corrupting than anything pornography can produce.
Tony Smythe: The Observer, 'Sayings of the Week', 18 Sept 1972

7 God forbid that any book should be banned. The practice is as indefensible as infanticide.
Rebecca West: The Strange Necessity, 'The Tosh Horse'

8 If you are a songwriter did anyone ask you if you wanted to spend the rest of your career modifying your lyric content to suit the spiritual needs of an imaginary eleven-year-old?
Frank Zappa: The Real Frank Zappa Book

CERTAINTY

1 If a man will begin with certainties, he shall end in doubts, but if he will be content to begin with doubts, he shall end in certainties.
Francis Bacon: The Advancement of Learning, Bk. I, Ch. 5

2 The mind longs for certainty, and perhaps it longs most for a certainty which clubs it down. What the mind can understand, what it can ploddingly prove and approve, might be what it most despises.
Julian Barnes: Staring at the Sun

CHANCE

See also accidents, luck, opportunity

1 Of all the gin joints in all the towns in all the world, she walks into mine!
Humphrey Bogart: Casablanca

2 I shot an arrow into the air, It fell to earth, I knew not where.
Henry Wadsworth Longfellow: The Arrow and the Song

3 Accidental and fortuitous concurrence of atoms.
Lord Palmerston: Speech, House of Commons, 1857

4 I have set my life upon a cast, And I will stand the hazard of the die.
William Shakespeare: Richard III, V:4

CHANGE

See also progress, transience

1 Can the Ethiopian change his skin, or the leopard his spots? then may ye also do good, that are accustomed to do evil.
Bible: Jeremiah: 13:23

2 Variety's the very spice of life That gives it all its flavour.
William Cowper: The Task

3 Most women set out to try to change a man, and when they have changed him they do not like him.
Marlene Dietrich: Attrib.

4 The Times They Are A-Changin'.
Bob Dylan: Song title

5 One must never lose time in vainly regretting the past nor in complaining about the changes which cause us discomfort, for change is the very essence of life.
Anatole France: Attrib.

6 Most of the change we think we see in life
Is due to truths being in and out of favor.
Robert Frost: The Black Cottage

7 Very often we support change, and then are swept away by the change. I think that...you just make your own response to your own generation. A response adequate to your time.
Nadine Gordimer: The Times, 1 June 1990

8 Everything flows and nothing stays.
Heraclitus: Cratylus (Plato), 402a

9 You can't step into the same river twice.
Heraclitus: Cratylus (Plato), 402a

10 Change is not made without inconvenience, even from worse to better.

Richard Hooker: English Dictionary (Johnson), Preface

11 Well, I find that a change of nuisances is as good as a vacation.

David Lloyd George: On being asked how he maintained his cheerfulness when beset by numerous political obstacles. Attrib.

12 The wind of change is blowing through the continent. Whether we like it or not, this growth of national consciousness is a political fact.

Harold Macmillan: Speech, South African Parliament, 3 Feb 1960

13 We meant to change a nation, and instead, we changed a world.

Ronald Reagan: Farewell address, 11 Jan 1989

14 Every reform movement has a lunatic fringe.

Theodore Roosevelt: Comment, 1913

CHARACTER

1 If you wish to know what a man is, place him in authority.

Yugoslav proverb

2 Every man is as Heaven made him, and sometimes a great deal worse.

Miguel de Cervantes: Don Quixote, Pt. II, Ch. 4

3 A patronizing disposition always has its meaner side.

George Eliot: Adam Bede

4 Talent develops in quiet places, character in the full current of human life.

Goethe: Torquato Tasso, I

5 What is character but the determination of incident? What is incident but the illustration of character?

Henry James: Partial Portraits, 'The Art of Fiction'

6 I recognize that I am made up of several persons and that the person that at the moment has the upper hand will inevitably give place to another. But which is the real one? All of them or none?

W. Somerset Maugham: A Writer's Notebook

7 It is with narrow-souled people as with narrow-necked bottles: the less they have in them, the more noise they make in pouring it out.

Alexander Pope: Thoughts on Various Subjects

8 There is no such thing as psychological. Let us say that one can improve the biography of the person.

Jean-Paul Sartre: The Divided Self (R. D. Laing), Ch. 8

9 A certain person may have, as you say, a wonderful presence: I do not know. What I do know is that he has a perfectly delightful absence.

Idries Shah: Reflections, 'Presence and Absence'

CHARITY

See also generosity

1 Private patients, if they do not like me, can go elsewhere; but the poor devils in the hospital I am bound to take care of.

35

John Abernethy: Memoirs of John Abernethy, Ch. 5 (George Macilwain)

2 The living need charity more than the dead.
George Arnold: The Jolly Old Pedagogue

3 In charity there is no excess.
Francis Bacon: Essays, 'Of Goodness, and Goodness of Nature'

4 Feed the World
Let them know it's Christmas.
Band Aid: Song written to raise money for the relief of famine in Ethiopia. Do They Know It's Christmas?

5 All our doings without charity are nothing worth.
The Book of Common Prayer: Collect, Quinquagesima Sunday

6 Charity begins at home, is the voice of the world.
Thomas Browne: Religio Medici, Pt. II

7 Charity is the power of defending that which we know to be indefensible. Hope is the power of being cheerful in circumstances which we know to be desperate.
G. K. Chesterton: Heretics, Ch. 12

8 No people do so much harm as those who go about doing good.
Mandell Creighton: Life

9 In medicine, charity offers to the poor the gains in medical skill, not the leavings.
Alan Gregg: The Bampton Lectures

10 The white man knows how to make everything, but he does not know how to distribute it.
Sitting Bull: Attrib.

11 The house which is not opened for charity will be opened to the physician.
The Talmud

12 I have always depended on the kindness of strangers.
Tennessee Williams: A Streetcar Named Desire, II:3

CHILDREN

See also babies, family, youth

1 Spare the rod and spoil the child.
Proverb

2 There's only one pretty child in the world, and every mother has it.
Proverb

3 It was no wonder that people were so horrible when they started life as children.
Kingsley Amis: One Fat Englishman, Ch. 14

4 Children sweeten labours, but they make misfortunes more bitter.
Francis Bacon: Essays, 'Of Parents and Children'

5 Children have never been very good at listening to their elders, but they have never failed to imitate them. They must, they have no other models.
James Baldwin: Nobody Knows My Name

6 I am married to Beatrice Salkeld, a painter. We have no children, except me.
Brendan Behan: Attrib.

7 Were we closer to the ground as children or is the grass emptier now?
Alan Bennett: Forty Years On, II

8 Having no children had been a kind of choice up to the moment when, from a choice, it became a sadness.
Bernardo Bertolucci: The Observer, 'Sayings of the Week', 1 May 1994

9 Desire not a multitude of unprofitable children, neither delight in ungodly sons.
Bible: Ecclesiasticus: 16:1

10 But when Jesus saw it, he was much displeased, and said unto them, Suffer the little children to come unto me, and forbid them not: for of such is the kingdom of God.
Bible: Mark: 10:14

11 You can do anything with children if you only play with them.
Bismarck: Attrib.

12 I guess that'll hold the little bastards.
Don Carney: Carney was ending a children's radio show and thought that he was off the air. Attrib.

13 Anybody who hates children and dogs can't be all bad.
W. C. Fields: Attrib.

14 To bear many children is considered not only a religious blessing but also an investment. The greater their number, some Indians reason, the more alms they can beg.
Indira Gandhi: New York Review of Books, 'Indira's Coup' (Oriana Fallaci)

15 You may house their bodies but not their souls,
For their souls dwell in the house of tomorrow, which you cannot visit, not even in your dreams.
Kahlil Gibran: The Prophet, 'On Children'

16 Common morality now treats childbearing as an aberration. There are practically no good reasons left for exercising one's fertility.
Germaine Greer

17 The business of being a child interests a child not at all. Children very rarely play at being other children.
David Holloway: The Daily Telegraph, 15 Dec 1966

18 One of the most obvious facts about grown-ups to a child is that they have forgotten what it is like to be a child.
Randall Jarrell: Third Book of Criticism

19 A child deserves the maximum respect; if you ever have something disgraceful in mind, don't ignore your son's tender years.
Juvenal: Satires, XIV

20 The real menace in dealing with a five-year-old is that in no time at all you begin to sound like a five-year-old.
Jean Kerr: Please Don't Eat the Daisies

21 At every step the child should be allowed to meet the real experiences of life; the thorns should never be plucked from his roses.
Ellen Key: The Century of the Child, Ch. 3

22 It is...sometimes easier to head an institute for the study of child guidance than it is to turn one brat into a decent human being.
Joseph Wood Krutch: If You Don't Mind My Saying, 'Whom Do We Picket Tonight?'

23 Boys are capital fellows in their own way, among their mates; but they are unwholesome companions for grown people.
Charles Lamb: Essays of Elia, 'The Old and the New Schoolmaster'

24 Man hands on misery to man. It deepens like a coastal shelf. Get out as early as you can, And don't have any kids yourself.
Philip Larkin: High Windows, 'This Be the Verse'

25 Literature is mostly about having sex and not much about having children; life is the other way round.
David Lodge: The British Museum is Falling Down, Ch. 4

26 There are only two things a child will share willingly — communicable diseases and his mother's age.
Benjamin Spock: Attrib.

CHIVALRY

See also courtesy

1 But there is another side to chivalry. If it dispenses leniency, it may with equal justification invoke control.
Freda Adler: Sisters in Crime, Ch. 4

2 Some say that the age of chivalry is past, that the spirit of romance is dead. The age of chivalry is never past, so long as there is a wrong left unredressed on earth.
Charles Kingsley: Life (Mrs C. Kingsley), Vol. II, Ch. 28

3 Remember, men, we're fighting for this woman's honour; which is probably more than she ever did.
Groucho Marx: Duck Soup

4 It is almost a definition of a gentleman to say that he is one who never inflicts pain.
Cardinal Newman: The Idea of a University, 'Knowledge and Religious Duty'

5 I have a truant been to chivalry.
William Shakespeare: Henry IV, Part One, V:1

6 Every man I meet wants to protect me. I can't figure out what from.
Mae West

CHRISTIANITY

See also religion

1 The Christian glories in the death of a pagan because thereby Christ himself is glorified.
St Bernard: Richard the Lionheart (J. Gillingham), Ch. 9

2 Where there is neither Greek nor Jew, circumcision nor uncircumcision, Barbarian, Scythian, bond nor free; but Christ is all, and in all.
Bible: Colossians: 3:11

3 Jesus said unto her, I am the resurrection, and the life: he that believeth in me, though he were dead, yet shall he live.
Bible: John: 11:25

4 The Christian ideal has not been tried and found wanting; it has been found difficult and left untried.
G. K. Chesterton: What's Wrong with the World, 'The Unfinished Temple'

5 He who begins by loving Christianity better than Truth will proceed by loving his own sect or church better than Christianity, and end by loving himself better than all.
Samuel Taylor Coleridge: Aids to Reflection: Moral and Religious Aphorisms

6 Christianity has done a great deal for love by making a sin of it.
Anatole France: The Garden of Epicurus

7 The Christian religion not only was at first attended with miracles, but even at this day cannot be believed by any reasonable person without one.
David Hume: Essays, 'Of Miracles'

8 Christianity accepted as given a metaphysical system derived from several already existing and mutually incompatible systems.
Aldous Huxley: Grey Eminence, Ch. 3

9 Fight the good fight with all thy might,
Christ is thy strength and Christ thy right,
Lay hold on life, and it shall be
Thy joy and crown eternally.
John Monsell: Hymn

10 No kingdom has ever had as many civil wars as the kingdom of Christ.
Baron de Montesquieu: Lettres persanes

11 Christianity has made of death a terror which was unknown to the gay calmness of the Pagan.
Ouida: The Failure of Christianity

12 Christianity is the most materialistic of all great religions.
William Temple: Reading in St John's Gospel, Vol. I, Introduction

13 The blood of the martyrs is the seed of the Church.
Tertullian: Traditional misquotation: more accurately, 'Our numbers increase as often as you cut us down: the blood of Christians is the seed'. Apologeticus, L

14 A Christian is a man who feels Repentance on a Sunday
For what he did on Saturday
And is going to do on Monday.
Thomas Russell Ybarra: The Christian

CHRISTMAS

1 I have often thought, says Sir Roger, it happens very well that Christmas should fall out in the Middle of Winter.
Joseph Addison: The Spectator, 269

2 I'm dreaming of a white Christmas.
Irving Berlin: Holiday Inn, 'White Christmas'

3 'Twas the night before Christmas, when all through the house Not a creature was stirring, not even a mouse;
The stockings were hung by the chimney with care,
In hopes that St Nicholas soon would be there.
Clement Clarke Moore: In Troy Sentinel, 23 Dec 1823, 'A Visit from St. Nicholas'

4 At Christmas play and make good cheer,

For Christmas comes but once a year.
Thomas Tusser: Five Hundred Points of Good Husbandry, 'The Farmer's Daily Diet'

5 To perceive Christmas through its wrapping becomes more difficult with every year.
Elwyn Brooks White: The Second Tree from the Corner

CHURCH

See also clergy, religion

1 The Vatican is an oppressive regime which, like a bat, fears the light.
Leonardo Boff: Said on leaving the Roman Catholic Church. The Observer, 5 July 1992

2 I see it as an elderly lady, who mutters away to herself in a corner, ignored most of the time.
George Carey: Referring to the Church of England. Reader's Digest, Mar 1991

3 And of all plagues with which mankind are curst,
Ecclesiastic tyranny's the worst.
Daniel Defoe: The True-Born Englishman, Pt. II

4 We Italians then owe to the Church of Rome and to her priests our having become irreligious and bad, but we owe her a still greater debt, and one that will be the cause of our ruin, namely that the Church has kept and still keeps our country divided.
Machiavelli: Discourses on First Ten Books of Livy

5 The Church should be no longer satisfied to represent only the Conservative Party at prayer.
Agnes Maude Royden: Speech, London, 16 July 1917

CINEMA

1 Hollywood – a place where people from Iowa mistake themselves for movie stars.
Fred Allen: Attrib.

2 To make a film is to create a world.
Lindsay Anderson: Halliwell's Filmgoer's and Video Viewer's Companion

3 Garbo Talks!
Anonymous: Promotional slogan.

4 What's up, Doc?
Anonymous: Used in 'Bugs Bunny' cartoons.

5 There's a big trend in Hollywood of taking very good European films and turning them into very bad American films. I've been offered a few of these, but it's really a perverse activity. I'd rather go on the dole.
Roddy Doyle: The Independent, 25 Apr 1994

6 I was born at the age of twelve on a Metro-Goldwyn-Mayer lot.
Judy Garland: The Observer, 'Sayings of the Week', 18 Feb 1951

7 The only thing I liked about films was looking at the back of my head which otherwise I could only see at the tailor's.
John Gielgud: Time, 15 Aug 1983

8 I like a film to have a beginning, a middle and an end, but not necessarily in that order.
Jean-Luc Godard: Attrib.

9 Photography is truth. And cinema is truth twenty-four times a second.
Jean-Luc Godard: Le Petit Soldat

10 A wide screen just makes a bad film twice as bad.
Samuel Goldwyn: Attrib.

11 The cinema is not a slice of life but a piece of cake.
Alfred Hitchcock: The Sunday Times, 6 Mar 1977

12 In Hollywood, if you don't have happiness you send out for it.
Rex Reed: Colombo's Hollywood, 'Hollywood the Bad' (J. R. Colombo)

13 When I grow up I still want to be a director.
Steven Spielberg: Time, 15 July 1985

14 The most expensive habit in the world is celluloid not heroin and I need a fix every two years.
Steven Spielberg: OM, Dec 1984

15 Westerns are closer to art than anything else in the motion picture business.
John Wayne: Halliwell's Filmgoer's and Video Viewer's Companion

16 Me? Tarzan?
Johnny Weissmuller: Reacting to an invitation to play Tarzan. Attrib.

CIVILIZATION

See also culture

1 Civilization is a method of living, an attitude of equal respect for all men.
Jane Addams: Speech, Honolulu, 1933

2 The modern world...has no no-

tion except that of simplifying something by destroying nearly everything.
G. K. Chesterton: All I Survey

3 In essence the Renaissance was simply the green end of one of civilization's hardest winters.
John Fowles: The French Lieutenant's Woman, Ch. 10

4 There is precious little in civilization to appeal to a Yeti.
Edmund Hillary: The Observer, 'Sayings of the Week', 3 June 1960

5 The degree of a nation's civilization is marked by its disregard for the necessities of existence.
W. Somerset Maugham: Our Betters, I

CLASS

See also aristocracy, snobbery

1 There's one law for the rich, and another for the poor.
Proverb

2 You can measure the social caste of a person by the distance between the husband's and wife's apartments.
Alfonso XIII: Attrib.

3 His Lordship may compel us to be equal upstairs, but there will never be equality in the servants' hall.
J. M. Barrie: The Admirable Crichton, I

4 Yet it is better to drop thy friends, O my daughter, than to drop thy 'H's'.
C. S. Calverley: Proverbial Philosophy, 'Of Friendship'

5 One of those refined people who go out to sew for the rich be-

cause they cannot bear contact with the poor.
Colette: The Other One

6 He bade me observe it, and I should always find, that the calamities of life were shared among the upper and lower part of mankind; but that the middle station had the fewest disasters.
Daniel Defoe: Robinson Crusoe, Pt. 1

7 All the world over, I will back the masses against the classes.
William Ewart Gladstone: Speech, Liverpool, 28 June 1886

8 'Bourgeois', I observed, 'is an epithet which the riff-raff apply to what is respectable, and the aristocracy to what is decent'.
Anthony Hope: The Dolly Dialogues

9 A Social-Democrat must never forget that the proletariat will inevitably have to wage a class struggle for Socialism even against the most democratic and republican bourgeoisie and petty bourgeoisie.
Lenin: The State and Revolution, Ch. 10

10 An Englishman's way of speaking absolutely classifies him
The moment he talks he makes some other Englishman despise him.
Alan Jay Lerner: My Fair Lady, I:1

11 Said Marx: 'Don't be snobbish, we seek to abolish
The 3rd Class, not the 1st.'
Christopher Logue: Christopher Logue's ABC, 'M'

12 The history of all hitherto existing society is the history of class struggles.
Karl Marx: The Communist Manifesto, 1

13 Britain is the society where the ruling class does not rule, the working class does not work and the middle class is not in the middle.
George Mikes: English Humour for Beginners

14 The one class you do *not* belong to and are not proud of at all is the lower-middle class. No one ever describes himself as belonging to the lower-middle class.
George Mikes: How to be Inimitable

15 Only on the third class tourist class passengers' deck was it a sultry overcast morning, but then if you do things on the cheap you must expect these things.
Spike Milligan: A Dustbin of Milligan

16 The worst fault of the working classes is telling their children they're not going to succeed, saying: 'There is a life, but it's not for you'.
John Mortimer: The Observer, 'Sayings of the Week', 5 June 1988

17 We have nothing to lose but our aitches.
George Orwell: Referring to the middle classes. The Road to Wigan Pier, Ch. 13

18 Since every Jack became a gentleman
There's many a gentle person made a Jack.

William Shakespeare: Richard III, I:3

19 There are two classes in good society in England. The equestrian classes and the neurotic classes.

George Bernard Shaw: Heartbreak House

20 I am a gentleman. I live by robbing the poor.

George Bernard Shaw: Man and Superman

21 It is impossible for one class to appreciate the wrongs of another.

Elizabeth Stanton: History of Woman Suffrage (with Susan B. Anthony and Mathilda Gage), Vol. I

22 The charm of Britain has always been the ease with which one can move into the middle class.

Margaret Thatcher: The Observer, 'Sayings of the Week', 27 Oct 1974

23 The ship follows Soviet custom: it is riddled with class distinctions so subtle, it takes a trained Marxist to appreciate them.

Paul Theroux: The Great Railway Bazaar, Ch. 30

24 No writer before the middle of the 19th century wrote about the working classes other than as grotesque or as pastoral decoration. Then when they were given the vote certain writers started to suck up to them.

Evelyn Waugh: Interview. Paris Review, 1963

25 Bricklayers kick their wives to death, and dukes betray theirs; but it is among the small clerks and shopkeepers nowadays that it comes most often to the cutting of throats.

H. G. Wells: Short Stories, 'The Purple Pileus'

26 The constitution does not provide for first and second class citizens.

Wendell Lewis Willkie: An American Programme, Ch. 2

CLASSICS

1 They were a tense and peculiar family, the Oedipuses, weren't they?

Max Beerbohm: Max: A Biography (D. Cecil)

2 So they told me how Mr Gladstone read Homer for fun, which I thought served him right.

Winston Churchill: My Early Life, Ch. 2

3 Thou hadst small Latin, and less Greek.

Ben Jonson: To the Memory of William Shakespeare

4 The classics are only primitive literature. They belong in the same class as primitive machinery and primitive music and primitive medicine.

Stephen Leacock: Homer and Humbug

5 Every man with a belly full of the classics is an enemy of the human race.

Henry Miller: Tropic of Cancer, 'Dijon'

6 Nobody can say a word against Greek: it stamps a man at once as an educated gentleman.

George Bernard Shaw: Major Barbara, I

CLEANNESS

1 Bathe early every day and sickness will avoid you.
Hindustani proverb

2 Bath twice a day to be really clean, once a day to be passably clean, once a week to avoid being a public menace.
Anthony Burgess: Mr Enderby, Pt. I, Ch. 2

3 MR PRITCHARD. I must dust the blinds and then I must raise them.
MRS OGMORE-PRITCHARD. And before you let the sun in, mind it wipes its shoes.
Dylan Thomas: Under Milk Wood

4 Have you ever taken anything out of the clothes basket because it had become, relatively, the cleaner thing?
Katharine Whitehorn: The Observer, 'On Shirts', 1964

CLERGY

See also Church, religion

1 As for the British churchman, he goes to church as he goes to the bathroom, with the minimum of fuss and no explanation if he can help it.
Ronald Blythe: The Age of Illusion

2 Make him a bishop, and you will silence him at once.
Earl of Chesterfield: When asked what steps might be taken to control the evangelical preacher George Whitefield. Attrib.

3 It is no accident that the symbol of a bishop is a crook, and the sign of an archbishop is a double-cross.
Dom Gregory Dix: Letter to The Times, 3 Dec 1977 (Francis Bown)

4 A man who is good enough to go to heaven, is good enough to be a clergyman.
Samuel Johnson: Life of Johnson (J. Boswell), Vol. II

5 If I were a cassowary
On the plains of Timbuctoo,
I would eat a missionary,
Cassock, band, and hymn-book too.
Samuel Wilberforce: Also attrib. to W. M. Thackeray.

6 The idea that only a male can represent Christ at the altar is a most serious heresy.
George Carey: Reader's Digest, Apr 1991

CLOTHES

See also fashion

1 Woollen clothing keeps the skin healthy.
Venetian proverb

2 She had a womanly instinct that clothes possess an influence more powerful over many than the worth of character or the magic of manners.
Louisa May Alcott: Little Women, Pt. II

3 To a woman, the consciousness of being well-dressed gives a sense of tranquility which religion fails to bestow.
Helen Olcott Bell: Letters and Social Aims: R. W. Emerson

4 I go to a better tailor than any of

you and pay more for my clothes. The only difference is that you probably don't sleep in yours.
Clarence Seward Darrow: Reply when teased by reporters about his appearance. 2500 Anecdotes (E. Fuller)

5 Those who make their dress a principal part of themselves, will, in general, become of no more value than their dress.
William Hazlitt: On the Clerical Character

6 Fine clothes are good only as they supply the want of other means of procuring respect.
Samuel Johnson: Life of Johnson (J. Boswell), Vol. II

7 Where did you get that hat? Where did you get that tile?
James Rolmaz: Where Did You Get That Hat?

8 Not a gentleman; dresses too well.
Bertrand Russell: Referring to Sir Anthony Eden, the Conservative statesman. Six Men (A. Cooke)

9 Her frocks are built in Paris but she wears them with a strong English accent.
Saki: Reginald on Women

10 All my clothes have stretch marks, darling.
Jennifer Saunders: Absolutely Fabulous

11 Costly thy habit as thy purse can buy,
But not express'd in fancy; rich, not gaudy;
For the apparel oft proclaims the man.
William Shakespeare: Hamlet, I:3

12 The only man who really needs a tail coat is a man with a hole in his trousers.
John Taylor: The Observer, 'Shouts and Murmurs'

13 You can say what you like about long dresses, but they cover a multitude of shins.
Mae West: Peel Me a Grape (J. Weintraub)

COLD WAR

1 Let us not be deceived – we are today in the midst of a cold war.
Bernard Baruch: Speech, South Carolina Legislature, 16 Apr 1947

2 An iron curtain has descended across the Continent.
Winston Churchill: The phrase 'iron curtain' was originally coined by Joseph Goebbels. Address, Westminster College, Fulton, USA, 5 Mar 1946

COMFORT

See also sympathy

1 When pain and anguish wring the brow,
A ministering angel thou!
Walter Scott: Marmion, VI: 30

2 I beg cold comfort.
William Shakespeare: King John, V:7

3 Like a bridge over troubled water,
I will ease your mind.
Paul Simon: Bridge Over Troubled Water

COMMERCIALISM

See also business, money

1 My fear will be that in 15 years

time Jerusalem, Bethlehem, once centres of strong Christian presence, might become a kind of Walt Disney Theme Park.
George Carey: The Observer, 12 Jan 1992

2 This town was made to make money in and it has no other function. It has no pretence to longevity because it was never designed like that in the first place.
Billy Connolly: Referring to Los Angeles. The Times, 15 Dec 1990

3 Our democratic capitalist society has converted Eros into an employee of Mammon.
Octavio Paz: The Observer, 'Sayings of the Week', 19 June 1994

COMMITMENT

1 In for a penny, in for a pound.
Proverb

2 One cannot be a part-time nihilist.
Albert Camus: The Rebel

3 Total commitment to family and total commitment to career is possible, but fatiguing.
Muriel Fox: New Woman, Oct 1971

4 Catholics and Communists have committed great crimes, but at least they have not stood aside, like an established society, and been indifferent. I would rather have blood on my hands than water like Pilate.
Graham Greene: The Comedians, Pt. III, Ch. 4

5 Miss Brodie said: 'Pavolova contemplates her swans in order to perfect her swan dance, she studies them. This is true dedication. You must all grow up to be dedicated women as I have dedicated myself to you.'
Muriel Spark: The Prime of Miss Jean Brodie, Ch. 3

COMMUNICATION

See also conversation, language, speech

1 Only connect!
E. M. Forster: Howards End, Epigraph

2 Unless one is a genius, it is best to aim at being intelligible.
Anthony Hope: The Dolly Dialogues

3 The medium is the message. This is merely to say that the personal and social consequences of any medium…result from the new scale that is introduced into our affairs by each extension of ourselves or by any new technology.
Marshall McLuhan: Understanding Media, Ch. 1

4 And this certainly has to be the most historic phone call ever made.
Richard Milhous Nixon: Telephone call to astronauts on moon, 20 July 1969.

COMMUNISM

See also Marxism, socialism

1 Are you now or have you ever been a member of a godless conspiracy controlled by a foreign power?

Richard Arens: Question put to people appearing at hearings of the House of Representatives Committee on Un-American Activities. The Fifties (P. Lewis)

2 Russian communism is the il-legitimate child of Karl Marx and Catherine the Great.
Clement Atlee: Speech, 11 Apr 1956

3 The state is not 'abolished', it withers away.
Friedrich Engels: Anti-Dühring

4 Every year humanity takes a step towards Communism. Maybe not you, but at all events your grandson will surely be a Communist.
Nikita Khrushchev: Said to Sir William Hayter, June 1956

5 Those who wait for that must wait until a shrimp learns to whistle.
Nikita Khrushchev: Referring to the chances of the Soviet Union rejecting communism. Attrib.

6 Communism is Soviet power plus the electrification of the whole country.
Lenin: Political slogan of 1920, promoting the programme of electrification.

7 It looks like a duck, walks like a duck, and quacks like a duck.
Joseph R. McCarthy: Suggested method of identifying a communist. Attrib.

8 Communism is like prohibition, it's a good idea but it won't work.
Will Rogers: Autobiography, Nov 1927

9 For us in Russia communism is a dead dog, while, for many people in the West, it is still a living lion.
Alexander Solzhenitsyn: The Listener, 15 Feb 1979

10 Every communist has a fascist frown, every fascist a communist smile.
Muriel Spark: The Girls of Slender Means, Ch. 4

11 Communism continued to haunt Europe as a spectre – a name men gave to their own fears and blunders. But the crusade against Communism was even more imaginary than the spectre of Communism.
A. J. P. Taylor: The Origins of the Second World War, Ch. 2

COMPLAINTS

1 We have first raised a dust and then complain we cannot see.
Bishop Berkeley: Principles of Human Knowledge, Introduction

2 The world is disgracefully managed, one hardly knows to whom to complain.
Ronald Firbank: Vainglory

3 If you are foolish enough to be contented, don't show it, but grumble with the rest.
Jerome K. Jerome: Idle Thoughts of an Idle Fellow

COMPROMISE

1 All government, indeed every human benefit and enjoyment, every virtue, and every prudent act, is founded on compromise and barter.

Edmund Burke: Speech on Conciliation with America (House of Commons, 22 Mar 1775)

2 A cockroach world of compromise.

Angela Carter: Wise Children

3 Compromise used to mean that half a loaf was better than no bread. Among modern statesmen it really seems to mean that half a loaf is better than a whole loaf.

G. K. Chesterton: What's Wrong with the World

CONCEIT

See also arrogance, egotism, pride

1 A man...must have a very good opinion of himself when he asks people to leave their own fireside, and encounter such a day as this, for the sake of coming to see him. He must think himself a most agreeable fellow.

Jane Austen: Emma, Ch. 13

2 If ever he went to school without any boots it was because he was too big for them.

Ivor Bulmer-Thomas: Referring to the Labour politician Harold Wilson. Remark, Conservative Party Conference, 1949

3 We are so vain that we even care for the opinion of those we don't care for.

Marie Ebner von Eschenbach: Aphorism

4 Conceit is the finest armour a man can wear.

Jerome K. Jerome: Idle Thoughts of an Idle Fellow

5 Vanity dies hard; in some obstinate cases it outlives the man.

Robert Louis Stevenson: Prince Otto

6 Isn't it? I know in my case I would grow intolerably conceited.

James Whistler: Replying to the pointed observaton that it was as well that we do not not see ourselves as others see us. The Man Whistler (H. Pearson)

7 No, no, Oscar, you forget. When you and I are together we never talk about anything except me.

James Whistler: Cable replying to Oscar Wilde's message: 'When you and I are together we never talk about anything except ourselves'. The Gentle Art of Making Enemies

CONFORMITY

See also orthodoxy

1 When in Rome, live as the Romans do: when elsewhere, live as they live elsewhere.

St Ambrose: Advice to St Augustine

2 Take the tone of the company you are in.

Earl of Chesterfield: Letter to his son, 9 Oct 1747

3 Why do you have to be a non-conformist like everybody else?

James Thurber: Attrib. Actually a cartoon caption by Stan Hunt in the New Yorker

CONFUSION

1 Anyone who isn't confused here doesn't really understand what's going on.

Anonymous: Referring to the sectarian problems in Northern Ireland.

2 I can't say I was ever lost, but I was bewildered once for three days.
Daniel Boone: Reply when asked if he had ever been lost. Attrib.

3 I believe that I have created a lot of cognitive dissonance in the minds of people who are comfortable with stereotypes.
Hillary Clinton: The Observer, 'Sayings of the Week', 15 May 1994

4 This world is very odd we see,
We do not comprehend it;
But in one fact we all agree,
God won't, and we can't mend it.
Arthur Hugh Clough: Dipsychus, Bk. II

5 I had nothing to offer anybody except my own confusion.
Jack Kerouac: On the Road, Pt. II

6 For mine own part, it was Greek to me.
William Shakespeare: Julius Caesar, I:2

CONSCIENCE

See also integrity

1 Conscience, I say, not thine own, but of the other: for why is my liberty judged of another man's conscience?
Bible: I Corinthians: 10:29

2 All a man can betray is his conscience.
Joseph Conrad: Under Western Eyes

3 Conscience is a coward, and those faults it has not strength enough to prevent it seldom has justice enough to accuse.
Oliver Goldsmith: The Vicar of Wakefield, Ch. 13

4 Those who follow their conscience directly are of my religion; and, for my part, I am of the same religion as all those who are brave and true.
Henri IV: Henri had become a Roman Catholic, as a political move, in 1576. Letter to M. de Batz, 1577

5 Conscience is the inner voice that warns us somebody may be looking.
H. L. Mencken: A Mencken Chrestomathy

6 A peace above all earthly dignities,
A still and quiet conscience.
William Shakespeare: Henry VIII, III:2

7 Foul whisperings are abroad. Unnatural deeds
Do breed unnatural troubles; infected minds
To their deaf pillows will discharge their secrets;
More needs she the divine than the physician.
William Shakespeare: Macbeth, V:1

8 Conscience is but a word that cowards use,
Devis'd at first to keep the strong in awe.
William Shakespeare: Richard III, V:3

CONSERVATION

See also ecology, environment

1 Contrary to popular mythology,

it is not my Department's mission in life to tarmac over the whole of England.
Paul Channon: Speech, Sept 1988

2 Population growth is the primary source of environmental damage.
Jacques Cousteau: Remark, Jan 1989

3 Trees are poems that the earth writes upon the sky. We fell them down and turn them into paper that we may record our emptiness.
Kahlil Gibran: Sand and Foam

4 Green politics is not about being far left or far right, but far-sighted.
David Icke: Speech, Green Party conference, Sept 1989

5 We are living beyond our means. As a people we have developed a life-style that is draining the earth of its priceless and irreplaceable resources without regard for the future of our children and people all around the world.
Margaret Mead: Redbook, 'The Energy Crises – Why Our World Will Never Again Be the Same', Apr 1974

6 Our English countryside is one of the most heavily man-made habitats in Europe. To make it into a green museum would be to belie its whole history.
Nicholas Ridley: Speech, Nov 1988

CONSERVATISM

See also change

1 The most conservative man in the world is the British Trade Unionist when you want to change him.
Ernest Bevin: Speech, Trade Union Congress, 8 Sept 1927

2 All conservatism is based upon the idea that if you leave things alone you leave them as they are. But you do not. If you leave a thing alone you leave it to a torrent of change.
G. K. Chesterton: Orthodoxy, Ch. 7

3 I do not know which makes a man more conservative – to know nothing but the present, or nothing but the past.
John Maynard Keynes: The End of Laisser-Faire, I

4 You can't teach an old dogma new tricks.
Dorothy Parker: Wit's End (R. E. Drennan)

5 The radical invents the views. When he has worn them out, the conservative adopts them.
Mark Twain: Notebooks

CONSTANCY

1 A foolish consistency is the hobgoblin of little minds, adored by little statesmen and philosophers and divines. With consistency a great soul has simply nothing to do.
Ralph Waldo Emerson: Essays, 'Self-reliance'

2 Consistency is contrary to nature, contrary to life. The only completely consistent people are the dead.
Aldous Huxley: Do What you Will

3 *Plus ça change, plus c'est la même chose.*

The more things change, the more they stay the same.
Alphonse Karr: Les Guêpes, Jan 1849

CONTENTMENT

See also happiness, satisfaction

1 Live with the gods. And he does so who constantly shows them that his soul is satisfied with what is assigned to him.
Marcus Aurelius: Meditations, Bk. V, Ch. 27

2 Here with a Loaf of Bread beneath the Bough,
A Flask of Wine, a Book of Verse – and Thou
Beside me singing in the Wilderness –
And Wilderness is Paradise enow.
Edward Fitzgerald: The Rubáiyát of Omar Khayyám

3 I earn that I eat, get that I wear, owe no man hate, envy no man's happiness, glad of other men's good, content with my harm.
William Shakespeare: As You Like It, III:2

CONTRACEPTION

See also sex

1 Vasectomy means not ever having to say you're sorry.
Larry Adler: Attrib.

2 I want to tell you a terrific story about oral contraception. I asked this girl to sleep with me and she said 'no'.

Woody Allen: Woody Allen: Clown Prince of American Humor (Adler and Feinman), Ch. 1

3 He no play-a-da game. He no make-a-da rules!
Earl Butz: Referring to the Pope's strictures against contraception. Remark, 1974

4 It is now quite lawful for a Catholic woman to avoid pregnancy by a resort to mathematics, though she is still forbidden to resort to physics and chemistry.
H. L. Mencken: Notebooks, 'Minority Report'

5 Contraceptives should be used on every conceivable occasion.
Spike Milligan: The Last Goon Show of All

6 We want far better reasons for having children than not knowing how to prevent them.
Dora Russell: Hypatia, Ch. 4

CONVERSATION

See also speech

1 Although there exist many thousand subjects for elegant conversation, there are persons who cannot meet a cripple without talking about feet.
Chinese proverb

2 Questioning is not the mode of conversation among gentlemen.
Samuel Johnson: Life of Johnson (J. Boswell), Vol. II

3 Beware of the conversationalist who adds 'in other words'. He is merely starting afresh.
Robert Morley: The Observer, 'Sayings of the Week', 6 Dec 1964

4 Ideal conversation must be an

exchange of thought, and not, as many of those who worry most about their shortcomings believe, an eloquent exhibition of wit or oratory.
Emily Post: Etiquette, Ch. 6

5 Conversation has a kind of charm about it, an insinuating and insidious something that elicits secrets from us just like love or liquor.
Seneca: Epistles

6 Teas,
Where small talk dies in agonies.
Percy Bysshe Shelley: Peter Bell the Third

7 There is no such thing as conversation. It is an illusion. There are intersecting monologues, that is all.
Rebecca West: There Is No Conversation, Ch. 1

8 A good listener is not someone who has nothing to say. A good listener is a good talker with a sore throat.
Katharine Whitehorn: Attrib.

CORRUPTION

1 Among a people generally corrupt, liberty cannot long exist.
Edmund Burke: Letter to the Sheriffs of Bristol, 1777

2 Corruption, the most infallible symptom of constitutional liberty.
Edward Gibbon: Decline and Fall of the Roman Empire, Ch. 21

3 I order you to hold a free election, but forbid you to elect anyone but Richard my clerk.
Henry II: Writ to the electors of the See of Winchester regarding the election of a new bishop. Recueil des historiens des Gaules et de la France, XIV

4 There will be no whitewash in the White House.
Richard Milhous Nixon: Referring to the Watergate scandal. Statement, 17 Apr 1973

5 All things can corrupt perverted minds.
Ovid: Tristia, Bk. II

6 Any institution which does not suppose the people good, and the magistrate corruptible is evil.
Robespierre: Déclaration des droits de l'homme, 24 Apr 1793

7 Something is rotten in the state of Denmark.
William Shakespeare: Hamlet, I:4

8 All those men have their price.
Robert Walpole: Memoirs of Sir Robert Walpole (W. Coxe)

COSMETICS

See also appearance

1 Most women are not so young as they are painted.
Max Beerbohm: A Defence of Cosmetics

2 All the cosmetics names seemed obscenely obvious to me in their promise of sexual bliss. They were all firming or uplifting or invigorating. They made you *tingle*. Or *glow*. Or feel *young*.
Erica Jong: How to Save your Own Life

3 Waits at the window wearing the face that she keeps in a jar by the door.

COUNTRYSIDE

John Lennon: Eleanor Rigby (with Paul McCartney)

4 In the factory we make cosmetics. In the store we sell hope.
Charles Revson: Fire and Ice (A. Tobias)

COUNTRYSIDE

See also ecology, flowers, nature, trees

1 God made the country, and man made the town.
William Cowper: The Task

2 Ever charming, ever new,
When will the landscape tire the view?
John Dyer: Grongar Hill

3 When I am in the country I wish to vegetate like the country.
William Hazlitt: On Going a Journey

4 Are not these woods
More free from peril than the envious court?
William Shakespeare: As You Like It, II:1

COURAGE

See also endurance, heroism

1 The sons of the prophet were brave men and bold,
And quite unaccustomed to fear,
But the bravest by far in the ranks of the Shah
Was Abdul the Bulbul Amir.
Anonymous: Abdul the Bulbul Amir

2 Who dares, wins.
Anonymous: Motto of the British Special Air Service regiment

3 And though hard be the task,

'Keep a stiff upper lip.'
Phoebe Cary: Keep a Stiff Upper Lip

4 I'll bell the cat.
Archibald Douglas: Of his proposed capture of Robert Cochrane (executed 1482); the phrase 'bell the cat' was earlier used by Eustache Deschamps in his Ballade: Le Chat et les souris

5 None but the Brave deserves the Fair.
John Dryden: Alexander's Feast

6 Courage is the price that Life exacts for granting peace.
Amelia Earhart: Courage

7 It is better to die on your feet than to live on your knees.
Dolores Ibarruri: Speech, Paris, 3 Sept 1936

8 We could never learn to be brave and patient, if there were only joy in the world.
Helen Keller: Atlantic Monthly (May 1890)

9 If the creator had a purpose in equipping us with a neck, he surely meant us to stick it out.
Arthur Koestler: Encounter, May 1970

10 He was a bold man that first eat an oyster.
Jonathan Swift: Polite Conversation, Dialogue 2

11 Fortune favours the brave.
Terence: Phormio

COURTESY

See also chivalry, etiquette, manners

1 Civility costs nothing.
Proverb

2 If a man be gracious and courteous to strangers, it shews he is a citizen of the world.
Francis Bacon: Essays, 'Of Goodness and Goodness of Nature'

3 The English are polite by telling lies. The Americans are polite by telling the truth.
Malcolm Bradbury: Stepping Westward, Bk. II, Ch. 5

Of thinking too precisely on th' event.
William Shakespeare: Hamlet, IV:4

7 Cowards die many times before their deaths:
The valiant never taste of death but once.
William Shakespeare: Julius Caesar, II:2

COWARDICE

1 Probably a fear we have of facing up to the real issues. Could you say we were guilty of Noël Cowardice?
Peter De Vries: Comfort me with Apples, Ch. 8

2 None but a coward dares to boast that he has never known fear.
Marshal Foch: Attrib.

3 He led his regiment from behind
He found it less exciting.
W. S. Gilbert: The Gondoliers, I

4 To a surprising extent the warlords in shining armour, the apostles of the martial virtues, tend not to die fighting when the time comes. History is full of ignominious getaways by the great and famous.
George Orwell: Who Are the War Criminals?

5 The summer soldier and the sunshine patriot will, in this crisis, shrink from the service of their country.
Thomas Paine: Pennsylvania Journal, 'The American Crisis'

6 Some craven scruple

CREATION

1 The Hand that made us is divine.
Joseph Addison: The Spectator, 465

2 In the beginning God created the heaven and the earth.
Bible: Genesis: 1:1

3 Little Lamb, who made thee? Dost thou know who made thee?
William Blake: Songs of Innocence, 'The Lamb'

4 Whan that the month in which the world bigan,
That highte March, whan God first maked man.
Geoffrey Chaucer: The Canterbury Tales, 'The Nun's Priest's Tale'

5 'Who *is* the Potter, pray, and who the Pot?'
Edward Fitzgerald: The Rubáiyát of Omar Khayyám

6 It took the whole of Creation
To produce my foot, my each feather:
Now I hold creation in my foot.
Ted Hughes: Hawk Roosting

7 I cannot forgive Descartes; in all his philosophy he did his best to dispense with God. But he

54

could not avoid making Him set the world in motion with a flip of His thumb; after that he had no more use for God.
Blaise Pascal: Pensées, II

8 'Do you know how made you?' 'Nobody, as I knows on,' said the child, with a short laugh... 'I 'spect I grow'd.'
Harriet Beecher Stowe: Uncle Tom's Cabin, Ch. 20

9 Which beginning of time according to our Chronologie, fell upon the entrance of the night preceding the twenty third day of Octob., in the year of the Julian Calendar, 710.
James Ussher: Referring to the Creation, as described in Genesis, which, he had calculated, took place on 22 Oct 4004 BC. The Annals of the World

10 God made everything out of nothing. But the nothingness shows through.
Paul Valéry: Mauvaises Pensées et autres

11 The art of creation is older than the art of killing.
Andrei Voznesensky: Poem with a Footnote

CRICKET

See also sport and games

1 It's not in support of cricket but as an earnest protest against golf.
Max Beerbohm: Said when giving a shilling towards W. G. Grace's testimonial. Carr's Dictionary of Extraordinary English Cricketers

2 I do love cricket – it's so very English.
Sarah Bernhardt: On seeing a game of football. Nijinsky (R. Buckle)

3 They came to see me bat not to see you bowl.
W. G. Grace: Refusing to leave the crease after being bowled first ball in front of a large crowd. Attrib.

4 I've always wanted to be one of the top cricketers in the world and I wouldn't want to be in any other situation. I've worked hard and given myself to the game, and this is the result.
Brian Lara: Arriving at Edgbaston, to play for Warwickshire. The Independent, 28 Apr 1994

5 I've proved it's not just a gentleman's game. I was born in Yorkshire and I'm available if they want me.
Kathryn Leng: The Times, 30 Dec 1993

6 I tend to believe that cricket is the greatest thing that God ever created on earth...certainly greater than sex, although sex isn't too bad either.
Harold Pinter: The Observer, 5 Oct 1980

7 I have always looked upon cricket as organised loafing.
William Temple: Address to parents when headmaster of Repton School

8 If the French noblesse had been capable of playing cricket with their peasants, their chateaux would never have been burnt.
George Macaulay Trevelyan: English Social History, Ch. XIII

9 It requires one to assume such indecent postures.

Oscar Wilde: Explaining why he did not play cricket. Attrib.

CRIME

See also murder, theft

1 If poverty is the mother of crime, stupidity is its father.
Jean de La Bruyère: Les Caractères

2 Crime, like virtue, has its degrees.
Jean Racine: Phèdre, IV:2

3 We're barking mad about crime in this country. We have an obsession with believing the worst, conning ourselves that there was a golden age – typically 40 years before the one we're living in.
Nick Ross: Radio Times, 26 June–2 July 1993

4 I came to the conclusion many years ago that almost all crime is due to the repressed desire for aesthetic expression.
Evelyn Waugh: Decline and Fall, Pt. III, Ch. 1

CRITICISM

See also insults, writing

1 Of all fatiguing, futile, empty trades, the worst, I suppose, is writing about writing.
Hilaire Belloc: The Silence of the Sea

2 And why beholdest thou the mote that is in thy brother's eye, but considerest not the beam that is in thine own eye?
Bible: Matthew: 7:3

3 A great deal of contemporary criticism reads to me like a man saying: 'Of course I do not like

green cheese: I am very fond of brown sherry.'
G. K. Chesterton: All I Survey

4 If you hear that someone is speaking ill of you, instead of trying to defend yourself you should say: 'He obviously does not know me very well, since there are so many other faults he could have mentioned'.
Epictetus: Enchiridion

5 You *may* abuse a tragedy, though you cannot write one. You may scold a carpenter who has made you a bad table, though you cannot make a table. It is not your trade to make tables.
Samuel Johnson: Referring to the qualifications needed to indulge in literary criticism. Life of Johnson (J. Boswell), Vol. I

6 The pleasure of criticizing robs us of the pleasure of being moved by some very fine things.
Jean de La Bruyère: Les Caractères

7 People who like this sort of thing will find this is the sort of thing they like.
Abraham Lincoln: A comment on a book. Attrib.

8 I was so long writing my review that I never got around to reading the book.
Groucho Marx: Attrib.

9 People ask you for criticism, but they only want praise.
W. Somerset Maugham: Of Human Bondage, Ch. 50

10 Prolonged, indiscriminate reviewing of books involves constantly *inventing* reactions towards books about which one

has no spontaneous feelings whatever.
George Orwell: Confessions of a Book Reviewer

11 'Tis hard to say, if greater want of skill
Appear in writing or in judging ill.
Alexander Pope: An Essay on Criticism

12 I never read anything concerning my work. I feel that criticism is a letter to the public which the author, since it is not directed to him, does not have to open and read.
Rainer Maria Rilke: Letters

CRITICS

1 I make my pictures for people, not for critics.
Cecil B. de Mille: Halliwell's Filmgoer's and Video Viewer's Companion

2 A good critic is one who narrates the adventures of his mind among masterpieces.
Anatole France: The Literary Life, Preface

3 Asking a working writer what he thinks about critics is like asking a lamp-post how it feels about dogs.
Christopher Hampton: The Sunday Times Magazine, 16 Oct 1977

4 A fly, Sir, may sting a stately horse and make him wince; but one is but an insect, and the other is a horse still.
Samuel Johnson: Life of Johnson (J. Boswell), Vol. I

5 Pay no attention to what the critics say; no statue has ever been put up to a critic.
Jean Sibelius: Attrib.

6 I had another dream the other day about music critics. They were small and rodent-like with padlocked ears, as if they had stepped out of a painting by Goya.
Igor Stravinsky: The Evening Standard, 29 Oct 1969

7 A critic is a man who knows the way but can't drive the car.
Kenneth Tynan: New York Times Magazine, 9 Jan 1966

CRUELTY

See also hurt, nastiness, violence

1 The wish to hurt, the momentary intoxication with pain, is the loophole through which the pervert climbs into the minds of ordinary men.
Jacob Bronowski: The Face of Violence, Ch. 5

2 Man's inhumanity to man
Makes countless thousands mourn!
Robert Burns: Man was Made to Mourn

3 Fear is the parent of cruelty.
J. A. Froude: Short Studies on Great Subjects, 'Party Politics'

4 A cruel story runs on wheels, and every hand oils the wheels as they run.
Ouida: Wisdom, Wit and Pathos, 'Moths'

5 I must be cruel only to be kind.
William Shakespeare: Hamlet, III:4

CULTURE

See also civilization, philistinism

1 Culture is the passion for sweetness and light, and (what is more) the passion for making them prevail.
Matthew Arnold: Literature and Dogma, Preface

2 Culture is an instrument wielded by professors to manufacture professors, who when their turn comes will manufacture professors.
Simone Weil: The Need for Roots

3 Mrs Ballinger is one of the ladies who pursue Culture in bands, as though it were dangerous to meet it alone.
Edith Wharton: Xingu, Ch. 1

CURIOSITY

See also wonder

1 Curiosity killed the cat.
Proverb

2 'If everybody minded their own business,' the Duchess said in a hoarse growl, 'the world would go round a deal faster than it does.'
Lewis Carroll: Alice's Adventures in Wonderland, Ch. 6

3 The world is but a school of inquiry.
Michel de Montaigne: Essais, III

4 Curiosity will conquer fear even more than bravery will.
James Stephens: The Crock of Gold

5 Disinterested intellectual curiosity is the life blood of real civilisation.
George Macaulay Trevelyan: English Social History, Preface

CYNICISM

1 Cynicism is an unpleasant way of saying the truth.
Lillian Hellman: The Little Foxes

2 A cynic is a man who, when he smells flowers, looks around for a coffin.
H. L. Mencken: Attrib.

3 Cynicism is humour in ill-health.
H. G. Wells: Short Stories, 'The Last Trump'

4 A man who knows the price of everything and the value of nothing.
Oscar Wilde: A cynic. Lady Windermere's Fan, III

D

DAMNATION

See also devil, hell

1 Blot out his name, then, record one lost soul more,
   One task more declined, one more footpath untrod,
   One more devils'-triumph and sorrow for angels,
   One wrong more to man, one more insult to God!
   Robert Browning: The Lost Leader

2 You will be damned if you do – And you will be damned if you don't.
   Lorenzo Dow: Reflections on the Love of God

DANGER

1 If you play with fire you get burnt.
   Proverb

2 Dangers by being despised grow great.
   Edmund Burke: Speech, House of Commons, 11 May 1792

3 Believe me! The secret of reaping the greatest fruitfulness and the greatest enjoyment from life is to *live dangerously!*
   Friedrich Nietzsche: Die Fröhliche Wissenschaft, Bk. IV

4 There's a snake hidden in the grass.
   Virgil: Eclogue, Bk. III

DAY

1 Awake! for Morning in the Bowl of Night
   Has flung the Stone that puts the Stars to Flight:
   And Lo! the Hunter of the East has caught
   The Sultan's Turret in a Noose of Light.
   Edward Fitzgerald: The Rubáiyát of Omar Khayyám

2 Oh, what a beautiful morning! Oh, what a beautiful day!
   Oscar Hammerstein: From the musical Oklahoma. Oh, What a Beautiful Morning

3 Sweet day, so cool, so calm, so bright,
   The bridal of the earth and sky.
   George Herbert: Virtue

4 Under the opening eye-lids of the morn.
   John Milton: Lycidas

5 Three o'clock is always too late or too early for anything you want to do.
   Jean-Paul Sartre: Nausea

DEATH

See also afterlife, epitaphs, last words, obituaries

1 Dead men tell no tales.
   Proverb

2 Death is the great leveller.
   Proverb

3 Never speak ill of the dead.
   Proverb

4 Nothing is certain but death and taxes.
   Proverb

5 There will be sleeping enough in the grave.
   Proverb

6 It's not that I'm afraid to die. I just don't want to be there when it happens.
Woody Allen: Without Feathers, 'Death (A Play)'

7 Swing low sweet chariot,
Comin' for to carry me home,
I looked over Jordan an' what did I see?
A band of Angels coming after me,
Comin' for to carry me home.
Anonymous: Swing Low, Sweet Chariot

8 I have often thought upon death, and I find it the least of all evils.
Francis Bacon: An Essay on Death

9 Men fear death, as children fear to go in the dark; and as that natural fear in children is increased with tales, so is the other.
Francis Bacon: Essays, 'Of Death'

10 To die will be an awfully big adventure.
J. M. Barrie: Peter Pan, III

11 Graveyards have a morbid reputation. Many people associate them with death.
Bishop of Bath and Wells: Remark, Apr 1988

12 The physician cutteth off a long disease; and he that is today a king tomorrow shall die.
Bible: Ecclesiasticus: 10:10

13 We all labour against our own cure, for death is the cure of all diseases.
Thomas Browne: Religio Medici

14 I am ready to meet my Maker. Whether my Maker is ready for the ordeal of meeting me is another matter.
Winston Churchill: On his 75th birthday. Speech, 30 Nov 1949

15 Strange, is it not? that of the myriads who
Before us pass'd the door of Darkness through,
Not one returns to tell us of the Road,
Which to discover we must travel too.
Edward Fitzgerald: The Rubáiyát of Omar Khayyám

16 Why fear death? It is the most beautiful adventure in life.
Charles Frohman: Said before going down with the liner Lusitania, alluding to 'To die will be an awfully big adventure' from Barrie's Peter Pan, which Frohman had produced. J. M. Barrie and the Lost Boys (A. Birkin)

17 I am told he makes a very handsome corpse, and becomes his coffin prodigiously.
Oliver Goldsmith: The Good-Natured Man, I

18 The doctors found, when she was dead –
Her last disorder mortal.
Oliver Goldsmith: Elegy on Mrs. Mary Blaize

19 Grieve not that I die young. Is it not well
To pass away ere life hath lost its brightness?
Lady Flora Hastings: Swan Song

20 Once you're dead, you're made for life.
Jimi Hendrix: Attrib.

21 It is the duty of a doctor to pro-

DEATH

22 Death...It's the only thing we haven't succeeded in completely vulgarizing.
Aldous Huxley: Eyeless in Gaza, Ch. 31

23 It matters not how a man dies, but how he lives. The act of dying is not of importance, it lasts so short a time.
Samuel Johnson: Life of Johnson (J. Boswell), Vol. II

24 Above ground I shall be food for kites; below I shall be food for mole-crickets and ants. Why rob one to feed the other?
Juang-zu: When asked on his deathbed what his wishes were regarding the disposal of his body. Famous Last Words (B. Conrad)

25 That is the road we all have to take – over the Bridge of Sighs into eternity.
Søren Kierkegaard: Kierkegaard Anthology (Auden)

26 The dead don't die. They look on and help.
D. H. Lawrence: Letter

27 I detest life-insurance agents. They always argue that I shall some day die, which is not so.
Stephen Leacock: Literary Lapses

28 There is a Reaper whose name is Death,
And, with his sickle keen,
He reaps the bearded grain at a breath,
And the flowers that grow between.
Henry Wadsworth Longfellow: The Reaper and the Flowers

29 Either he's dead or my watch has stopped.
Groucho Marx: A Day at the Races

30 Dying is a very dull, dreary affair. And my advice to you is to have nothing whatever to do with it.
W. Somerset Maugham: Escape from the Shadows (Robin Maugham)

31 Whom the gods love dies young.
Menander: Dis Exapaton

32 One dies only once, and it's for such a long time!
Molière: Le Dépit amoureux, V:3

33 It's not pining, it's passed on. This parrot is no more....It's an ex-parrot.
Monty Python's Flying Circus: Sketch, 14 Dec 1969

34 Oh well, no matter what happens, there's always death.
Napoleon I: Attrib.

35 Many men on the point of an edifying death would be furious if they were suddenly restored to life.
Cesare Pavese

36 He's gone to join the majority.
Petronius Arbiter: Referring to a dead man. Satyricon: Cena Trimalchionis, 42

37 Dying
is an art, like everything else.
I do it exceptionally well.
Sylvia Plath: Lady Lazarus

38 I mount! I fly!
O grave! where is thy victory?
O death! where is thy sting?
Alexander Pope: The Dying Christian to his Soul

39 I will be
A bridegroom in my death, and
run into 't
As to a lover's bed.
*William Shakespeare: Antony and
Cleopatra, IV:12*

40 He had rather
Groan so in perpetuity, than be
cured
By the sure physician, death.
William Shakespeare: Cymbeline

41 The worst is death, and death
will have his day.
*William Shakespeare: Richard II,
III:2*

42 After all, what *is* death? Just nature's way of telling us to slow
down.
*Dick Sharples: In Loving
Memory, Yorkshire Television,
1979*

43 Death is the veil which those
who live call life:
They sleep, and it is lifted.
*Percy Bysshe Shelley: Prometheus
Unbound, III*

44 I cannot forgive my friends for
dying: I do not find these vanishing acts of theirs at all amusing.
Logan Pearsall Smith: Trivia

45 Death must be distinguished
from dying, with which it is often confused.
*Sydney Smith: The Smith of
Smiths (Pearson)*

46 And Death Shall Have No
Dominion.
Dylan Thomas: Title of poem

47 Death is the price paid by life
for an enhancement of the com-
plexity of a live organism's structure.
Arnold Toynbee: Life After Death

48 While I thought that I was
learning how to live, I have
been learning how to die.
Leonardo da Vinci: Notebooks

49 The human race is the only
one that knows it must die, and
it knows this only through its experience. A child brought up
alone and transported to a
desert island would have no
more idea of death than a cat or
a plant.
*Voltaire: The Oxford Book of
Death (D. J. Enright)*

DEBAUCHERY

See also lust, pleasure, sex

1 A great many people have come
up to me and asked how I manage to get so much work done
and still keep looking so dissipated.
*Robert Benchley: Chips off the Old
Benchley, 'How to Get Things
Done'*

2 My problem lies in reconciling
my gross habits with my net income.
Errol Flynn: Attrib.

3 No one ever suddenly became
depraved.
Juvenal: Satires, II

4 Home is heaven and orgies are
vile
But you need an orgy, once in a
while.
Ogden Nash

5 Once: a philosopher; twice: a
pervert!
*Voltaire: Turning down an
invitation to an orgy, having
attended one the previous night for
the first time. Attrib.*

DECEPTION

See also appearances, hypocrisy, insincerity, lying

1 To deceive oneself is very easy.
Proverb

2 Beware of false prophets, which come to you in sheep's clothing, but inwardly they are ravening wolves.
Bible: Matthew: 7:15

3 Almost every man wastes part of his life in attempts to display qualities which he does not possess, and to gain applause which he cannot keep.
Samuel Johnson: The Rambler

4 You can fool some of the people all the time and all the people some of the time; but you can't fool all the people all the time.
Abraham Lincoln: Attrib.

5 You can fool too many of the people too much of the time.
James Thurber: Fables for Our Time, 'The Owl Who Was God'

DECISION

1 Tender-handed stroke a nettle,
And it stings you for your pains;
Grasp it like a man of mettle,
And it soft as silk remains.
Aaron Hill: Verses Written on Window

2 Like all weak men he laid an exaggerated stress on not changing one's mind.
W. Somerset Maugham: Of Human Bondage, Ch. 37

3 If someone tells you he is going to make 'a realistic decision', you immediately understand that he has resolved to do something bad.
Mary McCarthy: On the Contrary

DECLINE

1 More will mean worse.
Kingsley Amis: Encounter, July 1960

2 It is the logic of our times,
No subject for immortal verse –
That we who lived by honest dreams
Defend the bad against the worse.
C. Day Lewis: Where are the War Poets?

3 It is only a step from the sublime to the ridiculous.
Napoleon I: Remark following the retreat from Moscow, 1812. Attrib.

4 There may have been disillusionments in the lives of the medieval saints, but they would scarcely have been better pleased if they could have foreseen that their names would be associated nowadays chiefly with racehorses and the cheaper clarets.
Saki: Reginald at the Carlton

5 I shall be like that tree; I shall die from the top.
Jonathan Swift: Predicting his own mental decline on seeing a tree with a withered crown. Lives of the Wits (H. Pearson)

6 I started at the top and worked my way down.
Orson Welles: The Filmgoer's Book of Quotes (Leslie Halliwell)

DEFEAT

See also loss

1 As always, victory finds a hundred fathers, but defeat is an orphan.
Count Galeazzo Ciano: Diary entry, 9 Sept 1942

2 'Tis better to have fought and lost,
Than never to have fought at all.
Arthur Hugh Clough: Peschiera

3 A man can be destroyed but not defeated.
Ernest Hemingway: The Old Man and the Sea

4 We wuz robbed – We should have stood in bed.
Joe Jacobs: After Max Schmeling's defeat by Jack Sharkey. Strong Cigars and Lovely Women (J. Lardner)

5 Woe to the vanquished.
Livy: History, V:48

6 Every man meets his Waterloo at last.
Wendell Phillips: Speech, Brooklyn, 1 Nov 1859

7 Well, I have only one consolation, No candidate was ever elected ex-president by such a large majority!
William Howard Taft: Referring to his disastrous defeat in the 1912 presidential election. Attrib.

8 Please understand that there is no one depressed in *this* house; we are not interested in the possibilities of defeat; they do not exist.
Victoria: Referring to the Boer War; said to Balfour. Life of Salisbury (Lady G. Cecil)

9 Another year! – another deadly blow!
Another mighty empire overthrown!
And we are left, or shall be left, alone.
William Wordsworth: Napoleon defeated Prussia at the Battles of Jena and Anerstädt, 14 Oct 1806. Sonnets, 'Another year!'

DELUSION

1 But yet the light that led astray Was light from Heaven.
Robert Burns: The Vision

2 Take the life-lie away from the average man and straight away you take away his happiness.
Henrik Ibsen: The Wild Duck, V

3 Many people have delusions of grandeur but you're deluded by triviality.
Eugène Ionesco: Exit the King

DEMOCRACY

See also government, majority, public

1 One man shall have one vote.
John Cartwright: People's Barrier Against Undue Influence

2 Democracy means government by the uneducated, while aristocracy means government by the badly educated.
G. K. Chesterton: The New York Times, 1 Feb 1931

3 Democracy is the wholesome and pure air without which a socialist public organisation cannot live a full-blooded life.

Mikhail Gorbachov: Report to 27th Party Congress. Speech, 25 Feb 1986

4 Democracy is only an experiment in government, and it has the obvious disadvantage of merely counting votes instead of weighing them.
Dean Inge: Possible Recovery?

5 A democracy is a state which recognises the subjecting of the minority to the majority.
Lenin: The State and The Revolution

6 No man is good enough to govern another man without that other's consent.
Abraham Lincoln: Speech, 1854

7 The ballot is stronger than the bullet.
Abraham Lincoln: Speech, 19 May 1856

8 that government of the people, by the people, and for the people, shall not perish from the earth.
Abraham Lincoln: Speech, 19 Nov 1863, dedicating the national cemetery on the site of the Battle of Gettysburg

9 Man's capacity for evil makes democracy necessary and man's capacity for good makes democracy possible.
Reinhold Niebuhr: Quoted by Anthony Wedgwood Benn in The Times, 18 Jul 1977

10 Democracy passes into despotism.
Plato: Republic, Bk. 8

11 You won the elections, but I won the count.
Anastasio Somoza: The Guardian, 17 June 1977

12 It's not the voting that's democracy; it's the counting.
Tom Stoppard: Jumpers

13 Democracy means simply the bludgeoning of the people by the people for the people.
Oscar Wilde: The Soul of Man under Socialism

DESIRE

See also hunger, lust

1 Those who restrain Desire, do so because theirs is weak enough to be restrained.
William Blake: The Marriage of Heaven and Hell, 'Those who restrain Desire…'

2 Man's Desires are limited by his Perceptions; none can desire what he has not perceived.
William Blake: There is no Natural Religion

3 There is nothing like desire for preventing the thing one says from bearing any resemblance to what one has in mind.
Marcel Proust: A la recherche du temps perdu: Le Côté de Guermantes

4 There are two tragedies in life. One is to lose your heart's desire. The other is to gain it.
George Bernard Shaw: Man and Superman, IV

5 Desire is the very essence of man.
Benedict Spinoza: Ethics

DESPAIR

See also sorrow

1 Despair is better treated with hope, not dope.

Richard Asher: Lancet, I:954, 1958

2 The name of the slough was Despond.
John Bunyan: The Pilgrim's Progress, Pt. I

3 Don't despair, not even over the fact that you don't despair.
Franz Kafka: Diary

4 The mass of men lead lives of quiet desperation.
Henry David Thoreau: Walden, 'Economy'

DESTINY

See also purpose

1 Whatever may happen to you was prepared for you from all eternity; and the implication of causes was from eternity spinning the thread of your being.
Marcus Aurelius: Meditations, Bk. X, Ch. 5

2 I felt as if I were walking with destiny, and that all my past life had been but a preparation for this hour and this trial.
Winston Churchill: The Gathering Storm, Ch. 38

3 The Moving Finger writes; and, having writ,
Moves on: nor all thy Piety nor Wit
Shall lure it back to cancel half a Line,
Nor all thy Tears wash out a Word of it.
Edward Fitzgerald: The Rubáiyát of Omar Khayyám

4 Tempt not the stars, young man, thou canst not play
With the severity of fate.
John Ford: The Broken Heart, I:3

5 Anatomy is destiny.
Sigmund Freud

6 I go the way that Providence dictates with the assurance of a sleepwalker.
Adolf Hitler: Referring to his successful re-occupation of the Rhineland, despite advice against the attempt. Speech, Munich, 15 Mar 1936

7 Do not try to find out – we're forbidden to know – what end the gods have in store for me, or for you.
Horace: Odes, I

8 We may become the makers of our fate when we have ceased to pose as its prophets.
Karl Popper: The Observer, 28 Dec 1975

9 There's a divinity that shapes our ends,
Rough-hew them how we will.
William Shakespeare: Hamlet, V:2

10 The wheel is come full circle.
William Shakespeare: King Lear, V:3

11 We are merely the stars' tennis-balls, struck and bandied
Which way please them.
John Webster: The Duchess of Malfi, V:4

12 Every bullet has its billet.
William III: Journal (John Wesley), 6 June 1765

DETERMINATION

See also endurance, persistence

1 Where there's a will there's a way.
Proverb

DEVIL

2 There is no such thing as a great talent without great will-power.
Honoré de Balzac: La Muse du département

3 It will be conquered; I will not capitulate.
Samuel Johnson: Referring to his illness. Life of Johnson (J. Boswell), Vol. IV

4 We must just KBO ('Keep Buggering On').
Winston Churchill: Remark, Dec 1941. Finest Hour (M. Gilbert)

5 Look for me by moonlight;
Watch for me by moonlight;
I'll come to thee by moonlight, though hell should bar the way!
Alfred Noyes: The Highwayman

6 We are not now that strength which in old days
Moved earth and heaven; that which we are, we are;
One equal temper of heroic hearts,
Made weak by time and fate, but strong in will
To strive, to seek, to find, and not to yield.
Alfred, Lord Tennyson: Ulysses

7 I fight on, I fight to win.
Margaret Thatcher: Referring to the election for the leadership of the Conservative Party. The Times, 21 Nov 1990

8 I knew what I wanted and determined at an early age that no man would ever tell me what to do. I would make my own rules and down with the double standards.
Mae West: Working Woman, Feb 1979

DEVIL

1 The devil is not so black as he is painted.
Proverb

2 Talk of the devil, and he is bound to appear.
Proverb

3 And that no man might buy or sell, save he that had the mark, or the name of the beast, or the number of his name.
Here is wisdom. Let him that hath understanding count the number of the beast: for it is the number of a man; and his number is Six hundred threescore and six.
Bible: Revelations: 13:17–18

4 O Thou! Whatever title suit thee –
Auld Hornie, Satan, Nick, or Clootie.
Robert Burns: Address to the Devil

5 It is so stupid of modern civilization to have given up believing in the devil when he is the only explanation of it.
Ronald Knox: Let Dons Delight

6 The devil can cite Scripture for his purpose.
William Shakespeare: The Merchant of Venice, I:3

7 Sometimes
The Devil is a gentleman.
Percy Bysshe Shelley: Peter Bell the Third

DIARIES

1 Only good girls keep diaries. Bad girls don't have the time.
Tallulah Bankhead: Attrib.

2 I do not keep a diary. Never

have. To write a diary every day is like returning to one's own vomit.
Enoch Powell: Sunday Times, 6 Nov 1977

3 What is a diary as a rule? A document useful to the person who keeps it, dull to the contemporary who reads it, invaluable to the student, centuries afterwards, who treasures it!
Ellen Terry: The Story of My Life, Ch. 14

4 I never travel without my diary. One should always have something sensational to read in the train.
Oscar Wilde: The Importance of Being Earnest, II

DIPLOMACY

See also tact

1 It is better for aged diplomats to be bored than for young men to die.
Warren Austin: When asked if he got tired during long debates at the UN. Attrib.

2 There are three groups that no British Prime Minister should provoke: the Vatican, the Treasury and the miners.
Stanley Baldwin: A similar remark is often attributed to Harold Macmillan. Attrib.

3 To jaw-jaw is better than to war-war.
Winston Churchill: Speech, Washington, 26 June 1954

4 When you have to kill a man it costs nothing to be polite.
Winston Churchill: Justifying the fact that the declaration of war against Japan was made in the usual diplomatic language. The Grand Alliance

5 America has all that Russia has not. Russia has things America has not. Why will America not reach out a hand to Russia, as I have given my hand?
Isadora Duncan: Speaking in support of Russia following the 1917 Revolution. Speech, Symphony Hall, Boston, 1922

6 We have stood alone in that which is called isolation – our splendid isolation, as one of our colonial friends was good enough to call it.
George Joachim Goschen: Speech, Lewes, 26 Feb 1896

7 Megaphone diplomacy leads to a dialogue of the deaf.
Geoffrey Howe: The Observer, 'Sayings of the Week', 29 Sept 1985

8 Official dignity tends to increase in inverse ratio to the importance of the country in which the office is held.
Aldous Huxley: Beyond the Mexique Bay

9 Let us never negotiate out of fear, but let us never fear to negotiate.
John Fitzgerald Kennedy: Inaugural address, 20 Jan 1961

10 The great nations have always acted like gangsters, and the small nations like prostitutes.
Stanley Kubrick: The Guardian, 5 June 1963

11 All diplomacy is a continuation of war by other means.
Chou En Lai

12 *La cordiale entente qui existe entre mon gouvernement et le sien.* The friendly understanding that exists between my government and hers.
Louis Philippe: Referring to an informal understanding reached between Britain and France in 1843. The more familiar phrase, 'entente cordiale', was first used in 1844. Speech, 27 Dec 1843

13 Let them especially put their demands in such a way that Great Britain could say that she supported both sides.
Ramsey MacDonald: Referring to France and Germany. The Origins of the Second Word War (A. J. P. Taylor), Ch. 3

14 An ambassador is an honest man sent to lie abroad for the good of his country.
Henry Wotton: Life (Izaak Walton)

DISABILITY

See also blindness

1 If there are any of you at the back who do not hear me, please don't raise your hands because I am also nearsighted.
W. H. Auden: Starting a lecture in a large hall. In Book of the Month Club News, Dec 1946

2 I'm a coloured, one-eyed Jew.
Sammy Davis Jnr: When asked what his handicap was during a game of golf. Attrib.

3 I am happy...with who I am and I do not want to be 'fixed'.
Roslyn Rosen: President of the National Association of the Deaf. The Times, 16 June 1994

4 You are not crippled at all unless your mind is in a splint.
Frank Scully: Bartlett's Unfamiliar Quotations (Leonard Louis Levinson)

DISAPPOINTMENT

See also disillusion

1 Unhappiness is best defined as the difference between our talents and our expectations.
Edward de Bono: The Observer, 'Sayings of the Week', 12 June 1977

2 The best laid schemes o' mice an' men
Gang aft a-gley,
An' lea'e us nought but grief an' pain
For promis'd joy.
Robert Burns: To a Mouse

3 Oh, I wish that God had not given me what I prayed for! It was not so good as I thought.
Johanna Spyri: Heidi, Ch. 11

DISCONTENT

See also envy

1 And sigh that one thing only has been lent
To youth and age in common – discontent.
Matthew Arnold: Youth's Agitations

2 So have I loitered my life away, reading books, looking at pictures, going to plays, hearing, thinking, writing on what pleased me best. I have wanted only one thing to make me happy, but wanting that have wanted everything.

William Hazlitt: English Literature, Ch. XVII, 'My First Acquaintance with Poets'

3 Ever let the fancy roam,
Pleasure never is at home.

John Keats: Fancy, I

4 He disdains all things above his reach, and preferreth all countries before his own.

Thomas Overbury: Miscellaneous Works, 'An Affectate Traveller'

5 While not exactly disgruntled, he was far from feeling gruntled.

P. G. Wodehouse: The Code of the Woosters

DISCOVERY

See also exploration, science, space

1 *Eureka!*
I have found it!

Archimedes: An exclamation of joy supposedly uttered as, stepping into a bath and noticing the water overflowing, he saw the answer to a problem and began the train of thought that led to his principle of buoyancy. Attrib.

2 At daylight in the morning we discovered a bay, which appeared to be tolerably well sheltered from all winds, into which I resolved to go with the ship.

James Cook: On the discovery of Botany Bay. Journal, 28 Apr 1770

3 We have discovered the secret of life!

Francis Crick: Excitedly bursting into a Cambridge pub with James Watson to celebrate the fact that they had unravelled the structure of DNA. The Double Helix (J. D. Watson)

4 God could cause us considerable embarrassment by revealing all the secrets of nature to us: we should not know what to do for sheer apathy and boredom.

Goethe: Memoirs (Riemer)

5 I do not know what I may appear to the world, but to myself I seem to have been only like a boy playing on the sea-shore, and diverting myself in now and then finding a smoother pebble or a prettier shell than ordinary, whilst the great ocean of truth lay all undiscovered before me.

Isaac Newton: Isaac Newton (L. T. More)

6 The people – could you patent the sun?

Jonas E. Salk: On being asked who owned the patent on his polio vaccine. Famous Men of Science (S. Bolton)

7 We must also keep in mind that discoveries are usually not made by one man alone, but that many brains and many hands are needed before a discovery is made for which one man receives the credit.

Henry E. Sigerist: A History of Medicine, Vol. I, Introduction

8 Discovery consists of seeing what everybody has seen and thinking what nobody has thought.

Albert Szent-Györgyi: The Scientist Speculates (I. J. Good)

DISEASE

See also illness

1 A disease known is half cured.
Proverb

2 We are led to think of diseases as isolated disturbances in a healthy body, not as the phases of certain periods of bodily development.
Clifford Allbutt: Bulletin of the New York Academy of Medicine, 4:1000, 1928 (F. H. Garrison)

3 Before this strange disease of modern life,
With its sick hurry, its divided aims.
Matthew Arnold: The Scholar Gipsy

4 Cure the disease and kill the patient.
Francis Bacon: Essays, 'Of Friendship'

5 Life is an incurable disease.
Abraham Cowley: To Dr Scarborough

6 Epidemics have often been more influential than statesman and soldiers in shaping the course of political history, and diseases may also colour the moods of civilizations.
René Dubos: The White Plague, Ch. 5

7 Disease is an experience of mortal mind. It is fear made manifest on the body.
Mary Baker Eddy: Science and Health, Ch. 14

8 Some people are so sensitive they feel snubbed if an epidemic overlooks them.
Frank (Kin) Hubbard: Abe Martin's Broadcast

9 I have Bright's disease and he has mine.
S. J. Perelman: Attrib.

10 Diseases are the tax on pleasures.
John Ray: English Proverbs

11 The diseases which destroy a man are no less natural than the instincts which preserve him.
George Santayana: Dialogues in Limbo, 3

12 The art of medicine consists of amusing the patient while Nature cures the disease.
Voltaire: Attrib.

13 I would like to remind those responsible for the treatment of tuberculosis that Keats wrote his best poems while dying of this disease. In my opinion he would never have done so under the influence of modern chemotherapy.
Arthur M. Walker: Walkerisms (Julius L. Wilson)

DISILLUSION

See also disappointment

1 The price one pays for pursuing any profession or calling is an intimate knowledge of its ugly side.
James Baldwin: Nobody Knows My Name

2 If you live long enough, you'll see that every victory turns into a defeat.
Simone de Beauvoir: Tous les hommes sont mortels

3 I have protracted my work till most of those whom I wished to please have sunk into the grave; and success and miscarriage are empty sounds.
Samuel Johnson: Dictionary of the English Language

4 One stops being a child when one realizes that telling one's trouble does not make it better.
Cesare Pavese: The Business of Living: Diaries 1935–50

DISMISSAL

1 It is not fit that you should sit here any longer!...you shall now give place to better men.
Oliver Cromwell: Speech to the Rump Parliament, 22 Jan 1655

2 Go, and never darken my towels again!
Groucho Marx: Duck Soup

3 We Don't Want To Lose You But We Think You Ought To Go.
Paul Alfred Rubens: Song title

4 Stand not upon the order of your going,
But go at once.
William Shakespeare: Macbeth, III:4

5 Dropping the pilot.
John Tenniel: Caption of a cartoon. The cartoon refers to Bismarck's resignation portraying him as a ship's pilot walking down the gangway of the ship while Wilhelm II watches from the deck.
Punch, 29 Mar 1890

6 The son of a bitch isn't going to resign on me, I want him fired.

Harry S. Truman: To Omar Bradley, when Truman sacked MacArthur from his command of UN forces in Korea, 1951. Attrib.

DOCTORS

See also medicine, remedies

1 God heals, and the doctor takes the fee.
Proverb

2 I am dying with the help of too many physicians.
Alexander the Great: Attrib.

3 Fifty years ago the successful doctor was said to need three things; a top hat to give him Authority, a paunch to give him Dignity, and piles to give him an Anxious Expression.
Anonymous: Lancet, 1:169, 1951

4 They answered, as they took their fees,
'There is no cure for this disease.'
Hilaire Belloc: Cautionary Tales, 'Henry King'

5 BODY-SNATCHER, n. A robber of grave-worms. One who supplies the young physicians with that with which the old physicians have supplied the undertaker.
Ambrose Bierce: The Devil's Dictionary

6 Doctors are just the same as lawyers; the only difference is that lawyers merely rob you, whereas doctors rob you and kill you, too.
Anton Chekhov: Ivanov, I

7 The skilful doctor treats those

who are well but the inferior doctor treats those who are ill.
Ch'in Yueh-jen

8 There are more old drunkards than old doctors.
Benjamin Franklin: Attrib.

9 A physician who is a lover of wisdom is the equal to a god.
Hippocrates: Decorum, V

10 I suppose one has a greater sense of intellectual degradation after an interview with a doctor than from any human experience.
Alice James: The Diary of Alice James (ed. Leon Edel), 27 Sept 1890

11 A doctor is a man licensed to make grave mistakes.
Leonard Louis Levinson: Bartlett's Unfamiliar Quotations (Leonard Louis Levinson)

12 A physician who treats himself has a fool for a patient.
William Osler: Sir William Osler: Aphorisms, Ch. I (William B. Bean)

13 There is not a doctor who desires the health of his friends; not a soldier who desires the peace of his country.
Philemon: Fabulae Incertae, Fragment 46

14 Who shall decide when doctors disagree?
Alexander Pope: Moral Essays, III

15 The best doctor in the world is the Veterinarian. He can't ask his patients what is the matter – he's got to just know.
Will Rogers: The Autobiography of Will Rogers, 12

16 The most tragic thing in the world is a sick doctor.
George Bernard Shaw: The Doctor's Dilemma, I

17 There are worse occupations in the world than feeling a woman's pulse.
Laurence Sterne

18 Mr. Anaesthetist, if the patient can keep awake, surely you can.
Wilfred Trotter: Quoted in Lancet, 2:1340, 1965

19 A physician is one who pours drugs of which he knows little into a body of which he knows less.
Voltaire: Attrib.

20 Physicians are like kings, – they brook no contradiction.
John Webster: The Duchess of Malfi, V:2

DOGS

1 The great pleasure of a dog is that you may make a fool of yourself with him and not only will he not scold you, he will make a fool of himself too.
Samuel Butler: Notebooks

2 She was always attentive to the feelings of dogs, and very polite if she had to decline their advances.
George Eliot: Middlemarch, Ch. 39

3 The dog, to gain some private ends,
Went mad and bit the man.
Oliver Goldsmith: Elegy on the Death of a Mad Dog

4 You ain't nothin' but a hound dog,
Cryin' all the time.
Jerry Leiber: Hound Dog (with Mike Stoller)

5 A door is what a dog is perpetually on the wrong side of.
Ogden Nash: A Dog's Best Friend is his Illiteracy

6 A huge dog, tied by a chain, was painted on the wall and over it was written in capital letters 'Beware of the dog.'
Petronius Arbiter: Satyricon: Cena Trimalchionis, 29

7 I am His Highness' dog at Kew;
Pray tell me sir, whose dog are you?
Alexander Pope: On the collar of a dog given to Frederick, Prince of Wales

8 That indefatigable and unsavoury engine of pollution, the dog.
John Sparrow: Letter to The Times, 30 Sep 1975

9 I loathe people who keep dogs. They are cowards who haven't got the guts to bite people themselves.
August Strindberg: A Madman's Diary

DOUBT

See also indecision, scepticism, uncertainty

1 And immediately Jesus stretched forth his hand, and caught him, and said unto him, O thou of little faith, wherefore didst thou doubt?
Bible: Matthew: 14:31

2 His doubts are better than most people's certainties.
Lord Hardwicke: Referring to Dirleton's Doubts. Life of Johnson (J. Boswell)

3 The trouble with the world is that the stupid are cocksure and the intelligent full of doubt.
Bertrand Russell: Autobiography

DREAMS

1 So I awoke, and behold it was a dream.
John Bunyan: The Pilgrim's Progress, Pt. 1

2 I do not know whether I was then a man dreaming I was a butterfly, or whether I am now a butterfly dreaming I am a man.
Chuang Tse: Chuang Tse (H. A. Giles), Ch. 2

3 Castles in the air – they're so easy to take refuge in. So easy to build, too.
Henrik Ibsen: The Master Builder, III

4 Dreams are true while they last, and do we not live in dreams?
Alfred, Lord Tennyson: The Higher Pantheism

DRINKS

See also alcohol, drunkenness, water

1 If I had known there was no Latin word for tea I would have caught the vulgar stuff alone.
Hilaire Belloc: Attrib.

2 Drink no longer water, but use a little wine for thy stomach's sake and thine often infirmities.
Bible: I Timothy: 5:23

3 I am willing to taste any drink once.
James Cabell: Jurgen, Ch. 1

4 If someone asks for a soft drink

at a party, we no longer think he is a wimp.
Edwina Currie: Speech, Dec 1988

5 One more drink and I'd be under the host.
Dorothy Parker: You Might As Well Live (J. Keats)

6 I think it must be so, for I have been drinking it for sixty-five years and I am not dead yet.
Voltaire: On learning that coffee was considered a slow poison. Attrib.

DRUGS

1 A drug is that substance which, when injected into a rat, will produce a scientific report.
Anonymous

2 Half the modern drugs could well be thrown out the window except that the birds might eat them.
Martin H. Fischer: Fischerisms (Howard Fabing and Ray Marr)

3 Two great European narcotics, alcohol and Christianity.
Friedrich Nietzsche: The Twilight of the Idols, 'Things the Germans Lack'

4 Cocaine is God's way of saying you're making too much money.
Robin Williams: Screen International, 15 Dec 1990

5 Americans use drugs as if consumption bestowed a 'special license' to be an asshole.
Frank Zappa: The Real Frank Zappa Book

DRUNKENNESS

See also alcohol

1 What shall we do with the drunken sailor
Early in the morning?
Hoo-ray and up she rises
Early in the morning.
Anonymous: What shall we do with the Drunken Sailor?

2 One reason I don't drink is that I want to know when I am having a good time.
Nancy Astor: Attrib.

3 An alcoholic has been lightly defined as a man who drinks more than his own doctor.
Alvan L. Barach: Journal of the American Medical Association, 181:393, 1962

4 Wine is a mocker, strong drink is raging: and whosoever is deceived thereby is not wise.
Bible: Proverbs: 20:1

5 If merely 'feeling good' could decide, drunkenness would be the supremely valid human experience.
William James: Varieties of Religious Experience

6 Drunkenness is temporary suicide: the happiness that it brings is merely negative, a momentary cessation of unhappiness.
Bertrand Russell: The Conquest of Happiness

7 But I'm not so think as you drunk I am.
John Collings Squire: Ballade of Soporific Absorption

8 An alcoholic is someone you don't like who drinks as much as you do.
Dylan Thomas: Dictionary of 20th Century Quotations (Nigel Rees)

DUTY

1 Do your duty and leave the rest to the Gods.
Pierre Corneille: Horace, II:8

2 England expects every man will do his duty.
Lord Nelson: Signal hoisted prior to the Battle of Trafalgar, 1805

3 It is the highest and eternal duty of women – namely, to sacrifice their lives and to seek the good of their husbands.
Adi Parva: Hindu text, Mahabharata

4 When a stupid man is doing something he is ashamed of, he always declares that it is his duty.
George Bernard Shaw: Caesar and Cleopatra, III

E

ECOLOGY

See also conservation, environment

1 As cruel a weapon as the cave man's club, the chemical barrage has been hurled against the fabric of life.
Rachel Carson: The Silent Spring

2 Both biological and cultural diversity are now severely threatened and working for their preservation is a critical task.
Murray Gell-Mann: The Quark and the Jaguar

3 It will be said of this generation that it found England a land of beauty and left it a land of beauty spots.
Cyril Joad: The Observer, 'Sayings of Our Times', 31 May 1953

ECONOMICS

1 Don't spoil the ship for a ha'porth of tar.
Proverb

2 A budget is a method of worrying before you spend instead of afterwards.
Anonymous

3 Respectable Professors of the Dismal Science.
Thomas Carlyle: Referring to economists. Latter-Day Pamphlets

4 Annual income twenty pounds, annual expenditure nineteen nineteen six, result happiness. Annual income twenty pounds, annual expenditure twenty pounds ought and six, result misery.
Charles Dickens: David Copperfield, Ch. 12

5 If freedom were not so economically efficient it certainly wouldn't stand a chance.
Milton Friedman: Remark, Mar 1987

6 One nanny said, 'Feed a cold'; she was a neo-Keynesian. Another nanny said, 'Starve a cold'; she was a monetarist.
Harold Macmillan: Maiden speech, House of Lords, 1984

7 Recession is when a neighbour loses his job; depression is when you lose yours.
Ronald Reagan: The Observer, 'Sayings of the Week', 26 Oct 1980

8 If all economists were laid end to end, they would not reach a conclusion.
George Bernard Shaw: Attrib

9 Give me a one-handed economist! All my economists say, 'on the one hand...on the other'.
Harry S. Truman: Presidential Anecdotes (P. Boller)

10 One man's wage rise is another man's price increase.
Harold Wilson: The Observer, 'Sayings of the Week', 11 Jan 1970

EDUCATION

See also examinations

1 They know enough who know how to learn.

Henry Brooks Adams: The Education of Henry Adams

2 Universities incline wits to sophistry and affectation.
Francis Bacon: Valerius Terminus of the Interpretation of Nature, Ch. 26

3 The true University of these days is a collection of books.
Thomas Carlyle: Heroes and Hero-Worship, 'The Hero as Man of Letters'

4 This is to seyn, to syngen and to rede,
As smale children doon in hire childhede.
Geoffrey Chaucer: The Canterbury Tales, 'The Prioress's Tale'

5 His English education at one of the great public schools had preserved his intellect perfectly and permanently at the stage of boyhood.
G. K. Chesterton: The Man Who Knew Too Much

6 Public schools are the nurseries of all vice and immorality.
Henry Fielding: Joseph Andrews, Bk. III, Ch. 5

7 Shakespeare is fine for grammar school kids.
Nigel de Gruchy: The Observer, 5 July 1992

8 Education made us what we are.
Claude-Adrien Helvétius: Discours XXX, Ch. 30

9 And seek for truth in the groves of Academe.
Horace: Epistles, II

10 You sought the last resort of feeble minds with classical educations. You became a schoolmaster.
Aldous Huxley: Antic Hay

11 It is no matter what you teach them first, any more than what leg you shall put into your breeches first.
Samuel Johnson: Life of Johnson (J. Boswell), Vol. I

12 I find the three major administrative problems on a campus are sex for the students, athletics for the alumni and parking for the faculty.
Clark Kerr: Time, 17 Nov 1958

13 Universities are the cathedrals of the modern age. They shouldn't have to justify their existence by utilitarian criteria.
David Lodge: Nice Work, IV

14 If you educate a man you educate a person, but if you educate a woman you educate a family.
Ruby Manikan: The Observer, 'Sayings of the Week', 30 Mar 1947

15 One tongue is sufficient for a woman.
John Milton: On being asked whether he would allow his daughters to learn foreign languages. Attrib.

16 The schoolteacher is certainly underpaid as a childminder, but ludicrously overpaid as an educator.
John Osborne: The Observer, 'Sayings of the Week', 21 July 1985

17 A man who has never gone to school may steal from a freight car, but if he has a university education he may steal the whole railroad.
Franklin D. Roosevelt: Attrib.

18 You can't expect a boy to be

vicious till he's been to a good
school.
Saki: Reginald in Russia

19 For every person wishing to
teach there are thirty not
wanting to be taught.
W. C. Sellar: And Now All This

20 He who can, does. He who
cannot, teaches.
*George Bernard Shaw: Man and
Superman, 'Maxims for
Revolutionists'*

21 Education is what survives
when what has been learnt has
been forgotten.
*B. F. Skinner: New Scientist, 21
May 1964, 'Education in 1984'*

22 Education...has produced a
vast population able to read but
unable to distinguish what is
worth reading.
*George Macaulay Trevelyan:
English Social History, Ch. 18*

23 Soap and education are not
as sudden as a massacre, but
they are more deadly in the
long run.
*Mark Twain: The Facts
concerning the Recent Resignation*

24 Anyone who has been to an
English public school will always
feel comparatively at home in
prison.
*Evelyn Waugh: Decline and Fall,
Pt. III, Ch. 4*

25 The battle of Waterloo was
won on the playing fields of
Eton.
Duke of Wellington: Attrib.

EFFORT

See also work

1 If a job's worth doing, it's worth
doing well.
Proverb

2 Energy is Eternal Delight.
*William Blake: The Marriage of
Heaven and Hell, 'The Voice of the
Devil'*

3 I have nothing to offer but
blood, toil, tears and sweat.
*Winston Churchill: On becoming
prime minister. Speech, House of
Commons, 13 May 1940*

4 Please do not shoot the pianist.
He is doing his best.
*Oscar Wilde: Impressions of
America, 'Leadville'*

EGOTISM

See also arrogance, conceit, pride,
selfishness

1 EGOTIST, n. A person of low
taste, more interested in himself
than in me.
*Ambrose Bierce: The Devil's
Dictionary*

2 An author who speaks about his
own books is almost as bad as a
mother who talks about her own
children.
*Benjamin Disraeli: Speech in
Glasgow, 19 Nov 1873*

3 One had rather malign oneself
than not speak of oneself at all.
*Duc de la Rochefoucauld:
Maximes, 138*

4 No man thinks there is much
ado about nothing when the ado
is about himself.
*Anthony Trollope: The Bertrams,
Ch. 27*

5 I am the only person in the
world I should like to know
thoroughly.

Oscar Wilde: Lady Windermere's Fan, II

EMOTION

See also passion, sentimentality

1 There is a road from the eye to the heart that does not go through the intellect.
G. K. Chesterton: The Defendant

2 'There are strings', said Mr Tappertit, 'in the human heart that had better not be wibrated.'
Charles Dickens: Barnaby Rudge, Ch. 22

3 The intellect is always fooled by the heart.
Duc de la Rochefoucauld: Maximes, 102

ENDING

1 All good things must come to an end.
Proverb

2 All's well that ends well.
Proverb

3 This is the way the world ends Not with a bang but a whimper.
T. S. Eliot: The Hollow Men

ENDURANCE

See also courage, determination

1 What can't be cured, must be endured.
Proverb

2 Nothing happens to any man that he is not formed by nature to bear.
Marcus Aurelius: Meditations, Bk. V, Ch. 18

3 Job endured everything – until

his friends came to comfort him, then he grew impatient.
Søren Kierkegaard: Journal

4 Sorrow and silence are strong, and patient endurance is god-like.
Henry Wadsworth Longfellow: Evangeline

5 Still have I borne it with a patient shrug,
For sufferance is the badge of all our tribe.
William Shakespeare: The Merchant of Venice, I:3

6 Let's talk sense to the American people. Let's tell them the truth, that there are no gains without pains.
Adlai Stevenson: Speech, Chicago, 26 July 1952

7 If you can't stand the heat, get out of the kitchen.
Harry S. Truman: Perhaps proverbial in origin, it possibly echoes the expression 'kitchen cabinet'. Mr Citizen, Ch. 15

8 Maybe one day we shall be glad to remember even these hardships.
Virgil: Aeneid, Bk. I

ENEMIES

1 Better a thousand enemies outside the house than one inside.
Arabic proverb

2 But I say unto you, Love your enemies, bless them that curse you, do good to them that hate you, and pray for them which despitefully use you, and persecute you.
Bible: Matthew: 5:44

ENTHUSIASM

3 Even a paranoid can have enemies.
Henry Kissinger: Time, 24 Jan 1977

4 They made peace between us; we embraced, and we have been mortal enemies ever since.
Alain-René Lesage: Le Diable boiteux, Ch. 3

5 A very great man once said you should love your enemies and that's not a bad piece of advice. We can love them but, by God, that doesn't mean we're not going to fight them.
Norman Schwarzkopf: Referring to the Gulf War (1991). The Observer, 14 July 1991

6 He makes no friend who never made a foe.
Alfred, Lord Tennyson: Idylls of the King, 'Lancelot and Elaine'

ENTHUSIASM

1 It is unfortunate, considering that enthusiasm moves the world, that so few enthusiasts can be trusted to speak the truth.
Arthur Balfour: Letter to Mrs Drew, 1918

2 Nothing great was ever achieved without enthusiasm.
Ralph Waldo Emerson: Essays, 'Circles'

3 Every man loves what he is good at.
Thomas Shadwell: A True Widow, V:1

ENVIRONMENT

See also ecology

1 The first Care in building of Cities, is to make them airy and well perflated; infectious Distempers must necessarily be propagated amongst Mankind living close together.
John Arbuthnot: An Essay Concerning the Effects of Air on Human Bodies

2 They improvidentially piped growing volumes of sewage into the sea, the healing virtues of which were advertised on every railway station.
Robert Cecil: Referring to seaside resorts. Life in Edwardian England

3 Population growth is the primary source of environmental damage.
Jacques Cousteau: The Observer, 'Sayings of the Week', 15 Jan 1989

4 I am a pasenger on the spaceship, Earth.
Richard Buckminster Fuller: Operating Manual for Spaceship Earth

5 If sunbeams were weapons of war, we would have had solar energy long ago.
George Porter: The Observer, 'Sayings of the Week', 26 Aug 1973

ENVY

See also discontent, jealousy

1 Better be envied than pitied.
Proverb

2 I am sure the grapes are sour.
Aesop: Fables, 'The Fox and the Grapes'

3 Fools may our scorn, not envy raise,

For envy is a kind of praise.
John Gay: Fables

4 Moral indignation is in most cases 2 per cent moral, 48 per cent indignation and 50 per cent envy.
Vittorio de Sica: The Observer, 'Sayings of the Decade', 1961

5 Never having been able to succeed in the world, he took his revenge by speaking ill of it.
Voltaire: Zadig, Ch. 4

EPITAPHS

1 She sleeps alone at last.
Robert Benchley: Suggested epitaph for an actress. Attrib.

2 In lapidary inscriptions a man is not upon oath.
Samuel Johnson: Life of Johnson (J. Boswell), Vol. II

3 John Brown's body lies a-mouldering in the grave, His soul is marching on!
Charles Sprague Hall: The song commemorates the American hero who died in the cause of abolishing slavery. John Brown's Body

4 Over my dead body!
George S. Kaufman: On being asked to suggest his own epitaph. The Algonquin Wits (R. Drennan)

5 Beneath this slab John Brown is stowed. He watched the ads And not the road.
Ogden Nash: Lather as You Go

6 Alas, poor Yorick! I knew him, Horatio: a fellow of infinite jest, of most excellent fancy.
William Shakespeare: Hamlet, V:1

7 *Si monumentum requiris, circumspice.*
If you seek my monument, look around you.
Christopher Wren: Inscription in St Paul's Cathedral, London

EQUALITY

See also human rights

1 A cat may look at a king.
Proverb

2 All cats are grey in the dark.
Proverb

3 The Prophet Mohamed wanted equality for women. But when Islam went from the desert to the palaces, men put in certain loopholes.
Zeenat Ali: The Independent, 16 Sept 1993

4 Equality may perhaps be a right, but no power on earth can ever turn it into a fact.
Honoré de Balzac: La Duchesse de Langeais

5 What makes equality such a difficult business is that we only want it with our superiors.
Henry Becque: Querelles littéraires

6 The terrorist and the policeman both come from the same basket.
Joseph Conrad: The Secret Agent, Ch. 4

7 Men are made by nature unequal. It is vain, therefore, to treat them as if they were equal.
J. A. Froude: Short Studies on Great Subjects, 'Party Politics'

8 A just society would be one in which liberty for one person is constrained only by the de-

mands created by equal liberty for another.

Ivan Illich: Tools for Conviviality

9 His foreparents came to America in immigrant ships. My foreparents came to America in slave ships. But whatever the original ships, we are both in the same boat tonight.

Jesse Jackson: Speech, July 1988

10 I have a dream that one day this nation will rise up, live out the true meaning of its creed: we hold these truths to be self-evident, that all men are created equal.

Martin Luther King: He used the words 'I have a dream' in a number of speeches. Speech, Washington, 27 Aug 1963

11 Every man who comes to England is entitled to the protection of the English law, whatever oppression he may heretofore have suffered, and whatever may be the colour of his skin, whether it is black or whether it is white.

Lord Mansfield: From the judgment in the case of James Somersett, a fugitive Negro slave (May 1772); it established the principle that slaves enjoyed the benefits of freedom while in England.

12 This isn't going to be a good country for any of us to live in until it's a good country for all of us to live in.

Richard Milhous Nixon: The Observer, 'Sayings of the Week', 29 Sep 1968

13 All animals are equal but some animals are more equal than others.

George Orwell: Animal Farm, Ch. 10

14 In America everybody is of the opinion that he has no social superiors, since all men are equal, but he does not admit that he has no social inferiors.

Bertrand Russell: Unpopular Essays

15 *Declaration of Sentiments:* . . . We hold these truths to be self-evident: that all men and women are created equal.

Elizabeth Stanton: History of Woman Suffrage, Vol. I (with Susan B. Anthony and Mathilda Gage)

ETERNITY

See also immortality, time

1 As it was in the beginning, is now, and ever shall be: world without end.

The Book of Common Prayer: Morning Prayer, Gloria

2 Eternity's a terrible thought. I mean, where's it going to end?

Tom Stoppard: Rosencrantz and Guildenstern Are Dead, II

ETIQUETTE

See also manners

1 It is necessary to clean the teeth frequently, more especially after meals, but not on any account with a pin, or the point of a penknife, and it must never be done at table.

St Jean Baptiste de la Salle: The Rules of Christian Manners and Civility, I

2 At a dinner party one should eat

wisely but not too well, and talk
well but not too wisely.
*W. Somerset Maugham: A
Writer's Notebook*

3 'How did you think I managed
at dinner, Clarence?' 'Capitally!'
'I had a knife and two forks left
at the end,' she said regretfully.
*William Pett Ridge: Love at
Paddington Green, Ch. 6*

EUROPE

1 In Western Europe there are
now only small countries – those
that know it and those that don't
know it yet.
*Théo Lefèvre: The Observer,
'Sayings of the Year', 1963*

2 We are part of the community of
Europe and we must do our
duty as such.
*Marquess of Salisbury: Speech,
Caernarvon, 11 Apr 1888*

3 That Europe's nothin' on earth
but a great big auction, that's all
it is.
*Tennessee Williams: Cat on a Hot
Tin Roof, I*

EVIL

See also good and evil, sin, vice

1 *Honi soit qui mal y pense.*
Evil be to him who evil thinks.
*Anonymous: Motto for the Order
of the Garter*

2 The fearsome word-and-
thought-defying *banality of evil.*
*Hannah Arendt: Eichmann in
Jerusalem: A Report on the
Banality of Evil*

3 And this is the condemnation,
that light is come into the world,

and men loved darkness rather
than light, because their deeds
were evil.
Bible: John: 3:19

4 The belief in a supernatural
source of evil is not necessary;
men alone are quite capable of
every wickedness.
*Joseph Conrad: Under Western
Eyes, Part 2*

5 He who passively accepts evil is
as much involved in it as he who
helps to perpetrate it.
*Martin Luther King: Stride
Towards Freedom*

6 Farewell remorse! All good to
me is lost;
Evil, be thou my Good.
*John Milton: Paradise Lost,
Bk. IV*

7 There is scarcely a single man
sufficiently aware to know all the
evil he does.
*Duc de la Rochefoucauld:
Maximes, 269*

8 The evil that men do lives after
them;
The good is oft interred with
their bones.
*William Shakespeare: Julius
Caesar, III:2*

EVOLUTION

See also survival

1 A hen is only an egg's way of
making another egg.
*Samuel Butler: Life and Habit,
VIII*

2 Some call it Evolution
And others call it God.
*William H. Carruth: Each in His
Own Tongue*

3 The question is this: Is man an

ape or an angel? I, my lord, am on the side of the angels.
Benjamin Disraeli: Speech, 25 Nov 1864

4 How like us is that ugly brute, the ape!
Ennius: On the Nature of the Gods, I (Cicero)

5 I can trace my ancestry back to a protoplasmal primordial atomic globule.
W. S. Gilbert: The Mikado, I

6 Philip is a living example of natural selection. He was as fitted to survive in this modern world as a tapeworm in an intestine.
William Golding: Free Fall, Ch. 2

7 The probable fact is that we are descended not only from monkeys but from monks.
Elbert Hubbard: A Thousand and One Epigrams

EXAMINATIONS

See also education

1 Examinations are formidable even to the best prepared, for the greatest fool may ask more than the wisest man can answer.
Charles Caleb Colton: Lacon, Vol. II

2 Do not on any account attempt to write on both sides of the paper at once.
W. C. Sellar: 1066 And All That, Test Paper 5

EXAMPLE

1 Practise what you preach.
Proverb

2 Example is the school of mankind, and they will learn at no other.
Edmund Burke: Letters on a Regicide Peace, letter 1

3 What you do not want done to yourself, do not do to others.
Confucius: Analects

4 A precedent embalms a principle.
William Scott: An opinion given while Advocate-General. Attrib.; also quoted by Benjamin Disraeli (1848)

EXCESS

See also moderation

1 Nothing in excess.
Anonymous

2 L'embarras des richesses.
A superfluity of good things.
Abbé Lénor Jean d'Allainval: Play title

3 The road of excess leads to the palace of Wisdom.
William Blake: The Marriage of Heaven and Hell, 'Proverbs of Hell'

4 I would remind you that extremism in the defence of liberty is no vice. And let me remind you also that moderation in the pursuit of justice is no virtue!
Barry Goldwater: Speech, San Francisco, 17 July 1964

5 Well said; that was laid on with a trowel.
William Shakespeare: As You Like It, I:2

6 The lady doth protest too much, methinks.
William Shakespeare: Hamlet, III:2

7 It out-herods Herod.

William Shakespeare: Hamlet, III:2

8 Moderation is a fatal thing, Lady Hunstanton. Nothing succeeds like excess.

Oscar Wilde: A Woman of No Importance, III

EXECUTION

See also last words, martyrdom, punishment

1 And almost all things are by the law purged with blood; and without shedding of blood is no remission.

Bible: Hebrews: 9:22

2 And when they were come to the place, which is called Calvary, there they crucified him, and the malefactors, one on the right hand, and the other on the left.

Bible: Luke: 23:33

3 'Off with his head!'

Lewis Carroll: Alice's Adventures in Wonderland, Ch. 8

4 Thou wilt show my head to the people: it is worth showing.

Georges Jacques Danton: Said as he mounted the scaffold, 5 Apr 1794. French Revolution (Carlyle), Bk. VI, Ch. 2

5 To die for faction is a common evil,
But to be hanged for nonsense is the Devil.

John Dryden: Absalom and Achitophel, II

6 Depend upon it, Sir, when a man knows he is to be hanged in a fortnight, it concentrates his mind wonderfully.

Samuel Johnson: Life of Johnson (J. Boswell), Vol. III

7 The world itself is but a large prison, out of which some are daily led to execution.

Walter Raleigh: Said after his trial for treason, 1603. Attrib.

8 If you give me six lines written by the most honest man, I will find something in them to hang him.

Cardinal Richelieu: Exact wording uncertain. Attrib.

9 'O liberté! O liberté! Que de crimes on commet en ton nom!'
Oh liberty! Oh liberty! What crimes are committed in thy name!

Madame Roland: Said as she mounted the steps of the guillotine. Attrib.

EXISTENCE

1 Dear Sir, Your astonishment's odd:
I am always about in the Quad.
And that's why the tree
Will continue to be
Since observed by Yours faithfully, God.

Anonymous: The response to KNOX's limerick

2 Let us be moral. Let us contemplate existence.

Charles Dickens: Martin Chuzzlewit, Ch. 10

3 As far as we can discern, the sole purpose of human existence is to kindle a light in the darkness of mere being.

Carl Gustav Jung: Memories, Dreams, Reflections, Ch. 11

4 There once was a man who said
'God
Must think it exceedingly odd
If he find that this tree
Continues to be
When there's no one about in
the Quad.'
*Ronald Knox: For a reply, see
ANONYMOUS. Attrib.*

5 I know perfectly well that I don't
want to do anything; to do
something is to create existence
– and there's quite enough existence as it is.
Jean-Paul Sartre: Nausea

EXPECTATION

See also disappointment, hope

1 As I know more of mankind I
expect less of them, and am
ready now to call a man *a good
man*, upon easier terms than I
was formerly.
*Samuel Johnson: Life of Johnson
(J. Boswell), Vol. IV*

2 Dear Mary, We all knew you
had it in you.
*Dorothy Parker: Telegram sent to a
friend on the successful outcome of
her much publicized pregnancy.*

3 'Blessed is the man who expects
nothing, for he shall never be
disappointed' was the ninth
beatitude.
*Alexander Pope: Letter to
Fortescue, 23 Sept 1725*

4 This suspense is terrible. I hope
it will last.
*Oscar Wilde: The Importance of
Being Earnest, III*

EXPEDIENCY

1 Half a loaf is better than no
bread.
Proverb

2 Nobody is forgotten when it is
convenient to remember him.
Benjamin Disraeli: Attrib.

3 You can't learn too soon that the
most useful thing about a principle is that it can always be sacri-
ficed to expediency.
*W. Somerset Maugham: The
Circle, III*

4 Death and taxes and childbirth!
There's never any convenient
time for any of them!
*Margaret Mitchell: Gone with the
Wind*

5 No man is justified in doing evil
on the ground of expediency.
*Theodore Roosevelt: The Strenuous
Life*

EXPERIENCE

1 Experience is the mother of
wisdom.
Proverb

2 Practice makes perfect.
Proverb

3 One should try everything once,
except incest and folk-dancing.
Arnold Bax: Farewell to My Youth

4 You will think me lamentably
crude: my experience of life has
been drawn from life itself.
*Max Beerbohm: Zuleika Dobson,
Ch. 7*

5 How many roads must a man
walk down
Before you call him a man?
Bob Dylan: Blowin' in the Wind

6 A moment's insight is sometimes worth a life's experience.
Oliver Wendell Holmes: The Professor at the Breakfast Table, Ch. 10

7 Nothing ever becomes real till it is experienced – even a proverb is no proverb to you till your life has illustrated it.
John Keats: Letter to George and Georgiana Keats, 19 Mar 1819

EXPERTS

1 An expert is a man who has made all the mistakes, which can be made, in a very narrow field.
Niels Bohr: Attrib.

2 An expert is someone who knows some of the worst mistakes that can be made in his subject, and how to avoid them.
Werner Heisenberg: Physics and Beyond

3 Specialist – A man who knows more and more about less and less.
William James Mayo: Also attributed to Nicholas Butler.

4 The trouble with specialists is that they tend to think in grooves.
Elaine Morgan: The Descent of Woman, Ch. 1

EXPLORATION

See also discovery

1 Go West, young man, and grow up with the country.
Horace Greeley: Also attributed to the US writer John Soule (1815–91), Terre Haute (Indiana) Express, 1851. Hints toward Reform

2 Nothing easier. One step beyond the pole, you see, and the north wind becomes a south one.
Robert Edwin Peary: Explaining how he knew he had reached the North Pole. Attrib.

3 Had we lived, I should have had a tale to tell of the hardihood, endurance, and courage of my companions which would have stirred the heart of every Englishman. These rough notes and our dead bodies must tell the tale.
Captain Robert Falcon Scott: Message to the Public

4 Dr Livingstone, I presume?
Henry Morton Stanley: On finding David Livingstone at Ujiji on Lake Tanganyika, Nov 1871. How I found Livingstone, Ch. 11

EXTRAVAGANCE

See also excess, luxury, money, ostentation

1 Riches are for spending.
Francis Bacon: Essays, 'Of Expense'

2 He sometimes forgets that he is Caesar, but I always remember that I am Caesar's daughter.
Julia: Replying to suggestions that she should live in the simple style of her father, which contrasted with her own extravagance. Saturnalia (Macrobius)

3 I suppose that I shall have to die beyond my means.
Oscar Wilde: When told that an operation would be expensive. He is also believed to have said 'I am dying beyond my means' on accepting a glass of champagne as he lay on his deathbed. Life of Wilde (Sherard)

EYES

1 The eyes are the window of the soul.
Proverb

2 That youthful sparkle in his eyes is caused by his contact lenses, which he keeps highly polished.
Sheilah Graham: Referring to Ronald Reagan. The Times, 22 Aug 1981

3 Jeepers Creepers – where'd you get them peepers?
Johnny Mercer: Jeepers Creepers

4 Out vile jelly! Where is thy lustre now?
William Shakespeare: Spoken by Cornwall as he puts out Gloucester's remaining eye. King Lear, III:7

F

FACTS

See also truth

1 Now, what I want is Facts…
Facts alone are wanted in life.
*Charles Dickens: Hard Times,
Bk. I, Ch. 1*

2 Facts are not science – as the
dictionary is not literature.
*Martin H. Fischer: Fischerisms
(Howard Faber and Ray Marr)*

3 Facts do not cease to exist because they are ignored.
Aldous Huxley: Proper Studies

4 Once a newspaper touches a
story, the facts are lost forever,
even to the protagonists.
*Norman Mailer: The Presidential
Papers*

5 Facts speak louder than statistics.
*Geoffrey Streatfield: The Observer,
'Sayings of the Week', 19 Mar
1950*

FAILURE

See also defeat, loss, success

1 A miss is as good as a mile.
Proverb

2 She knows there's no success
like failure
And that failure's no success at
all.
*Bob Dylan: Love Minus Zero No
Limit*

3 It doesn't hurt to lose my
crown, it hurts to lose.
*Steffi Graf: The Independent,
22 June 1994*

4 Failure is inevitable. Success is
elusive.
Steven Spielberg: OM, Dec 1984

5 Failure? Do you remember what
Queen Victoria once said?
'Failure' – the possibilities do
not exist.'
*Margaret Thatcher: Queen
Victoria had been speaking about
the Boer War. TV news interview,
at start of Falklands War, 5 Apr
1982*

FAIRIES

See also supernatural

1 Every time a child says 'I don't
believe in fairies' there is a little
fairy somewhere that falls down
dead.
J. M. Barrie: Peter Pan

2 There are fairies at the bottom
of our garden.
*Rose Fyleman: Fairies and
Chimneys*

FAITH

See also belief, God, religion,
trust

1 Faith will move mountains.
Proverb

2 Now faith is the substance of
things hoped for, the evidence of
things not seen.
Bible: Hebrews: 11:1

3 I feel no need for any other faith
than my faith in human beings.
Pearl Buck: I Believe

4 My dear child, you must believe

in God in spite of what the clergy tell you.
Benjamin Jowett: Autobiography (Asquith), Ch. 8

5 Faith may be defined briefly as an illogical belief in the occurrence of the improbable.
H. L. Mencken: Prejudices, 'Types of Men'

6 Life is doubt, and faith without doubt is nothing but death.
Miguel de Unamuno y Jugo: Poesias

7 Faith consists in believing when it is beyond the power of reason to believe. It is not enough that a thing be possible for it to be believed.
Voltaire: Questions sur l'encyclopédie

FAME

See also popularity, reputation

1 A celebrity is a person who works hard all his life to become known, then wears dark glasses to avoid being recognized.
Fred Allen: Treadmill to Oblivion

2 Fame is like a river, that beareth up things light and swollen, and drowns things weighty and solid.
Francis Bacon: Essays, 'Of Praise'

3 The celebrity is a person who is known for his well-knownness.
Daniel J. Boorstin: The Image, 'From Hero to Celebrity: The Human Pseudo-event'

4 Being a star has made it possible for me to get insulted in places where the average Negro could never hope to get insulted.
Sammy Davis Jnr: Yes I Can

5 A big man has no time really to

do anything but just sit and be big.
F. Scott Fitzgerald: This Side of Paradise, Bk. III, Ch. 2

6 I'm into pop because I want to get rich, get famous and get laid.
Bob Geldof: Attrib.

7 Fame is a powerful aphrodisiac.
Graham Greene: Radio Times, 10 Sept 1964

8 Fame is the spur that the clear spirit doth raise
(That last infirmity of noble mind)
To scorn delights, and live laborious days.
John Milton: Lycidas

9 'What are you famous for?'
'For nothing. I am just famous.'
Iris Murdoch: The Flight from the Enchanter

10 In the future, everyone will be famous for 15 minutes.
Andy Warhol: Attrib.

11 There is only one thing in the world worse than being talked about, and that is not being talked about.
Oscar Wilde: The Picture of Dorian Gray, Ch. 1

FAMILIARITY

1 Familiarity breeds contempt.
Proverb

2 No man is a hero to his valet.
Anne-Marie Bigot de Cornuel: Lettres de Mlle Aïssé, 13 Aug 1728

3 I like familiarity. In me it does not breed contempt. Only more familiarity.
Gertrude Stein: Dale Carnegie's Scrapbook

FAMILY

See also children, marriage

1 Blood is thicker than water.
Proverb

2 Every family has a skeleton in the cupboard.
Proverb

3 Like father, like son.
Proverb

4 Parents are the last people on earth who ought to have children.
Samuel Butler: Notebooks

5 If one is not going to take the necessary precautions to avoid having parents one must undertake to bring them up.
Quentin Crisp: The Naked Civil Servant

6 Fate chooses your relations, you choose your friends.
Jacques Delille: Malheur et pitié, I

7 There are times when parenthood seems nothing but feeding the mouth that bites you.
Peter De Vries: Tunnel of Love

8 It is a melancholy truth that even great men have their poor relations.
Charles Dickens: Bleak House, Ch. 28

9 My father was frightened of his mother. I was frightened of my father, and I'm damned well going to make sure that my children are frightened of me.
George V: Attrib.

10 They fuck you up, your mum and dad.
They may not mean to, but they do.
They fill you with the faults they had

And add some extra, just for you.
Philip Larkin: This be the Verse

11 I have a wife, I have sons: all of them hostages given to fate.
Lucan: Works, VII

12 A group of closely related persons living under one roof; it is a convenience, often a necessity, sometimes a pleasure, sometimes the reverse; but who first exalted it as admirable, an almost religious ideal?
Rose Macaulay: The World My Wilderness, Ch. 20

13 The sink is the great symbol of the bloodiness of family life. All life is bad, but family life is worse.
Julian Mitchell: As Far as You Can Go, Pt. I, Ch. 1

14 The worst misfortune that can happen to an ordinary man is to have an extraordinary father.
Austin O'Malley

15 Men are generally more careful of the breed of their horses and dogs than of their children.
William Penn: Some Fruits of Solitude, in Reflections and Maxims relating to the conduct of Humane Life, Pt. I, No 52

16 There is only one person an English girl hates more than she hates her elder sister; and that is her mother.
George Bernard Shaw: Man and Superman

17 All happy families resemble one another, each unhappy family is unhappy in its own way.
Leo Tolstoy: Anna Karenina, Pt. I, Ch. 1

18 We could improve world wide mental health if we acknowledged that parents can make you crazy.
Frank Zappa: The Real Frank Zappa Book

FASCISM ·

See also Nazism

1 Il Duce ha sempre ragione.
The Duce is always right.
Anonymous: Referring to the Italian dictator, Benito Mussolini (1883–1945). Fascist Slogan

2 The final solution of the Jewish problem.
Adolf Hitler: Referring to the Nazi concentration camps. The Final Solution (G. Geitlinger)

3 Fascism is a religion; the twentieth century will be known in history as the century of Fascism.
Benito Mussolini: On Hitler's seizing power. Sawdust Caesar (George Seldes), Ch. 24

4 Every communist has a fascist frown, every fascist a communist smile.
Muriel Spark: The Girls of Slender Means, Ch. 4

5 Fascism means war.
John St Loe Strachey: Slogan, 1930s

FASHION

See also clothes

1 Fashion is architecture: it is a matter of proportions.
Coco Chanel: Coco Chanel, Her Life, Her Secrets (Marcel Haedrich)

2 One had as good be out of the world, as out of the fashion.
Colley Cibber: Love's Last Shift, II

3 Her frocks are built in Paris but she wears them with a strong English accent.
Saki: Reginald on Women

4 For an idea ever to be fashionable is ominous, since it must afterwards be always old-fashioned.
George Santayana: Winds of Doctrine, 'Modernism and Christianity'

5 Fashions, after all, are only induced epidemics.
George Bernard Shaw: Doctor's Dilemma, Preface

FEAR

1 In the Nineteenth Century men lost their fear of God and acquired a fear of microbes.
Anonymous

2 It is a miserable state of mind to have few things to desire and many things to fear.
Francis Bacon: Essays, 'Of Empire'

3 Fear has many eyes and can see things underground.
Miguel de Cervantes: Don Quixote, Pt. I, Ch. 20

4 Let me assert my firm belief that the only thing we have to fear is fear itself.
Franklin D. Roosevelt: First Inaugural Address, 4 Mar 1933

5 Fear lent wings to his feet.
Virgil: Aeneid, Bk. VIII

FEMINISM

See also equality, sexes, woman's role, women

1 Men their rights and nothing more; women their rights and nothing less.
Susan B. Anthony: The Revolution, Motto

2 Women fail to understand how much men hate them.
Germaine Greer: The Female Eunuch

3 You can now see the Female Eunuch the world over...Wherever you see nail varnish, lipstick, brassieres, and high heels, the Eunuch has set up her camp.
Germaine Greer: The Female Eunuch

4 The most important thing women have to do is to stir up the zeal of women themselves.
John Stuart Mill: Letter to Alexander Bain, 14 July 1869

5 In both fiction and non-fiction, women are making their voices heard. My interpretation of women's rights in Islam, like that of countless other Muslim-born feminists, clashes strongly with the conservative, official interpretation.
Taslima Nasreen: The Times, 18 June 1994

6 The vote, I thought, means nothing to women. We should be armed.
Edna O'Brien: Quoted as epigraph to Fear of Flying (Erica Jong), Ch. 16

7 Women had always fought for men, and for their children. Now they were ready to fight for their own human rights. Our militant movement was established.
Emmeline Pankhurst: My Own Story

8 The *divine right* of husbands, like the divine right of kings, may, it is hoped, in this enlightened age, be contested without danger.
Mary Wollstonecraft: A Vindication of the Rights of Woman, Ch. 3

FICTION

See also books, literature, novels, writing

1 Science fiction is no more written for scientists than ghost stories are written for ghosts.
Brian Aldiss: Penguin Science Fiction, Introduction

2 Drunk in charge of a narrative.
Angela Carter: Wise Children

3 There are many reasons why novelists write, but they all have one thing in common – a need to create an alternative world.
John Fowles: The Sunday Times Magazine, 2 Oct 1977

4 Contentment and fulfilment don't make for very good fiction.
Joanna Trollope: The Times, 25 June 1994

FLATTERY

See also insincerity, praise, servility

1 Imitation is the sincerest form of flattery.
Proverb

2 It is happy for you that you pos-

sess the talent of flattering with delicacy. May I ask whether these pleasing attentions proceed from the impulse of the moment, or are the result of previous study?
Jane Austen: Pride and Prejudice, Ch. 14

3 Madam, before you flatter a man so grossly to his face, you should consider whether or not your flattery is worth his having.
Samuel Johnson: Diary and Letters (Mme D'Arblay), Vol. I, Ch. 2

4 Be advised that all flatterers live at the expense of those who listen to them.
Jean de La Fontaine: Fables, I, 'Le Corbeau et le Renard'

5 Flattery is all right so long as you don't inhale.
Adlai Stevenson: Attrib.

6 'Tis an old maxim in the schools,
That flattery's the food of fools;
Yet now and then your men of wit
Will condescend to take a bit.
Jonathan Swift: Cadenus and Vanessa

FLOWERS

See also gardens

1 And I will make thee beds of roses
And a thousand fragrant posies.
Christopher Marlowe: The Passionate Shepherd to his Love

2 Gather the flowers, but spare the buds.
Andrew Marvell: The Picture of Little T.C. in a Prospect of Flowers

3 Say it with flowers.
Patrick O'Keefe: Slogan for Society of American Florists

4 They are for prima donnas or corpses – I am neither.
Arturo Toscanini: Refusing a floral wreath at the end of a performance. The Elephant that Swallowed a Nightingale (C. Galtey)

FLYING

See also travel

1 Had I been a man I might have explored the Poles or climbed Mount Everest, but as it was my spirit found outlet in the air.
Amy Johnson: Myself When Young (ed. Margot Asquith)

2 I feel about airplanes the way I feel about diets. It seems to me that they are wonderful things for other people to go on.
Jean Kerr: The Snake Has All the Lines, 'Mirror, Mirror, on the Wall'

3 A man with wings large enough and duly attached might learn to overcome the resistance of the air, and conquering it succeed in subjugating it and raise himself upon it.
Leonardo da Vinci: Flight of Birds

FOOD

See also greed, hunger

1 Bread is the staff of life.
Proverb

2 I'm a man
More dined against than dining.

Maurice Bowra: *Echoing King
Lear's 'I am a man more sinn'd
against than sinning'.* (III:2).
Summoned by Bells (J. Betjeman)

3 A good Kitchen is a good
Apothicaries shop.
*William Bullein: The Bulwark
Against All Sickness*

4 Some hae meat, and canna eat,
And some wad eat that want it,
But we hae meat and we can eat,
And sae the Lord be thankit.
Robert Burns: The Selkirk Grace

5 A good eater must be a good
man; for a good eater must have
a good digestion, and a good digestion depends upon a good
conscience.
*Benjamin Disraeli: The Young
Duke*

6 The way to a man's heart is
through his stomach.
Fanny Fern: Willis Parton

7 Food is an important part of a
balanced diet.
*Fran Lebowitz: Metropolitan Life,
'Food for Thought and Vice Versa'*

8 I told my doctor I get very tired
when I go on a diet, so he gave
me pep pills. Know what happened? I ate faster.
Joe E. Lewis

9 The Chinese do not draw any
distinction between food and
medicine.
*Lin Yutang: The Importance of
Living, Ch. 9, Sect. 7*

10 Many children are suffering
from muesli-belt malnutrition.
*Vincent Marks: Remark, June
1986*

11 One should eat to live, not live
to eat.
Molière: L'Avare, III:2

12 An army marches on its
stomach.
Napoleon I: Attrib.

13 I think food is, actually, very
beautiful in itself.
*Delia Smith: The Times, 17 Oct
1990*

14 He was a bold man that first
eat an oyster.
*Jonathan Swift: Polite
Conversation, Dialogue 2*

15 You breed babies and you eat
chips with everything.
*Arnold Wesker: Chips with
Everything, I:2*

FOOLISHNESS

See also gullibility, ignorance, stupidity

1 A fool and his money are soon
parted.
Proverb

2 A fool at forty is a fool indeed.
Proverb

3 Better be a fool than a knave.
Proverb

4 Empty vessels make the greatest
sound.
Proverb

5 Mix a little foolishness with
your serious plans: it's lovely to
be silly at the right moment.
Horace: Odes, IV

6 Fools are in a terrible, overwhelming majority, all the wide
world over.
*Henrik Ibsen: An Enemy of the
People, IV*

7 You cannot fashion a wit out of
two half-wits.
Neil Kinnock: The Times, 1983

8 The portrait of a blinking idiot.

William Shakespeare: The
Merchant of Venice, II:9

FOOTBALL

1 Professional football is no
longer a game. It's a war. And it
brings out the same primitive instincts that go back thousands of
years.
Malcolm Allison: The Observer,
'Sayings of the Week', 14 Mar
1973

2 One of the secrets of football is
the simplicity of its laws.
Joseph Blatter: FIFA News, 1987

3 Wherein is nothing but beastly
fury and extreme violence,
whereof proceedeth hurt; and
consequently rancour and mal-
ice do remain with them that be
wounded.
Thomas Elyot: Referring to
football. Boke called the
Governour

4 The goal stands up, the keeper
Stands up to keep the goal.
A. E. Housman: A Shropshire
Lad, 'Bredon Hill'

5 The goal was scored a little bit
by the hand of God and a little
bit by the head of Maradona.
Diego Maradona: Referring to a
goal he scored against England in
the 1986 World Cup quarter-final;
although scored illegally with the
hand, the referee allowed it to
stand. Interview after the game

6 In England, soccer is a grey
game played by grey people on
grey days.
Rodney Marsh: Describing football
to an audience on Florida
television, 1979.

7 Football isn't a matter of life
and death – it's much more important than that.
Bill Shankly: Attrib.

8 Football…causeth fighting,
brawling, contention, quarrel
picking, murder, homicide and
great effusion of bloode, as daily
experience teacheth.
Philip Stubbes: Anatomie of
Abuses

FORGIVENESS

1 Forgive and forget.
Proverb

2 Even if someone throws a stone
at you, respond with food.
Kazakh proverb: The
Independent, 29 Nov 1993

3 Once a woman has forgiven her
man, she must not reheat his
sins for breakfast.
Marlene Dietrich: Marlene
Dietrich's ABC

4 She intended to forgive. Not to
do so would be un-Christian;
but did not intend to do so soon,
nor forget how much she had to
forgive.
Jessamyn West: The Friendly
Perusation, 'The Buried Leaf'

FRANKNESS

See also honesty, sincerity, truth

1 But of all plagues, good Heaven,
thy wrath can send,
Save me, oh, save me, from the
candid friend.
George Canning: New Morality

2 The great consolation in life is
to say what one thinks.
Voltaire: Letter, 1765

3 On an occasion of this kind it becomes more than a moral duty to speak one's mind. It becomes a pleasure.
Oscar Wilde: The Importance of Being Earnest, II

FREEDOM

See also human rights

1 There is a wind of nationalism and freedom blowing round the world, and blowing as strongly in Asia as elsewhere.
Stanley Baldwin: Speech, London, 4 Dec 1934

2 So free we seem, so fettered fast we are!
Robert Browning: Andrea del Sarto

3 Liberty, too, must be limited in order to be possessed.
Edmund Burke: Letter to the Sheriffs of Bristol, 1777

4 Hereditary bondsmen! know ye not
Who would be free themselves must strike the blow?
Lord Byron: Childe Harold's Pilgrimage, I

5 The condition upon which God hath given liberty to man is eternal vigilance.
John Philpot Curran: Speech on the Right of Election of Lord Mayor of Dublin, 10 July 1790

6 Yes, 'n' how many years can some people exist
Before they're allowed to be free?
Bob Dylan: Blowin' in the Wind

7 O Freedom, what liberties are taken in thy name!
Daniel George: The Perpetual Pessimist, a parody of Marie Jeanne Philip on Roland's (1754–93; French revolutionary) last words before her execution.

8 The love of liberty is the love of others; the love of power is the love of ourselves.
William Hazlitt: The Times, 1819

9 I know not what course others may take; but as for me, give me liberty or give me death.
Patrick Henry: Speech, Virginia Convention, 23 Mar 1775

10 It's often safer to be in chains than to be free.
Franz Kafka: The Trial, Ch. 8

11 Freedom's just another word for nothing left to lose.
Kris Kristofferson: Me and Bobby McGee

12 It is true that liberty is precious – so precious that it must be rationed.
Lenin: Attrib.

13 Those who deny freedom to others, deserve it not for themselves.
Abraham Lincoln: Speech, 19 May 1856

14 It would be better that England should be free than that England should be compulsorily sober.
William Connor Magee: Speech on the Intoxicating Liquor Bill, House of Lords, 2 May 1872

15 I cannot and will not give any undertaking at a time when I, and you, the people, are not free. Your freedom and mine cannot be separated.
Nelson Mandela: Message read by his daughter to a rally in Soweto, 10 Feb 1985

16 Emancipate yourselves from mental slavery.
None but ourselves can free our minds.
Bob Marley: Uprising, 'Redemption Song'

17 The liberty of the individual must be thus far limited; he must not make himself a nuisance to other people.
John Stuart Mill: On Liberty, Ch. 3

18 None can love freedom heartily, but good men; the rest love not freedom, but licence.
John Milton: Tenure of Kings and Magistrates

19 Freedom is the right to tell people what they do not want to hear.
George Orwell: The Road to Wigan Pier

20 Man was born free and everywhere he is in chains.
Jean Jacques Rousseau: Du contrat social, Ch. 1

21 No human being, however great, or powerful, was ever so free as a fish.
John Ruskin: The Two Paths, Lecture V

22 Man is condemned to be free.
Jean-Paul Sartre: Existentialism is a Humanism

23 You took my freedom away a long time ago and you can't give it back because you haven't got it yourself.
Alexander Solzhenitsyn: The First Circle, Ch. 17

24 My definition of a free society is a society where it is safe to be unpopular.

Adlai Stevenson: Speech, Detroit, Oct. 1952

25 I disapprove of what you say, but I will defend to the death your right to say it.
Voltaire: Attrib.

26 Liberty does not consist in mere declarations of the rights of man. It consists in the translation of those declarations into definite action.
Woodrow Wilson: Speech, 4 July 1914

FRIENDS

1 Books and friends should be few but good.
Proverb

2 Forsake not an old friend; for the new is not comparable to him: a new friend is as new wine; when it is old, thou shalt drink it with pleasure.
Bible: Ecclesiasticus: 9:10

3 Have no friends not equal to yourself.
Confucius: Analects

4 Fate chooses your relations, you choose your friends.
Jacques Delille: Malheur et pitié, I

5 I get by with a little help from my friends.
John Lennon: With a Little Help from My Friends (with Paul McCartney)

6 It is more shameful to distrust one's friends than to be deceived by them.
Duc de la Rochefoucauld: Maximes, 84

FRIENDSHIP

See also love and friendship

1 A friend in need is a friend indeed.
Proverb

2 God defend me from my friends; from my enemies I can defend myself.
Proverb

3 I've noticed your hostility towards him…I ought to have guessed you were friends.
Malcolm Bradbury: The History Man, Ch. 7

4 I don't trust him. We're friends.
Bertolt Brecht: Mother Courage, III

5 Should auld acquaintance be forgot,
And never brought to min'?
Robert Burns: Auld Lang Syne

6 Two may talk together under the same roof for many years, yet never really meet; and two others at first speech are old friends.
Mary Catherwood: Mackinac and Lake Stories, 'Marianson'

7 It is not so much our friends' help that helps us as the confident knowledge that they will help us.
Epicurus

8 Sir, I look upon every day to be lost, in which I do not make a new acquaintance.
Samuel Johnson: Life of Johnson (J. Boswell), Vol. IV

9 Friendship is unnecessary, like philosophy, like art…It has no survival value; rather it is one of those things that give value to survival.
C. S. Lewis: The Four Loves, Friendship

10 To like and dislike the same things, that is indeed true friendship.
Sallust: Bellum Catilinae

11 I might give my life for my friend, but he had better not ask me to do up a parcel.
Logan Pearsall Smith: Trivia

FUNERALS

See also death

1 I bet you a hundred bucks he ain't in there.
Charles Bancroft Dillingham: Referring to the escapologist Harry Houdini; said at his funeral, while carrying his coffin. Attrib.

2 Many funerals discredit a physician.
Ben Jonson

3 Why should I go? She won't be there.
Arthur Miller: When asked if he would attend his wife Marilyn Monroe's funeral. Attrib.

4 It proves what they say, give the public what they want to see and they'll come out for it.
Red Skelton: Said while attending the funeral in 1958 of Hollywood producer Harry Cohn. It has also been attributed to Samuel Goldwyn while attending Louis B. Mayer's funeral in 1957.

5 Not a drum was heard, not a funeral note,
As his corse to the rampart we hurried.
Charles Wolfe: The Burial of Sir John Moore at Corunna, I

FUTURE

See also past, present, time

1 Tomorrow never comes.
Proverb

2 Boast not thyself of tomorrow; for thou knowest not what a day may bring forth.
Bible: Proverbs: 27:1

3 You've no idea how pleasant it is not to have any future. It's like having a totally efficient contraceptive.
Anthony Burgess: Honey for the Bears, Pt. II, Ch. 6

4 I never think of the future. It comes soon enough.
Albert Einstein: Interview, 1930

5 The future will one day be the present and will seem as unimportant as the present does now.
W. Somerset Maugham: The Summing Up

6 The future is made of the same stuff as the present.
Simone Weil: On Science, Necessity, and the Love of God (ed. Richard Rees), 'Some Thoughts on the Love of God'

G

GARDENS

See also flowers

1 Mary, Mary, quite contrary,
How does your garden grow?
Anonymous: Tommy Thumb's Pretty Song Book

2 And the Lord God planted a garden eastward in Eden; and there he put the man whom he had formed.
Bible: Genesis: 2:6

3 To get the best results you must talk to your vegetables.
Charles, Prince of Wales: The Observer, 'Sayings of the Week', 28 Sept 1986

GENERALIZATIONS

1 To generalize is to be an idiot.
William Blake: Life of Blake (Gilchrist)

2 All generalizations are dangerous, even this one.
Alexandre Dumas, fils: Attrib.

3 All Stanislavsky ever said was: 'Avoid generalities.'
Anthony Hopkins: Films Illustrated, Dec 1980

GENEROSITY

See also charity, kindness

1 A bit of fragrance always clings to the hand that gives you roses.
Chinese proverb

2 God loveth a cheerful giver.
Bible: II Corinthians: 9:7

3 Experience was to be taken as

showing that one might get a five-pound note as one got a light for a cigarette; but one had to check the friendly impulse to ask for it in the same way.
Henry James: The Awkward Age

GENIUS

See also talent

1 Genius (which means transcendent capacity of taking trouble, first of all).
Thomas Carlyle: Frederick the Great, Vol. IV, Ch. 3

2 Genius is one per cent inspiration and ninety-nine per cent perspiration.
Thomas Edison: Attrib.

3 True genius walks along a line, and, perhaps, our greatest pleasure is in seeing it so often near falling, without being ever actually down.
Oliver Goldsmith: The Bee, 'The Characteristics of Greatness'

4 A genius! For thirty-seven years I've practiced fourteen hours a day, and now they call me a genius!
Pablo Sarasate: On being hailed as a genius by a critic. Attrib.

5 When a true genius appears in the world, you may know him by this sign, that the dunces are all in confederacy against him.
Jonathan Swift: Thoughts on Various Subjects

GLORY

1 May God deny you peace but give you glory!
Miguel de Unamuno y Jugo: Closing words. The Tragic Sense of Life

2 Sic transit gloria mundi.
Thus the glory of the world passes away.
Thomas à Kempis: The Imitation of Christ, I

GOD

See also atheism, faith, prayer, religion

1 Every man thinks God is on his side. The rich and powerful know that he is.
Jean Anouilh: The Lark

2 Then Peter opened his mouth, and said, Of a truth I perceive that God is no respecter of persons.
Bible: Acts: 10:34

3 A God who let us prove his existence would be an idol.
Dietrich Bonhoeffer: No Rusty Swords

4 Thou shalt have one God only; who
Would be at the expense of two?
Arthur Hugh Clough: The Latest Decalogue, 1

5 God moves in a mysterious way
His wonders to perform;
He plants his footsteps in the sea,
And rides upon the storm.
William Cowper: Olney Hymns, 35

6 God is subtle but he is not malicious.

Albert Einstein: Inscribed over the fireplace in the Mathematical Institute, Princeton. It refers to Einstein's objection to the quantum theory. Albert Einstein (Carl Seelig), Ch. 8

7 At bottom God is nothing more than an exalted father.
Sigmund Freud: Totem and Taboo

8 O worship the King, all glorious above!
O gratefully sing his power and his love!
Our Shield and Defender – the Ancient of Days,
Pavilioned in splendour, and girded with praise.
Robert Grant: Hymn

9 I have no need of that hypothesis.
Marquis de Laplace: On being asked by Napoleon why he had made no mention of God in his book about the universe, Mécanique céleste. Men of Mathematics (E. Bell)

10 Man has never been the same since God died.
He has taken it very hard.
Edna St Vincent Millay: Conversation at Midnight, 4

11 God is dead: but considering the state the species man is in, there will perhaps be caves, for ages yet, in which his shadow will be shown.
Friedrich Nietzsche: Die Fröhliche Wissenschaft, Bk. III

12 God is a gentleman. He prefers blondes.
Joe Orton: Loot, II

13 God can stand being told by Professor Ayer and Marghanita Laski that he doesn't exist.

J. B. Priestley: The Listener, 1 July 1965, 'The BBC's Duty to Society'

14 It is a mistake to assume that God is interested only, or even chiefly, in religion.
William Temple: Attrib.

15 If God did not exist, it would be necessary to invent Him.
Voltaire: Epîtres, 'A l'auteur du livre des trois Imposteurs'

16 If God made us in His image, we have certainly returned the compliment.
Voltaire: Le Sottisier

GOOD

See also good and evil, righteousness, virtue

1 Men have never been good, they are not good, they never will be good.
Karl Barth: Time, 12 Apr 1954

2 He who would do good to another must do it in Minute Particulars.
General Good is the plea of the scoundrel, hypocrite, and flatterer.
William Blake: Jerusalem

3 *Summum bonum.*
The greatest good.
Cicero: De Officiis, I

4 Goodness does not more certainly make men happy than happiness makes them good.
Walter Savage Landor: Imaginary Conversations, 'Lord Brooke and Sir Philip Sidney'

5 The good is the beautiful.
Plato: Lysis

6 Do good by stealth, and blush to find it fame.

Alexander Pope: Epilogue to the Satires, Dialogue I

7 How far that little candle throws his beams!
So shines a good deed in a naughty world.
William Shakespeare: The Merchant of Venice, V:1

8 Nothing can harm a good man, either in life or after death.
Socrates: Apology (Plato)

9 You shouldn't say it is not good. You should say you do not like it; and then, you know, you're perfectly safe.
James Whistler: Whistler Stories (D. Seitz)

GOOD AND EVIL

See also virtue and vice

1 Good can imagine Evil; but Evil cannot imagine Good.
W. H. Auden: A Certain World: A Commonplace Book

2 The good die early, and the bad die late.
Daniel Defoe: Character of the late Dr. Annesley

3 A good man can be stupid and still be good. But a bad man must have brains.
Maxim Gorky: The Lower Depths

4 The web of our life is of a mingled yarn, good and ill together.
William Shakespeare: All's Well that Ends Well, IV:3

GOSSIP

1 The gossip of two women will destroy two houses.
Arabic proverb

2 Don't wash your dirty linen in public.
Proverb

3 There's no smoke without fire.
Proverb

4 Throw dirt enough, and some will stick.
Proverb

5 Walls have ears.
Proverb

6 Listeners never hear good of themselves.
Proverb

7 How these curiosities would be quite forgot, did not such idle fellows as I am put them down.
John Aubrey: Brief Lives, 'Venetia Digby'

8 No one gossips about other people's secret virtues.
Bertrand Russell: On Education

9 I remember that a wise friend of mine did usually say, 'that which is everybody's business is nobody's business'.
Izaak Walton: The Compleat Angler, Ch. 2

GOVERNMENT

See also democracy, monarchy, politics

1 I will undoubtedly have to seek what is happily known as gainful employment, which I am glad to say does not describe holding public office.
Dean Acheson: Remark made on leaving his post as secretary of state, 1952; he subsequently returned to private legal practice

2 The danger is not that a particular class is unfit to govern. Every class is unfit to govern.
Lord Acton: Letter to Mary Gladstone, 1881

3 Where some people are very wealthy and others have nothing, the result will be either extreme democracy or absolute oligarchy, or despotism will come from either of those excesses.
Aristotle: Politics, Bk. IV

4 One to mislead the public, another to mislead the Cabinet, and the third to mislead itself.
Herbert Henry Asquith: Explaining why the War Office kept three sets of figures. The Price of Glory (Alastair Horne), Ch. 2

5 Too bad all the people who know how to run the country are busy driving cabs and cutting hair.
George Burns

6 A small acquaintance with history shows that all Governments are selfish and the French Governments more selfish than most.
David Eccles: The Observer, 'Sayings of the Year', 29 Dec 1962

7 A government that is big enough to give you all you want is big enough to take it all away.
Barry Goldwater: Bachman's Book of Freedom Quotations (M. Ivens and R. Dunstan)

8 We give the impression of being in office but not in power.
Norman Lamont: The Observer, 13 June 1993

9 Government has no other end but the preservation of property.
John Locke: Second Treatise on Civil Government

10 Every country has the government it deserves.
Joseph de Maistre: Lettres et Opuscules Inédits, 15 Aug 1811

11 The worst government is the most moral. One composed of cynics is often very tolerant and human. But when fanatics are on top there is no limit to oppression.
H. L. Mencken: Notebooks, 'Minority Report'

12 One day the don't-knows will get in, and then where will we be?
Spike Milligan: Attributed remark made about a pre-election poll

13 Government, even in its best state, is but a necessary evil; in its worst state, an intolerable one.
Thomas Paine: Common Sense, Ch. 1

14 Let the people think they govern and they will be governed.
William Penn: Some Fruits of Solitude, 337

15 We live under a government of men and morning newspapers.
Wendell Phillips: Address: The Press

16 Secrecy is the first essential in affairs of the State.
Cardinal Richelieu: Testament Politique, Maxims

17 I don't make jokes – I just watch the government and report the facts.
Will Rogers: Saturday Review, 'A Rogers Thesaurus', 25 Aug 1962

18 Parliament is the longest running farce in the West End.
Cyril Smith: The Times, 23 Sept 1977

19 Many people consider the things which government does for them to be social progress, but they consider the things government does for others as socialism.
Earl Warren: Peter's Quotations (Laurence J. Peter)

20 The people's government, made for the people, made by the people, and answerable to the people.
Daniel Webster: Second speech on Foote's resolution, 26 Jan 1830

GRAMMAR

See also language, words

1 When I split an infinitive, god damn it, I split it so it stays split.
Raymond Chandler: Letter to his English publisher

2 This is the sort of English up with which I will not put.
Winston Churchill: The story is that Churchill wrote the comment in the margin of a report in which a civil servant had used an awkward construction to avoid ending a sentence with a preposition. An alternative version substitutes 'bloody nonsense' for 'English'. Plain Words (E. Gowers), Ch. 9

3 Grammar, which can govern even kings.
Molière: Les Femmes savantes, II:6

4 I am the Roman Emperor, and am above grammar.
Sigismund: Responding to criticism of his Latin. Attrib.

GREATNESS

GREATNESS

1 A truly great man never puts away the simplicity of a child.
Chinese proverb

2 Great men are but life-sized. Most of them, indeed, are rather short.
Max Beerbohm: And Even Now

3 No great man lives in vain. The history of the world is but the biography of great men.
Thomas Carlyle: Heroes and Hero-Worship, 'The Hero as Divinity'

4 To be great is to be misunderstood.
Ralph Waldo Emerson: Essays, 'Self-Reliance'

5 To be alone is the fate of all great minds – a fate deplored at-times, but still always chosen as the less grievous of two evils.
Arthur Schopenhauer: Aphorismen zur Lebensweisheit

6 Some are born great, some achieve greatness, and some have greatness thrust upon 'em.
William Shakespeare: Twelfth Night, II:5

7 A great city is that which has the greatest men and women.
Walt Whitman: Song of the Broad-Axe, 5

GREED

See also food, materialism, obesity

1 He that eats till he is sick must fast till he is well.
Hebrew proverb

2 The eye is bigger than the belly.
Proverb

3 Gluttony is an emotional escape, a sign something is eating us.
Peter De Vries: Comfort me with Apples, Ch. 7

4 More die in the United States of too much food than of too little.
John Kenneth Galbraith: The Affluent Society, Ch. 9

5 Wealth is like sea-water; the more we drink, the thirstier we become; and the same is true of fame.
Arthur Schopenhauer: Parerga and Paralipomena

6 People will swim through shit if you put a few bob in it.
Peter Sellers: Halliwell's Filmgoer's and Video Viewer's Companion

GUILT

See also conscience, crime, justice, regret

1 When Pilate saw that he could prevail nothing, but that rather a tumult was made, he took water, and washed his hands before the multitude, saying, I am innocent of the blood of this just person: see ye to it.
Then answered all the people, and said, His blood be on us, and on our children.
Bible: Matthew: 27:24–25

2 St. Thomas, guard for me my kingdom! To you I declare myself guilty of that for which others bear the blame.

Henry II: Said at the outbreak of the Great Rebellion, 1173–74; one of Henry's first actions was to perform a public penance for Thomas Becket's murder.
Chronique de la guerre entre les Anglois et les Ecossais en 1173 et 1174 (Jordan Fantosme)

3 Love bade me welcome; yet my soul drew back,
    Guilty of dust and sin.
George Herbert: Love

4 O! my offence is rank, it smells to heaven.
William Shakespeare: Hamlet, III:3

5 Suspicion always haunts the guilty mind;
    The thief doth fear each bush an officer.
William Shakespeare: Henry VI, Part Three, V:6

6 Here's the smell of the blood still. All the perfumes of Arabia will not sweeten this little hand.
William Shakespeare: Macbeth, V:1

GULLIBILITY

See also foolishness, impressionability

1 There's a sucker born every minute.
Phineas Taylor Barnum: Attrib.

2 Man is a dupable animal. Quacks in medicine, quacks in religion, and quacks in politics know this, and act upon that knowledge.
Robert Southey: The Doctor, Ch. 87

HABIT

1 Old habits die hard.
Proverb

2 Curious things, habits. People themselves never knew they had them.
Agatha Christie: Witness for the Prosecution

3 Men's natures are alike; it is their habits that carry them far apart.
Confucius: Analects

HALF MEASURES

1 Two half-truths do not make a truth, and two half-cultures do not make a culture.
Arthur Koestler: The Ghost in the Machine, Preface

2 I'm not really a Jew; just Jewish, not the whole hog.
Jonathan Miller: Beyond the Fringe

HAPPINESS

See also contentment, laughter, pleasure

1 One joy scatters a hundred griefs.
Chinese proverb

2 I wonder why happiness is despised nowadays: dismissively confused with comfort or complacency, judged an enemy of social – even technological – progress.
Julian Barnes: Metroland

3 If you haven't been happy very young, you can still be happy later on, but it's much harder. You need more luck.
Simone de Beauvoir: The Observer, 'Sayings of the Week', 19 May 1975

4 Happiness is a mystery like religion, and should never be rationalized.
G. K. Chesterton: Heretics, Ch. 7

5 That action is best, which procures the greatest happiness for the greatest numbers.
Francis Hutcheson: Inquiry into the Original of our Ideas of Beauty and Virtue, Treatise II, 'Concerning Moral Good and Evil'

6 Happiness is like coke – something you get as a by-product in the process of making something else.
Aldous Huxley: Point Counter Point

7 Happiness is not an ideal of reason but of imagination.
Immanuel Kant: Grundlegung zur Metaphysik der Sitten, II

8 Ask yourself whether you are happy, and you cease to be so.
John Stuart Mill: Autobiography, Ch. 5

9 To be without some of the things you want is an indispensable part of happiness.
Bertrand Russell: Attrib.

10 There is only one happiness in life, to love and be loved.
George Sand: Letter to Lina Calamatta, 31 March 1862

11 Happiness? That's nothing

more than health and a poor
memory.
Albert Schweitzer: Attrib.

12 A lifetime of happiness: no
man alive could bear it: it would
be hell on earth.
*George Bernard Shaw: Man and
Superman, I*

13 A man is happy so long as he
choose to be happy and nothing
can stop him.
*Alexander Solzhenitsyn: Cancer
Ward*

14 Happiness is an imaginary
condition, formerly often attributed by the living to the dead,
now usually attributed by adults
to children, and by children to
adults.
Thomas Szasz: The Second Sin

15 Happiness is no laughing
matter.
Richard Whately: Apophthegms

16 Happy Days Are Here Again.
*Jack Yellen: Used by Roosevelt as
a campaign song in 1932. Song title*

HASTE

See also impetuosity

1 Don't throw the baby out with
the bathwater.
Proverb

2 Haste makes waste.
Proverb

3 More haste, less speed.
Proverb

4 In skating over thin ice, our
safety is in our speed.
*Ralph Waldo Emerson: Essays,
'Prudence'*

5 Never before have we had so little time in which to do so much.
*Franklin D. Roosevelt: Radio
address, 23 Feb 1942*

6 If it were done when 'tis done,
then 'twere well
It were done quickly.
*William Shakespeare: Macbeth,
I:7*

7 Hurry! I never hurry. I have no
time to hurry.
*Igor Stravinsky: Responding to his
publisher's request that he hurry his
completion of a composition.
Attrib.*

HATE

See also love and hate

1 It does not matter much what a
man hates, provided he hates
something.
Samuel Butler: Notebooks

2 I am free of all prejudice. I hate
everyone equally.
W. C. Fields: Attrib.

3 If you hate a person, you hate
something in him that is part of
yourself. What isn't part of ourselves doesn't disturb us.
Hermann Hesse: Demian, Ch. 6

4 Few people can be happy unless
they hate some other person, nation or creed.
Bertrand Russell: Attrib.

5 An intellectual hatred is the
worst.
*W. B. Yeats: A Prayer for My
Daughter*

HEALTH AND HEALTHY LIVING

See also medicine

1 An apple a day keeps the doctor
away.
Proverb

2 Nutritional research, like a modern star of Bethlehem, brings hope that sickness need not be a part of life.
Adelle Davis: The New York Times Magazine, 'The Great Adelle Davis Controversy', 20 May 1973

3 A wise man ought to realize that health is his most valuable possession.
Hippocrates: A Regimen for Health, 9

4 *Orandum est ut sit mens sana in corpore sano.*
Your prayer must be for a sound mind in a sound body.
Juvenal: Satires, X

5 Early to rise and early to bed makes a male healthy and wealthy and dead.
James Thurber: Fables for Our Time, 'The Shrike and the Chipmunks'

HEAVEN

See also afterlife

1 And he dreamed, and behold a ladder set up on the earth, and the top of it reached to heaven: and behold the angels of God ascending and descending on it.
Bible: Genesis: 28:12

2 Even the paradise of fools is not an unpleasant abode while it is inhabitable.
Dean Inge: Attrib.

3 Probably no invention came more easily to man than Heaven.
Georg Christoph Lichtenberg: Aphorisms

4 For observe, that to hope for

Paradise is to live in Paradise, a very different thing from actually getting there.
Vita Sackville-West: Passenger to Tehran, Ch. 1

5 If you go to Heaven without being naturally qualified for it you will not enjoy yourself there.
George Bernard Shaw: Man and Superman

6 Grant me paradise in this world; I'm not so sure I'll reach it in the next.
Tintoretto: Arguing that he be allowed to paint the Paradiso in the doge's palace in Venice, despite his advanced age. Attrib.

7 There is a happy land,
Far, far away,
Where saints in glory stand,
Bright, bright as day.
Andrew Young: 'There is a Happy Land'

HELL

See also damnation, devil

1 Abandon hope, all ye who enter here.
Dante: The inscription at the entrance to Hell. Divine Comedy, Inferno, III

2 Hell is oneself;
Hell is alone, the other figures in it
Merely projections. There is nothing to escape from
And nothing to escape to. One is always alone.
T. S. Eliot: The Cocktail Party, I:3

3 Hell is other people.
Jean-Paul Sartre: Huis clos

4 Hell is a city much like London — A populous and smoky city.

Percy Bysshe Shelley: Peter Bell the Third

5 The way down to Hell is easy.
Virgil: Aeneid, Bk. VI

HEROISM

See also courage, endurance, patriotism, war

1 Some talk of Alexander, and some of Hercules,
Of Hector and Lysander, and such great names as these;
But of all the world's brave heroes there's none that can compare
With a tow, row, row, row, row, row for the British Grenadier.
Anonymous: The British Grenadiers

2 They died to save their country and they only saved the world.
Hilaire Belloc: The English Graves

3 ANDREA. Unhappy the land that has no heroes.

GALILEO. No, unhappy the land that needs heroes.
Bertolt Brecht: Galileo, 13

4 Every hero becomes a bore at last.
Ralph Waldo Emerson: Representative Men, 'Uses of Great Men'

5 Show me a hero and I will write you a tragedy.
F. Scott Fitzgerald: The Crack-Up, 'Notebooks, E'

6 I'm a hero with coward's legs. I'm a hero from the waist up.
Spike Milligan: Puckoon

7 Being a hero is about the shortest-lived profession on earth.
Will Rogers: Saturday Review, 'A Rogers Thesaurus', 25 Aug 1962

HISTORY

See also past

1 History repeats itself.
Proverb

2 History is the sum total of the things that could have been avoided.
Konrad Adenauer

3 Man is a history-making creature who can neither repeat his past nor leave it behind.
W. H. Auden: The Dyer's Hand, 'D. H. Lawrence'

4 History does not repeat itself. Historians repeat each other.
Arthur Balfour: Attrib.

5 The history of every country begins in the heart of a man or woman.
Willa Cather: O Pioneers!, Pt. II, Ch. 4

6 History is philosophy teaching by examples.
Dionysius of Halicarnassus: Ars rhetorica, XI:2

7 History is an endless repetition of the wrong way of living.
Lawrence Durrell: The Listener, 1978

8 History is more or less bunk. It's tradition. We don't want tradition. We want to live in the present and the only history that is worth a tinker's damn is the history we make today.
Henry Ford: Chicago Tribune, 25 May 1916

9 History never looks like history when you are living through it. It always looks confusing and messy, and it always feels uncomfortable.

HOME

John W. Gardner: No Easy Victories

10 Events in the past may roughly be divided into those which probably never happened and those which do not matter.
Dean Inge: Assessments and Anticipations, 'Prognostications'

11 It takes a great deal of history to produce a little literature.
Henry James: Life of Nathaniel Hawthorne, Ch. 1

12 'History', Stephen said, 'is a nightmare from which I am trying to awake'.
James Joyce: Ulysses

13 Hegel says somewhere that all great events and personalities in world history reappear in one fashion or another. He forgot to add: the first time as tragedy, the second as farce.
Karl Marx: The Eighteenth Brumaire of Louis Napoleon

14 History is past politics, and politics present history.
John Robert Seeley: Quoting the historian E. A. Freeman. The Growth of British Policy

15 The Cavaliers (Wrong but Wromantic) and the Roundheads (Right but Repulsive).
W. C. Sellar: 1066 And All That

16 America became top nation and history came to a full stop.
W. C. Sellar: 1066 And All That

HOME

1 East, west, home's best.
Proverb

2 Home is where the heart is.
Proverb

3 A House Is Not a Home.
Polly Adler: Title of memoirs

4 Home is home, though it be never so homely.
John Clarke: Paroemiologia Anglo-Latina

5 Home is the place where, when you have to go there,
They have to take you in.
Robert Frost: The Death of the Hired Man

6 A man travels the world over in search of what he needs and returns home to find it.
George Moore: The Brook Kerith, Ch. 11

7 Keep the Home Fires Burning.
Ivor Novello: Song title (written with Lena Guilbert Ford)

8 Mid pleasures and palaces though we may roam,
Be it ever so humble, there's no place like home;
John Howard Payne: Clari, or the Maid of Milan

HOMOSEXUALITY

See also sex

1 Out of the closets and into the streets.
Anonymous: Slogan for US Gay Liberation Front

2 Between women love is contemplative.
Simone de Beauvoir: Le Deuxième Sexe

3 But the men of Sodom were wicked and sinners before the Lord exceedingly.
Bible: Genesis: 13:13

4 I became one of the stately homos of England.

Quentin Crisp: The Naked Civil Servant

5 I am the Love that dare not speak its name.
Lord Alfred Douglas: Two Loves

6 Constant conditioning in my youth and social pressure in every department of my life all failed to convert me to heterosexuality.
Ian McKellen: The Times, 5 Dec 1991

7 There's nothing I'd like better than to live in a world where my sexuality was utterly irrelevant.
Armistead Maupin: The Sunday Times, 4 Feb 1990

8 This sort of thing may be tolerated by the French, but we are British – thank God.
Lord Montgomery: Comment on a bill to relax the laws against homosexuals. Daily Mail, 27 May 1965

9 Wilde's captors were the police. But his persecutors were to be found on the letters page of the *Daily Telegraph*.
Matthew Parris: The Times, 7 Apr 1993

10 If Michelangelo had been straight, the Sistine Chapel would have been wallpapered.
Robin Tyler: Speech to gay-rights rally, Washington, 9 Jan 1988

HONESTY

See also frankness, integrity, sincerity, truth

1 Honesty is the best policy.
Proverb

2 Though I be poor, I'm honest.
Thomas Middleton: The Witch, III:2

3 To make your children *capable of* honesty is the beginning of education.
John Ruskin: Time and Tide, Letter VIII

4 Honesty is the best policy; but he who is governed by that maxim is not an honest man.
Richard Whately: Apophthegms

5 If you do not tell the truth about yourself you cannot tell it about other people.
Virginia Woolf: The Moment and Other Essays

HOPE

See also optimism

1 A drowning man will clutch at a straw.
Proverb

2 Hope for the best.
Proverb

3 While there's life there's hope.
Proverb

4 Comin' in on a Wing and a Prayer.
Harold Adamson: Film and song title

5 Hope is the power of being cheerful in circumstances which we know to be desperate.
G. K. Chesterton: Heretics, Ch. 12

6 He that lives upon hope will die fasting.
Benjamin Franklin: The Way to Wealth

7 Confidence and hope do be more good than physic.
Galen

8 After all, tomorrow is another day.
Margaret Mitchell: The closing words of the book, Gone with the Wind

9 Hope springs eternal in the human breast;
Man never is, but always to be blest.
Alexander Pope: An Essay on Man, I

10 For hope is but the dream of those that wake.
Matthew Prior: Solomon, II

HORSES

See also hunting, sport and games

1 When I appear in public people expect me to neigh, grind my teeth, paw the ground and swish my tail – none of which is easy.
Princess Anne: The Observer, 'Sayings of the Week', 22 May 1977

2 I sprang to the stirrup, and Joris, and he;
I galloped, Dirck galloped, we galloped all three.
Robert Browning: How they brought the Good News from Ghent to Aix

3 Gwine to run all night!
Gwine to run all day!
I bet my money on the bob-tail nag.
Somebody bet on the bay.
Stephen Foster: Camptown Races

4 A horse! a horse! my kingdom for a horse.
William Shakespeare: Richard III, V:4

HOUSES

See also architecture, stately homes

1 Houses are built to live in and not to look on; therefore let use be preferred before uniformity, except where both may be had.
Francis Bacon: Essays, 'Of Building'

2 A house is a machine for living in.
Le Corbusier: Towards an Architecture

3 They're all made out of ticky-tacky, and they all look just the same.
Malvina Reynolds: Song describing a housing scheme built in the hills south of San Francisco. Little Boxes

HOUSEWORK

See also woman's role

1 Housekeeping ain't no joke.
Louisa May Alcott: Little Women, Pt. I

2 There was no need to do any housework at all. After the first four years the dirt doesn't get any worse.
Quentin Crisp: The Naked Civil Servant

3 The whole process of home-making, house-keeping and cooking, which ever has been woman's special province, should be looked on as an art and a profession.
Sarah Joseph Hale: Editorial, Godey's Lady's Book

HUMAN CONDITION

See also life, mankind

1 We mortals cross the ocean of
this world
Each in his average cabin of a
life.
*Robert Browning: Bishop
Blougram's Apology*

2 If God were suddenly condemned to live the life which he
has inflicted on men, He would
kill Himself.
*Alexandre Dumas, fils: Pensées
d'album*

3 Oh wearisome condition of
humanity!
Born under one law, to another
bound.
Fulke Greville: Mustapha, V:6

4 Man hands on misery to man.
It deepens like a coastal shelf.
Get out as early as you can,
And don't have any kids your-
self.
*Philip Larkin: High Windows,
'This Be the Verse'*

5 You come into the world alone,
you go out alone. In between it's
nice to know a few people, but
being alone is a fundamental
quality of human life, depressing
as that is.
Helen Mirren: Remark, Jan 1989

6 All the world's a stage,
And all the men and women
merely players;
They have their exits and their
entrances;
And one man in his time plays
many parts,
His acts being seven ages.
*William Shakespeare: As You Like
It, II:7*

HUMAN NATURE

See also mankind

1 Human nature is so well disposed towards those who are in
interesting situations, that a
young person, who either marries or dies, is sure to be kindly
spoken of.
Jane Austen: Emma, Ch. 22

2 Nature is often hidden, sometimes overcome, seldom extin-
guished.
*Francis Bacon: Essays, 'Of Nature
in Men'*

3 I got disappointed in human nature as well and gave it up because I found it too much like
my own.
*J. P. Donleavy: Fairy Tales of New
York*

4 Most human beings have an almost infinite capacity for taking
things for granted.
*Aldous Huxley: Themes and
Variations*

5 We need more understanding of
human nature, because the only
real danger that exists is man
himself...His psyche should be
studied because we are the
origin of all coming evil.
Carl Gustav Jung: Interview

6 Out of the crooked timber of
humanity no straight thing can
ever be made.
*Immanuel Kant: Idee zu einer
allgemeinen Geschichte in
weltbürgerlicher Absicht*

7 Scenery is fine – but human
nature is finer.
*John Keats: Letter to Benjamin
Bailey, 13 Mar 1818*

8 'Tis the way of all flesh.

HUMAN RIGHTS

Thomas Shadwell: The Sullen Lovers, V:2

HUMAN RIGHTS

See also equality, freedom

1 All human beings are born free and equal in dignity and rights.
Anonymous: Universal Declaration of Human Rights (1948), Article 1

2 Liberté! Égalité! Fraternité! Freedom! Equality! Brotherhood!
Anonymous: Motto for French Revolutionaries

3 We look forward to a world founded upon four essential human freedoms. The first is freedom of speech and expression – everywhere in the world. The second is freedom of every person to worship God in his own way – everywhere in the world. The third is freedom from want…everywhere in the world. The fourth is freedom from fear…anywhere in the world.
Franklin D. Roosevelt: Speech to Congress, 6 Jan 1941

4 None ought to be lords or landlords over another, but the earth is free for every son and daughter of mankind to live free upon.
Gerrard Winstanley: Letter to Lord Fairfax, 1649

HUMILITY

See also servility

1 Blessed are the meek: for they shall inherit the earth.
Bible: Matthew: 5:5

2 Humility is only doubt,

And does the sun and moon blot out.
William Blake: The Everlasting Gospel

3 It is difficult to be humble. Even if you aim at humility, there is no guarantee that when you have attained the state you will not be proud of the feat.
Bonamy Dobrée: John Wesley

4 The meek do not inherit the earth unless they are prepared to fight for their meekness.
H. J. Laski: Attrib.

HUMOUR

See also laughter, puns

1 I have a fine sense of the ridiculous, but no sense of humour.
Edward Albee: Who's Afraid of Virginia Woolf?, I

2 The marvellous thing about a joke with a double meaning is that it can only mean one thing.
Ronnie Barker: Sauce, 'Daddie's Sauce'

3 Comedy is tragedy that happens to other people.
Angela Carter: Wise Children

4 A joke's a very serious thing.
Charles Churchill: The Ghost

5 Men will confess to treason, murder, arson, false teeth, or a wig. How many of them will own up to a lack of humour?
Frank More Colby: Essays, I

6 No mind is thoroughly well organized that is deficient in a sense of humour.
Samuel Taylor Coleridge: Table Talk

7 Total absence of humour renders life impossible.

Colette: Chance Acquaintances

8 A different taste in jokes is a great strain on the affections.
George Eliot: Daniel Deronda

9 Funny peculiar, or funny ha-ha?
Ian Hay: The Housemaster, III

10 Every man has, some time in his life, an ambition to be a wag.
Samuel Johnson: Diary and Letters (Mme D'Arblay), Vol. III, Ch. 46

11 The coarse joke proclaims that we have here an animal which finds its own animality either objectionable or funny.
C. S. Lewis: Miracles

12 Impropriety is the soul of wit.
W. Somerset Maugham: The Moon and Sixpence, Ch. 4

13 It is not for nothing that, in the English language alone, to accuse someone of trying to be funny is highly abusive.
Malcolm Muggeridge: Tread Softly For You Tread on My Jokes

14 Everything is funny, as long as it's happening to somebody else.
Will Rogers: The Illiterate Digest

15 People no longer need the jokes explained; everyone gets irony nowadays.
John Waters: The Times, 11 June 1994

16 Why have they been telling us women lately that we have no sense of humor – when we are always laughing?…And when we're not laughing, we're smiling.
Naomi Weisstein: All She Needs, Introduction (Ellen Levine)

HUNGER

See also desire, food

1 Hunger is the best sauce.
Proverb

2 Poverty is an anomaly to rich people. It is very difficult to make out why people who want dinner do not ring the bell.
Walter Bagehot: Literary Studies, II

3 When he told men to love their neighbour, their bellies were full. Nowadays things are different.
Bertolt Brecht: Mother Courage, II

4 If only it were as easy to banish hunger by rubbing the belly as it is to masturbate.
Diogenes: Lives and Opinions of Eminent Philosophers (Diogenes Laertius)

5 They that die by famine die by inches.
Matthew Henry: Exposition of the Old and New Testaments

6 The war against hunger is truly mankind's war of liberation.
John Fitzgerald Kennedy: Speech, World Food Congress, 4 June 1963

7 Let them eat cake.
Marie-Antoinette: On being told that the people had no bread to eat; in fact she was repeating a much older saying. Attrib.

HUNTING

See also sport and games

1 Happy the hare at morning, for she cannot read
The Hunter's waking thoughts.
W. H. Auden: The Dog Beneath the Skin

2 Detested sport,

That owes its pleasures to another's pain.
William Cowper: The Task

3 Wild animals never kill for sport. Man is the only one to whom the torture and death of his fellow-creatures is amusing in itself.
J. A. Froude: Oceana, Ch. 5

4 It isn't mere convention. Everyone can see that the people who hunt are the right people and the people who don't are the wrong ones.
George Bernard Shaw: Heartbreak House

5 The English country gentleman galloping after a fox – the unspeakable in full pursuit of the uneatable.
Oscar Wilde: A Woman of No Importance, I

HURT

See also cruelty, nastiness

1 Those have most power to hurt us that we love.
Francis Beaumont: The Maid's Tragedy, V:6

2 It takes your enemy and your friend, working together, to hurt you to the heart; the one to slander you and the other to get the news to you.
Mark Twain: Following the Equator

HYPOCRISY

See also insincerity

1 All are not saints that go to church.
Proverb

2 Prisons are built with stones of Law, brothels with bricks of Religion.
William Blake: The Marriage of Heaven and Hell

3 Man is the only animal that can remain on friendly terms with the victims he intends to eat until he eats them.
Samuel Butler: Notebooks

4 We ought to see far enough into a hypocrite to see even his sincerity.
G. K. Chesterton: Heretics, Ch. 5

5 Man is the only animal that learns by being hypocritical. He pretends to be polite and then, eventually, he *becomes* polite.
Jean Kerr: Finishing Touches

6 For neither man nor angel can discern
Hypocrisy, the only evil that walks
Invisible, except to God alone.
John Milton: Paradise Lost, Bk. III

7 Hypocrisy is the homage paid by vice to virtue.
Duc de la Rochefoucauld: Maximes, 218

8 I hope you have not been leading a double life, pretending to be wicked and being really good all the time. That would be hypocrisy.
Oscar Wilde: The Importance of Being Earnest, II

9 A Christian is a man who feels
Repentance on a Sunday
For what he did on Saturday
And is going to do on Monday.
Thomas Russell Ybarra: The Christia

I

IDEALISM

1 You can't be a true idealist without being a true realist.
Jacques Delors: Speech, European Union Corfu Summit, 21 June 1994

2 If a man hasn't discovered something that he would die for, he isn't fit to live.
Martin Luther King: Speech, Detroit, 23 June 1963

3 Ideal mankind would abolish death, multiply itself million upon million, rear up city upon city, save every parasite alive, until the accumulation of mere existence is swollen to a horror.
D. H. Lawrence: St Mawr

4 An idealist is one who, on noticing that a rose smells better than a cabbage, concludes that it will also make better soup.
H. L. Mencken: Sententiae

5 A radical is a man with both feet firmly planted in the air.
Franklin D. Roosevelt: Broadcast, 26 Oct 1939

6 If a woman like Eva Peron with no ideals can get that far, think how far I can go with all the ideals that I have.
Margaret Thatcher: The Sunday Times, 1980

IDEAS

See also opinions

1 Paradoxes are useful to attract attention to ideas.
Mandell Creighton: Life and Letters

2 What was once thought can never be unthought.
Friedrich Dürrenmatt: The Physicists

3 Man is ready to die for an idea, provided that idea is not quite clear to him.
Paul Eldridge: Horns of Glass

4 Many ideas grow better when transplanted into another mind than in the one where they sprang up.
Oliver Wendell Holmes Jnr

5 A stand can be made against invasion by an army; no stand can be made against invasion by an idea.
Victor Hugo: Histoire d'un Crime, 'La Chute'

6 An idea isn't responsible for the people who believe in it.
Don Marquis: New York Sun

7 A society made up of individuals who were all capable of original thought would probably be unendurable. The pressure of ideas would simply drive it frantic.
H. L. Mencken: Notebooks, 'Minority Report'

IDLENESS

See also bed, laziness

1 The devil finds work for idle hands to do.
Proverb

2 The dreadful burden of having nothing to do.

Nicolas Boileau: Épitres, XI

3 Idleness is only the refuge of weak minds.
Earl of Chesterfield: Letter to his son, 20 July 1749

4 It is impossible to enjoy idling thoroughly unless one has plenty of work to do.
Jerome K. Jerome: Idle Thoughts of an Idle Fellow

5 We would all be idle if we could.
Samuel Johnson: Life of Johnson (J. Boswell), Vol. III

6 Young people ought not to be idle. It is very bad for them.
Margaret Thatcher: The Times, 1984

IGNORANCE

See also foolishness, innocence, stupidity

1 He that knows little, often repeats it.
Proverb

2 What you don't know can't hurt you.
Proverb

3 IGNORAMUS, n. A person unacquainted with certain kinds of knowledge familiar to yourself, and having certain other kinds that you know nothing about.
Ambrose Bierce: The Devil's Dictionary

4 Ignorance is preferable to error; and he is less remote from the truth who believes nothing, than he who believes what is wrong.
Thomas Jefferson: Notes on the State of Virginia

5 Nothing in the world is more dangerous than sincere ignorance and conscientious stupidity.
Martin Luther King: Strength To Love

6 His ignorance was an Empire State Building of ignorance. You had to admire it for its size.
Dorothy Parker: Referring to Harold Ross. Attrib.

7 From ignorance our comfort flows,
The only wretched are the wise.
Matthew Prior: To the Hon. Charles Montague

ILLNESS

See also disease, medicine, remedies

1 Feed a cold and starve a fever.
Commonly interpreted as meaning that one should eat with a cold but not with a fever. An alternative explanation is that if one 'feeds' a cold, by not taking care of it, one will end up having to deal with a fever. Proverb

2 If you are too smart to pay the doctor, you had better be too smart to get ill.
African (Transvaal) proverb

3 Coughs and sneezes spread diseases.
Anonymous: Wartime health slogan in the UK, c. 1942 Dictionary of 20th Century Quotations (Nigel Rees)

4 A long illness seems to be placed between life and death, in order to make death a comfort both to those who die and to those who remain.
Jean de La Bruyère: Caractères, Ch. 11

5 I reckon being ill as one of the greatest pleasures of life, provided one is not too ill and is not obliged to work till one is better.
Samuel Butler: The Way of All Flesh, Ch. 80

6 Much of the world's work, it has been said, is done by men who do not feel quite well. Marx is a case in point.
John Kenneth Galbraith: The Age of Uncertainty, Ch. 3

7 Every time you sleep with a boy you sleep with all his old girlfriends.
Government-sponsored AIDS advertisement, 1987

8 If you start to think about your physical or moral condition, you usually find that you are sick.
Goethe: Sprüche in Prosa, Pt. I, Bk. II

9 If my next-door neighbour is to be allowed to let his children go unvaccinated, he might as well be allowed to leave strychnine lozenges about in the way of mine.
T. H. Huxley: Method and Results, 'Administrative Nihilism'

10 One who is ill has not only the right but also the duty to seek medical aid.
Maimonides

11 The sick are the greatest danger for the healthy; it is not from the strongest that harm comes to the strong, but from the weakest.
Friedrich Nietzsche: Genealogy of Morals, Essay 3

12 They do certainly give very strange and new-fangled names to diseases.
Plato: Republic, III

13 Every man who feels well is a sick man neglecting himself.
Jules Romains: Knock, ou le triomphe de la médecine

14 Most of the time we think we're sick, it's all in the mind.
Thomas Wolfe: Look Homeward, Angel, Pt. I, Ch. 1

IMAGINATION

1 The primary imagination I hold to be the living power and prime agent of all human perception, and as a repetition in the finite mind of the eternal act of creation in the infinite I AM.
Samuel Taylor Coleridge: Biographia Literaria, Ch. 13

2 Art is ruled uniquely by the imagination.
Benedetto Croce: Esthetic, Ch. 1

3 She has no imagination and that means no compassion.
Michael Foot: Referring to the Conservative politician and prime minister Margaret Thatcher. Attrib.

4 Imagination and fiction make up more than three quarters of our real life.
Simone Weil: Gravity and Grace

IMITATION

See also originality

1 A lotta cats copy the Mona Lisa, but people still line up to see the original.
Louis Armstrong: When asked whether he objected to people copying his style. Attrib.

2 Imitation is the sincerest form of flattery.
Charles Caleb Colton: Lacon, Vol. I

3 When people are free to do as they please, they usually imitate each other.
Eric Hoffer: The Passionate State of Mind

4 You will, Oscar, you will.
James Whistler: Replying to Oscar Wilde's exclamation 'I wish I had said that!' Attrib.

IMMORTALITY

See also eternity, mortality, posterity

1 I don't want to achieve immortality through my work...I want to achieve it through not dying.
Woody Allen: Woody Allen and His Comedy (E. Lax)

2 He had decided to live for ever or die in the attempt.
Joseph Heller: Catch-22, Ch. 3

3 We feel and know that we are eternal.
Benedict Spinoza: Ethics

IMPERFECTION

See also mistakes

1 To err is human.
Proverb

2 When you have faults, do not fear to abandon them.
Confucius: Analects

3 Even imperfection itself may have its ideal or perfect state.
Thomas De Quincey: Murder Considered as one of the Fine Arts

4 I'm aggrieved when sometimes even excellent Homer nods.

Horace: Ars Poetica

5 If we had no faults of our own, we would not take so much pleasure in noticing those of others.
Duc de la Rochefoucauld: Maximes, 31

IMPERTINENCE

1 He has to learn that petulance is not sarcasm, and that insolence is not invective.
Benjamin Disraeli: Said of Sir C. Wood. Speech, House of Commons, 16 Dec 1852

2 The right people are rude. They can afford to be.
W. Somerset Maugham: Our Betters, II

3 JUDGE WILLIS. You are extremely offensive, young man.
F. E. SMITH. As a matter of fact, we both are, and the only difference between us is that I am trying to be, and you can't help it.
F. E. Smith: Frederick Elwin, Earl of Birkenhead (Lord Birkenhead), Vol. I, Ch. 9

IMPETUOSITY

See also haste, spontaneity

1 There are some who speak one moment before they think.
Jean de La Bruyère: Les Caractères

2 Celerity is never more admir'd Than by the negligent.
William Shakespeare: Antony and Cleopatra, III:7

3 When a prisoner sees the door of his dungeon open he dashes for it without stopping to think where he shall get his dinner.

George Bernard Shaw: Back to Methuselah, Preface

IMPORTANCE

1 Are not five sparrows sold for two farthings, and not one of them is forgotten before God?
Bible: Luke: 12:6

2 Not to be sneezed at.
George Colman, the Younger: Heir-at-Law, II:1

3 Art and religion first; then philosophy; lastly science. That is the order of the great subjects of life, that's their order of importance.
Muriel Spark: The Prime of Miss Jean Brodie, Ch. 2

4 If this is God's world there are no unimportant people.
George Thomas: Remark, in a TV interview

IMPRESSIONABILITY

See also gullibility

1 She had
A heart – how shall I say? – too soon made glad,
Too easily impressed.
Robert Browning: My Last Duchess

2 Like a cushion, he always bore the impress of the last man who sat on him.
David Lloyd George: Referring to Lord Derby. Attrib. In The Listener, 7 Sep 1978. This remark is also credited to Earl Haig

3 They'll take suggestion as a cat laps milk.
William Shakespeare: The Tempest, II:1

4 Give me a girl at an impressionable age, and she is mine for life.
Muriel Spark: The Prime of Miss Jean Brodie, Ch. 1

IMPRISONMENT

See also oppression, punishment, slavery

1 A robin redbreast in a cage
Puts all Heaven in a rage.
William Blake: Auguries of Innocence

2 O! dreadful is the check – intense the agony
When the ear begins to hear, and the eye begins to see;
When the pulse begins to throb – the brain to think again –
The soul to feel the flesh, and the flesh to feel the chain.
Emily Brontë: The Prisoner

3 Oh they're taking him to prison for the colour of his hair.
A. E. Housman: Collected Poems, Additional Poems

4 Stone walls do not a prison make,
Nor iron bars a cage.
Richard Lovelace: To Althea, from Prison

5 We think caged birds sing, when indeed they cry.
John Webster: The White Devil, V:4

6 I never saw a man who looked
With such a wistful eye
Upon that little tent of blue
Which prisoners call the sky.
Oscar Wilde: The Ballad of Reading Gaol, I:3

7 If this is the way Queen Victoria

INCOMPETENCE

deserve to have any.
*Oscar Wilde: Complaining at
having to wait in the rain for
transport to take him to prison.
Attrib.*

INCOMPETENCE

1 This island is almost made of
coal and surrounded by fish.
Only an organizing genius could
produce a shortage of coal and
fish in Great Britain at the same
time.
*Aneurin Bevan: Speech,
Blackpool, 18 May 1945*

2 Work is accomplished by those
employees who have not yet
reached their level of incompetence.
*Laurence J. Peter: The Peter
Principle*

INDECISION

See also uncertainty

1 I will have nothing to do with a
man who can blow hot and cold
with the same breath.
*Aesop: Fables, 'The Man and the
Satyr'*

2 Nothing is so exhausting as
indecision, and nothing is so
futile.
Bertrand Russell: Attrib.

3 I must have a prodigious quantity of mind; it takes me as much
as a week, sometimes, to make it
up.
*Mark Twain: The Innocents
Abroad, Ch. 7*

1 But what is past my help is past
my care.
*Francis Beaumont: With John
Fletcher. The Double Marriage,
I:1*

2 Sir, I view the proposal to hold
an international exhibition at
San Francisco with an equanim-
ity bordering on indifference.
*W. S. Gilbert: Gilbert, His Life
and Strife (Hesketh Pearson)*

3 At length the morn and cold
indifference came.
*Nicholas Rowe: The Fair Penitent,
I:1*

4 I hear it was charged against me
that I sought to destroy institutions,
But really I am neither for nor
against institutions.
*Walt Whitman: I Hear It was
Charged against Me*

INDIVIDUALITY

1 Nature made him, and then
broke the mould.
*Ludovico Ariosto: Referring to
Charlemagne's paladin, Roland.
Orlando furioso*

2 It is the common wonder of all
men, how among so many million of faces, there should be
none alike.
*Thomas Browne: Religio Medici,
Pt. II*

3 Without deviation from the
norm 'progress' is not possible.
*Frank Zappa: The Real Frank
Zappa Book*

INFERIORITY

See also mediocrity

1 Wherever an inferiority complex exists, there is a good reason for it.
Carl Gustav Jung: Interview, 1943

2 It is an infallible sign of the second-rate in nature and intellect to make use of everything and everyone.
Ada Beddington Leverson: The Limit

3 There's no such thing as a bad Picasso, but some are less good than others.
Pablo Picasso: Come to Judgment (A. Whitman)

4 No one can make you feel inferior without your consent.
Eleanor Roosevelt: This is My Story

INFLUENCE

See also power

1 How to Win Friends and Influence People.
Dale Carnegie: Book title

2 The proper time to influence the character of a child is about a hundred years before he is born.
Dean Inge: The Observer, 21 June, 1929

3 We have met too late. You are too old for me to have any effect on you.
James Joyce: On meeting the Irish poet, W. B. Yeats. James Joyce (R. Ellmann)

4 Athens holds sway over all Greece; I dominate Athens; my wife dominates me; our new-born son dominates her.
Themistocles: Explaining an earlier remark to the effect that his young son ruled all Greece. Attrib.

5 The man who can dominate a London dinner-table can dominate the world.
Oscar Wilde: Attrib. by R. Aldington in his edition of Wilde

INJUSTICE

1 Give a dog a bad name and hang him.
Proverb

2 If I had been born a man, I would have conquered Europe.
Marie Konstantinovna Bashkirtseff: The Journal of a Young Artist, 25 June 1884

3 Those who have had no share in the good fortunes of the mighty often have a share in their misfortunes.
Bertolt Brecht: The Caucasian Chalk Circle

4 When one has been threatened with a great injustice, one accepts a smaller as a favour.
Jane Welsh Carlyle: Journal, 21 Nov 1855

5 Justice is the means by which established injustices are sanctioned.
Anatole France: Crainquebille

6 Undeservedly you will atone for the sins of your fathers.
Horace: Odes, III

7 I am a man
More sinn'd against than sinning.
William Shakespeare: King Lear, III:2

INNOCENCE

See also conscience, ignorance

1 No, it is not only our fate but our business to lose innocence, and once we have lost that, it is futile to attempt a picnic in Eden.
Elizabeth Bowen: In Orion III, 'Out of a Book'

2 Ralph wept for the end of innocence, the darkness of man's heart, and the fall through the air of the true, wise friend called Piggy.
William Golding: Lord of the Flies, Ch. 12

INSINCERITY

See also hypocrisy

1 Experience teaches you that the man who looks you straight in the eye, particularly if he adds a firm handshake, is hiding something.
Clifton Fadiman: Enter, Conversing

2 He who praises everybody praises nobody.
Samuel Johnson: Life of Johnson (J. Boswell), Vol. III

3 Most friendship is feigning, most loving mere folly.
William Shakespeare: As You Like It, II:7

INSPIRATION

1 That I make poetry and give pleasure (if I give pleasure) are because of you.
Horace: Odes, IV

2 Biting my truant pen, beating myself for spite:
'Fool!' said my Muse to me, 'look in thy heart and write.'
Philip Sidney: Sonnet, Astrophel and Stella

INSULTS

See also criticism

1 Sticks and stones may break my bones, but words will never hurt me.
Proverb

2 Lloyd George could not see a belt without hitting below it.
Margot Asquith: Referring to the Liberal statesman. The Autobiography of Margot Asquith

3 If there is anyone here whom I have not insulted, I beg his pardon.
Johannes Brahms: Said on leaving a gathering of friends. Brahms (P. Latham)

4 An injury is much sooner forgotten than an insult.
Earl of Chesterfield: Letter to his son, 9 Oct 1746

5 Calumnies are answered best with silence.
Ben Jonson: Volpone, II:2

INTEGRITY

See also honesty, morality, righteousness

1 Be so true to thyself, as thou be not false to others.
Francis Bacon: Essays, 'Of Wisdom for a Man's Self'

2 Integrity without knowledge is weak and useless, and knowl-

edge without integrity is dangerous and dreadful.
Samuel Johnson: Rasselas, Ch. 41

3 My strength is as the strength of ten,
Because my heart is pure.
Alfred, Lord Tennyson: Sir Galahad

INTELLECT

See also mind, thinking

1 Hercule Poirot tapped his forehead. 'These little grey cells, It is "up to them" – as you say over here.'
Agatha Christie: The Mysterious Affair at Styles

2 We should take care not to make the intellect our god; it has, of course, powerful muscles, but no personality.
Albert Einstein: Out of My Later Life, 51

3 The voice of the intellect is a soft one, but it does not rest till it has gained a hearing.
Sigmund Freud: The Future of an Illusion

4 Man is an intellectual animal, and therefore an everlasting contradiction to himself. His senses centre in himself, his ideas reach to the ends of the universe; so that he is torn in pieces between the two, without a possibility of its ever being otherwise.
William Hazlitt: Characteristics

5 We are thinking beings, and we cannot exclude the intellect from participating in any of our functions.

William James: Varieties of Religious Experience

6 Intellect is invisible to the man who has none.
Arthur Schopenhauer: Aphorismen zur Lebensweisheit

INTELLIGENCE

See also knowledge, understanding

1 He has a brilliant mind until he makes it up.
Margot Asquith: Referring to the Labour statesman, Sir Stafford Cripps. The Wit of the Asquiths

2 NORA. But if God had wanted us to think with our womb, why did He give us a brain?
Clare Boothe Luce: Slam the Door Softly

3 No one ever went broke underestimating the intelligence of the American people.
H. L. Mencken: Attrib.

4 A really intelligent man feels what other men only know.
Baron de Montesquieu: Essai sur les causes qui peuvent affecter les esprits et les caractères

5 The height of cleverness is to be able to conceal it.
Duc de la Rochefoucauld: Maximes, 245

6 Intelligence is quickness to apprehend as distinct from ability, which is capacity to act wisely on the thing apprehended.
A. N. Whitehead: Dialogues, 135

7 All the unhappy marriages come from the husbands having brains. What good are brains to a man? They only unsettle him.

P. G. Wodehouse: The Adventures of Sally

Noël Coward: Future Indefinite

INTRIGUE

1 Ay, now the plot thickens very much upon us.
Duke of Buckingham: The Rehearsal, III:1

2 Everybody was up to something, especially, of course, those who were up to nothing.

IRREVOCABILITY

1 The die is cast.
Julius Caesar: Said on crossing the Rubicon (49 BC) at the beginning of his campaign against Pompey. Attrib.

2 The Gods themselves cannot recall their gifts.
Alfred, Lord Tennyson: Tithonus

J

JEALOUSY

See also envy

1 For the ear of jealousy heareth all things; and the noise of murmurings is not hid.
Bible: Wisdom: 1:10

2 The 'Green-Eyed Monster' causes much woe, but the absence of this ugly serpent argues the presence of a corpse whose name is Eros.
Minna Antrim: Naked Truth and Veiled Allusions

3 Jealousy is no more than feeling alone among smiling enemies.
Elizabeth Bowen: The House in Paris

4 Though jealousy be produced by love, as ashes are by fire, yet jealousy extinguishes love as ashes smother the flame.
Margaret of Navarre: 'Novel XLVIII, the Fifth Day'

5 O, beware, my lord, of jealousy;
It is the green-ey'd monster which doth mock
The meat it feeds on.
William Shakespeare: Othello, III:3

JOURNALISM

See also media, newspapers

1 Have you noticed that life, real honest to goodness life, with murders and catastrophes and fabulous inheritances, happens almost exclusively in newspapers?
Jean Anouilh: The Rehearsal

2 'Christianity, of course but why journalism?'
Arthur Balfour: In reply to Frank Harris's remark, '...all the faults of the age come from Christianity and journalism'. Autobiography (Margot Asquith), Ch. 10

3 Who's in charge of the clattering train?
Lord Beaverbrook: Attrib.

4 Journalists say a thing that they know isn't true, in the hope that if they keep on saying it long enough it will be true.
Arnold Bennett: The Title, II

5 No news is good news; no journalists is even better.
Nicolas Bentley: Attrib.

6 There is a bias in television journalism. It is not against any particular party or point of view – it is a bias against *understanding*.
John Birt: This launched a series of articles written jointly with Peter Jay. The Times, 28 Feb 1975

7 Journalism largely consists of saying 'Lord Jones is dead' to people who never knew Lord Jones was alive.
G. K. Chesterton: Attrib.

8 I hesitate to say what the functions of the modern journalist may be; but I imagine that they do not exclude the intelligent anticipation of facts even before they occur.
Lord Curzon: Speech, House of Commons, 29 Mar 1898

9 Backward ran sentences until reeled the mind.

JUDGMENT

Wolcott Gibbs: Parodying the style of Time magazine. More in Sorrow

10 Good taste is, of course, an utterly dispensable part of any journalist's equipment.
Michael Hogg: The Daily Telegraph, 2 Dec 1978

11 A good newspaper, I suppose, is a nation talking to itself.
Arthur Miller: The Observer, 'Sayings of the Week', 26 Nov 1961

12 SIXTY HORSES WEDGED IN A CHIMNEY
The story to fit this sensational headline has not turned up yet.
J. B. Morton: The Best of Beachcomber, 'Mr Justice Cocklecarrot: Home Life'

13 Journalism – an ability to meet the challenge of filling the space.
Rebecca West: The New York Herald Tribune, 22 April 1956

14 There is much to be said in favour of modern journalism. By giving us the opinions of the uneducated, it keeps us in touch with the ignorance of the community.
Oscar Wilde: The Critic as Artist, Pt. 2

15 Rock journalism is people who can't write interviewing people who can't talk for people who can't read.
Frank Zappa: Attrib.

JUDGMENT

1 Judge not, that ye be not judged.
Bible: Matthew: 7:1

2 And why beholdest thou the mote that is in thy brother's eye, but considerest not the beam that is in thine own eye?
Bible: Matthew: 7:3

3 No man can justly censure or condemn another, because indeed no man truly knows another.
Thomas Browne: Religio Medici, Pt. II

4 You shall judge of a man by his foes as well as by his friends.
Joseph Conrad: Lord Jim, Ch. 34

5 Force, if unassisted by judgement, collapses through its own mass.
Horace: Odes, III

6 Everyone complains of his memory, but no one complains of his judgement.
Duc de la Rochefoucauld: Maximes, 89

JUSTICE

See also law, lawyers

1 When I came back to Dublin, I was court-martialled in my absence and sentenced to death in my absence, so I said they could shoot me in my absence.
Brendan Behan: The Hostage, I

2 It is better that ten guilty persons escape than that one innocent suffer.
William Blackstone: Commentaries on the Laws of England, Bk. IV, Ch. 27

3 Ah, colonel, all's fair in love and war, you know.
Nathan Bedford Forrest: Remark to a captured enemy officer who had been tricked into surrendering. A Civil War Treasury (B. Botkin)

4 Justice should not only be done, but should manifestly and undoubtedly be seen to be done.
Gordon Hewart: The Chief (R. Jackson)

5 I have come to regard the law courts not as a cathedral but rather as a casino.
Richard Ingrams: The Guardian, 30 July 1977

6 I am a warrior in the time of women warriors; the longing for justice is the sword I carry, the love of womankind my shield.
Sonia Johnson: From Housewife to Heretic

7 Justice is the constant and perpetual wish to render to every one his due.
Justinian I: Institutes, I

8 Justice is such a fine thing that we cannot pay too dearly for it.
Alain-René Lesage: Crispin rival de son maître, IX

9 The love of justice in most men is simply the fear of suffering injustice.
Duc de la Rochefoucauld: Maximes, 78

10 Haste still pays haste, and leisure answers leisure;
Like doth quit like, and Measure still for Measure.
William Shakespeare: Measure for Measure, V:1

11 This is a British murder inquiry and some degree of justice must be seen to be more or less done.
Tom Stoppard: Jumpers, II

12 The end may justify the means as long as there is something that justifies the end.
Leon Trotsky: Antonio Gramsci: an introduction to his thought (A. Pozzolini), Preface

KILLING

See also assassination, death, murder, suicide

1 Difficult as it may be to cure, it is always easy to poison and to kill.
Elisha Bartlett: Philosophy of Medical Science, Pt. II, Ch. 16

2 Euthanasia is a long, smooth-sounding word, and it conceals its danger as long, smooth words do, but the danger is there, nevertheless.
Pearl Buck: The Child Who Never Grew, Ch. 2

3 Thou shalt not kill; but needst not strive
Officiously to keep alive.
Arthur Hugh Clough: The Latest Decalogue, 11

4 Ask any soldier. To kill a man is to merit a woman.
Jean Giraudoux: Tiger at the Gates, I

5 To save a man's life against his will is the same as killing him.
Horace: Ars Poetica

6 To kill a human being is, after all, the least injury you can do him.
Henry James: My Friend Bingham

7 There's no difference between one's killing and making decisions that will send others to kill. It's exactly the same thing, or even worse.
Golda Meir: L'Europeo (Oriana Fallaci)

8 Kill a man, and you are a murderer. Kill millions of men, and you are a conqueror. Kill everyone, and you are a god.
Jean Rostand: Pensées d'un biologiste

KINDNESS

See also charity, generosity

1 One kind word can warm three winter months.
Japanese proverb

2 A word of kindness is better than a fat pie.
Russian proverb

3 Recompense injury with justice, and recompense kindness with kindness.
Confucius: Analects

4 True kindness presupposes the faculty of imagining as one's own the suffering and joy of others.
André Gide

5 People pay the doctor for his trouble; for his kindness they still remain in his debt.
Seneca

6 Yet do I fear thy nature;
It is too full o' th' milk of human kindness
To catch the nearest way.
William Shakespeare: Macbeth, I:5

7 This is a way to kill a wife with kindness.
William Shakespeare: The Taming of the Shrew, IV:1

KNOWLEDGE

See also learning, self-knowledge, wisdom

1 Learning is a treasure which accompanies its owner everywhere.
Chinese proverb

2 Knowledge is the mother of all virtue; all vice proceeds from ignorance.
Proverb

3 *Nam et ipsa scientia potestas est.*
Knowledge itself is power.
Francis Bacon: Religious Meditations, 'Of Heresies'

4 For in much wisdom is much grief: and he that increaseth knowledge increaseth sorrow.
Bible: Ecclesiastes 1:18

5 But of the tree of the knowledge of good and evil, thou shalt not eat of it: for in the day that thou eatest thereof thou shalt surely die.
Bible: Genesis: 2:15

6 A smattering of everything, and a knowledge of nothing.
Charles Dickens: Sketches by Boz, 'Tales', Ch. 3

7 For lust of knowing what should not be known,
We take the Golden Road to Samarkand.
James Elroy Flecker: Hassan, V:2

8 The clever men at Oxford
Know all that there is to be knowed.
But they none of them know one half as much
As intelligent Mr Toad.
Kenneth Grahame: The Wind in the Willows, Ch. 10

9 It is the province of knowledge to speak and it is the privilege of wisdom to listen.
Oliver Wendell Holmes: The Poet at the Breakfast Table, Ch. 10

10 If a little knowledge is dangerous, where is the man who has so much as to be out of danger?
T. H. Huxley: On Elementary Instruction in Physiology

11 There was never an age in which useless knowledge was more important than in our own.
Cyril Joad: The Observer, 'Sayings of the Week', 30 Sept 1951

12 All knowledge is of itself of some value. There is nothing so minute or inconsiderable, that I would not rather know it than not.
Samuel Johnson: Life of Johnson (J. Boswell)

13 The greater our knowledge increases the more our ignorance unfolds.
John Fitzgerald Kennedy: Speech, Rice University, 12 Sept 1962

14 A study of history shows that civilizations that abandon the quest for knowledge are doomed to disintegration.
Bernard Lovell: The Observer, 'Sayings of the Week', 14 May 1972

15 A little learning is a dangerous thing;
Drink deep, or taste not the Pierian spring:
There shallow draughts intoxicate the brain,
And drinking largely sobers us again.

Alexander Pope: An Essay on Criticism

16 Our knowledge can only be finite, while our ignorance must necessarily be infinite.
Karl Popper: Conjectures and Refutations

17 Beware you be not swallowed up in books! An ounce of love is worth a pound of knowledge.
John Wesley: Life of Wesley (R. Southey), Ch. 16

LANGUAGE

See also communication, grammar, malapropisms

1 The Greeks Had a Word for It.
Zoë Akins: Play title

2 Therefore is the name of it called Babel; because the Lord did there confound the language of all the earth: and from thence did the Lord scatter them abroad upon the face of all the earth.
Bible: Genesis: 11:9

3 A silly remark can be made in Latin as well as in Spanish.
Miguel de Cervantes: The Dialogue of the Dogs

4 I speak Spanish to God, Italian to women, French to men, and German to my horse.
Charles V: Attrib.

5 All slang is metaphor, and all metaphor is poetry.
G. K. Chesterton: The Defendant

6 Bring on the empty horses!
Michael Curtiz: Said during the filming of The Charge of the Light Brigade. Curtiz, who was not noted for his command of the English language, meant 'riderless horses'. When people laughed at his order he became very angry, shouting, 'You think I know fuck-nothing, when I know fuck-all!'

7 The liberation of language is rooted in the liberation of ourselves.
Mary Daly: The Church and the Second Sex

8 Imagine the Lord talking French! Aside from a few odd words in Hebrew, I took it completely for granted that God had never spoken anything but the most dignified English.
Clarence Shepard Day: Life With Father, 'Father interferes'

9 I am always sorry when any language is lost, because languages are the pedigree of nations.
Samuel Johnson: Tour to the Hebrides (J. Boswell)

10 I include 'pidgin-English'... even though I am referred to in that splendid language as 'Fella belong Mrs Queen'.
Prince Philip: Speech, English-Speaking Union Conference, Ottawa, 29 Oct 1958

11 Life is too short to learn German.
Richard Porson: Gryll Grange (T. L. Peacock), Ch. 3

12 Sign language is the equal of speech, lending itself equally to the rigorous and the poetic, to philosophical analysis or to making love.
Oliver Sacks: The Times, 16 June 1994

13 England and America are two countries separated by the same language.
George Bernard Shaw: Attrib.

14 Language and knowledge are indissolubly connected; they are interdependent.
Annie Sullivan: Speech, American Association to Promote the Teaching of Speech to the Deaf, July 1894

15 We dissect nature along lines laid down by our native language… Language is not simply a reporting device for experience but a defining framework for it.
Benjamin Lee Whorf: New Directions in the Study of Language (ed. Hoyer), 'Thinking in Primitive Communities'

LAST WORDS

Not always the actual last words said, but including remarks made when dying. Many are apocryphal, hence the fact that some people have more than one set of attributed 'last words'.

1 Ave Caesar, morituri te salutant.
Hail Caesar; those who are about to die salute you.
Anonymous: Greeting to the Roman Emperor by gladiators

2 Thank you, sister. May you be the mother of a bishop!
Brendan Behan: Said to a nun nursing him on his deathbed. Attrib.

3 And when Jesus had cried with a loud voice, he said, Father, into thy hands I commend my spirit: and having said thus, he gave up the ghost.
Bible: Luke: 23:46

4 Et tu, Brute?
You too, Brutus?
Julius Caesar

5 All right, then, I'll say it: Dante makes me sick.
Lope Félix de Vega Carpio: On being informed he was about to die. Attrib.

6 Let not poor Nelly starve.
Charles II: Referring to his mistress Nell Gwynne. Said on his death bed

7 I'm so bored with it all.
Winston Churchill: Said to be his last words. Clementine (M. Soames)

8 Goodnight, my darlings. I'll see you tomorrow.
Noël Coward: The Life of Noël Coward (C. Lesley)

9 No, it is better not. She will only ask me to take a message to Albert.
Benjamin Disraeli: On his deathbed, declining an offer of a visit from Queen Victoria.

10 Goodbye, my friends, I go on to glory.
Isadora Duncan: She was strangled when her long scarf became entangled in the wheel of a sports car. Attrib.

11 All my possessions for a moment of time.
Elizabeth I

12 I have spent a lot of time searching through the Bible for loopholes.
W. C. Fields: Said during his last illness. Attrib.

13 I feel nothing, apart from a certain difficulty in continuing to exist.
Bernard de Fontenelle: Remark on his deathbed. Famous Last Words (B. Conrad)

14 I don't mind if my life goes in the service of the nation. If I die today every drop of my blood will invigorate the nation.

Indira Gandhi: Said the night before she was assassinated by Sikh militants, 30 Oct 1984. The Sunday Times, 3 Dec 1989

15 Bugger Bognor.

George V: His alleged last words, when his doctor promised him he would soon be well enough to visit Bognor Regis.

16 Mehr Licht!
More light!

Goethe: Attrib. last words. In fact he asked for the second shutter to be opened, to allow more light in.

17 It is. But not as hard as farce.

Edmund Gwenn: On his deathbed, in reply to the comment 'It must be very hard'. Time, 30 Jan 1984

18 Well, I've had a happy life.
William Hazlitt

19 Only one man ever understood me…And he didn't understand me.

Hegel: Said on his deathbed. Famous Last Words (B. Conrad)

20 I am about to take my last voyage, a great leap in the dark.
Thomas Hobbes

21 If heaven had granted me five more years, I could have become a real painter.

Hokusai: Said on his deathbed. Famous Last Words (B. Conrad)

22 On the contrary!

Henrik Ibsen: His nurse had just remarked that he was feeling a little better. True Remarkable Occurrences (J. Train)

23 It's all been rather lovely.
John Le Mesurier: The Times, 15 Nov 1983

24 Why are you weeping? Did you imagine that I was immortal?

Louis XIV: Noticing as he lay on his deathbed that his attendants were crying. Louis XIV (V. Cronin).

25 Tête d'Armée.
Chief of the Army.
Napoleon I: Last words. Attrib.

26 I do not have to forgive my enemies, I have had them all shot.

Ramón María Narváez: Said on his deathbed, when asked by a priest if he forgave his enemies. Famous Last Words (B. Conrad)

27 Kiss me, Hardy.

Lord Nelson: Spoken to Sir Thomas Hardy, captain of the Victory, during the Battle of Trafalgar, 1805.

28 Too kind, too kind.

Florence Nightingale: When given the Order of Merit on her deathbed. Life of Florence Nightingale, Vol. II, Pt. 7, Ch. 9 (E. Cook)

29 I am just going outside and may be some time.

Captain Lawrence Oates: Before leaving the tent and vanishing into the blizzard on the ill-fated Antarctic expedition (1910–12). Oates was afraid that his lameness would slow down the others. Journal (R. F. Scott), 17 Mar 1912

30 Die, my dear Doctor, that's the last thing I shall do!
Lord Palmerston

31 I have not told half of what I saw.

Marco Polo: The Story of Civilization (W. Durant), Vol. I

32 I owe much; I have nothing; the rest I leave to the poor.
François Rabelais

33 My dear hands. Farewell, my poor hands.
Sergei Rachmaninov: On being informed that he was dying from cancer. The Great Pianists (H. Schonberg)

34 I have a long journey to take, and must bid the company farewell.
Walter Raleigh: Sir Walter Raleigh (Edward Thompson), Ch. 26

35 So little done, so much to do.
Cecil Rhodes

36 Dear World, I am leaving you because I am bored. I am leaving you with your worries. Good luck.
George Sanders: Suicide note

37 Nonsense, they couldn't hit an elephant at this distance
John Sedgwick: In response to a suggestion that he should not show himself over the parapet during the Battle of the Wilderness. Attrib.

38 Crito, we owe a cock to Aesculapius; please pay it and don't let it pass.
Socrates: Before his execution by drinking hemlock. Phaedo (Plato), 118

39 What *is* the answer?…In that case, what is the question?
Gertrude Stein:

40 If this is dying, I don't think much of it.
Lytton Strachey: Lytton Strachey (Michael Holroyd), Pt. V, Ch. 17

41 Ah, a German and a genius! a prodigy, admit him!
Jonathan Swift: Learning of the arrival of the composer Handel (1685–1759).

42 I did not know that we had ever quarrelled.
Henry David Thoreau: On being urged to make his peace with God. Attrib.

43 God bless … God damn.
James Thurber

44 I have had no real gratification or enjoyment of any sort more than my neighbor on the next block who is worth only half a million.
William Henry Vanderbilt: Famous Last Words (B. Conrad)

45 Dear me, I believe I am becoming a god. An emperor ought at least to die on his feet.
Vespasian: Lives of the Caesars (Suetonius)

46 Either that wallpaper goes, or I do.
Oscar Wilde: As he lay dying in a drab Paris bedroom. Time, 16 Jan 1984

LAUGHTER

See also happiness, humour

1 Laughter is the best medicine.
Proverb

2 I make myself laugh at everything, so that I do not weep.
Beaumarchais: Le Barbier de Séville, I:2

3 One must laugh before one is happy, or one may die without ever laughing at all.
Jean de La Bruyère: Les Caractères

4 Laugh, and the world laughs with you;
Weep, and you weep alone,
For the sad old earth must borrow its mirth,
But has trouble enough of its own.

Ella Wheeler Wilcox: Solitude

LAW

See also crime, justice

1 Every one is innocent until he is
proved guilty.
Proverb

2 Possession is nine points of the
law.
Proverb

3 The good of the people is the
chief law.
Cicero: De Legibus, III

4 'If the law supposes that,' said
Mr Bumble..., 'the law is a ass
– a idiot.'
*Charles Dickens: Oliver Twist,
Ch. 51*

5 Although we have some laws
which are unfair to women,
some women can live their
whole lives and not know the law
as it affects them.
*Taujan Faisal: The Times, 15 June
1994*

6 Public opinion is always in advance of the law.
John Galsworthy: Windows

7 The Law is the true embodi-
ment
Of everything that's excellent.
It has no kind of fault or flaw,
And I, my lords, embody the
Law.
W. S. Gilbert: Iolanthe, I

8 Laws grind the poor, and rich
men rule the law.
Oliver Goldsmith: The Traveller

9 The Common Law of England
has been laboriously built about
a mythical figure – the figure of
'The Reasonable Man'.
A. P. Herbert: Uncommon Law

10 In university they don't tell you
that the greater part of the law is
learning to tolerate fools.
*Doris Lessing: Martha Quest,
Pt. III, Ch. 2*

11 Laws were made to be broken.
*Christopher North: Noctes
Ambrosianae, 24 May 1830*

12 Ignorance of the law excuses
no man; not that all men know
the law, but because 'tis an excuse every man will plead, and
no man can tell how to confute
him.
John Selden: Table Talk

13 Laws are like spider's webs: if
some poor weak creature come
up against them, it is caught; but
a bigger one can break through
and get away.
*Solon: Lives of the Eminent
Philosophers (Diogenes Laertius),
I*

14 It is only those with the deepest
pockets who can risk going to
law.
*Lord Woolf: The Times, 23 June
1994*

LAWYERS

1 He that is his own lawyer has a
fool for a client.
Proverb

2 Lawyers are the only persons in
whom ignorance of the law is
not punished.
Jeremy Bentham: Attrib.

3 A lawyer with his briefcase can
steal more than a thousand men
with guns.
Mario Puzo: The Godfather

LAZINESS

See also idleness

1 We grow old more through indolence, than through age.
Christina of Sweden: Maxims (1660–1680)

2 Happy is the man with a wife to tell him what to do and a secretary to do it.
Lord Mancroft: The Observer, 'Sayings of the Week', 18 Dec 1966

3 Henry has always led what could be called a sedentary life, if only he'd ever got as far as actually sitting up.
Henry Reed: Not a Drum was Heard: The War Memoirs of General Gland

4 It is better to have loafed and lost than never to have loafed at all.
James Thurber: Fables for Our Time, 'The Courtship of Arthur and Al'

LEADERSHIP

1 And he shall rule them with a rod of iron; as the vessels of a potter shall they be broken to shivers: even as I received of my Father.
Bible: Revelations: 2:27

2 I believe in benevolent dictatorship provided I am the dictator.
Richard Branson: Remark, Nov 1984

3 Captains of industry.
Thomas Carlyle: Past and Present, Bk. IV, Ch. 4

4 Let me pass, I have to follow them, I am their leader.

Alexandre Auguste Ledru-Rollin: Trying to force his way through a mob during the Revolution of 1848, of which he was one of the chief instigators. A similar remark is attributed to the British Conservative Statesman, Bonar Law. The Fine Art of Political Wit (L. Harris)

LEARNING

See also education, knowledge

1 What we have to learn to do, we learn by doing.
Aristotle: Nicomachean Ethics, Bk. II

2 Read, mark, learn and inwardly digest.
The Book of Common Prayer: Collect, 2nd Sunday in Advent

3 An art can only be learned in the workshop of those who are winning their bread by it.
Samuel Butler: Erewhon, Ch. 20

4 I am always ready to learn although I do not always like being taught.
Winston Churchill: The Observer, 9 Nov 1952

5 It is the true nature of mankind to learn from mistakes, not from example.
Fred Hoyle: Into Deepest Space

6 That is what learning is. You suddenly understand something you've understood all your life, but in a new way.
Doris Lessing: The Four-Gated City

7 Some for renown, on scraps of learning dote,
And think they grow immortal as they quote.

Edward Young: Love of Fame, I

LEXICOGRAPHY

1 Like Webster's Dictionary
We're Morocco bound.
Johnny Burke: Song, 'Road to Morocco' from the film The Road to Morocco

2 The responsibility of a dictionary is to record a language, not set its style.
Philip Babcock Gove: Letter to Life Magazine, 17 Nov 1961

3 Lexicographer. A writer of dictionaries, a harmless drudge.
Samuel Johnson: Dictionary of the English Language

LIBERALISM

1 You Liberals think that goats are just sheep from broken homes.
Malcolm Bradbury: After Dinner Game (with Christopher Bigsby)

2 When a liberal is abused, he says: Thank God they didn't beat me. When he is beaten, he thanks God they didn't kill him. When he is killed, he will thank God that his immortal soul has been delivered from its mortal clay.
Lenin: Lenin heard this characterization at a meeting, and repeated it with approval. The Government's Falsification of the Duma and the Tasks of the Social-Democrats, 'Proletary', Dec 1906.

LIFE

See also afterlife, death, human condition, mortality

1 Life begins at forty.
Proverb

2 Life is just a bowl of cherries.
Proverb

3 Life is sweet.
Proverb

4 Life, the Universe and Everything.
Douglas Adams: Book title

5 Before this strange disease of modern life,
With its sick hurry, its divided aims.
Matthew Arnold: The Scholar Gipsy

6 Remember that no man loses any other life than this which he now lives, nor lives any other than this which he now loses.
Marcus Aurelius: Meditations, Bk. II, Ch. 14

7 You don't get to choose how you're going to die. Or when. You can only decide how you're going to live. Now.
Joan Baez: Daybreak

8 Life is rather like a tin of sardines – we're all of us looking for the key.
Alan Bennett: Beyond the Fringe

9 One should not exaggerate the importance of trifles. Life, for instance, is much too short to be taken seriously.
Nicolas Bentley: Attrib.

10 For everything that lives is holy, life delights in life.
William Blake: America

11 Life is one long process of getting tired.
Samuel Butler: Notebooks

12 Life is the art of drawing suffi-

cient conclusions from insufficient premises.
Samuel Butler: Notebooks

13 Life is a dusty corridor, I say, Shut at both ends.
Roy Campbell: The Flaming Terrapin

14 It's as large as life, and twice as natural!
Lewis Carroll: Through the Looking-Glass, Ch. 7

15 Life is an incurable disease.
Abraham Cowley: To Dr Scarborough

16 Life was a funny thing that happened to me on the way to the grave.
Quentin Crisp: The Naked Civil Servant, Ch. 18

17 People do not live nowadays – they get about ten percent out of life.
Isadora Duncan: This Quarter Autumn, 'Memoirs'

18 Life is a sexually transmitted disease.
Graffiti

19 I'm more and more convinced that life is a dream. What has happened to me is surely a dream.
Anthony Hopkins: The Independent, 12 Feb 1994

20 Life is just one damned thing after another.
Elbert Hubbard: A Thousand and One Epigrams

21 Life isn't all beer and skittles.
Thomas Hughes: Tom Brown's Schooldays, Pt. I, Ch. 2

22 The art of life is the art of avoiding pain.
Thomas Jefferson: Letter to Maria Cosway, 12 Oct 1786

23 Life is something to do when you can't get to sleep.
Fran Lebowitz: The Observer, 21 Jan 1979

24 Life is like a sewer. What you get out of it depends on what you put into it.
Tom Lehrer: We Will all Go together When We Go

25 Life is what happens to you while you're busy making other plans.
John Lennon: Beautiful Boy

26 The living are just the dead on holiday.
Maurice Maeterlinck: Attrib.

27 The aim of life is to live, and to live means to be aware, joyously, drunkenly, serenely, divinely aware.
Henry Miller: The Wisdom of the Heart, 'Creative Death'

28 Life is a foreign language: all men mispronounce it.
Christopher Morley: Thunder on the Left, Ch. 14

29 Life itself is a mystery which defies solution.
John Mortimer: The Sunday Times, 1 Apr 1990

30 Life is for each man a solitary cell whose walls are mirrors.
Eugene O'Neill: Lazarus Laughed

31 There is no cure for birth and death save to enjoy the interval.
George Santayana: Soliloquies in England, 24, 'War Shrines'

32 It is only in the microscope that our life looks so big. It is an indivisible point, drawn out and

magnified by the powerful lenses of Time and Space.
Arthur Schopenhauer: Parerga and Paralipomena, 'The Vanity of Existence'

33 Life is as tedious as a twice-told tale
Vexing the dull ear of a drowsy man.
William Shakespeare: King John, III:4

34 Life's but a walking shadow, a poor player,
That struts and frets his hour upon the stage,
And then is heard no more; it is a tale
Told by an idiot, full of sound and fury,
Signifying nothing.
William Shakespeare: Macbeth, V:5

35 Living well and beautifully and justly are all one thing.
Socrates: Crito (Plato)

36 Life is a gamble, at terrible odds – if it was a bet, you wouldn't take it.
Tom Stoppard: Rosencrantz and Guildenstern Are Dead, III

37 Oh, isn't life a terrible thing, thank God?
Dylan Thomas: Under Milk Wood

38 We begin to live when we have conceived life as a tragedy.
W. B. Yeats: Autobiography

LIFE AND DEATH

1 The first breath is the beginning of death.
Proverb

2 Dying is as natural as living.
Proverb

3 Every moment dies a man,
Every moment one and one sixteenth is born.
Charles Babbage: A parody of TENNYSON's Vision of Sin. Letter to Tennyson

4 Life, the permission to know death.
Djuna Barnes: Nightwood

5 This world nis but a thurghfare ful of wo,
And we ben pilgrimes, passinge to and fro;
Deeth is an ende of every worldly sore.
Geoffrey Chaucer: The Canterbury Tales, 'The Knight's Tale'

6 Birth, and copulation, and death.
That's all the facts when you come to brass tacks.
T. S. Eliot: Sweeney Agonistes, 'Fragment of an Agon'

7 A man is not completely born until he be dead.
Benjamin Franklin: Letters to Miss Hubbard

8 The most rational cure after all for the inordinate fear of death is to set a just value on life.
William Hazlitt: Table Talk, 'On the Fear of Death'

9 Many men would take the death-sentence without a whimper to escape the life-sentence which fate carries in her other hand.
T. E. Lawrence: The Mint, Pt. I, Ch. 4

10 Every moment dies a man,
Every moment one is born.

Alfred, Lord Tennyson: For a parody, see BABBAGE. The Vision of Sin

11 Because there is no difference.
Thales: His reply when asked why he chose to carry on living after saying there was no difference between life and death. The Story of Civilization (W. Durant), Vol. 2

12 All say, 'How hard it is that we have to die' — a strange complaint to come from the mouths of people who have had to live.
Mark Twain: Pudd'nhead Wilson

13 Science says: 'We must live,' and seeks the means of prolonging, increasing, facilitating and amplifying life, of making it tolerable and acceptable; wisdom says: 'We must die,' and seeks how to make us die well.
Miguel de Unamuno y Jugo: Essays and Soliloquies, 'Arbitrary Reflections'

LITERATURE

See also books, criticism, fiction, novels, plays, poetry, writing

1 The reading of all good books is like a conversation with the finest men of past centuries.
René Descartes: Le Discours de la méthode

2 Only two classes of books are of universal appeal. The very best and the very worst.
Ford Maddox Ford: Joseph Conrad

3 I'm able to bolt down a cheap thriller but I couldn't read Troilus and Cressida or Coriolanus with any great pleasure.
John Gielgud: The Observer, 'Sayings of the Week', 17 Apr 1994

4 He knew everything about literature except how to enjoy it.
Joseph Heller: Catch-22, Ch. 8

5 The proper study of mankind is books.
Aldous Huxley: Chrome Yellow

6 Sturm und Drang.
Storm and stress.
Friedrich Maximilian von Klinger: Used to designate a late 18th-century literary movement in Germany. Play title

7 Our American professors like their literature clear and cold and pure and very dead.
Sinclair Lewis: Speech, on receiving the Nobel Prize, 1930

8 Literature is mostly about having sex and not much about having children; life is the other way round.
David Lodge: The British Museum is Falling Down, Ch. 4

9 Suddenly I realized this literary stuff doesn't just come out of a hat. It has a mechanism which you can take apart like a watch.
David Lodge: The Times Educational Supplement, 18 May 1990

10 Literature and butterflies are the two sweetest passions known to man.
Vladimir Nabokov: Radio Times, Oct 1962

11 Literature is news that STAYS news.
Ezra Pound: ABC of Reading, Ch. 2

12 Great Literature is simply lan-

guage charged with meaning to
the utmost possible degree.
Ezra Pound: How to Read

3 Something that everybody
wants to have read and nobody
wants to read.
*Mark Twain: Definition of a
classic of literature. Speech at
Nineteenth Century Club, New
York, 20 Nov 1900*

4 Literature is the orchestration
of platitudes.
Thornton Wilder: Time magazine

LOGIC

See also philosophy

LOGIC, n. The art of thinking
and reasoning in strict accor-
dance with the limitations and
incapacities of the human understanding.
*Ambrose Bierce: The Devil's
Dictionary*

'Contrariwise,' continued
Tweedledee, 'if it was so, it
might be; and if it were so, it
would be: but as it isn't, it ain't.
That's logic.'
*Lewis Carroll: Through the
Looking-Glass, Ch. 4*

You can only find truth with
logic if you have already found
truth without it.
*G. K. Chesterton: The Man who
was Orthodox*

Logic must take care of itself.
*Ludwig Wittgenstein: Tractatus
Logico-Philosophicus, Ch. 5*

LONELINESS

See also solitude
Oh! why does the wind blow

upon me so wild? – It is because
I'm nobody's child?
*Phila Henrietta Case: Nobody's
Child*

2 Pray that your loneliness may
spur you into finding something
to live for, great enough to die
for.
*Dag Hammarskjöld: Diaries,
1951*

3 So lonely am I
My body is a floating weed
Severed at the roots
Were there water to entice me,
I would follow it, I think.
*Ono no Komachi: Kokinshu,
Anthology of Japanese Literature
(ed. Donald Keene)*

4 All the lonely people, where do
they all belong?
*John Lennon: Eleanor Rigby (with
Paul McCartney)*

5 My heart is a lonely hunter that
hunts on a lonely hill.
*Fiona Macleod: The Lonely
Hunter*

6 Loneliness and the feeling of
being unwanted is the most terrible poverty.
*Mother Teresa: Time, 'Saints
Among Us', 29 Dec 1975*

LONGEVITY

See also age, life, old age

1 Ageing seems to be the only
available way to live a long time.
*Daniel-François-Esprit Auber:
Dictionnaire Encyclopédique
(E. Guérard)*

2 LONGEVITY, n. Uncommon ex-
tension of the fear of death.
*Ambrose Bierce: The Devil's
Dictionary*

3 Despair of all recovery spoils longevity,
And makes men's miseries of alarming brevity.
Lord Byron: Don Juan, II

4 Longevity is the revenge of talent upon genius.
Cyril Connolly: The Sunday Times, 19 June 1966

5 Life protracted is protracted woe.
Samuel Johnson: The Vanity of Human Wishes

6 The brain is the organ of longevity.
George Alban Sacher: Perspectives in Experimental Gerontology

7 Do not try to live forever. You will not succeed.
George Bernard Shaw: The Doctor's Dilemma, 'Preface on Doctors'

8 If you live long enough, the venerability factor creeps in; you get accused of things you never did and praised for virtues you never had.
I. F. Stone: Peter's Quotations (Laurence J. Peter)

9 Keep breathing.
Sophie Tucker: Her reply, at the age of 80, when asked the secret of her longevity. Attrib.

LOSS

See also defeat, mourning

1 'Tis better to have loved and lost than never to have lost at all.
Samuel Butler: The Way of All Flesh, Ch. 77

2 What's lost upon the roundabouts we pulls up on the swings!
Patrick Reginald Chalmers: Green Days and Blue Days: Roundabouts and Swings

3 To lose one parent, Mr Worthing, may be regarded as a misfortune; to lose both looks like carelessness.
Oscar Wilde: The Importance of Being Earnest, I

LOVE

See also admiration, love and death, love and friendship, love

1 All the world loves a lover.
Proverb

2 Love laughs at locksmiths.
Proverb

3 Love makes the world go round
Proverb

4 Lucky at cards, unlucky in love
Proverb

5 When poverty comes in at the door, love flies out of the window.
Proverb

6 Tell me about yourself – your struggles, your dreams, your telephone number.
Peter Arno: Caption to a cartoon a man takes to a woman

7 Falling in love, we said; I fell for him. We were falling women. We believed in it, this downward motion: so lovely, like flying, and yet at the same time so dire, so extreme, so unlikely.
Margaret Atwood: The Handmaid's Tale

8 We must love one another or die.
W. H. Auden: September 1, 1939

9 Nuptial love maketh mankind;

friendly love perfecteth it; but wanton love corrupteth and embaseth it.
Francis Bacon: Essays, 'Of Love'

10 Love is just a system for getting someone to call you darling after sex.
Julian Barnes: Talking It Over, Ch. 16

11 Love ceases to be a pleasure, when it ceases to be a secret.
Aphra Behn: The Lover's Watch, 'Four o'clock'

12 He that loveth not knoweth not God; for God is love.
Bible: I John: 4:7

13 Thou shalt love thy neighbour as thyself.
Bible: Matthew: 22:37

14 Love seeketh not itself to please,
Nor for itself hath any care,
But for another gives its ease,
And builds a Heaven in Hell's despair.
William Blake: Songs of Experience, 'The Clod and the Pebble'

15 My love is like a red red rose
That's newly sprung in June:
My love is like the melodie
That's sweetly play'd in tune.
Robert Burns: A Red, Red Rose

16 God is Love – I dare say. But what a mischievous devil Love is!
Samuel Butler: Notebooks

17 Many a man has fallen in love with a girl in a light so dim he would not have chosen a suit by it.
Maurice Chevalier: Attrib.

8 To the men and women who own men and women

those of us meant to be lovers
we will not pardon you
for wasting our bodies and time
Leonard Cohen: The Energy of Slaves

19 Say what you will, 'tis better to be left than never to have been loved.
William Congreve: The Way of the World, II:1

20 Mad about the boy.
Noël Coward: Song title

21 It has been said that love robs those who have it of their wit, and gives it to those who have none.
Denis Diderot: Paradoxe sur le comédien

22 Come live with me, and be my love,
And we will some new pleasures prove
Of golden sands, and crystal brooks,
With silken lines, and silver hooks.
John Donne: The Bait

23 Love built on beauty, soon as beauty, dies.
John Donne: Elegies, 2, 'The Anagram'

24 Love one another, but make not a bond of love:
Let it rather be a moving sea between the shores of your souls.
Kahlil Gibran: The Prophet

25 In love as in sport, the amateur status must be strictly maintained.
Robert Graves: Occupation: Writer

26 Hello, Young Lovers, Wherever You Are.

Oscar Hammerstein: From the musical The King and I Song title

27 I know nothing about platonic love except that it is not to be found in the works of Plato.

Edgar Jepson: EGO 5 (James Agate)

28 Come, my Celia, let us prove,
While we can, the sports of love,
Time will not be ours for ever,
He, at length, our good will
sever.

Ben Jonson: Volpone, III:6

29 All You Need Is Love.

John Lennon: Song title (with Paul McCartney)

30 Two souls with but a single thought,
Two hearts that beat as one.

Maria Lovell: Ingomar the Barbarian, II (transl. of Friedrich Halm)

31 Come live with me, and be my love;
And we will all the pleasures prove
That hills and valleys, dales and fields,
Woods or steepy mountain yields.

Christopher Marlowe: The Passionate Shepherd to his Love

32 Falling out of love is very enlightening. For a short while you see the world with new eyes.

Iris Murdoch: The Observer, 'Sayings of the Week', 4 Feb 1968

33 By the time you swear you're his,
Shivering and sighing,
And he vows his passion is
Infinite, undying—
Lady, make a note of this:
One of you is lying.

Dorothy Parker: Unfortunate Coincidence

34 Ye gods! annihilate but space and time.
And make two lovers happy.

Alexander Pope: The Art of Sinking in Poetry, 11

35 Let's Do It; Let's Fall in Love.

Cole Porter: Paris, song title

36 There are very few people who are not ashamed of having been in love when they no longer love each other.

Duc de la Rochefoucauld: Maximes, 71

37 It takes a woman twenty years to make a man of her son, and another woman twenty minutes to make a fool of him.

Helen Rowland: Reflections of a Bachelor Girl

38 Of all forms of caution, caution in love is perhaps the most fatal to true happiness.

Bertrand Russell: Autobiography

39 Every little girl knows about love. It is only her capacity to suffer because of it that increases.

Françoise Sagan: Daily Express

40 Liszt said to me today that God alone deserves to be loved. It may be true, but when one has loved a man it is very different to love God.

George Sand: Intimate Journal

41 But love is blind, and lovers cannot see
The pretty follies that themselves commit.

William Shakespeare: The Merchant of Venice, II:6

42 For aught that I could ever read,

Could ever hear by tale or history,
The course of true love never did run smooth.
William Shakespeare: A Midsummer Night's Dream, I:1

43 And all for love, and nothing for reward.
Edmund Spenser: The Faerie Queene

44 A woman despises a man for loving her, unless she returns his love.
Elizabeth Drew Stoddard: Two Men, Ch. 32

45 'Tis strange what a man may do, and a woman yet think him an angel.
William Makepeace Thackeray: Henry Esmond, Ch. 7

46 One can't live on love alone; and I am so stupid that I can do nothing but think of him.
Sophie Tolstoy: A Diary of Tolstoy's Wife, 1860–1891

47 Those who have courage to love should have courage to suffer.
Anthony Trollope: The Bertrams, Ch. 27

48 I doubt whether any girl would be satisfied with her lover's mind if she knew the whole of it.
Anthony Trollope: The Small House at Allington, Ch. 4

49 Love conquers all things: let us too give in to Love.
Virgil: Eclogue, Bk. X

50 It is like a cigar. If it goes out, you can light it again but it never tastes quite the same.
Lord Wavell: Attrib.

LOVE AND DEATH

See also death

1 Love is my religion – I could die for that.
John Keats: Letter to Fanny Brawne, 13 Oct 1819

2 How alike are the groans of love to those of the dying.
Malcolm Lowry: Under the Volcano, Ch. 12

3 Men have died from time to time, and worms have eaten them, but not for love.
William Shakespeare: As You Like It, IV:1

4 I kiss'd thee ere I kill'd thee, no way but this,
Killing myself to die upon a kiss.
William Shakespeare: Othello, V:2

LOVE AND FRIENDSHIP

See also friendship

1 Love is blind; friendship closes its eyes.
Proverb

2 A woman can become a man's friend only in the following stages – first an acquaintance, next a mistress, and only then a friend.
Anton Chekhov: Uncle Vanya, II

3 No human relation gives one possession in another – every two souls are absolutely different. In friendship or in love, the two side by side raise hands together to find what one cannot reach alone.
Kahlil Gibran: Beloved Prophet (Virginia Hilu)

4 Most friendship is feigning, most loving mere folly.

William Shakespeare: As You Like It, II:7

5 Friendship is constant in all other things
Save in the office and affairs of love.
William Shakespeare: Much Ado About Nothing, II:1

LOVE AND HATE

See also hate

1 Odi et amo.
I hate and love.
Catullus: Carmina, LXXXV

2 Heaven has no rage like love to hatred turned,
Nor hell a fury like a woman scorned.
William Congreve: The Mourning Bride, III

3 Oh, I have loved him too much to feel no hate for him.
Jean Racine: Andromaque, II:1

4 If one judges love by its visible effects, it looks more like hatred than like friendship.
Duc de la Rochefoucauld: Maximes, 72

5 My only love sprung from my only hate!
Too early seen unknown, and known too late!
William Shakespeare: Romeo and Juliet, I:5

LOVE AND MARRIAGE

See also marriage

1 Love and marriage, love and marriage,
Go together like a horse and carriage.
Sammy Cahn: Our Town, 'Love and Marriage'

2 ALMA. I rather suspect her of being in love with him.
MARTIN. Her own husband? Monstrous! What a selfish woman!
Jennie Jerome Churchill: His Borrowed Plumes

3 Love is moral even without legal marriage, but marriage is immoral without love.
Ellen Key: The Morality of Woman and Other Essays, 'The Morality of Woman'

4 Many a man in love with a dimple makes the mistake of marrying the whole girl.
Stephen Leacock: Literary Lapses

5 Any one must see at a glance that if men and women marry those whom they do not love, they must love those whom they do not marry.
Harriet Martineau: Society in America, Vol. III, 'Marriage'

LOYALTY

See also betrayal, patriotism, support

1 There is honour among thieves.
Proverb

2 You cannot run with the hare and hunt with the hounds.
Proverb

3 The State, in choosing men to serve it, takes no notice of their opinions. If they be willing faithfully to serve it, that satisfies.
Oliver Cromwell: Said before the Battle of Marston Moor, 2 July 1644

4 A man who will steal *for me* will steal *from me*.

Theodore Roosevelt: Firing a cowboy who had applied Roosevelt's brand to a steer belonging to a neighbouring ranch. Roosevelt in the Bad Lands (Herman Hagedorn)

5 If this man is not faithful to his God, how can he be faithful to me, a mere man?

Theodoric: Explaining why he had had a trusted minister, who had said he would adopt his master's religion, beheaded. Dictionnaire Encyclopédique (E. Guérard)

LUCK

See also chance, superstition

1 There, but for the grace of God, goes John Bradford.

John Bradford: Said on seeing some criminals being led to execution. Attrib.

2 Fortune, that favours fools.

Ben Jonson: The Alchemist, Prologue

3 I am a great believer in luck, and I find the harder I work the more I have of it.

Stephen Leacock: Literary Lapses

LUST

See also desire, love, sex

1 For all that is in the world, the lust of the flesh, and the lust of the eyes, and the pride of life, is not of the Father, but is of the world.

Bible: I John: 2:16

2 What is commonly called love, namely the desire of satisfying a voracious appetite with a certain quantity of delicate white human flesh.

Henry Fielding: Tom Jones, Bk. VI, Ch. 1

3 I'll come no more behind your scenes, David; for the silk stockings and white bosoms of your actresses excite my amorous propensities.

Samuel Johnson: Said to the actor-manager David Garrick. Life of Johnson (J. Boswell), Vol. I

4 Lolita, light of my life, fire of my loins. My sin, my Soul.

Vladimir Nabokov: Lolita

5 All witchcraft comes from carnal lust which in women is insatiable.

Jacob Sprenger and Hendrich Kramer: The indispensable handbook for the Inquisition. Malleus Maleficarum

6 Outside every thin girl there is a fat man trying to get in.

Katharine Whitehorn: Attrib.

LUXURY

See also extravagance, wealth

1 The saddest thing I can imagine is to get used to luxury.

Charlie Chaplin: My Autobiography

2 In the affluent society no useful distinction can be made between luxuries and necessaries.

John Kenneth Galbraith: The Affluent Society, Ch. 21

3 How many things I can do without!

Socrates: *Examining the range of goods on sale at a market.* Lives of the Eminent Philosophers (Diogenes Laertius), II

4 Beulah, peel me a grape.
Mae West: I'm No Angel, film 1933

LYING

See also deception, truth

1 A liar is worse than a thief.
Proverb

2 The boy cried 'Wolf, wolf!' and the villagers came out to help him.
Aesop: Fables, 'The Shepherd's Boy'

3 It contains a misleading impression, not a lie. I was being economical with the truth.
Robert Armstrong: Giving evidence on behalf of the British Government in an Australian court case, Nov 1986. Armstrong was, in fact, quoting Edmund Burke (1729–97).

4 A lie can be half-way round the world before the truth has got its boots on.
James Callaghan: Speech, 1 Nov 1976

5 It cannot in the opinion of His Majesty's Government be classified as slavery in the extreme acceptance of the word without some risk of terminological inexactitude.
Winston Churchill: Speech, House of Commons, 22 Feb 1906

6 Whoever would lie usefully should lie seldom.
Lord Hervey: Memoirs of the Reign of George II, Vol. I

7 The broad mass of a nation... will more easily fall victim to a big lie than to a small one.
Adolf Hitler: Mein Kampf, Ch. 10

8 Unless a man feels he has a good enough memory, he should never venture to lie.
Michel de Montaigne: Also quoted in Le Menteur, IV:5 by Pierre Corneille (1606–84). Essais, I

9 He led a double life. Did that make him a liar? He did not feel a liar. He was a man of two truths.
Iris Murdoch: The Sacred and Profane Love Machine

10 He who does not need to lie is proud of not being a liar.
Friedrich Nietzsche: Nachgelassene Fragmente

11 O what a tangled web we weave,
When first we practise to deceive!
Walter Scott: Marmion, VI:17

12 In our country the lie has become not just a moral category but a pillar of the State.
Alexander Solzhenitsyn: The Observer, 'Sayings of the Year', 29 Dec 1974

13 A lie is an abomination unto the Lord and a very present help in trouble.
Adlai Stevenson: Speech, Jan 19

MADNESS

See also psychiatry, psychology

1 We all are born mad. Some remain so.
Samuel Beckett: Waiting for Godot, II

2 A knight errant who turns mad for a reason deserves neither merit nor thanks. The thing is to do it without cause.
Miguel de Cervantes: Don Quixote, Pt. I, Ch. 25

3 The madman is not the man who has lost his reason. The madman is the man who has lost everything except his reason.
G. K. Chesterton: Orthodoxy, Ch. 1

4 Much Madness is divinest Sense –
To a discerning Eye –
Much Sense – the starkest Madness.
Emily Dickinson: Poems, 'Much Madness is Divinest Sense'

5 There is less harm to be suffered in being mad among madmen than in being sane all by oneself.
Denis Diderot: Supplement to Bougainville's 'Voyage'

6 Those whom God wishes to destroy, he first makes mad.
Euripides: Fragment

7 It is his reasonable conversation which mostly frightens us in a madman.
Anatole France

8 Insanity is a kind of innocence.
Graham Greene: The Quiet American, Ch. 3, Pt. 2

9 Insanity is often the logic of an accurate mind overtaxed.
Oliver Wendell Holmes

10 Show me a sane man and I will cure him for you.
Carl Gustav Jung: The Observer, 19 July 1975

11 Madness need not be all breakdown. It may also be breakthrough. It is potential liberation and renewal as well as enslavement and existential death.
R. D. Laing: The Politics of Experience, Ch. 16

12 Insanity is hereditary – you can get it from your children.
Sam Levinson

13 Insanity in individuals is something rare – but in groups, parties, nations, and epochs it is the rule.
Friedrich Nietzsche: Beyond Good and Evil, Ch. 4

14 Men are so necessarily mad, that not to be mad would amount to another form of madness.
Blaise Pascal: Pensées, 414

15 His father's sister had bats in the belfry and was put away.
Eden Phillpotts: Peacock House, 'My First Murder'

16 Our occasional madness is less wonderful than our occasional sanity.
George Santayana: Interpretations of Poetry and Religion

17 Though this be madness, yet there is method in't.
William Shakespeare: Hamlet, II:2

MAJORITY

18 If you talk to God, you are praying; if God talks to you, you have schizophrenia.
Thomas Szasz: The Second Sin

19 Men will always be mad and those who think they can cure them are the maddest of all.
Voltaire: Letter, 1762

MAJORITY

See also democracy, minority, public

1 The one pervading evil of democracy is the tyranny of the majority.
Lord Acton: The History of Freedom

2 When great changes occur in history, when great principles are involved, as a rule the majority are wrong.
Eugene V. Debs: Speech, 12 Aug 1918

3 'It's always best on these occasions to do what the mob do.'
'But suppose there are two mobs?' suggested Mr Snodgrass.
'Shout with the largest,' replied Mr Pickwick.
Charles Dickens: Pickwick Papers, Ch. 13

4 The majority has the might – more's the pity – but it hasn't right...The minority is always right.
Henrik Ibsen: An Enemy of the People, IV

5 It is time for the great silent majority of Americans to stand up and be counted.
Richard Milhous Nixon: Election speech, Oct 1970

MALAPROPISMS

Remarks of a type associated with Mrs Malaprop in Sheridan's play The Rivals

1 Our watch, sir, have indeed comprehended two aspicious persons.
William Shakespeare: Much Ado About Nothing, III:5

2 Comparisons are odorous.
William Shakespeare: Much Ado About Nothing, III:5

3 Illiterate him, I say, quite from your memory.
Richard Brinsley Sheridan: The Rivals, II

4 As headstrong as an allegory on the banks of the Nile.
Richard Brinsley Sheridan: The Rivals, III

5 If I reprehend any thing in this world, it is the use of my oracular tongue, and a nice derangement of epitaphs!
Richard Brinsley Sheridan: The Rivals, III

MANKIND

See also human condition, human nature

1 I am a human being: Do not fold, spindle or mutilate.
Anonymous: Hippy slogan

2 Man, when perfected, is the best of animals, but, when separated from law and justice, he is the worst of all.
Aristotle: Politics, Bk. I

3 Drinking when we are not thirsty and making love all year round, madam; that is all there

is to distinguish us from other animals.
Beaumarchais: Le Mariage de Figaro, II:21

4 MAN, n. An animal so lost in rapturous contemplation of what he thinks he is as to overlook what he indubitably ought to be.
Ambrose Bierce: The Devil's Dictionary

5 What is man, when you come to think upon him, but a minutely set, ingenious machine for turning, with infinite artfulness, the red wine of Shiraz into urine?
Karen Blixen: Seven Gothic Tales, 'The Dreamers'

6 Man is a noble animal, splendid in ashes, and pompous in the grave.
Thomas Browne: Urn Burial, Ch. 5

7 A single sentence will suffice for modern man: he fornicated and read the papers.
Albert Camus: The Fall

8 The true science and the true study of man is man.
Pierre Charron: Traité de la sagesse, Bk. I, Ch. 1

9 Mankind is not a tribe of animals to which we owe compassion. Mankind is a club to which we owe our subscription.
G. K. Chesterton: Daily News, 10 Apr 1906

10 The evolution of the human race will not be accomplished in the ten thousand years of tame animals, but in the million years of wild animals, because man is and will always be a wild animal.

Charles Darwin: The Next Ten Million Years, Ch. 4

11 Human beings are like timid punctuation marks sprinkled among the incomprehensible sentences of life.
Jean Giraudoux: Siegfried, 2

12 The human race will be the cancer of the planet.
Julian Huxley

13 Man appears to be the missing link between anthropoid apes and human beings.
Konrad Lorenz: The New York Times Magazine, 11 Apr 1965 (John Pfeiffer)

14 I'll give you my opinion of the human race... their heart's in the right place, but their head is a thoroughly inefficient organ.
W. Somerset Maugham: The Summing Up

15 A human being is an ingenious assembly of portable plumbing.
Robert Morley: Human Being

16 There are one hundred and ninety-three living species of monkeys and apes. One hundred and ninety-two of them are covered with hair. The exception is a naked ape self-named *Homo sapiens*.
Desmond Morris: The Naked Ape, Introduction

17 Man is not a solitary animal, and so long as social life survives, self-realization cannot be the supreme principle of ethics.
Bertrand Russell: History of Western Philosophy, 'Romanticism'

18 I love mankind – it's people I can't stand.

Charles M. Schultz: Go Fly a Kite, Charlie Brown

19 After all, for mankind as a whole there are no exports. We did not start developing by obtaining foreign exchange from Mars or the moon. Mankind is a closed society.
E. F. Schumacher: Small is Beautiful, A Study of Economics as if People Mattered, Ch. 14

20 What a piece of work is a man! How noble in reason! how infinite in faculties!...And yet, to me, what is this quintessence of dust? Man delights not me – no, nor woman neither.
William Shakespeare: Hamlet, II:2

21 How beauteous mankind is! O brave new world
That has such people in't!
William Shakespeare: The Tempest, V:1

22 Physically there is nothing to distinguish human society from the farm-yard except that children are more troublesome and costly than chickens and women are not so completely enslaved as farm stock.
George Bernard Shaw: Getting Married, Preface

23 I am a man, I count nothing human foreign to me.
Terence: Heauton Timorumenos

24 The noblest work of God? Man. Who found it out? Man.
Mark Twain: Autobiography

25 One thousand years more. That's all *Homo sapiens* has before him.
H. G. Wells: Diary (Harold Nicolson)

26 If anything is sacred the human body is sacred.
Walt Whitman: I Sing the Body Electric, 8

27 We're all of us guinea pigs in the laboratory of God. Humanity is just a work in progress.
Tennessee Williams: Camino Real, 12

MANNERS

See also courtesy, etiquette

1 Don't tell your friends about your indigestion:
'How are you!' is a greeting, not a question.
Arthur Guiterman: A Poet's Proverbs, 'Of Tact'

2 On the Continent people have good food; in England people have good table manners.
George Mikes: How to be an Alien

3 Politeness is organised indifference.
Paul Valéry: Tel Quel

4 Manners are especially the need of the plain. The pretty can get away with anything.
Evelyn Waugh: The Observer, 'Sayings of the Year', 1962

5 Manners maketh man.
William of Wykeham: Motto of Winchester College and New College, Oxford

MARRIAGE

See also love and marriage

1 Better be an old man's darling than a young man's slave.
Proverb

2 Marriages are made in heaven.
Proverb

3 Marry in haste, and repent at leisure.
Proverb

4 The first wife is matrimony, the second company, the third heresy.
Proverb

5 I married beneath me – all women do.
Nancy Astor: Dictionary of National Biography

6 It is a truth universally acknowledged, that a single man in possession of a good fortune must be in want of a wife.
Jane Austen: The opening words of the book. Pride and Prejudice, Ch. 1

7 Happiness in marriage is entirely a matter of chance.
Jane Austen: Pride and Prejudice, Ch. 6

8 He was reputed one of the wise men, that made answer to the question, when a man should marry? A young man not yet, an elder man not at all.
Francis Bacon: Essays, 'Of Marriage and Single Life'

9 No man should marry until he has studied anatomy and dissected at least one woman.
Honoré de Balzac: La Physiologie du mariage

10 I think weddings is sadder than funerals, because they remind you of your own wedding. You can't be reminded of your own funeral because it hasn't happened.
Brendan Behan: Richard's Cork Leg, I

11 Being a husband is a whole-time job. That is why so many husbands fail. They cannot give their entire attention to it.
Arnold Bennett: The Title, I

12 Husbands, love your wives, and be not bitter against them.
Bible: Colossians: 3:19

13 But if they cannot contain, let them marry: for it is better to marry than to burn.
Bible: I Corinthians: 7:9

14 To have and to hold from this day forward, for better for worse, for richer for poorer, in sickness and in health, to love and to cherish, till death us do part.
The Book of Common Prayer: Solemnization of Matrimony

15 Splendid couple – slept with both of them.
Maurice Bowra: Referring to a well-known literary couple. Attrib.

16 'We stay together, but we distrust one another.'
'Ah, yes...but isn't that a definition of marriage?'
Malcolm Bradbury: The History Man, Ch. 3

17 Wedlock – the deep, deep peace of the double bed after the hurly-burly of the chaise-longue.
Mrs Patrick Campbell: Jennie (Ralph G. Martin), Vol. II

18 They call it 'serial monogamy'.
Angela Carter: Wise Children

19 The one advantage about marrying a princess – or someone from a royal family – is that they do know what happens.
Charles, Prince of Wales: Attrib.

20 An archaeologist is the best husband any woman can have:

the older she gets, the more interested he is in her.
Agatha Christie: Attrib.

21 The most happy marriage I can picture or imagine to myself would be the union of a deaf man to a blind woman.
Samuel Taylor Coleridge: Recollections (Allsop)

22 Courtship to marriage, as a very witty prologue to a very dull Play.
William Congreve: The Old Bachelor, V:10

23 Marriage is a wonderful invention; but then again so is a bicycle repair kit.
Billy Connolly: The Authorized Version

24 Dear Mrs A., hooray hooray, At last you are deflowered On this as every other day I love you. Noël Coward.
Noël Coward: Telegram to Gertrude Lawrence on her marriage to Richard S. Aldrich

25 Here lies my wife; here let her lie!
Now she's at rest, and so am I.
John Dryden: Epitaph Intended for Dryden's Wife

26 So that ends my first experience with matrimony, which I always thought a highly overrated performance.
Isadora Duncan: The New York Times, 1923

27 When widows exclaim loudly against second marriages, I would always lay a wager, that the man, if not the wedding-day, is absolutely fixed on.
Henry Fielding: Amelia, Bk. VI, Ch. 8

28 One fool at least in every married couple.
Henry Fielding: Amelia, Bk. IX, Ch. 4

29 A man in love is incomplete until he has married. Then he's finished.
Zsa Zsa Gabor: Newsweek, 28 Mar 1960

30 The concept of two people living together for 25 years without having a cross word suggests a lack of spirit only to be admired in sheep.
A. P. Herbert: News Chronicle, 1940

31 If a man avoids
Marriage and all the troubles women bring
And never takes a wife, at last he comes
To a miserable old age, and does not have
Anyone to care for the old man.
Hesiod: Theogony, 602–7

32 Marriage has many pains, but celibacy has no pleasures.
Samuel Johnson: Rasselas, Ch. 26

33 It has been discovered experimentally that you can draw laughter from an audience anywhere in the world, of any class or race, simply by walking on to a stage and uttering the words 'I am a married man'.
Ted Kavanagh: News Review, 10 July 1947

34 He married a woman to stop her getting away
Now she's there all day.
Philip Larkin: Self's The Man

35 Being married six times shows a degree of optimism over wis-

dom, but I am incorrigibly optimistic.
Norman Mailer: The Observer, 'Sayings of the Week', 17 Jan 1988

36 Marriage is like a cage; one sees the birds outside desperate to get in, and those inside equally desperate to get out.
Michel de Montaigne: Essais, III

37 One doesn't have to get anywhere in a marriage. It's not a public conveyance.
Iris Murdoch: A Severed Head

38 Marriage is an insult and women shouldn't touch it.
Jenni Murray: The Independent, 20 June 1992

39 It is now known…that men enter local politics solely as a result of being unhappily married.
Cyril Northcote Parkinson: Parkinson's Law, Ch. 10

40 Marriage may often be a stormy lake, but celibacy is almost always a muddy horsepond.
Thomas Love Peacock: Melincourt

41 I don't think a prostitute is more moral than a wife, but they are doing the same thing.
Prince Philip: Remark, Dec 1988

42 When you're bored with yourself, marry and be bored with someone else.
David Pryce-Jones: Owls and Satyrs

43 It doesn't much signify whom one marries, for one is sure to find next morning that it was someone else.
Samuel Rogers: Table Talk (ed. Alexander Dyce)

44 A married couple are well suited when both partners usually feel the need for a quarrel at the same time.
Jean Rostand: Le Mariage

45 When you see what some girls marry, you realize how they must hate to work for a living.
Helen Rowland: Reflections of a Bachelor Girl

46 It takes two to make a marriage a success and only one a failure.
Herbert Samuel: A Book of Quotations

47 Have you not heard
When a man marries, dies, or turns Hindoo,
His best friends hear no more of him?
Percy Bysshe Shelley: Referring to the novelist Thomas Love Peacock, who worked for the East India Company and had recently married. Letter to Maria Gisborne, I

48 Married women are kept women, and they are beginning to find it out.
Logan Pearsall Smith: Afterthoughts, 'Other people'

49 In marriage, a man becomes slack and selfish and undergoes a fatty degeneration of his moral being.
Robert Louis Stevenson: Virginibus Puerisque

50 Remember, it is as easy to marry a rich woman as a poor woman.
William Makepeace Thackeray: Pendennis, Ch. 28

51 Every night of her married life she has been late for school.
Dylan Thomas: Under Milk Wood

52 It should be a very happy mar-

riage – they are both so much in love with *him*.
Irene Thomas: Attrib.

53 Divorce? Never. But murder often!
Sybil Thorndike: Replying to a query as to whether she had ever considered divorce during her long marriage to Sir Lewis Casson. Attrib.

54 A man should not insult his wife publicly, at parties. He should insult her in the privacy of the home.
James Thurber: Thurber Country

55 Marriage is the only adventure open to the cowardly.
Voltaire: Thoughts of a Philosopher

56 Marriage is a great institition, but I'm not ready for an institution, yet.
Mae West

57 Twenty years of romance makes a woman look like a ruin; but twenty years of marriage make her something like a public building.
Oscar Wilde: A Woman of No Importance, I

58 Of course, I do have a slight advantage over the rest of you. It helps in a pinch to be able to remind your bride that you gave up a throne for her.
Duke of Windsor: Discussing the maintenance of happy marital relations. Attrib.

59 Marriage isn't a process of prolonging the life of love, but of mummifying the corpse.
P. G. Wodehouse: Bring on the Girls (with Guy Bolton)

60 Wondering why one's friends chose to marry the people they

did is unprofitable, but recurrent. One could so often have done so much better for them.
John Wyndham: The Kraken Wakes

MARTYRDOM

See also execution

1 The king has been very good to me. He promoted me from a simple maid to be a marchioness. Then he raised me to be a queen. Now he will raise me to be a martyr.
Anne Boleyn: Notable Women in History (W. Abbot)

2 To die for a religion is easier than to live it absolutely.
Jorge Luis Borges: Labyrinthes

3 'Dying for an idea,' again, sounds well enough, but why not let the idea die instead of you?
Wyndham Lewis: The Art of Being Ruled, Pt. 1, Ch. 1

4 A thing is not necessarily true because a man dies for it.
Oscar Wilde: Oscariana

MARXISM

See also Communism, socialism

1 The Marxist analysis has got nothing to do with what happened in Stalin's Russia; it's like blaming Jesus Christ for the Inquisition in Spain.
Tony Benn: The Observer, 27 Apr 1980

2 Karl Marx wasn't a Marxist all the time. He got drunk in the Tottenham Court Road.

*Michael Foot: Behind The Image
(Susan Barnes)*

3 The workers have nothing to
lose but their chains. They have
a world to gain. Workers of the
world, unite.
*Karl Marx: The Communist
Manifesto*

4 From each according to his
abilities, to each according to
his needs.
*Karl Marx: Criticism of the Gotha
Programme*

5 Capitalist production begets,
with the inexorability of a law of
nature, its own negation.
Karl Marx: Das Kapital, Ch. 15

MATERIALISM

See also commercialism, greed,
money, wealth

1 Thinking to get at once all the
gold the goose could give,
he killed it, and opened it only
to find – nothing.
*Aesop: Fables, 'The Goose with the
Golden Eggs'*

2 You don't want no pie in the sky
when you die,
You want something here on the
ground while you're still around.
Muhammad Ali: Attrib.

3 For gold in phisik is a cordial,
Therfore he lovede gold in
special.
*Geoffrey Chaucer: Referring to the
doctor. The Canterbury Tales,
Prologue*

4 To be clever enough to get all
that money, one must be stupid
enough to want it.
*G. K. Chesterton: The Innocence
of Father Brown*

5 I never hated a man enough to
give him diamonds back.
*Zsa Zsa Gabor: The Observer,
'Sayings of the Week', 28 Aug
1957*

6 Increase of material comforts, it
may be generally laid down,
does not in any way whatsoever
conduce to moral growth.
*Mahatma Gandhi: Obituary,
News Chronicle*

7 Man must choose whether to be
rich in things or in the freedom
to use them.
*Ivan Illich: Deschooling Society,
Ch. 4*

8 In a consumer society there are
inevitably two kinds of slaves:
the prisoners of addiction and
the prisoners of envy.
Ivan Illich: Tools for Conviviality

9 Kissing your hand may make
you feel very very good but a
diamond and safire bracelet
lasts forever.
*Anita Loos: Gentlemen Prefer
Blondes, Ch. 4*

10 Years ago a person, he was unhappy, didn't know what to do
with himself – he'd go to church,
start a revolution – *something*.
Today you're unhappy? Can't
figure it out? What is the salvation? Go shopping.
Arthur Miller: The Price, I

11 Diamonds Are A Girl's Best
Friend.
*Leo Robin: Gentlemen Prefer
Blondes, song title*

12 What do you not drive human
hearts into, cursed
craving for gold!
Virgil: Aeneid, Bk. III

13 A gold rush is what happens

when a line of chorus girls spot a man with a bank roll.
Mae West: Klondike Annie, film 1936

MATHEMATICS

See also numbers

1 All science requires mathematics.
Roger Bacon: Opus Maius, Pt. IV

2 I never could make out what those damned dots meant.
Lord Randolph Churchill: Referring to decimal points. Lord Randolph Churchill (W. S. Churchill)

3 As far as the laws of mathematics refer to reality, they are not certain, and as far as they are certain, they do not refer to reality.
Albert Einstein: The Tao of Physics (F. Capra), Ch. 2

4 There is no 'royal road' to geometry.
Euclid: Said to Ptolemy I when asked if there were an easier way to solve theorems. Comment on Euclid (Proclus)

5 Quod erat demonstrandum.
Which was to be proved.
Euclid: Hence, of course, Q.E.D. Elements, I:5

6 The only way I can distinguish proper from improper fractions Is by their actions.
Ogden Nash: Ask Daddy, He Won't Know

7 One geometry cannot be more true than another; it can only be more convenient. Geometry is not true, it is advantageous.
Robert T. Pirsig: Zen and the Art of Motorcycle Maintenance, Pt. III, Ch. 22

8 Let no one ignorant of mathematics enter here.
Plato: Inscription written over the entrance to the Academy. Biographical Encyclopedia (I. Asimov)

9 Mathematics, rightly viewed, possesses not only truth but supreme beauty – a beauty cold and austere like that of sculpture.
Bertrand Russell: Mysticism and Logic

10 Numbers constitute the only universal language.
Nathaniel West: Miss Lonelyhearts

MEDIA

See also journalism, newspapers, television

1 When a dog bites a man that is not news, but when a man bites a dog that is news.
John B. Bogart: Sometimes attributed to Charles Dana and Amos Cummings. Attrib.

2 I try to find Radio 4 but I can't with all those bloody music channels.
Jack Charlton: The Guardian, June 1994

3 TV…is our latest medium – we call it a medium because nothing's well done.
Ace Goodman: Letter to Groucho Marx, 1954 The Groucho Letters

4 The Liberty of the press is the *Palladium* of all the civil, political and religious rights of an Englishman.

Junius: Letters, 'Dedication'

5 Freedom of the press in Britain is freedom to print such of the proprietor's prejudices as the advertisers don't object to.
Hannen Swaffer: Attrib.

6 Facing the press is more difficult than bathing a leper.
Mother Teresa: Eileen Egan, Such a Vision of the Street

MEDICINE

See also doctors, remedies

1 Nature, time and patience are the three great physicians.
Bulgarian proverb

2 Medicine can only cure curable diseases, and then not always.
Chinese proverb

3 The poets did well to conjoin Music and Medicine in Apollo: because the office of medicine is but to tune this curious harp of man's body and to reduce it to harmony.
Francis Bacon: The Advancement of Learning, Bk. II

4 HOMEOPATHY, n. A school of medicine midway between Allopathy and Christian Science. To the last both the others are distinctly inferior, for Christian Science will cure imaginary diseases, and they can not.
Ambrose Bierce: The Devil's Dictionary

5 Vaccination is the medical sacrament corresponding to baptism.
Samuel Butler

6 Patience is the best medicine.
John Florio: First Frutes

7 Comedy is medicine.

8 I swear by Apollo the physician, by Asclepius, by Health, by Panacea and by all the gods and goddesses, making them my witnesses, that I will carry out, according to my ability and judgment, this oath and this indenture.
Hippocrates: The Hippocratic Oath

9 A miracle drug is any drug that will do what the label says it will do.
Eric Hodgins: Episode

10 One of the most difficult things to contend with in a hospital is the assumption on the part of the staff that because you have lost your gall bladder you have also lost your mind.
Jean Kerr: Please Don't Eat the Daisies

11 Medicine may be defined as the art or the science of keeping a patient quiet with frivolous reasons for his illness and amusing him with remedies good or bad until nature kills him or cures him.
Gilles Ménage: Ménagiana, Pt. III

12 The aim of medicine is surely not to make men virtuous; it is to safeguard and rescue them from the consequences of their vices.
H. L. Mencken: Prejudices, 'Types of Men: the Physician'

13 Medicine is for the patient. Medicine is the people. It is not for the profits.
George Merck

14 Medicine for the dead is too late.
Quintilian

15 Medical science is as yet very imperfectly differentiated from common curemongering witchcraft.
George Bernard Shaw: The Doctor's Dilemma, 'Preface on Doctors'

16 I've already had medical attention – a dog licked me when I was on the ground.
Neil Simon: Only When I Laugh (screenplay)

17 Formerly, when religion was strong and science weak, men mistook magic for medicine, now, when science is strong and religion weak, men mistake medicine for magic.
Thomas Szasz: The Second Sin

18 He preferred to know the power of herbs and their value for curing purposes, and, heedless of glory, to exercise that quiet art.
Virgil: Aeneid

MEDIOCRITY

See also inferiority

1 The most insidious influence on the young is not violence, drugs, tobacco, drink or sexual perversion, but our pursuit of the trivial and our tolerance of the third-rate.
Eric Anderson: The Observer, 'Sayings of the Week', 12 June 1994

2 Only mediocrity can be trusted to be always at its best.
Max Beerbohm: Conversations with Max (S.N. Behrman)

3 Some men are born mediocre, some men achieve mediocrity, and some men have mediocrity thrust upon them. With Major Major it had been all three.
Joseph Heller: Catch-22, Ch. 9

4 Women want mediocre men, and men are working to be as mediocre as possible.
Margaret Mead: Quote Magazine, 15 May 1958

5 It isn't evil that is ruining the earth, but mediocrity. The crime is not that Nero played while Rome burned, but that he played badly.
Ned Rorem: The Final Diary

6 Much of a muchness.
John Vanbrugh: The Provok'd Husband, I:1

MELANCHOLY

See also despair, sorrow

1 Nothing's so dainty sweet as lovely melancholy.
Francis Beaumont: The Nice Valour, III:3

2 If there is a hell upon earth, it is to be found in a melancholy man's heart.
Robert Burton: Anatomy of Melancholy, Pt. I

3 Ay, in the very temple of delight Veil'd Melancholy has her sovran shrine.
John Keats: Ode on Melancholy

4 I was told I am a true cosmopolitan. I am unhappy everywhere.
Stephen Vizinczey: The Guardian, 7 Mar 1968

MEMORIALS

See also epitaphs, obituaries, reputation

1 Their bodies are buried in peace; but their name liveth for evermore.
Bible: Ecclesiasticus: 44:14

2 They shall grow not old, as we that are left grow old:
Age shall not weary them, nor the years condemn.
At the going down of the sun and in the morning
We will remember them.
Laurence Binyon: Poems For the Fallen

3 In Flanders fields the poppies blow
Between the crosses, row on row,
That mark our place.
John McCrae: In Flanders Fields, 'Ypres Salient', 3 May 1915

4 I was told that the Chinese said they would bury me by the Western Lake and build a shrine to my memory. I have some slight regret that this did not happen, as I might have become a god, which would have been very *chic* for an atheist.
Bertrand Russell: The Autobiography of Bertrand Russell, Vol. II, Ch. 3

5 Remembrance is the secret of reconciliation.
Rudolf Scharping: The Observer, 'Sayings of the Week', 17 Apr 1994

6 Move Queen Anne? Most certainly not! Why it might some day be suggested that *my* statue should be moved, which I should much dislike.
Victoria: Said at the time of her Diamond Jubilee (1897), when it was suggested that the statue of Queen Anne should be moved from outside St. Paul's. Men, Women and Things (Duke of Portland), Ch. 5

MEMORY

See also nostalgia, past

1 Memories are hunting horns whose sound dies on the wind.
Guillaume Apollinaire: Cors de Chasse

2 Memory is the thing you forget with.
Alexander Chase: Perspectives

3 To endeavour to forget anyone is a certain way of thinking of nothing else.
Jean de La Bruyère: Les Caractères

4 I never forget a face, but I'll make an exception in your case.
Groucho Marx: The Guardian, 18 June 1965

5 These foolish things
Remind me of you.
Eric Maschwitz: Song

6 Memory is history recorded in our brain, memory is a painter, it paints pictures of the past and of the day.
Grandma Moses: Grandma Moses, My Life's History (ed. Aotto Kallir), Ch. 1

7 Thanks For the Memory.
Leo Robin: Big Broadcast, song title

8 Better by far you should forget and smile

MEN

MEN

Than that you should remember
and be sad.
Christina Rossetti: Remember

9 To expect a man to retain everything that he has ever read is like
expecting him to carry about in
his body everything that he has
ever eaten.
*Arthur Schopenhauer: Parerga
and Paralipomena*

10 Old men forget; yet all shall be
forgot,
But he'll remember, with advan-
tages,
What feats he did that day.
*William Shakespeare: Henry V,
IV:3*

11 There are three things I always
forget. Names, faces and—the
third I can't remember.
Italo Svevo: Attrib.

MEN

See also sexes, women

1 One cannot be always laughing
at a man without now and then
stumbling on something witty.
*Jane Austen: Pride and Prejudice,
Ch. 40*

2 A man's a man for a' that.
*Robert Burns: For a' that and a'
that*

3 All men are rapists and that's all
they are. They rape us with their
eyes, their laws and their codes.
*Marilyn French: The Women's
Room*

4 Probably the only place where a
man can feel really secure is in a
maximum security prison, except for the imminent threat of
release.

*Germaine Greer: The Female
Eunuch*

5 Christ called as his Apostles
only men. He did this in a totally
free and sovereign way.
*John Paul II: The Observer,
'Sayings of the Week', 25 Sept
1988*

6 How beastly the bourgeois is
especially the male of the
species.
*D. H. Lawrence: How beastly
the bourgeois is*

7 Why can't a woman be more
like a man?
Men are so honest, so thorough-
ly square;
Eternally noble, historically fair.
*Alan Jay Lerner: My Fair Lady,
II:4*

8 A man in the house is worth two
in the street.
*Mae West: Belle of the Nineties,
film 1934*

MERIT

1 A good dog deserves a good
bone.
Proverb

2 I don't deserve this, but I have
arthritis, and I don't deserve
that either.
*Jack Benny: Said when accepting
an award. Attrib.*

3 I guess this is the week I earn my
salary.
*John Fitzgerald Kennedy:
Comment made during the Cuban
missile crisis. Nobody Said It
Better (M. Ringo)*

4 I wasn't lucky. I deserved it.

*Margaret Thatcher: Said after
receiving school prize, aged nine.
Attrib.*

5 The Rise of the Meritocracy.
Michael Young: Book title

METAPHYSICS

See also philosophy

1 A blind man in a dark room –
looking for a black hat – which
isn't there.
*Lord Bowen: Characterization of a
metaphysician. Attrib.*

2 Metaphysics is the finding of
bad reasons for what we believe
upon instinct; but to find these
reasons is no less an instinct.
*F. H. Bradley: Appearance and
Reality, Preface*

3 In other words, apart from the
known and the unknown, what
else is there?
*Harold Pinter: The Homecoming,
II*

MIND

See also intellect, intelligence,
thinking

1 A great many open minds
should be closed for repairs.
Toledo Blade

2 The brain is not an organ to be
relied upon. It is developing
monstrously. It is swelling like a
goitre.
Aleksandr Blok

3 As long as our brain is a mystery, the universe, the reflection
of the structure of the brain will
also be a mystery.
*Santiago Ramón y Cajal: Charlas
de Café*

4 The mind is an iceberg it floats
with only 17 of its bulk above
water.
*Sigmund Freud: Bartlett's
Unfamiliar Quotations (Leonard
Louis Levinson)*

5 Little minds are interested in
the extraordinary; great minds
in the commonplace.
*Elbert Hubbard: Roycroft
Dictionary and Book of Epigrams*

6 The natural course of the human mind is certainly from
credulity to scepticism.
*Thomas Jefferson: Letter to Dr.
Caspar Wistar, 21 June 1807*

7 The pendulum of the mind os-
cillates between sense and nonsense, not between right and
wrong.
*Carl Gustav Jung: Memories,
Dreams, Reflections, Ch. 5*

8 A mind not to be changed by
place or time.
The mind is its own place, and
in itself
Can make a Heaven of Hell, a
Hell of Heaven.
John Milton: Paradise Lost, Bk. I

9 Mind is ever the ruler of the
universe.
Plato: Philebus

10 Our minds are lazier than our
bodies.
*Duc de la Rochefoucauld:
Bartlett's Unfamiliar Quotations
(Leonard Louis Levinson)*

11 The dogma of the Ghost in the
Machine.
*Gilbert Ryle: The Concept of
Mind, Ch. 1*

12 If it is for mind that we are
seaching the brain, then we are
supposing the brain to be much

more than a telephone-exchange. We are supposing it a telephone-exchange along with the subscribers as well.
Charles Scott Sherrington: Man on his Nature

13 Mind over matter.
Virgil: Aeneid, Bk. VI

MINORITY

See also majority

1 What's a cult? It just means not enough people to make a minority.
Robert Altman: The Observer, 1981

2 Minorities…are almost always in the right.
Sydney Smith: The Smith of Smiths (H. Pearson), Ch. 9

MISANTHROPY

See also mankind

1 I've always been interested in people, but I've never liked them.
W. Somerset Maugham: The Observer, 'Sayings of the Week', 28 Aug 1949

2 A young, earnest American brought up the subject of nuclear warfare which, he said might well destroy the entire human race. 'I can't wait' P. G. Wodehouse murmured.
Malcolm Muggeridge: Tread Softly for You Tread On My Jokes

3 Other people are quite dreadful. The only possible society is oneself.
Oscar Wilde: An Ideal Husband, III

MISFORTUNE

See also sorrow

1 It is easy to bear the misfortunes of others.
Proverb

2 It never rains but it pours.
Proverb

3 Calamities are of two kinds. Misfortune to ourselves and good fortune to others.
Ambrose Bierce: The Devil's Dictionary

4 A chapter of accidents.
Earl of Chesterfield: Letter to his son, 16 Feb 1753

5 We are all strong enough to bear the misfortunes of others.
Duc de la Rochefoucauld: Maximes, 19

6 When sorrows come, they come not single spies,
But in battalions!
William Shakespeare: Hamlet, IV:5

MISOGYNY

See also women

1 How can I possibly dislike a sex to which Your Majesty belongs?
Cecil Rhodes: Replying to Queen Victoria's suggestion that he disliked women. Rhodes (Lockhart)

2 Would you have me speak after my custom, as being a professed tyrant to their sex?
William Shakespeare: Much Ado About Nothing, I:1

MISQUOTATIONS

1 Misquotations are the only

quotations that are never mis-quoted.

Hesketh Pearson: Common Misquotations

2 We have ways of making men talk.

Anonymous: Film catchphrase, often repeated as 'We have ways of making you talk'. Lives of a Bengal Lancer

3 That's one small step for man, one giant leap for mankind.

Neil Armstrong: Said on stepping onto the moon. Often quoted as, 'small step for a man…' (which is probably what he intended). Remark, 21 July 1969

4 Then said Jesus unto him, Put up again thy sword into his place: for all they that take the sword shall perish with the sword.

Bible: Matthew 26:52: Often misquoted as 'They that live by the sword shall die by the sword'.

5 Pride goeth before destruction, and an haughty spirit before a fall.

Bible: Proverbs 16:18: Often misquoted as 'Pride goeth before a fall'.

6 Play it, Sam. Play 'As Time Goes By.'

Humphrey Bogart: Often misquoted as 'Play it again, Sam'. Casablanca

7 You dirty double-crossing rat!

James Cagney: Usually misquoted by impressionists as 'You dirty rat'. Blonde Crazy

8 'Excellent!' I cried. 'Elementary,' said he.

Arthur Conan Doyle: Watson talking to Sherlock Holmes; Holmes's reply is often misquoted as 'Elementary, my dear Watson'. The Crooked Man

9 I got there fustest with the mostest.

Nathan Bedford Forrest: Popular misquotation of his explanation of his success in capturing Murfreesboro; his actual words were, 'I just took the short cut and got there first with the most men'. A Civil War Treasury (B. Botkin)

10 I never said, 'I want to be alone.' I only said, 'I want to be *left* alone.' There is all the difference.

Greta Garbo: Garbo (John Bainbridge)

11 I am happy now that Charles calls on my bedchamber less frequently than of old. As it is, I now endure but two calls a week and when I hear his steps outside my door I lie down on my bed, close my eyes, open my legs and think of England.

Lady Alice Hillingdon: Often mistakenly attributed to Queen Victoria. Journal (1912)

12 Alas, poor Yorick! I knew him, Horatio: a fellow of infinite jest, of most excellent fancy.

William Shakespeare: Often misquoted as 'I knew him well'. Hamlet, V:1

13 I always did like a man in uniform. And that one fits you grand. Why don't you come up sometime and see me?

Mae West: Often misquoted as 'Come up and see me some time'. She Done Him Wrong, film 1933

MISTAKES

1 Two wrongs do not make a right.
Proverb

2 It is worse than immoral, it's a mistake.
Dean Acheson: Describing the Vietnam war. Quoted by Alistair Cooke in his radio programme Letter from America

3 The weak have one weapon: the errors of those who think they are strong.
Georges Bidault: The Observer, 1962

4 What we call experience is often a dreadful list of ghastly mistakes.
J. Chalmers Da Costa: The Trials and Triumphs of the Surgeon, Ch. 1

5 Yes, once – many, many years ago. I thought I had made a wrong decision. Of course, it turned out that I had been right all along. But I was wrong to have *thought* that I was wrong.
John Foster Dulles: On being asked whether he had ever been wrong. Facing the Music (H. Temianka)

6 The man who makes no mistakes does not usually make anything.
Edward John Phelps: Speech, Mansion House, London, 24 Jan 1899

7 Dentopedology is the science of opening your mouth and putting your foot in it. I've been practising it for years.
Prince Philip: Attrib.

8 To err is human, to forgive, divine.

Alexander Pope: An Essay on Criticism

9 What time is the next swan?
Leo Slezak: When the mechanical swan left the stage without him during a performance of Lohengrin. What Time Is the Next Swan? (Walter Slezak)

10 Human blunders usually do more to shape history than human wickedness.
A. J. P. Taylor: The Origins of the Second World War, Ch. 10

11 Well, if I called the wrong number, why did you answer the phone?
James Thurber: Cartoon caption

12 The physician can bury his mistakes, but the architect can only advise his client to plant vines.
Frank Lloyd Wright: The New York Times Magazine, 4 Oct 1953

MISTRUST

1 While I see many hoof-marks going in, I see none coming out.
Aesop: Fables, 'The Lion, the Fox, and the Beasts'

2 The lion and the calf shall lie down together but the calf won't get much sleep.
Woody Allen: Without Feathers, 'The Scrolls'

3 But if he does really think that there is no distinction between virtue and vice, why, Sir, when he leaves our houses let us count our spoons.
Samuel Johnson: Life of Johnson (J. Boswell), Vol. I

4 Quis custodiet ipsos custodes?

Who is to guard the guards
themselves?
Juvenal: Satires, VI

5 *Equo ne credite, Teucri.*
Quidquid id est timeo Danaos et
dona ferentis.
Do not trust the horse, Trojans.
Whatever it is, I fear the Greeks
even when they bring gifts.
Virgil: Aeneid, Bk. II

MIXED METAPHORS

1 If you open that Pandora's Box
you never know what Trojan
'orses will jump out.
Ernest Bevin: Referring to the
Council of Europe. Ernest Bevin
and the Foreign Office (Sir
Roderick Barclay)

2 Every director bites the hand
that lays the golden egg.
Samuel Goldwyn: Attrib.

3 Mr Speaker, I smell a rat; I see
him forming in the air and dark-
ening the sky; but I'll nip him in
the bud.
Boyle Roche: Attrib.

MODERATION

1 Moderation in all things.
Proverb

2 I have changed my ministers,
but I have not changed my
measures; I am still for moderation and will govern by it.
Queen Anne: To members of the
new Tory ministry, Jan 1711

3 Moderation is a virtue only in
those who are thought to have
an alternative.
Henry Kissinger: The Observer,
24 Jan 1982

4 What have I gained by health?
intolerable dullness. What by
early hours and moderate
meals? – a total blank.
Charles Lamb: Letter to William
Wordsworth, 22 Jan 1830

MODESTY

1 Nurse, take away the candle and
spare my blushes.
Henry James: On being informed,
whilst confined to his bed, that he
had been awarded the Order of
Merit. The American Treasury
(C. Fadiman)

2 In some remote regions of Islam
it is said, a woman caught un-
veiled by a stranger will raise her
skirt to cover her face.
Raymond Mortimer: Colette

3 Be modest! It is the kind of
pride least likely to offend.
Jules Renard: Journal

4 The nuns who never take a bath
without wearing a bathrobe all
the time. When asked why, since
no man can see them, they reply
'Oh, but you forget the good
God.'
Bertrand Russell: The Basic
Writings, Pt. II, Ch. 7

5 Put off your shame with your
clothes when you go in to your
husband, and put it on again
when you come out.
Theano: Lives, Teachings, and
Sayings of Famous Philosophers;
Pythagoras, Bk VIII (Diogenes
Laertius)

MONARCHY

See also royalty

1 *Rex illiteratus, asinus coronatus.*
An unlettered king is a crowned
ass.
Anonymous

2 The Sovereign has, under a constitutional monarchy such as
ours, three rights – the right to
be consulted, the right to encourage, the right to warn.
*Walter Bagehot: The English
Constitution, 'The Monarchy'*

3 If everything became entirely
based on politics, I think this
country would lose a great deal.
*Charles, Prince of Wales: His
views on the abolition of the
monarchy. ITV programme
Charles: The Private Man, the
Public Role, 29 June 1994*

4 There is no middle course between the throne and the scaffold.
*Charles X: Said to Talleyrand,
who is said to have replied 'You are
forgetting the postchaise'. Attrib.*

5 The influence of the Crown has
increased, is increasing, and
ought to be diminished.
*John Dunning: Motion passed by
the House of Commons, 1780*

6 There will soon be only five
kings left – the Kings of England, Diamonds, Hearts, Spades
and Clubs.
*Farouk I: Remark made to Lord
Boyd-Orr*

7 The right divine of kings to govern wrong.
Alexander Pope: The Dunciad, IV

8 Every subject's duty is the
King's; but every subject's soul
is his own.
*William Shakespeare: Henry V,
IV:1*

9 The monarchy is a labour-
intensive industry.
*Harold Wilson: The Observer,
13 Feb 1977*

MONEY

See also economics, extravagance,
greed, materialism

1 Take care of the pence, and the
pounds will take care of themselves.
Proverb

2 I can't afford to waste my time
making money.
*Jean Louis Rodolphe Agassiz:
When asked to give a lecture for a
fee. Attrib.*

3 It does seem to be true that the
more you get the more you
spend. It is rather like being on a
golden treadmill.
Charles Allsop: Remark, Dec 1988

4 Money, it turned out, was exactly like sex, you thought of
nothing else if you didn't have it
and thought of other things if
you did.
*James Baldwin: Nobody Knows
My Name*

5 For the love of money is the root
of all evil: which while some coveted after, they have erred from
the faith, and pierced themselves through with many sorrows.
Bible: I Timothy: 6:10

6 It has been said that the love of
money is the root of all evil. The
want of money is so quite as
truly.
Samuel Butler: Erewhon, Ch. 20

7 It is a kind of spiritual snobbery
that makes people think that

they can be happy without money.
Albert Camus: Notebooks, 1935–1942

8 Where large sums of money are concerned, it is advisable to trust nobody.
Agatha Christie: Endless Night, Bk. II, Ch. 15

9 Making money is pretty pointless and it needs constant attention.
Adam Faith: The Observer, 'Sayings of the Week', 8 May 1994

10 It is only the poor who pay cash, and that not from virtue, but because they are refused credit.
Anatole France: A Cynic's Breviary (J. R. Solly)

11 If possible honestly, if not, somehow, make money.
Horace: Epistles, I

12 We all know how the size of sums of money appears to vary in a remarkable way according as they are being paid in or paid out.
Julian Huxley: Essays of a Biologist, I

13 You don't seem to realize that a poor person who is unhappy is in a better position than a rich person who is unhappy. Because the poor person has hope. He thinks money would help.
Jean Kerr: Poor Richard

14 For I don't care too much for money,
For money can't buy me love.
John Lennon: Can't Buy Me Love (with Paul McCartney)

15 Money can't buy friends, but you can get a better class of enemy.
Spike Milligan: Puckoon, Ch. 6

16 Money is like manure. If you spread it around it does a lot of good. But if you pile it up in one place it stinks like hell.
Clint Murchison Jnr: Time Magazine, 16 June 1961

17 Some people's money is merited
And other people's is inherited.
Ogden Nash: The Terrible People

18 Check enclosed.
Dorothy Parker: Giving her version of the two most beautiful words in the English language. Attrib.

19 Lack of money is the root of all evil.
George Bernard Shaw: Man and Superman, 'Maxims for Revolutionists.'

20 I think I could be a good woman if I had five thousand a year.
William Makepeace Thackeray: Vanity Fair, Ch. 36

21 No one would have remembered the Good Samaritan if he'd only had good intentions. He had money as well.
Margaret Thatcher: Television interview, 1980

22 The easiest way for your children to learn about money is for you not to have any.
Katharine Whitehorn: How to Survive Children

MOON

See also space, universe

1 who knows if the moon's

a balloon, coming out of a keen
city
in the sky – filled with pretty
people?
e. e. cummings

2 So sicken waning moons too
near the sun,
And blunt their crescents on the
edge of day.
John Dryden: Annus Mirabilis

3 For years politicians have
promised the moon, I'm the first
one to be able to deliver it.
*Richard Milhous Nixon: Radio
message to astronauts on the moon,
20 Jul 1969*

MORALITY

See also integrity, principles,
righteousness

1 No morality can be founded on
authority, even if the authority
were divine.
A. J. Ayer: Essay on Humanism

2 Morality's not practical. Morality's a gesture. A complicated
gesture learnt from books.
*Robert Bolt: A Man for All
Seasons*

3 What is moral is what you feel
good after, and what is immoral
is what you feel bad after.
*Ernest Hemingway: Death in the
Afternoon*

4 Morality which is based on
ideas, or on an ideal, is an un-
mitigated evil.
*D. H. Lawrence: Fantasia of the
Unconscious, Ch. 1*

5 We know no spectacle so ridiculous as the British public in one
of its periodical fits of morality.

*Lord Macaulay: Literary Essays
Contributed to the 'Edinburgh
Review', 'Moore's 'Life of Lord
Byron''*

6 Morality in Europe today is
herd-morality.
*Friedrich Nietzsche: Jenseits von
Gut und Böse*

7 We have, in fact, two kinds of
morality side by side; one which
we preach but do not practise,
and another which we practise
but seldom preach.
Bertrand Russell: Sceptical Essays

8 Morality consists in suspecting
other people of not being legally
married.
*George Bernard Shaw: The
Doctor's Dilemma*

9 The so-called new morality is
too often the old immorality
condoned.
*Lord Shawcross: The Observer,
17 Nov 1963*

10 Moral indignation is in most
cases 2 percent moral, 48 percent indignation and 50 percent
envy.
*Vittorio de Sica: The Observer,
1961*

11 If your morals make you
dreary, depend upon it, they are
wrong.
*Robert Louis Stevenson: Across the
Plains*

12 Victorian values…were the values when our country became
great.
*Margaret Thatcher: Television
interview, 1982*

MORTALITY

See also death, human condition

1 All men are mortal.
Proverb

2 Mortality, behold and fear!
What a change of flesh is here!
Francis Beaumont: On the Tombs in Westminster Abbey

3 I was not unaware that I had begotten a mortal.
Goethe: On learning of his son's death. The Story of Civilization (W. Durant), Vol. X

4 Life's short span forbids us to enter on far-reaching hopes.
Horace: Odes, I

5 I am moved to pity, when I think of the brevity of human life, seeing that of all this host of men not one will still be alive in a hundred years' time.
Xerxes: On surveying his army.

MOTHERHOOD

See also babies, birth, children

1 The best thing that could happen to motherhood already has. Fewer women are going into it.
Victoria Billings: Womansbook, 'Meeting Your Personal Needs'

2 Motherhood meant I have written four fewer books, but I know more about life.
A. S. Byatt: The Sunday Times, 21 Oct 1990

3 An author who speaks about his own books is almost as bad as a mother who talks about her own children.
Benjamin Disraeli: Speech in Glasgow, 19 Nov 1873

4 Claudia...had realised with astonishment that the perfect couple consisted of a mother and child and not, as she had always supposed, a man and woman.
Alice Thomas Ellis: The Other Side of the Fire

5 Mother is the dead heart of the family; spending father's earnings on consumer goods to enhance the environment in which he eats, sleeps and watches the television.
Germaine Greer: The Female Eunuch

6 Now, as always, the most automated appliance in a household is the mother.
Beverly Jones: The Florida Paper on Women's Liberation

7 Who has not watched a mother stroke her child's cheek or kiss her child *in a certain way* and felt a nervous shudder at the possessive outrage born to a free solitary human soul?
John Cowper Powys: The Meaning of Culture

8 A mother! What are we worth really? They all grow up whether you look after them or not.
Christina Stead: The Man Who Loved Children, Ch. 10

MOTIVE

See also purpose

1 Never ascribe to an opponent motives meaner than your own.
J. M. Barrie: Speech, St Andrews, 3 May 1922

2 Because it is there.
George Mallory: Answer to the question 'Why do you want to climb Mt. Everest?' George Mallory (D. Robertson)

3 Men are rewarded and pun-

ished not for what they do, but
rather for how their acts are defined. This is why men are more
interested in better justifying
themselves than in better behaving themselves.
Thomas Szasz: The Second Sin

MOURNING

See also death, loss, regret, sorrow

1 We met...Dr Hall in such very
deep mourning that either his
mother, his wife, or himself
must be dead.
*Jane Austen: Letter to Cassandra
Austen, 17 May 1799*

2 With proud thanksgiving, a
mother for her children,
England mourns for her dead
across the sea.
*Laurence Binyon: In response to
the slaughter of World War I.
Poems For the Fallen*

3 What we call mourning for our
dead is perhaps not so much
grief as not being able to call
them back as it is grief at not being able to want to do so.
*Thomas Mann: The Magic
Mountain*

4 Alas, poor Yorick! I knew him,
Horatio: a fellow of infinite jest,
of most excellent fancy.
*William Shakespeare: Hamlet,
V:1*

5 Home they brought her warrior
dead.
She nor swoon'd, nor utter'd
cry:
All her maidens, watching said,
'She must weep or she will die.'
*Alfred, Lord Tennyson: The
Princess, VI*

MURDER

See also assassination, killing

1 And the Lord said unto Cain,
Where is Abel thy brother? And
he said, I know not: Am I my
brother's keeper?
And he said, What hast thou
done? the voice of thy brother's
blood crieth unto me from the
ground.
Bible: Genesis: 4:9

2 I've been accused of every death
except the casualty list of the
World War.
*Al Capone: The Bootleggers
(Kenneth Allsop), Ch. 11*

3 Mordre wol out, that see we day
by day.
*Geoffrey Chaucer: The
Canterbury Tales, 'The Nun's
Priest's Tale'*

4 Murder considered as one of the
Fine Arts.
Thomas De Quincey: Essay title

5 Murder, like talent, seems occa-
sionally to run in families.
*G. H. Lewes: The Physiology of
Common Life, Ch. 12*

6 Murder most foul, as in the best
it is;
But this most foul, strange, and
unnatural.
William Shakespeare: Hamlet, I:5

7 Other sins only speak; murder
shrieks out.
*John Webster: The Duchess of
Malfi, IV:2*

8 The person by far the most likely to kill you is yourself.
*Jock Young: The Observer,
'Sayings of the Week', 8 May
1994*

MUSIC

See also opera

1 Nothing is capable of being well set to music that is not non-sense.
Joseph Addison: The Spectator, 18

2 A musicologist is a man who can read music but can't hear it.
Thomas Beecham: Beecham Remembered (H. Procter-Gregg)

3 The English may not like music – but they absolutely love the noise it makes.
Thomas Beecham: The Wit of Music (L. Ayre)

4 When I composed that, I was conscious of being inspired by God Almighty. Do you think I can consider your puny little fiddle when He speaks to me?
Ludwig van Beethoven: Said when a violinist complained that a passage was unplayable. Music All Around Me (A. Hopkins)

5 Down South where I come from you don't go around hitting too many white keys.
Eubie Blake: When asked why his compositions contained so many sharps and flats. Attrib.

6 Music has charms to soothe a savage breast.
William Congreve: The Mourning Bride, I

7 Strange how potent cheap music is.
Noël Coward: Private Lives

8 Music is the arithmetic of sounds as optics is the geometry of light.
Claude Debussy: Attrib.

9 There is music in the air, music all round us: the world is full of it, and you simply take as much as you require.
Edward Elgar: Basil Maine, Elgar, his Life and Works

10 The hills are alive with the sound of music
With the songs they have sung
For a thousand years.
Oscar Hammerstein: The Sound of Music, title song

11 Never compose anything unless the not composing of it becomes a positive nuisance to you.
Gustav Holst: Letter to W. G. Whittaker

12 The only sensual pleasure without vice.
Samuel Johnson: Referring to music. Johnsonian Miscellanies (ed. G. B. Hill), Vol. II

13 There's sure no passion in the human soul,
But finds its food in music.
George Lillo: Fatal Curiosity, I:2

14 Music, Maestro, Please.
Herb Magidson: Song title

15 Every day people come forward with new songs. Music goes on forever.
Bob Marley: Attrib.

16 Music is not written in red, white and blue. It is written in the heart's blood of the composer.
Nellie Melba: Melodies and Memories

17 Music is your own experience, your thoughts, your wisdom. If you don't live it, it won't come out of your horn.
Charlie Parker: Hear Me Talkin' to Ya (Nat Shapiro and Nat Hentoff)

18 If music be the food of love,
play on,
Give me excess of it, that, sur-
feiting,
The appetite may sicken and so
die.
*William Shakespeare: Twelfth
Night, I:1*

19 I don't write modern music. I
only write good music.
*Igor Stravinsky: To journalists on
his first visit to America, 1925*

MUSICIANS

1 Musicians don't retire; they stop
when there's no more music in
them.
*Louis Armstrong: The Observer,
'Sayings of the Week', 21 Apr
1968*

2 The public doesn't want a new
music: the main thing it demands of a composer is that he
be dead.
Arthur Honegger: Attrib.

3 The conductor has the advantage of not seeing the audience.
André Kostalenetz: Attrib.

MYTHS

1 Science must begin with myths,
and with the criticism of myths.
*Karl Popper: British Philosophy in
the Mid-Century (ed. C. A.
Mace)*

2 A myth is, of course, not a fairy
story. It is the presentation of
facts belonging to one category
in the idioms appropriate to another. To explode a myth is ac-
cordingly not to deny the facts
but to re-allocate them.
*Gilbert Ryle: The Concept of
Mind, Introduction*

NAKEDNESS

1 Lives there the man that can figure a naked Duke of Windlestraw addressing a naked House of Lords?
Thomas Carlyle: Sartor Resartus, Bk. I, Ch. 9

2 a pretty girl who naked is
is worth a million statues.
e. e. cummings: Collected Poems, 133

3 How idiotic civilization is! Why be given a body if you have to keep it shut up in a case like a rare, rare fiddle?
Katherine Mansfield: Bliss and Other Stories, 'Bliss'

4 JOURNALIST. Didn't you have anything on?
M. M. I had the radio on.
Marilyn Monroe: Attrib.

NAMES

1 A nickname is the heaviest stone that the devil can throw at a man.
William Hazlitt: Nicknames

2 No, Groucho is not my real name. I'm breaking it in for a friend.
Groucho Marx: Attrib.

3 What's in a name? That which we call a rose
By any other name would smell as sweet.
William Shakespeare: Romeo and Juliet, II:2

NASTINESS

See also cruelty, hurt

1 I do not want people to be very agreeable, as it saves me the trouble of liking them a great deal.
Jane Austen: Letter, 24 Dec 1798

2 One of the worst things about life is not how nasty the nasty people are. You know that already. It is how nasty the nice people can be.
Anthony Powell: A Dance to the Music of Time: The Kindly Ones, Ch. 4

3 I can't see that she could have found anything nastier to say if she'd thought it out with both hands for a fortnight.
Dorothy L. Sayers: Busman's Holiday, 'Prothalamion'

4 'I grant you that he's not two-faced,' I said. 'But what's the use of that when the one face he has got is so peculiarly unpleasant?'
C. P. Snow: The Affair, Ch. 4

NATIONALITY

1 The French are wiser than they seem, and the Spaniards seem wiser than they are.
Francis Bacon: Essays, 'Of Seeming Wise'

2 One of themselves, even a prophet of their own, said, The Cretians are alway liars, evil beasts, slow bellies.
Bible: Titus: 1:12

3 Great artists have no country.

Alfred de Musset: Lorenzaccio, I:5

4 I am not an Athenian or a Greek, but a citizen of the world.
Socrates: Of Banishment (Plutarch)

5 We are all American at puberty; we die French.
Evelyn Waugh: Diaries, 'Irregular Notes', 18 July 1961

NATURE

See also animals, countryside, ecology

1 Nature admits no lie.
Thomas Carlyle: Latter-Day Pamphlets, 5

2 Is ditchwater dull? Naturalists with microscopes have told me that it teems with quiet fun.
G. K. Chesterton: The Spice of Life

3 All my life through, the new sights of Nature made me rejoice like a child.
Marie Curie: Pierre Curie

4 By viewing Nature, Nature's handmaid, art,
Makes mighty things from small beginnings grow.
John Dryden: Annus Mirabilis

5 The irregular side of nature, the discontinuous and erratic side – these have been puzzles to science, or worse, monstrosities.
James Gleick: Chaos (1987)

6 Though you drive away Nature with a pitchfork she always returns.
Horace: Epistles, I

7 Nature is as wasteful of promising young men as she is of fish spawn.

Richard Hughes: The Fox in the Attic

8 The whole of nature is a conjugation of the verb to eat, in the active and the passive.
Dean Inge: Outspoken Essays

9 Nature is very consonant and conformable with herself.
Isaac Newton: Opticks, Bk. III

10 Nature abhors a vacuum.
François Rabelais: Attrib.

11 Nature has always had more power than education.
Voltaire: Vie de Molière

12 Nature is usually wrong.
James Whistler: The Gentle Art of Making Enemies

13 A vacuum is a hell of a lot better than some of the stuff that nature replaces it with.
Tennessee Williams: Cat On A Hot Tin Roof

NAVY

See also boats, officers, sea, war

1 We joined the Navy, to see the world
And what did we see? We saw the sea.
Irving Berlin: Song

2 Don't talk to me about naval tradition. It's nothing but rum, sodomy, and the lash.
Winston Churchill: Former Naval Person (Sir Peter Gretton), Ch. 1

3 I do not say the French cannot come, I only say they cannot come by sea.
John Jervis, Earl St Vincent: Remark to the Cabinet, 1803

NAZISM

See also fascism, World War II

1 *Ein Reich, Ein Volk, Ein Führer.*
One Realm, One People, One
Leader.
*Anonymous: Slogan of the Nazi
Party; first used at Nuremberg,
Sept 1934*

2 In Germany, the Nazis came for
the Communists and I didn't
speak up because I was not a
Communist. Then they came
for the Jews and I didn't speak
up because I was not a Jew.
Then they came for the trade
unionists and I didn't speak up
because I was not a trade unionist. Then they came for the
Catholics and I was a Protestant
so I didn't speak up. Then they
came for me...By that time there
was no one to speak up for anyone.
*Martin Niemöller: Concise
Dictionary of Religious Quotations
(W. Neil)*

NECESSITY

1 Beggars can't be choosers.
Proverb

2 Necessity is the mother of invention.
Proverb

3 Needs must when the devil dri-
ves.
Proverb

4 Necessity is the plea for every
infringement of human freedom. It is the argument of
tyrants; it is the creed of slaves.
*William Pitt the Younger: Speech,
House of Commons, 18 Nov 1783*

5 Teach thy necessity to reason
thus:
There is no virtue like necessity.
*William Shakespeare: Richard II,
I:3*

6 Necessity knows no law.
Publilius Syrus: Attrib.

NEGLECT

1 A little neglect may breed mischief...for want of a nail, the
shoe was lost; for want of a shoe
the horse was lost; and for want
of a horse the rider was lost.
*Benjamin Franklin: Poor
Richard's Almanack*

2 What time he can spare from
the adornment of his person he
devotes to the neglect of his du-
ties.
*William Hepworth Thompson:
Referring to the Cambridge
Professor of Greek, Sir Richard
Jebb. With Dearest Love to All
(M. R. Bobbit), Ch. 7*

NEIGHBOURS

1 Love your neighbour, yet pull
not down your hedge.
Proverb

2 Thou shalt love thy neighbour
as thy self.
Bible: Matthew: 22:39

3 For it is your business, when the
wall next door catches fire.
Horace: Epistles, I

NEUROSIS

See also psychiatry, psychology
1 Neurosis is always a substitute
for legitimate suffering.

Carl Gustav Jung

2 This is, I think, very much the Age of Anxiety, the age of the neurosis, because along with so much that weighs on our minds there is perhaps even more that grates on our nerves.
Louis Kronenberger: Company Manners, 'The Spirit of the Age'

3 Modern neurosis began with the discoveries of Copernicus. Science made man feel small by showing him that the earth was not the center of the universe.
Mary McCarthy: On the Contrary, 'Tyranny of the Orgasm'

4 Freud is all nonsense; the secret of neurosis is to be found in the family battle of wills to see who can refuse longest to help with the dishes.
Julian Mitchell: As Far as You Can Go, I, Ch. 1

5 Everything great in the world is done by neurotics; they alone founded our religions and created our masterpieces.
Marcel Proust: The Perpetual Pessimist (Sagittarius and George)

6 Neurosis is the way of avoiding non-being by avoiding being.
Paul Tillich: The Courage to Be

NEWSPAPERS

See also journalism, media

1 Reading someone else's newspaper is like sleeping with someone else's wife. Nothing seems to be precisely in the right place, and when you find what you are looking for, it is not clear then how to respond to it.

Malcolm Bradbury: Stepping Westward, Bk. I, Ch. 1

2 *The Times* is speechless and takes three columns to express its speechlessness.
Winston Churchill: Referring to Irish Home Rule. Speech, Dundee, 14 May 1908

3 Nothing is news until it has appeared in *The Times*.
Ralph Deakin: Attrib.

4 And when it's gay priests, even the tabloids suddenly find they have a religious affairs correspondent.
David Hare: The Sunday Times, 11 Feb 1990

5 All the news that's fit to print.
Adolph Simon Ochs: The motto of The New York Times

6 Never believe in mirrors or newspapers.
John Osborne: The Hotel in Amsterdam

7 They have been just as spiteful to me in the American press as the Soviet press was.
Alexander Solzhenitsyn: The Observer, 'Sayings of the Week', 1 May 1994

8 News is what a chap who doesn't care much about anything wants to read. And it's only news until he's read it. After that it's dead.
Evelyn Waugh: Scoop, Bk. I, Ch. 5

NOBILITY

See also aristocracy

1 Real nobility is based on scorn, courage, and profound indifference.

Albert Camus: Notebooks

2 *Noblesse oblige.*
Nobility has its own obligations.
Duc de Lévis: Maximes et Réflexions

3 Thou hast a grim appearance,
and thy face
Bears a command in't; though
thy tackle's torn,
Thou show'st a noble vessel.
What's thy name?
William Shakespeare: Coriolanus, IV:5

NOSTALGIA

See also memory, past

1 The 'good old times' – all times
when old are good –
Are gone.
Lord Byron: The Age of Bronze, I

2 Nothing recalls the past so po-
tently as a smell.
Winston Churchill: My Early Life

3 Despair abroad can always
nurse pleasant thoughts of
home.
Christopher Fry: A Phoenix Too Frequent

4 Yesterday, all my troubles
seemed so far away.
John Lennon: Yesterday (with Paul McCartney)

5 Fings Ain't Wot They Used
T'Be.
Frank Norman: Title of musical

6 Before the war, and especially
before the Boer War, it was summer all the year round.
George Orwell: Coming Up for Air, Pt. II, Ch. 1

7 They spend their time mostly
looking forward to the past.

John Osborne: Look Back in Anger, I

8 The earth's about five thousand
million years old. Who can afford to live in the past?
Harold Pinter: The Homecoming

9 We have seen better days.
William Shakespeare: Timon of Athens, IV:2

10 Sweet childish days, that were
as long
As twenty days are now.
William Wordsworth: To a Butterfly, I've Watched You Now

NOTHING

1 Nothing can be created out of
nothing.
Lucretius: On the Nature of the Universe, I

2 Nothing, like something, happens anywhere.
Philip Larkin: I Remember, I Remember

NOVELS

See also books, fiction, literature,
writing

1 My scrofulous French novel
On grey paper with blunt type!
Robert Browning: Soliloquy of the Spanish Cloister

2 When I want to read a novel I
write one.
Benjamin Disraeli: Attrib.

3 Historians tell the story of the
past, novelists the story of the
present.
Edmond de Goncourt: Journal

4 Far too many relied on the classic formula of a beginning, a
muddle, and an end.

Philip Larkin: Referring to modern novels. New Fiction, 15 (January 1978)

5 It is the sexless novel that should be distinguished: the sex novel is now normal.
George Bernard Shaw: Table-Talk of G.B.S.

6 A novel is a mirror walking along a main road.
Stendhal: Le Rouge et le noir, Ch. 49

7 The novel being dead, there is no point to writing made-up stories. Look at the French who will not and the Americans who cannot.
Gore Vidal: Myra Breckinridge, Ch. 2

NOVELTY

See also conservatism, progress

1 There are three things which the public will always clamour for, sooner or later: namely, Novelty, novelty, novelty.
Thomas Hood: Announcement of Comic Annual, 1836

2 It is the customary fate of new truths to begin as heresies and to end as superstitions.
T. H. Huxley: The Coming of Age of the Origin of Species

3 New opinions are always suspected, and usually without any other reason but because they are not already common.
John Locke: An Essay Concerning Human Understanding, dedicatory epistle

4 There is always something new out of Africa.
Pliny the Elder: Natural History, VIII

5 All great truths begin as blasphemies.
George Bernard Shaw: Annajanska

6 If we do not find anything pleasant, at least we shall find something new.
Voltaire: Candide, Ch. 17

NUCLEAR WEAPONS

See also weapons

1 Ban the bomb.
Anonymous: Slogan of nuclear disarmament campaigners

2 Better red than dead.
Anonymous: Slogan of the British nuclear disarmament movement

3 The way to win an atomic war is to make certain it never starts.
Omar Nelson Bradley: The Observer, 'Sayings of the Week', 20 Apr 1952

4 The Bomb brought peace but man alone can keep that peace.
Winston Churchill: Speech, House of Commons, 16 Aug 1945

5 If only I had known, I should have become a watchmaker.
Albert Einstein: Reflecting on his role in the development of the atom bomb. New Statesman, 16 Apr 1965

6 Surely the right course is to test the Russians, not the bombs.
Hugh Gaitskell: The Observer, 'Sayings of the Week', 23 June 1957

7 Hitherto man had to live with the idea of death as an individual; from now onward mankind

will have to live with the idea of its death as a species.
Arthur Koestler: Referring to the development of the atomic bomb. Peter's Quotations (Laurence J. Peter)

8 At first it was a giant column that soon took the shape of a supramundane mushroom.
William L. Laurence: Referring to the explosion of the first atomic bomb, over Hiroshima, 6 Aug 1945. The New York Times, 26 Sept 1945

9 The atom bomb is a paper tiger which the United States reactionaries use to scare people.
Mao Tse-Tung: Interview, Aug 1946

10 I am become death, the destroyer of worlds.
J. Robert Oppenheimer: Quoting Vishnu from the Gita, at the first atomic test in New Mexico, 16 July 1945. Attrib.

11 To adopt nuclear disarmament would be akin to behaving like a virgin in a brothel.
David Penhaligon: The Guardian, 1980

12 You may reasonably expect a man to walk a tightrope safely for ten minutes; it would be unreasonable to do so without accident for two hundred years.
Bertrand Russell: On the subject of nuclear war. The Tightrope Men (D. Bagley)

13 Man has wrested from nature the power to make the world a desert or to make the deserts bloom. There is no evil in the atom, only in men's souls.
Adlai Stevenson: Speech, Hartford, Connecticut, 18 Sept 1952

14 For Hon. Members opposite the deterrent is a phallic symbol. It convinces them that they are men.
George Wigg: The Observer, 'Sayings of the Week', 8 Mar 1964

NUMBERS

See also mathematics, statistics

1 Round numbers are always false.
Samuel Johnson: Life of Johnson (J. Boswell), Vol. III

2 No, I don't know his telephone number. But it was up in the high numbers.
John Maynard Keynes: Attrib.

3 No, it is a very interesting number, it is the smallest number expressible as a sum of two cubes in two different ways.
Srinivasa Ramanujan: The mathematician G. H. Hardy had referred to the number '1729' as 'dull'. Collected Papers of Srinivasa Ramanujan

OBESITY

See also food, greed

1 Outside every fat man there is an even fatter man trying to close in.
Kingsley Amis: See also CONNOLLY, ORWELL. One Fat Englishman, Ch. 3

2 Just the other day in the Underground I enjoyed the pleasure of offering my seat to three ladies.
G. K. Chesterton: Suggesting that fatness has its consolations. Das Buch des Lachens (W. Scholz)

3 Imprisoned in every fat man a thin one is wildly signalling to be let out.
Cyril Connolly: See also AMIS, ORWELL. The Unquiet Grave

4 Obesity is a mental state, a disease brought on by boredom and disappointment.
Cyril Connolly: The Unquiet Grave

5 I'm fat, but I'm thin inside. Has it ever struck you that there's a thin man inside every fat man, just as they say there's a statue inside every block of stone?
George Orwell: See also AMIS, CONNOLLY. Coming Up For Air, Pt. I, Ch. 3

6 Enclosing every thin man, there's a fat man demanding elbow-room.
Evelyn Waugh: Officers and Gentlemen, Interlude

7 Outside every thin girl there is a fat man trying to get in.
Katharine Whitehorn: Attrib.

8 The Right Hon. was a tubby little chap who looked as if he had been poured into his clothes and had forgotten to say 'When!'
P. G. Wodehouse: Very Good Jeeves!, 'Jeeves and the Impending Doom'

OBITUARIES

See also death, epitaphs, funerals, memorials

1 I have never killed a man, but I have read many obituaries with a lot of pleasure.
Clarence Seward Darrow: Medley

2 I've just read that I am dead. Don't forget to delete me from your list of subscribers.
Rudyard Kipling: Writing to a magazine that had mistakenly published an announcement of his death. Anekdotenschatz (H. Hoffmeister)

3 You should have known that it was not easy for me to die. But, tell me, were my obituaries good?
Makarios

4 Reports of my death are greatly exaggerated.
Mark Twain: On learning that his obituary had been published. Cable to the Associated Press

OBJECTIVITY

1 I am a camera with its shutter open, quite passive, recording, not thinking.
Christopher Isherwood: Goodbye to Berlin

2 The man who sees both sides of a question is a man who sees absolutely nothing at all.
Oscar Wilde: The Critic as Artist, Pt. 2

OBSTRUCTION

1 I'll put a spoke among your wheels.
Francis Beaumont: The Mad Lover, III:6

2 If any of you know cause, or just impediment.
The Book of Common Prayer: Solemnization of Matrimony

OCCUPATIONS

1 Jack of all trades, master of none.
Proverb

2 Doctors bury their mistakes. Lawyers hang them. But journalists put theirs on the front page.
Anonymous

3 The ugliest of trades have their moments of pleasure. Now, if I were a grave-digger, or even a hangman, there are some people I could work for with a great deal of enjoyment.
Douglas William Jerrold: Wit and Opinions of Douglas Jerrold, 'Ugly Trades'

4 The best careers advice to give to the young is 'Find out what you like doing best and get someone to pay you for doing it.'
Katharine Whitehorn: The Observer, 1975

OFFICERS

See also army, navy, soldiers, war

1 Any officer who shall behave in a scandalous manner, unbecoming the character of an officer and a gentleman shall…be cashiered.
Anonymous: The words 'conduct unbecoming the character of an officer' are a direct quotation from the Naval Discipline Act (10 Aug 1860), Article 24. Articles of War (1872), Disgraceful Conduct, 79

2 War is too important to be left to the generals.
Georges Clemenceau: A similar remark is attributed to another French statesman, Talleyrand (1754–1838). Attrib.

3 It is not the business of generals to shoot one another.
Duke of Wellington: Refusing an artillery officer permission to fire upon Napoleon himself during the Battle of Waterloo, 1815. Attrib.

OLD AGE

See also age, longevity

1 Man fools himself. He prays for a long life, and he fears an old age.
Chinese proverb

2 Forty is the old age of youth; fifty is the youth of old age.
French proverb

3 Old men are twice children.
Greek proverb

4 Dying while young is a boon in old age.
Yiddish proverb

5 Everyone faces at all times two

fateful possibilities: one is to grow older, the other not.
Anonymous

6 I will never be an old man. To me, old age is always fifteen years older than I am.
Bernard Baruch: The Observer 'Sayings of the Week', 21 Aug 1955

7 No one ever speaks of 'a beautiful old woman'.
Simone de Beauvoir: The Coming of Age

8 Tranquillity comes with years, and that horrid thing which Freud calls sex is expunged.
E. F. Benson: Mapp and Lucia

9 To be old is to be part of a huge and ordinary multitude…the reason why old age was venerated in the past was because it was extraordinary.
Ronald Blythe: The View in Winter

10 'You are old, Father William,' the young man said,
'And your hair has become very white;
And yet you incessantly stand on your head –
Do you think at your age, it is right?'
Lewis Carroll: See also SOUTHEY. Alice's Adventures in Wonderland, Ch. 5

11 I prefer old age to the alternative.
Maurice Chevalier: Attrib.

12 Oh to be seventy again.
Georges Clemenceau: Remark on his eightieth birthday, noticing a pretty girl in the Champs Elysées. Ego 3 (James Agate)

13 I grow old…I grow old…

I shall wear the bottoms of my trousers rolled.
T. S. Eliot: The Love Song of J. Alfred Prufrock

14 No skill or art is needed to grow old; the trick is to endure it.
Goethe

15 Time goes by: reputation increases, ability declines.
Dag Hammarskjöld: Diaries, 1964

16 Some people reach the age of 60 before others.
Lord Hood: The Observer, 'Sayings of the Week', 23 Feb 1964

17 It is so comic to hear oneself called old, even at ninety I suppose!
Alice James: Letter to William James, 14 June 1889. The Diary of Alice James (ed. Leon Edel)

18 A medical revolution has extended the life of our elder citizens without providing the dignity and security those later years deserve.
John Fitzgerald Kennedy: Acceptance speech, Democratic National Convention, Los Angeles, 15 July 1960

19 Old age is woman's hell.
Ninon de Lenclos: Attrib.

20 From the earliest times the old have rubbed it into the young that they are wiser than they, and before the young had discovered what nonsense this was they were old too, and it profited them to carry on the imposture.
W. Somerset Maugham: Cakes and Ale, Ch. 9

21 Growing old is a bad habit which a busy man has no time to form.
André Maurois: The Ageing American

22 Being seventy is not a sin.
Golda Meir: Reader's Digest (July 1971), 'The Indestructible Golda Meir'

23 Age only matters when one is ageing. Now that I have arrived at a great age, I might just as well be twenty.
Pablo Picasso: The Observer, Shouts and Murmurs, 'Picasso in Private' (John Richardson)

24 As you get older you become more boring and better behaved.
Simon Raven: The Observer 'Sayings Of the Week', 22 Aug 1976

25 Darling, I am growing old, Silver threads among the gold.
Eben Rexford: Silver Threads Among the Gold

26 Old age is a disease which we cannot cure.
Seneca: Epistulae ad Lucilium, CVIII

27 Last scene of all, That ends this strange eventful history, Is second childishness and mere oblivion; Sans teeth, sans eyes, sans taste, sans every thing.
William Shakespeare: As You Like It, II:7

28 Old men are dangerous; it doesn't matter to them what is going to happen to the world.
George Bernard Shaw: Heartbreak House

29 You are old, Father William, the young man cried, The few locks which are left you are grey; You are hale, Father William, a hearty old man, Now tell me the reason, I pray.
Robert Southey: See also CARROLL. The Old Man's Comforts, and How He Gained Them

30 Being over seventy is like being engaged in a war. All our friends are going or gone and we survive amongst the dead and the dying as on a battlefield.
Muriel Spark: Memento Mori, Ch. 4

31 Sleeping as quiet as death, side by wrinkled side, toothless, salt and brown, like two old kippers in a box.
Dylan Thomas: Under Milk Wood

32 He was either a man of about a hundred and fifty who was rather young for his years or a man of about a hundred and ten who had been aged by trouble.
P. G. Wodehouse: Wodehouse at Work to the End (Richard Usborne), Ch. 6

ONE-UPMANSHIP

See also snobbery, superiority

1 Keeping up with the Joneses was a full-time job with my mother and father. It was not until many years later when I lived alone that I realized how much cheaper it was to drag the Joneses down to my level.

Quentin Crisp: The Naked Civil Servant

2 *How to be one up* – how to make the other man feel that something has gone wrong, however slightly.

Stephen Potter: Lifemanship, Introduction

OPERA

See also music

1 Opera is like a husband with a foreign title: expensive to support, hard to understand, and therefore a supreme social challenge.

Cleveland Amory: NBC TV, 6 Apr 1960

2 I do not mind what language an opera is sung in so long as it is a language I don't understand.

Edward Appleton: The Observer, 'Sayings of the Week,' 28 Aug 1955

3 No good opera plot can be sensible, for people do not sing when they are feeling sensible.

W. H. Auden: Time, 29 Dec 1961

4 The opera isn't over till the fat lady sings.

Dan Cook: Washington Post, 13 June 1978

5 People are wrong when they say the opera isn't what it used to be. It is what it used to be. That's what's wrong with it.

Noël Coward: Design for Living

6 Opera is when a guy gets stabbed in the back and instead of bleeding he sings.

Ed Gardener: Duffy's Tavern (American radio show)

7 I sometimes wonder which

would be nicer – an opera without an interval, or an interval without an opera.

Ernest Newman: Berlioz, Romantic and Classic (ed. Peter Heyworth)

OPINIONS

See also ideas

1 We must say that the same opinions have arisen among men in cycles, not once, twice, nor a few times, but infinitely often.

Aristotle: Meteorologica

2 A man's opinion on tramcars matters; his opinion on Botticelli matters; his opinion on all things does not matter.

G. K. Chesterton: Heretics

3 Science is the father of knowledge, but opinion breeds ignorance.

Hippocrates: The Canon Law, IV

4 They that approve a private opinion, call it opinion; but they that mislike it, heresy: and yet heresy signifies no more than private opinion.

Thomas Hobbes: Leviathan, Pt. I, Ch. 11

5 The superiority of one man's opinion over another's is never so great as when the opinion is about a woman.

Henry James: The Tragic Muse, Ch. 9

6 The average man's opinions are much less foolish than they would be if he thought for himself.

Bertrand Russell: Autobiography

7 The fact that an opinion has

been widely held is no evidence whatever that it is not utterly absurd.
Bertrand Russell: Attrib.

8 I agree with no man's opinion. I have some of my own.
Ivan Turgenev: Fathers and Sons, Ch. 13

9 It is just when opinions universally prevail and we have added lip service to their authority that we become sometimes most keenly conscious that we do not believe a word that we are saying.
Virginia Woolf: The Common Reader

OPPORTUNITY

See also chance

1 Make hay while the sun shines.
Proverb

2 Nothing ventured, nothing gained.
Proverb

3 Opportunity seldom knocks twice.
Proverb

4 Strike while the iron is hot.
Proverb

5 Whenever you fall, pick up something.
Oswald Theodore Avery: Attrib.

6 A wise man will make more opportunities than he finds.
Francis Bacon: Essays, 'Of Ceremonies and Respects'

7 Cast thy bread upon the waters: for thou shalt find it after many days.
Bible: Ecclesiastes: 11:1

8 *Carpe diem, quam minimum credula postero.*
Seize today, and put as little trust as you can in the morrow.
Horace: Odes, I

9 One can present people with opportunities. One cannot make them equal to them.
Rosamond Lehmann: The Ballad and the Source

10 Grab a chance and you won't be sorry for a might have been.
Arthur Ransome: We Didn't Mean to Go to Sea

11 A man who never missed an occasion to let slip an opportunity.
George Bernard Shaw: Referring to Lord Rosebery. Attrib.

12 Never miss a chance to have sex or appear on television.
Gore Vidal: Attrib.

OPPOSITES

1 Fish die belly-upward and rise to the surface; it is their way of falling.
André Gide: Journals

2 War is Peace, Freedom is Slavery, Ignorance is Strength.
George Orwell: Nineteen Eighty-Four

OPPOSITION

See also government, politics

1 When I invented the phrase 'His Majesty's Opposition' he paid me a compliment on the fortunate hit.

OPPRESSION

John Cam Hobhouse: Speaking about the British statesman, Earl Canning (1812–62). Recollections of a Long Life, II, Ch. 12

2 One fifth of the people are against everything all the time.
Robert Kennedy: The Observer, 'Sayings of the Week', 10 May 1964

3 I have spent many years of my life in opposition and I rather like the role.
Eleanor Roosevelt: Letter to Bernard Baruch, 18 Nov 1952

4 The tragedy of the Police State is that it always regards all opposition as a crime, and there are no degrees.
Lord Vansittart: Speech, House of Lords, June 1947

OPPRESSION

See also imprisonment, power politics, slavery

1 When Israel was in Egypt land,
Let my people go,
Oppressed so hard they could not stand,
Let my people go.
Anonymous: Negro spiritual

2 To the capitalist governors Timor's petroleum smells better than Timorese blood and tears.
Distant Voices (John Pilger; 1994)

3 Christ in this country would quite likely have been arrested under the Suppression of Communism Act.
Joost de Blank: Referring to South Africa. The Observer, 'Sayings of the Week', 27 Oct 1963

4 All the government gives us is

charity at election time…Afterwards, death returns to our homes.
Marcos: The Independent, 12 Jan 1994

5 If you want a picture of the future, imagine a boot stamping on a human face – for ever.
George Orwell: Nineteen Eighty-Four

OPTIMISM

See also hope

1 After a storm comes a calm.
Proverb

2 Every cloud has a silver lining.
Proverb

3 It will all come right in the wash.
Proverb

4 The darkest hour is just before the dawn.
Proverb

5 When one door shuts, another opens.
Proverb

6 So, pack up your troubles in your old kit-bag,
And smile, smile, smile.
George Asaf: Pack up Your Troubles in Your Old Kit-bag

7 The pessimist is the man who believes things couldn't possibly be worse, to which the optimist replies 'Oh yes they could.'
Vladimir Bukovsky: The Guardian Weekly, 10 July 1977

8 Don't you know each cloud contains
Pennies from Heaven?
Johnny Burke: Pennies from Heaven

9 The optimist proclaims we live in the best of all possible worlds; and the pessimist fears this is true.
James Cabell: The Silver Stallion

10 But you have no silver linings without a cloud.
Angela Carter: Wise Children

11 The place where optimism most flourishes is the lunatic asylum.
Havelock Ellis: The Dance of Life

12 Optimism is the content of small men in high places.
F. Scott Fitzgerald: The Crack-Up

13 Cheer up, the worst is yet to come.
Philander Chase Johnson: Shooting Stars

14 An optimist is a guy that never had much experience.
Don Marquis: archy and mehitabel

15 All is for the best in the best of possible worlds.
Voltaire: Candide, Ch. 30

16 We are all in the gutter, but some of us are looking at the stars.
Oscar Wilde: Lady Windermere's Fan, III

17 I'm an optimist, but I'm an optimist who carries a raincoat.
Harold Wilson: Attrib.

ORDER

1 Order is heaven's first law.
Alexander Pope: An Essay on Man, IV

2 A place for everything, and everything in its place.
Samuel Smiles: Thrift, Ch. 5

ORIGINALITY

1 Anything that is worth doing has been done frequently. Things hitherto undone should be given, I suspect, a wide berth.
Max Beerbohm: Mainly on the Air

2 A thought is often original, though you have uttered it a hundred times.
Oliver Wendell Holmes: The Autocrat of the Breakfast Table, Ch. 1

3 Nothing has yet been said that's not been said before.
Terence: Eunuchus, Prologue

ORTHODOXY

See also conformity

1 The difference between Orthodoxy or My-doxy and Heterodoxy or Thy-doxy.
Thomas Carlyle: A similar remark is attributed to the British churchman William Warburton (1698–1779). History of the French Revolution, Pt. II, Bk. IV, Ch. 2

2 Worldly wisdom teaches that it is better for the reputation to fail conventionally than to succeed unconventionally.
John Maynard Keynes: The General Theory of Employment, Interest and Money, Bk. IV, Ch. 12

OSTENTATION

1 That's it, baby, if you've got it, flaunt it.
Mel Brooks: The Producers

2 When I meet those remarkable

OSTENTATION

people whose company is coveted, I often wish they would show off a little more.
Desmond MacCarthy: Theatre, 'Good Talk'

3 With the great part of rich people, the chief employment of riches consists in the parade of riches.
Adam Smith: The Wealth of Nations

PAINTING

See also art, artists

1 One picture is worth ten thousand words.
Frederick R. Barnard: Ascribed to Chinese origin. Printer's Ink, 8 Dec 1921

2 PAINTING, n. The art of protecting flat surfaces from the weather and exposing them to the critic.
Ambrose Bierce: The Devil's Dictionary

3 The day is coming when a single carrot, freshly observed, will set off a revolution.
Paul Cézanne: Attrib.

4 I do not paint a portrait to look like the subject, rather does the person grow to look like his portrait.
Salvador Dali: Attrib.

5 If people only knew as much about painting as I do, they would never buy my pictures.
Edwin Landseer: Said to W. P. Frith. Landseer the Victorian Paragon (Campbell Lennie), Ch. 12

6 A picture has been said to be something between a thing and a thought.
Samuel Palmer: Life of Blake (Arthur Symons)

7 I paint objects as I think them, not as I see them.
Pablo Picasso: Attrib.

8 Every time I paint a portrait I lose a friend.
John Singer Sargent: Attrib.

9 My business is to paint not what I know, but what I see.
Joseph Turner: Responding to a criticism of the fact that he had painted no portholes on the ships in a view of Plymouth. Proust: The Early Years (G. Painter)

PARASITES

1 Many a man who thinks to found a home discovers that he has merely opened a tavern for his friends.
Norman Douglas: South Wind, Ch. 24

2 So, naturalist observe, a flea
Hath smaller fleas that on him prey,
And these have smaller fleas to bite 'em.
And so proceed *ad infinitum*.
Jonathan Swift: On Poetry

PARTIES

See also society

1 The sooner every party breaks up the better.
Jane Austen: Emma, Ch. 25

2 I entertained on a cruising trip that was so much fun that I had to sink my yacht to make my guests go home.
F. Scott Fitzgerald: The Crack-Up, 'Notebooks, K'

3 What a swell party this is.
Cole Porter: High Society 'Well, Did You Evah!'

4 Certainly, there is nothing else here to enjoy.

George Bernard Shaw: Said at a party when his hostess asked him whether he was enjoying himself. Pass the Port (Oxfam)

5 The Life and Soul, the man who will never go home while there is one man, woman or glass of anything not yet drunk.
Katharine Whitehorn: Sunday Best, 'Husband-Swapping'

PARTING

1 Fare thee well, for I must leave thee,
Do not let this parting grieve thee,
And remember that the best of friends must part.
Anonymous: There is a Tavern in the Town

2 Parting is all we know of heaven,
And all we need of hell.
Emily Dickinson: My Life Closed Twice Before its Close

3 Good night, good night! Parting is such sweet sorrow
That I shall say good night till it be morrow.
William Shakespeare: Romeo and Juliet, II:2

PASSION

See also emotion, love

1 The man who is master of his passions is Reason's slave.
Cyril Connolly: Turnstile One (ed. V. S. Pritchett)

2 Nothing kills passion faster than an exploding harpoon in the guts.
Ben Elton: Stark

3 A man who has not passed

through the inferno of his passions has never overcome them.
Carl Gustav Jung: Memories, Dreams, Reflections, Ch. 9

4 It is with our passions as it is with fire and water, they are good servants, but bad masters.
Roger L'Estrange: Aesop's Fables, 38

PAST

See also history, memory, nostalgia

1 Even God cannot change the past.
Agathon: Nicomachean Ethics (Aristotle), VI

2 There was a house we all had in common and it was called the past.
Angela Carter: Wise Children

3 Study the past, if you would divine the future.
Confucius: Analects

4 The past is a foreign country: they do things differently there.
L. P. Hartley: The Go-Between

5 The past is the only dead thing that smells sweet.
Edward Thomas: Early One Morning

6 Each has his past shut in him like the leaves of a book known to him by heart and his friends can only read the title.
Virginia Woolf: Jacob's Room

PATIENCE

See also endurance, persistence

1 A watched pot never boils.
Proverb

2 Everything comes to him who waits.
Proverb

3 Patience is a virtue.
Proverb

4 Rome was not built in a day.
Proverb

5 Wait and see.
Herbert Henry Asquith: In various speeches, 1910

6 PATIENCE, n. A minor form of despair, disguised as a virtue.
Ambrose Bierce: The Devil's Dictionary

7 Beware the Fury of a Patient Man.
John Dryden: Absalom and Achitophel, I

8 With regard to the problem of the Sudeten Germans, my patience is now at an end.
Adolf Hitler: Speech, Berlin, 26 Sept 1938

9 Patience and passage of time do more than strength and fury.
Jean de La Fontaine: Fables, II, 'Le Lion et le Rat'

10 It is very strange...that the years teach us patience; that the shorter our time, the greater our capacity for waiting.
Elizabeth Taylor: A Wreath of Roses, Ch. 10

PATRIOTISM

See also loyalty, war

1 What pity is it
That we can die but once to serve our country!
Joseph Addison: Cato, IV:4

2 Patriotism is seen not only as the last refuge of the scoundrel but as the first bolt-hole of the hypocrite.
Melvyn Bragg: Speak for England, Introduction

3 The religion of Hell is patriotism and the government is an enlightened democracy.
James Cabell: Jurgen

4 'My country, right or wrong' is a thing that no patriot would think of saying, except in a desperate case. It is like saying 'My mother, drunk or sober.'
G. K. Chesterton: The Defendant

5 I have never understood why one's affections must be confined, as once with women, to a single country.
John Kenneth Galbraith: A Life in our Times

6 That kind of patriotism which consists in hating all other nations.
Elizabeth Gaskell: Sylvia's Lovers, Ch. 1

7 Dulce et decorum est pro patria mori.
It is a sweet and seemly thing to die for one's country.
Horace: Odes, III

8 Patriotism is the last refuge of a scoundrel.
Samuel Johnson: Life of Johnson (J. Boswell), Vol. II

9 Patriotism is often an arbitrary veneration of real estate above principles.
G. J. Nathan: Testament of a Critic

10 The old Lie: Dulce et decorum est
Pro patria mori.
Wilfred Owen: See also HORACE.
Dulce et decorum est

11 Patriots always talk of dying for their country and never of killing for their country.
Bertrand Russell: The Autobiography of Bertrand Russell

12 You'll never have a quiet world till you knock the patriotism out of the human race.
George Bernard Shaw: O'Flaherty V.C.

13 Patriotism to the Soviet State is a revolutionary duty, whereas patriotism to a bourgeois State is treachery.
Leon Trotsky: Disputed Barricade (Fitzroy Maclean)

PEACE

See also war and peace

1 'Here you are – don't lose it again.'
Anonymous: Caption to cartoon showing a wounded soldier handing over 'victory and peace in Europe'. Daily Mirror, 8 May 1945

2 The wolf also shall dwell with the lamb, and the leopard shall lie down with the kid; and the calf and the young lion and the fatling together: and a little child shall lead them.
Bible: Isaiah: 11:6

3 There is no peace, saith the Lord, unto the wicked.
Bible: Isaiah: 48:22

4 Give peace in our time, O Lord.
The Book of Common Prayer: Morning Prayer, Versicles

5 Don't tell me peace has broken out.
Bertolt Brecht: Mother Courage, VIII

6 Anythin' for a quiet life, as the man said wen he took the sitivation at the lighthouse.
Charles Dickens: Pickwick Papers, Ch. 43

7 Arms alone are not enough to keep the peace – it must be kept by men.
John Fitzgerald Kennedy: The Observer, 'Sayings of the Decade', 1962

8 The issues are the same. We wanted peace on earth, love, and understanding between everyone around the world. We have learned that change comes slowly.
Paul McCartney: The Observer, 'Sayings of the Week', 7 June 1987

9 Nation shall speak peace unto nation.
Montague John Rendall: Motto of BBC, 1927

10 When peace has been broken anywhere, the peace of all countries everywhere is in danger.
Franklin D. Roosevelt: Radio broadcast, 3 Sept 1939

11 We are the true peace movement.
Margaret Thatcher: The Times, 1983

PERCEPTION

1 If the doors of perception were cleansed everything would appear to man as it is, infinite.
William Blake: The Marriage of Heaven and Hell, 'A Memorable Fancy'

2 I saw it, but I did not realize it.

*Elizabeth Peabody: Giving a
Transcendentalist explanation for
her accidentally walking into a
tree. The Peabody Sisters of Salem
(L. Tharp)*

PERFECTION

1 Be ye therefore perfect, even as
your Father which is in heaven is
perfect.
Bible: Matthew: 5:48

2 Perfection has one grave defect;
it is apt to be dull.
*W. Somerset Maugham: The
Summing Up*

3 The essence of being human is
that one does not seek perfection.
*George Orwell: Shooting an
Elephant, 'Reflections on Gandhi'*

4 Finality is death. Perfection is finality. Nothing is perfect. There
are lumps in it.
*James Stephens: The Crock of
Gold*

PERSISTENCE

See also determination, endurance, patience

1 If the mountain will not come to
Mahomet, Mahomet must go to
the mountain.
Proverb

2 Never say die.
Proverb

3 If at first you don't succeed,
Try, try again.
*William Edward Hickson: Try and
Try Again*

4 Keep Right on to the End of the
Road.
Harry Lauder: Song title

5 Constant dripping hollows out a
stone.
*Lucretius: On the Nature of the
Universe, I.*

6 I am a kind of burr; I shall stick.
*William Shakespeare: Measure for
Measure, IV:3*

PERSUASION

1 They will conquer, but they will
not convince.
*Miguel de Unamuno y Jugo:
Referring to the Franco rebels.
Attrib.*

2 There is a holy, mistaken zeal in
politics, as well as religion. By
persuading others we convince
ourselves.
Junius: Letter, 19 Dec 1769

PERVERSITY

See also stubbornness

1 Let's find out what everyone is
doing,
And then stop everyone from
doing it.
*A. P. Herbert: Let's Stop
Somebody*

2 Adam was but human – this explains it all. He did not want the
apple for the apple's sake, he
wanted it only because it was
forbidden.
*Mark Twain: Pudd'nhead
Wilson's Calendar, Ch. 2*

PESSIMISM

1 Pessimism, when you get used
to it, is just as agreeable as optimism.

Arnold Bennett: Things that have Interested Me, 'The Slump in Pessimism'

2 Scratch a pessimist, and you find often a defender of privilege.

Lord Beveridge: The Observer, 'Sayings of the Week', 17 Dec 1943

3 Nothing to do but work,
Nothing to eat but food,
Nothing to wear but clothes,
To keep one from going nude.

Benjamin Franklin King: The Pessimist

4 If we see light at the end of the tunnel it is the light of an oncoming train.

Robert Lowell: Day by Day

5 How many pessimists end up by desiring the things they fear, in order to prove that they are right.

Robert Mallet: Apostilles

6 A pessimist is a man who looks both ways before crossing a one-way street.

Laurence J. Peter: Peter's Quotations

PHILISTINISM

See also culture

1 For this class we have a designation which now has become pretty well known, and which we may as well still keep for them, the designation of Philistines.

Matthew Arnold: Referring to the middle class. Culture and Anarchy, Ch. 3

2 When I hear anyone talk of Culture, I reach for my revolver.

Hermann Goering: Attrib. to Goering but probably said by Hanns Johst

3 Particularly against books the Home Secretary is. If we can't stamp out literature in the country, we can at least stop it being brought in from outside.

Evelyn Waugh: Vile Bodies, Ch. 2

4 Listen! There never was an artistic period. There never was an Art-loving nation.

James Whistler: Attrib.

PHILOSOPHERS

1 All are lunatics, but he who can analyze his delusion is called a philosopher.

Ambrose Bierce: Epigrams

2 There is nothing so absurd but some philosopher has said it.

Cicero: De Divinatione, II

3 To a philosopher no circumstance, however trifling, is too minute.

Oliver Goldsmith: The Citizen of the World

4 The philosophers have only interpreted the world in various ways; the point is to change it.

Karl Marx: Theses on Feuerbach

5 Not to care for philosophy is to be a true philosopher.

Blaise Pascal: Pensées, I

6 There will be no end to the troubles of states, or indeed, my dear Glaucon, of humanity itself, till philosophers become kings in this world, or till those we now call kings and rulers really and truly become philosophers.

Plato: Republic, Bk. 5

7 There are now-a-days professors of philosophy but not philosophers.
Henry David Thoreau: Walden, 'Economy'

8 A philosopher of imposing stature doesn't think in a vacuum. Even his most abstract ideas are, to some extent, conditioned by what is or what is not known in the time when he lives.
A. N. Whitehead: Dialogues

PHILOSOPHY

See also logic, metaphysics, thinking

1 The principles of logic and metaphysics are true simply because we never allow them to be anything else.
A. J. Ayer: Language, Truth and Logic

2 Do not all charms fly
At the mere touch of cold philosophy?
John Keats: Lamia, II

3 We thought philosophy ought to be patient and unravel people's mental blocks. Trouble with doing that is, once you've unravelled them, their heads fall off.
Frederic Raphael: The Glittering Prizes: A Double Life, III:2

4 Science is what you know, philosophy is what you don't know.
Bertrand Russell

5 It is a great advantage for a system of philosophy to be substantially true.
George Santayana: The Unknowable

6 Philosophy is the product of wonder.

A. N. Whitehead: Nature and Life, Ch. 1

7 Philosophy, as we use the word, is a fight against the fascination which forms of expression exert upon us.
Ludwig Wittgenstein: The Blue Book

8 Philosophy is not a theory but an activity.
Ludwig Wittgenstein: Tractatus Logico-Philosophicus, Ch. 4

PHOTOGRAPHY

1 Photography can never grow up if it imitates some other medium. It has to walk alone. It has to be itself.
Berenice Abbott: Infinity, 'It Has to Walk Alone'

2 Most things in life are moments of pleasure and a lifetime of embarrassment; photography is a moment of embarrassment and a lifetime of pleasure.
Tony Benn: The Sunday Times, 31 Dec 1989

3 The camera cannot lie. But it can be an accessory to untruth.
Harold Evans: Pictures on a Page

4 I have for instance among my purchases...several original Mona Lisas and all painted (according to the Signature) by the great artist Kodak.
Spike Milligan: A Dustbin of Milligan, 'Letters to Harry Secombe'

5 A photograph is not only an image (as a painting is an image), an interpretation of the real; it is also a trace, something directly

stencilled off the real, like a footprint or a death mask.
Susan Sontag: On Photography

PLACES

See also Europe

1 All roads lead to Rome.
Proverb

2 See Naples and die.
Proverb

3 I don't even know what street
Canada is on.
Al Capone: Attrib.

4 Hollywood is a world with all
the personality of a paper cup.
Raymond Chandler: Attrib.

5 India is a geographical term. It
is no more a united nation than
the Equator.
*Winston Churchill: Speech, Royal
Albert Hall, 18 Mar 1931*

6 I find it hard to say, because
when I was there it seemed to be
shut.
*Clement Freud: On being asked for
his opinion of New Zealand.
Similar remarks have been
attributed to others. BBC radio,
12 Apr 1978*

7 Some word that teems with hidden meaning – like Basingstoke.
W. S. Gilbert: Ruddigore, II

8 Liverpool is the pool of life.
Carl Gustav Jung: Attrib.

9 The whole city is arrayed in
squares just like a chess-board,
and disposed in a manner so
perfect and masterly that it is
impossible to give a description
that should do it justice.
*Marco Polo: Referring to Kublai
Khan's capital, Cambaluc (later
Peking). The Book of Marco Polo*

10 Great God! this is an awful
place.
*Captain Robert Falcon Scott:
Referring to the South Pole.
Journal, 17 Jan 1912*

PLAYS

See also acting, actors, literature,
theatre

1 Now a whole is that which has a
beginning, a middle, and an
end.
*Aristotle: Referring specifically to
the dramatic form of tragedy.
Poetics, Ch. 7*

2 One of Edward's Mistresses was
Jane Shore, who has had a play
written about her, but it is a
tragedy and therefore not worth
reading.
*Jane Austen: The History of
England*

3 In the theatre the audience want
to be surprised – but by things
that they expect.
*Tristan Bernard: Contes,
Repliques et Bon Mots*

4 I'd say award winning plays are
written only for the critics.
*Lew Grade: The Observer,
'Sayings of the Week', 18 Oct
1970*

5 Depending upon shock tactics is
easy, whereas writing a good
play is difficult. Pubic hair is no
substitute for wit.
J. B. Priestley: Outcries and Asides

6 If it be true that good wine
needs no bush, 'tis true that a
good play needs no epilogue.
*William Shakespeare: As You Like
It, Epilogue*

7 The play's the thing

Wherein I'll catch the con-
science of the King.
*William Shakespeare: Hamlet,
II:2*

8 The play was a great success,
but the audience was a disaster.
*Oscar Wilde: Referring to a play
that had recently failed. Attrib*

PLEASURE

See also debauchery, happiness

1 No pleasure without pain.
Proverb

2 One half of the world cannot
understand the pleasures of the
other.
Jane Austen: Emma, Ch. 9

3 Pleasure after all is a safer guide
than either right or duty.
*Samuel Butler: The Way of All
Flesh, Ch. 19*

4 Though sages may pour out
their wisdom's treasure,
There is no sterner moralist
than Pleasure.
Lord Byron: Don Juan, III

5 It was a miracle of rare device,
A sunny pleasure-dome with
caves of ice!
*Samuel Taylor Coleridge: Kubla
Khan*

6 People must not do things for
fun. We are not here for fun.
There is no reference to fun in
any Act of Parliament.
A. P. Herbert: Uncommon Law

7 No man is a hypocrite in his
pleasures.
*Samuel Johnson: Life of Johnson
(J. Boswell), Vol. IV*

8 A Little of What You Fancy
Does You Good.
Marie Lloyd: Song title

9 Great lords have their pleasures,
but the people have fun.
*Baron de Montesquieu: Pensées
diverses*

10 A life of pleasure requires an
aristocratic setting to make it interesting.
*George Santayana: Life of Reason,
'Reason in Society'*

11 Pleasure is nothing else but the
intermission of pain.
John Selden: Table Talk

12 A Good Time Was Had by All.
Stevie Smith: Book title

13 All the things I really like to do
are either immoral, illegal, or
fattening.
Alexander Woollcott: Attrib

POETRY

See also criticism, literature, writing

1 For this reason poetry is something more philosophical and
more worthy of serious attention
than history.
Aristotle: Poetics, Ch. 9

2 A criticism of life under the conditions fixed for such a criticism
by the laws of poetic truth and
poetic beauty.
*Matthew Arnold: Essays in
Criticism, Second Series, 'The
Study of Poetry'*

3 Poetry makes nothing happen,
it survives
In the valley of its saying.
*W. H. Auden: In Memory of W. B.
Yeats*

4 It is a pretty poem, Mr Pope,
but you must not call it Homer.

Richard Bentley: Referring to Alexander Pope's Iliad. Samuel Johnson, Life of Pope

5 Too many people in the modern world view poetry as a luxury, not a necessity like petrol. But to me it's the oil of life.
John Betjeman: The Observer, 'Sayings of the Year', 1974

6 I have nothing to say, I am saying it, and that is poetry.
John Cage: The Sunday Times (quoted by Cyril Connolly), 10 Sept 1972

7 For the godly poet must be chaste himself, but there is no need for his verses to be so.
Catullus: Carmina, XVI

8 You don't make a poem with thoughts; you must make it with words.
Jean Cocteau: The Sunday Times, 20 Oct 1963

9 That willing suspension of disbelief for the moment, which constitutes poetic faith.
Samuel Taylor Coleridge: Biographia Literaria, Ch. 14

10 Poetry is not a turning loose of emotion, but an escape from emotion; it is not the expression of personality, but an escape from personality.
T. S. Eliot: Tradition and the Individual Talent

11 All one's inventions are true, you can be sure of that. Poetry is as exact a science as geometry.
Gustave Flaubert: Letter to Louise Colet, 14 Aug 1853

12 We all write poems; it is simply that poets are the ones who write in words.

John Fowles: The French Lieutenant's Woman, Ch. 19

13 Poetry is the language in which man explores his own amazement.
Christopher Fry: Time, 3 Apr 1950

14 Rightly thought of there is poetry in peaches...even when they are canned.
Harley Granville-Barker: The Madras House, I

15 If Galileo had said in verse that the world moved, the Inquisition might have let him alone.
Thomas Hardy: The Later Years of Thomas Hardy (F. E. Hardy)

16 If poetry comes not as naturally as leaves to a tree it had better not come at all.
John Keats: Letter to John Taylor, 27 Feb 1818

17 Perhaps no person can be a poet, or can even enjoy poetry, without a certain unsoundness of mind.
Lord Macaulay: Literary Essays Contributed to the 'Edinburgh Review', 'Milton'

18 Poem me no poems.
Rose Macaulay: Poetry Review, Autumn 1963

19 Verse libre; a device for making poetry easier to read and harder to write.
H. L. Mencken: A Book of Burlesques

20 The truest poetry is the most feigning.
William Shakespeare: As You Like It, III:3

21 My poems are hymns of praise to the glory of life.

Edith Sitwell: Collected Poems, 'Some Notes on My Poetry'

22 A poem is never finished, only abandoned.
Paul Valéry: A Certain World (W. H. Auden)

23 There are no poetic ideas; only poetic utterances.
Evelyn Waugh: Books On Trial

24 No one will ever get at my verses who insists upon viewing them as a literary performance.
Walt Whitman: A Backward Glance O'er Travel'd Roads

25 Out of the quarrel with others we make rhetoric; out of the quarrel with ourselves we make poetry.
W. B. Yeats: Essay

POETRY AND PROSE

See also prose

1 I wish our clever young poets would remember my homely definitions of prose and poetry; that is, prose = words in their best order; – poetry = the best words in the best order.
Samuel Taylor Coleridge: Table Talk

2 Prose on certain occasions can bear a great deal of poetry: on the other hand, poetry sinks and swoons under a moderate weight of prose.
Walter Savage Landor: Imaginary Conversations, 'Archdeacon Hare and Walter Landor'

3 Poetry is to prose as dancing is to walking.
John Wain: Talk, BBC radio, 13 Jan 1976

POETS

See also criticism, poetry, writers

1 Poets and painters are outside the class system, or rather they constitute a special class of their own, like the circus people and the gipsies.
Gerald Brenan: Thoughts in a Dry Season, 'Writing'

2 A poet without love were a physical and metaphysical impossibility.
Thomas Carlyle: Critical and Miscellaneous Essays, 'Burns'

3 A true poet does not bother to be poetical. Nor does a nursery gardener scent his roses.
Jean Cocteau: Professional Secrets

4 Immature poets imitate; mature poets steal.
T. S. Eliot: Philip Massinger

5 To be a poet is a condition rather than a profession.
Robert Graves: Horizon

6 Not gods, nor men, nor even booksellers have put up with poets being second-rate.
Horace: Ars Poetica

POLICE

1 I have never seen a situation so dismal that a policeman couldn't make it worse.
Brendan Behan: Attrib.

2 When constabulary duty's to be done –
A policeman's lot is not a happy one.
W. S. Gilbert: The Pirates of Penzance, II

3 Policemen are numbered in case they get lost.

Spike Milligan: The Last Goon Show of All

4 A thing of duty is a boy for ever.
Flann O'Brien: About policemen always seeming to be young-looking. The Listener, 24 Feb 1977

5 Reading isn't an occupation we encourage among police officers. We try to keep the paper work down to a minimum.
Joe Orton: Loot, II

6 My father didn't create you to arrest me.
Lord Peel: Protesting against his arrest by the police, recently established by his father. Attrib.

7 One always has the air of someone who is lying when one speaks to a policeman.
Charles-Louis Philippe: Les Chroniques du canard sauvage

POLITICIANS

See also government

1 Men who have greatness within them don't go in for politics.
Albert Camus: Notebooks, 1935–42

2 a politician is an arse upon which everyone has sat except a man.
e. e. cummings: A Politician

3 When I was a boy I was told that anybody could become President of the United States. I am beginning to believe it.
Clarence Seward Darrow: Attrib.

4 I have come to the conclusion that politics are too serious a matter to be left to the politicians.
Charles de Gaulle: Attrib.

5 I always voted at my party's call,
And I never thought of thinking for myself at all.
W. S. Gilbert: HMS Pinafore, I

6 'Do you pray for the senators, Dr Hale?' 'No, I look at the senators and I pray for the country.'
Edward Everett Hale: New England Indian Summer (Van Wyck Brooks)

7 Politicians are the same everywhere. They promise to build bridges even where there are no rivers.
Nikita Khrushchev: Attrib., Oct 1960

8 A politician is a person with whose politics you don't agree; if you agree with him he is a statesman.
David Lloyd George: Attrib.

9 When you're abroad you're a statesman: when you're at home you're just a politician.
Harold Macmillan: Speech, 1958

10 Above any other position of eminence, that of Prime Minister is filled by fluke.
Enoch Powell: The Observer, 'Sayings of the Week' 8 Mar 1987

11 All politicians have vanity. Some wear it more gently than others.
David Steel: The Observer, 'Sayings of the Week', 14 July 1985

12 A politician is a statesman who approaches every question with an open mouth.
Adlai Stevenson: Also attrib. to Arthur Goldberg. The Fine Art of Political Wit (L. Harris)

13 A statesman is a politician who's been dead ten or fifteen years.

Harry S. Truman: New York World Telegram and Sun, 12 Apr 1958

14 It is a pity, as my husband says, that more politicians are not bastards by birth instead of vocation.

Katharine Whitehorn: The Observer, 1964

POLITICS

See also democracy, diplomacy, government

1 When the political columnists say 'Every thinking man' they mean themselves and when the candidates appeal to 'Every intelligent voter' they mean everybody who is going to vote for them.

Franklin P. Adams: Nods And Becks

2 Politics, as a practice, whatever its professions, has always been the systematic organisation of hatreds.

Henry Brooks Adams: The Education of Henry Adams

3 Don't tell my mother I'm in politics – she thinks I play the piano in a whorehouse.

Anonymous: US saying.

4 Man is by nature a political animal.

Aristotle: Politics, Bk. I

5 The connection between humbug and politics is too long established to be challenged.

Ronald Bell: Speech, 5 Dec 1979

6 Politics is a blood sport.

Aneurin Bevan: My Life with Nye (Jennie Lee)

7 Politics is not an exact science.

Bismarck: Speech, Prussian Chamber, 18 Dec 1863

8 Politics are usually the executive expression of human immaturity.

Vera Brittain: The Rebel Passion

9 Politics is the art of the possible.

R. A. Butler: Often attrib. to Butler but used earlier by others, including Bismarck. The Art of the Possible, Epigraph

10 I am not made for politics because I am incapable of wishing for, or accepting the death of my adversary.

Albert Camus: The Rebel

11 Do not criticize your government when out of the country. Never cease to do so when at home.

Winston Churchill: Attrib.

12 There are times in politics when you must be on the right side and lose.

John Kenneth Galbraith: The Observer, 'Sayings of the Week', 11 Feb 1968

13 Never judge a country by its politics. After all, we English are quite honest by nature, aren't we?

Alfred Hitchcock: The Lady Vanishes

14 The essential thing is the formation of the political will of the nation: that is the starting point for political action.

Adolf Hitler: Speech, Düsseldorf, 27 Jan 1932

15 You can't adopt politics as a profession and remain honest.

Louis McHenry Howe: Speech, Columbia University, 17 Jan 1933

16 Mothers all want their sons to

grow up to become president, but they don't want them to become politicians in the process.
John Fitzgerald Kennedy: Attrib.

17 In every age the vilest specimens of human nature are to be found among demagogues.
Lord Macaulay: History of England, Vol. I, Ch. 5

18 There are three groups that no prime minister should provoke: the Treasury, the Vatican, and the National Union of Mineworkers.
Harold Macmillan: First used by Stanley Baldwin. Attrib.

19 Every intellectual attitude is latently political.
Thomas Mann: The Observer, 11 Aug 1974

20 I used to say that politics was the second lowest profession and I have come to know that it bears a great similarity to the first.
Ronald Reagan: The Observer, 13 May 1979

21 The collection of prejudices which is called political philosophy is useful provided that it is not called philosophy.
Bertrand Russell: The Observer, 'Sayings of the Year', 1962

22 Go back to your constituencies and prepare for government!
David Steel: Speech to party conference, 1985

23 An independent is a guy who wants to take the politics out of politics.
Adlai Stevenson: The Art Of Politics.

24 Politics is perhaps the only profession for which no preparation is thought necessary.
Robert Louis Stevenson: Familiar Studies of Men and Books, 'Yoshida-Torajiro'

25 In politics, if you want anything said, ask a man; if you want anything done, ask a woman.
Margaret Thatcher: The Changing Anatomy of Britain (Anthony Sampson)

26 Real politics, not the kind one reads and writes about...has little to do with ideas, values and imagination...and everything to do with manoeuvres, intrigues, plots, paranoias, betrayals, a great deal of calculation, no little cynicism and every kind of con game.
Mario Vargas Llosa: A Fish in the Water

27 Politics come from man. Mercy, compassion and justice come from God.
Terry Waite: The Observer, 'Sayings of the Week', 13 Jan 1985

28 A week is a long time in politics.
Harold Wilson: First said in 1965 or 1966, and repeated on several occasions. Attrib.

29 Politics is the entertainment branch of Industry.
Frank Zappa

POPULARITY

See also fame

1 Everybody hates me because I'm so universally liked.

Peter De Vries: The Vale of Laughter, Pt. I

2 Popularity is a crime from the moment it is sought; it is only a virtue where men have it whether they will or no.
Lord Halifax: Political, Moral and Miscellaneous Thoughts and Reflections

3 Popularity? It's glory's small change.
Victor Hugo: Ruy Blas, III

4 The worse I do, the more popular I get.
John Fitzgerald Kennedy: Referring to his popularity following the failure of the US invasion of Cuba. The People's Almanac (D. Wallechinsky)

5 We're more popular than Jesus Christ now. I don't know which will go first. Rock and roll or Christianity.
John Lennon: The Beatles Illustrated Lyrics

6 He's liked, but he's not well liked.
Arthur Miller: Death of a Salesman, I

7 He hasn't an enemy in the world, and none of his friends like him.
Oscar Wilde: Said of G. B. Shaw. Sixteen Self Sketches (Shaw), Ch. 17

POPULAR MUSIC

1 Rock'n'roll is part of a pest to undermine the morals of the youth of our nation. It...brings people of both races together.
Anonymous: Statement by the North Alabama Citizens' Council in the 1950s

2 Listen kid, take my advice, never hate a song that has sold half a million copies.
Irving Berlin: Giving advice to the composer Cole Porter. Attrib.

3 Roll Over Beethoven.
Chuck Berry: Song title.

4 Canned music is like audible wallpaper.
Alistair Cooke: Attrib.

5 Strange how potent cheap music is.
Noël Coward: Private Lives

6 Rock Around the Clock.
Bill Haley and The Comets: Song title

7 Everybody is sleeping with everybody else in this business, but the artist is the only one that's getting screwed.
Billy Joel: The Independent, 24 June 1994

8 It's only rock and roll But I like it.
The Rolling Stones: It's Only Rock and Roll

9 Jazz will endure just as long as people hear it through their feet instead of their brains.
John Philip Sousa: Attrib.

10 No change in musical style... will survive unless it is accompanied by a change in clothing style.
Frank Zappa: The Real Frank Zappa Book

POSSIBILITY

1 The grand Perhaps!

*Robert Browning: Bishop
Blougram's Apology*

2 However, one cannot put a
quart in a pint cup.
*Charlotte Perkins Gilman: The
Living of Charlotte Perkins
Gilman*

3 Your If is the only peace-maker;
much virtue in If.
*William Shakespeare: As You Like
It, V:4*

POSTERITY

*See also fame, future, immor-
tality, reputation*

1 We are always doing something
for posterity, but I would fain
see posterity do something for
us.
*Joseph Addison: The Spectator,
583*

2 Posterity is as likely to be wrong
as anybody else.
*Heywood Broun: Sitting on the
World*

3 Damn the age. I'll write for
antiquity.
*Charles Lamb: Referring to his
lack of payment for the Essays of
Elia. English Wits (L. Russell)*

4 My time has not yet come
either; some are born posthu-
mously.
Friedrich Nietzsche: Ecce Homo

POVERTY

See also hunger

1 From clogs to clogs in three
generations.
Proverb

2 Poverty is not a crime.
Proverb

3 To some extent, if you've seen
one city slum you've seen them
all.
*Spiro Agnew: Election speech,
Detroit, 18 Oct 1968*

4 To be poor and independent is
very nearly an impossibility.
*William Cobbett: Advice to Young
Men*

5 Poverty, therefore, was comparative. One measured it by a
sliding scale. One was always
poor, in terms of those who
were richer.
*Margaret Drabble: The Radiant
Way*

6 There's no scandal like rags,
nor any crime so shameful as
poverty.
*George Farquhar: The Beaux'
Stratagem, I:1*

7 The very poor are unthinkable
and only to be approached by
the statistician and the poet.
E. M. Forster: Howards End

8 It is only the poor who are forbidden to beg.
Anatole France: Crainquebille

9 For every talent that poverty has
stimulated, it has blighted a
hundred.
John W. Gardner: Excellence

10 Is it possible that my people
live in such awful conditions?…I
tell you, Mr Wheatley, that if I
had to live in conditions like that
I would be a revolutionary myself.
*George V: On being told Mr
Wheatley's life story. The Tragedy
of Ramsay MacDonald
(L. MacNeill Weir), Ch. 16*

11 People who are much too sensitive to demand of cripples that

they run races ask of the poor that they get up and act just like everyone else in society.
Michael Harrington: The Other America

12 Oh! God! that bread should be so dear,
And flesh and blood so cheap!
Thomas Hood: The Song of the Shirt

13 This Administration here and now declares unconditional war on poverty in America.
Lyndon B. Johnson: State of the Union message, 8 Jan 1964

14 It's not easy for people to rise out of obscurity when they have to face straitened circumstances at home.
Juvenal: Satires, III

15 I (Who Have Nothing).
Jerry Leiber: Credited to 'Donida; Leiber, Stoller, Mogol'. Song title

16 Look at me: I worked my way up from nothing to a state of extreme poverty.
Groucho Marx: Monkey Business

17 The forgotten man at the bottom of the economic pyramid.
Franklin D. Roosevelt: Speech on radio, 7 Apr 1932

18 The poor don't know that their function in life is to exercise our generosity.
Jean-Paul Sartre: Words

19 Disease creates poverty and poverty disease.
Henry E. Sigerist: Medicine and Human Welfare, Ch. 1

20 The poor are our brothers and sisters....people in the world who need love, who need care, who have to be wanted.
Mother Teresa: Time, 'Saints Among Us', 29 Dec 1975

21 There were times my pants were so thin I could sit on a dime and tell if it was heads or tails.
Spencer Tracy: Spencer Tracy (L. Swindell)

POVERTY AND WEALTH

See also money, wealth

1 If the rich could hire other people to die for them, the poor could make a wonderful living.
Yiddish proverb

2 There are only two families in the world, my old grandmother used to say, The Haves and the Have-Nots.
Miguel de Cervantes: Don Quixote, Pt. II, Ch. 20

3 Errors look so very ugly in persons of small means — one feels they are taking quite a liberty in going astray; whereas people of fortune may naturally indulge in a few delinquencies.
George Eliot: Janet's Repentance, Ch. 25

4 When the rich wage war it is the poor who die.
Jean-Paul Sartre: The Devil and the Good Lord

POWER

See also influence, leadership

1 Divide and rule.
Proverb

2 He who pays the piper calls the tune.
Proverb

3 Power tends to corrupt, and ab-

POWER POLITICS

solute power corrupts absolutely. Great men are almost always
bad men...There is no worse
heresy than that the office sanctifies the holder of it.
*Lord Acton: Often misquoted as
'Power corrupts...' Letter to
Bishop Mandell Creighton, 5 Apr
1887*

4 A friend in power is a friend
lost.
*Henry Brooks Adams: The
Education of Henry Adams*

5 The greater the power, the more
dangerous the abuse.
*Edmund Burke: Speech, House of
Commons, 7 Feb 1771*

6 Men of power have not time to
read; yet men who do not read
are unfit for power.
Michael Foot: Debts Of Honour

7 Power is the ultimate aphrodisiac.
*Henry Kissinger: The Guardian,
28 Nov 1976*

8 To reign is worth ambition,
though in Hell:
Better to reign in Hell than serve
in Heaven.
John Milton: Paradise Lost, Bk. I

9 It could never be a correct justification that, because the whites
oppressed us yesterday when
they had power, that the blacks
must oppress them today because they have power.
*Robert Mugabe: Speech, Mar
1980*

10 Who controls the past controls
the future. Who controls the
present controls the past.
*George Orwell: Nineteen Eighty-
Four*

11 Unlimited power is apt to cor-

rupt the minds of those who
possess it.
*William Pitt the Elder: See also
Lord ACTON. Speech, House of
Lords, 9 Jan 1770*

12 You only have power over people so long as you don't take
everything away from them. But
when you've robbed a man of
everything he's no longer in your
power – he's free again.
*Alexander Solzhenitsyn: The First
Circle, Ch. 17*

13 Power corrupts, but lack of
power corrupts absolutely.
*Adlai Stevenson: The Observer,
Jan 1963*

14 The balance of power.
*Robert Walpole: Speech, House of
Commons*

15 The wrong sort of people are
always in power because they
would not be in power if they
were not the wrong sort of
people.
*Jon Wynne-Tyson: Times Literary
Supplement*

POWER POLITICS

See also oppression, violence,
weapons

1 Whatever happens, we have got
The Maxim Gun, and they have
not.
*Hilaire Belloc: Referring to
African natives. The Modern
Traveller*

2 Guns will make us powerful;
butter will only make us fat.
*Hermann Goering: Radio
broadcast, 1936*

3 A man may build himself a

throne of bayonets, but he cannot sit on it.
Dean Inge: Wit and Wisdom of Dean Inge (ed. Marchant)

4 There is a homely adage which runs 'Speak softly and carry a big stick, you will go far'.
Theodore Roosevelt: Speech, Minnesota State Fair, 2 Sept 1901

5 God is always on the side of the big battalions.
Vicomte de Turenne: Attrib.

6 God is on the side not of the heavy battalions, but of the best shots.
Voltaire: Notebooks

PRAISE

See also admiration, flattery

1 Self-praise is no recommendation.
Proverb

2 Watch how a man takes praise and there you have the measure of him.
Thomas Burke: T. P.'s Weekly, 8 June 1928

3 The advantage of doing one's praising for oneself is that one can lay it on so thick and exactly in the right places.
Samuel Butler: The Way of All Flesh, Ch. 34

4 To refuse praise reveals a desire to be praised twice over.
Duc de la Rochefoucauld: Maximes, 149

PRAYER

See also Christianity, faith, God, religion

1 PRAY, v. To ask that the rules of the universe be annulled on behalf of a single petitioner, confessedly unworthy.
Ambrose Bierce: The Devil's Dictionary

2 To Mercy, Pity, Peace, and Love All pray in their distress.
William Blake: Songs of Innocence, 'The Divine Image'

3 Your cravings as a human animal do not become a prayer just because it is God whom you must ask to attend to them.
Dag Hammarskjöld: Markings

4 If thou shouldst never see my face again,
Pray for my soul. More things are wrought by prayer
Than this world dreams of.
Alfred, Lord Tennyson: Idylls of the King, 'The Passing of Arthur'

5 Whatever a man prays for, he prays for a miracle. Every prayer reduces itself to this: 'Great God grant that twice two be not four.'
Ivan Turgenev: Prayer

PREJUDICE

1 Mother is far too clever to understand anything she does not like.
Arnold Bennett: The Title

2 Don't half-quote me to reinforce your own prejudices.
Brian Clark: Kipling

3 Common sense is the collection of prejudices acquired by age eighteen.
Albert Einstein: Scientific American, Feb 1976

4 I am free of all prejudice. I hate everyone equally.
W. C. Fields: Attrib.

5 My corns ache, I get gouty, and my prejudices swell like varicose veins.
James Gibbons Huneker: Old Fogy, Ch. 1

PRESENT

See also future, opportunity, past, time

1 No time like the present.
Proverb

2 Gather ye rosebuds while ye may,
Old time is still a-flying:
And this same flower that smiles today
Tomorrow will be dying.
Robert Herrick: Hesperides, 'To the Virgins, to Make Much of Time'

3 *Carpe diem.*
Seize the day.
Horace: Odes, I

4 We live in stirring times – tea-stirring times.
Christopher Isherwood: Mr Norris Changes Trains

PRIDE

See also arrogance, conceit, egotism

1 Pride goeth before destruction, and an haughty spirit before a fall.
Bible: Proverbs: 16:18

2 The moment of greatest humiliation is the moment when the spirit is proudest.
Christabel Pankhurst: Speech, Albert Hall, London, 19 Mar 1908

3 Yes; I am proud, I must be proud to see
Men not afraid of God, afraid of me.
Alexander Pope: Epilogue to the Satires, Dialogue II

4 There is false modesty, but there is no false pride.
Jules Renard: Journal

PRINCIPLES

See also integrity, morality

1 It is easier to fight for one's principles than to live up to them.
Alfred Adler: Alfred Adler (P. Bottome)

2 Ethics and Science need to shake hands.
Richard Clarke Cabot: The Meaning of Right and Wrong, Introduction

3 If one sticks too rigidly to one's principles one would hardly see anybody.
Agatha Christie: Towards Zero, I

4 Whenever two good people argue over principles, they are both right.
Marie Ebner von Eschenbach: Aphorism

PRIVACY

1 The house of every one is to him as his castle and fortress.
Edward Coke: Semayne's Case

2 I never said, 'I want to be alone.' I only said, 'I want to be *left* alone.' There is all the difference.
Greta Garbo: Garbo (John Bainbridge)

3 This is a free country, madam.

We have a right to share your privacy in a public place.
Peter Ustinov: Romanoff and Juliet, I

PROCRASTINATION

1 Never put off till tomorrow what you can do today.
Proverb

2 The road to hell is paved with good intentions.
Proverb

3 Give me chastity and continence, but not yet.
St Augustine of Hippo: Confessions, Bk. VIII, Ch. 7

4 Procrastination is the thief of time.
Edward Young: Night Thoughts

PROGRESS

See also change, conservatism, novelty

1 The people who live in the past must yield to the people who live in the future. Otherwise the world would begin to turn the other way round.
Arnold Bennett: Milestones

2 As enunciated today, 'progress' is simply a comparative of which we have not settled the superlative.
G. K. Chesterton: Heretics, Ch. 2

3 A man of destiny knows that beyond this hill lies another and another. The journey is never complete.
F. W. de Klerk: Referring to Nelson Mandela. The Observer, 'Sayings of the Week', 8 May 1994

4 What we call progress is the exchange of one nuisance for another nuisance.
Havelock Ellis: Attrib.

5 All that is human must retrograde if it does not advance.
Edward Gibbon: Decline and Fall of the Roman Empire, Ch. 71

6 You cannot fight against the future. Time is on our side.
William Ewart Gladstone: Advocating parliamentary reform. Speech, 1866

7 If I have seen further it is by standing on the shoulders of giants.
Isaac Newton: Letter to Robert Hooke, 5 Feb 1675

8 Organic life, we are told, has developed gradually from the protozoon to the philosopher, and this development, we are assured, is indubitably an advance. Unfortunately it is the philosopher, not the protozoon, who gives us this assurance.
Bertrand Russell: Mysticism and Logic, Ch. 6

9 Man's 'progress' is but a gradual discovery that his questions have no meaning.
Antoine de Saint-Exupéry: The Wisdom of the Sands

PROMISCUITY

See also sex

1 Every time you sleep with a boy you sleep with all his old girlfriends.
Government advert warning about AIDS, 1987

2 I see – she's the original good time that was had by all.

Bette Davis: Referring to a starlet of the time. The Filmgoer's Book of Quotes (Leslie Halliwell)

3 You mustn't think I advocate perpetual sex. Far from it. Nothing nauseates me more than promiscuous sex in and out of season.
D. H. Lawrence: Letter to Lady Ottoline Morrell, 20 Dec 1928

4 You were born with your legs apart. They'll send you to the grave in a Y-shaped coffin.
Joe Orton: What the Butler Saw, I

5 You know, she speaks eighteen languages. And she can't say 'No' in any of them.
Dorothy Parker: Speaking of an acquaintance. Attrib.

6 I have made love to ten thousand women.
Georges Simenon: Interview with Die Tat, 1977

7 I'm glad you like my Catherine. I like her too. She ruled thirty million people and had three thousand lovers. I do the best I can in two hours.
Mae West: After her performance in Catherine the Great. Speech from the stage

PROMISES

1 Better is it that thou shouldest not vow, than that thou shouldest vow and not pay.
Bible: Ecclesiastes: 5:5

2 A promise made is a debt unpaid.
Robert William Service: The Cremation of Sam McGee

3 Promises and pie-crust are made to be broken.

Jonathan Swift: Polite Conversation, Dialogue 1

PROMPTNESS

1 Punctuality is the politeness of kings.
Louis XVIII: Attrib.

2 Better never than late.
George Bernard Shaw: Responding to an offer by a producer to present one of Shaw's plays, earlier rejected it. The Unimportance of Being Oscar (Oscar Levant)

3 He gives twice who gives promptly.
Publilius Syrus: Attrib.

4 Punctuality is the virtue of the bored.
Evelyn Waugh: Diaries, 'Irregular Notes', 26 Mar 1962

PROPAGANDA

1 Propaganda is that branch of the art of lying which consists in nearly deceiving your friends without quite deceiving your enemies.
F. M. Cornford: New Statesman, 15 Sept 1978

2 The greater the lie, the greater the chance that it will be believed.
Adolf Hitler: Mein Kampf

3 I wonder if we could contrive… some magnificent myth that would in itself carry conviction to our whole community.
Plato: Republic, Bk. 5

PROSE

See also literature, poetry

1 Yet no one hears his own remarks as prose.
W. H. Auden: At a Party

2 Men will forgive a man anything except bad prose.
Winston Churchill: Election speech, Manchester, 1906

3 The pulpit was the cradle of English prose.
A. G. Little: English Historical Review, xlix (1934)

4 Good heavens! I have been talking prose for over forty years without realizing it.
Molière: Le Bourgeois Gentilhomme, II:4

PRUDENCE

See also caution, wisdom

1 Forewarned is forearmed.
Proverb

2 Prevention is better than cure.
Proverb

3 One does not insult the river god while crossing the river.
Anonymous: Chinese proverb.

4 Put your trust in God, my boys, and keep your powder dry.
Valentine Blacker: Oliver Cromwell's Advice

5 I'd much rather have that fellow inside my tent pissing out, than outside my tent pissing in.
Lyndon B. Johnson: When asked why he retained J. Edgar Hoover at the FBI. Guardian Weekly, 18 Dec 1971

6 Be nice to people on your way up because you'll meet 'em on your way down.
Wilson Mizner: Also attributed to Jimmy Durante. A Dictionary of Catch Phrases (Eric Partridge)

PRUDERY

See also censorship, puritanism

1 We have long passed the Victorian Era when asterisks were followed after a certain interval by a baby.
W. Somerset Maugham: The Constant Wife

2 Age will bring all things, and everyone knows, Madame, that twenty is no age to be a prude.
Molière: Le Misanthrope, III:4

3 An orgy looks particularly alluring seen through the mists of righteous indignation.
Malcolm Muggeridge: The Most of Malcolm Muggeridge, 'Dolce Vita in a Cold Climate'

PSYCHIATRY

See also madness, neurosis

1 The new definition of psychiatry is the care of the id by the odd.
Anonymous

2 Just because you're paranoid doesn't mean you're not being followed.
Anonymous

3 Psychiatrist: A man who asks you a lot of expensive questions your wife asks you for nothing.
Sam Bardell

4 No man is a hero to his wife's psychiatrist.
Eric Berne: Bartlett's Unfamiliar Quotations (Leonard Louis Levinson)

5 Psychiatry's chief contribution to philosophy is the discovery that the toilet is the seat of the soul.
Alexander Chase: Perspectives

6 A mental stain can neither be blotted out by the passage of time nor washed away by any waters.
Cicero: De Legibus, Bk. II

7 Sometimes a cigar is just a cigar.
Sigmund Freud: When asked by one of his students whether there was any symbolism in the large cigars that Freud smoked. Attrib.

8 Anybody who goes to see a psychiatrist ought to have his head examined.
Samuel Goldwyn: Attrib.

9 Freud is the father of psychoanalysis. It has no mother.
Germaine Greer: The Female Eunuch

10 Schizophrenic behaviour is a special strategy that a person invents in order to live in an unlivable situation.
R. D. Laing: The Politics of Experience

11 The mystic sees the ineffable, and the psychopathologist the unspeakable.
W. Somerset Maugham: The Moon and Sixpence, Ch. 1

12 If the nineteenth century was the age of the editorial chair, ours is the century of the psychiatrist's couch.
Marshall McLuhan: Understanding Media, Introduction

13 The care of the human mind is the most noble branch of medicine.
Aloysius Sieffert: Medical and Surgical Practitioner's Memorandum

14 One should only see a psychiatrist out of boredom.
Muriel Spark

15 A psychiatrist is a man who goes to the Folies-Bergère and looks at the audience.
Mervyn Stockwood: The Observer, 'Sayings of the Week', 15 Oct 1961

16 Psychiatrists classify a person as neurotic if he suffers from his problems in living, and a psychotic if he makes others suffer.
Thomas Szasz: The Second Sin

17 A neurotic is the man who builds a castle in the air. A psychotic is the man who lives in it. And a psychiatrist is the man who collects the rent.
Lord Robert Webb-Johnstone: Collected Papers

PSYCHOLOGY

See also mind

1 An animal psychologist is a man who pulls habits out of rats.
Anonymous

2 It seems a pity that psychology should have destroyed all our knowledge of human nature.
G. K. Chesterton: The Observer, 9 Dec 1934

3 Psychology has a long past, but only a short history.
Hermann Ebbinghaus: Summary of Psychology

4 The separation of psychology from the premises of biology is purely artificial, because the hu-

man psyche lives in indissoluble union with the body.
Carl Gustav Jung: Factors Determining Human Behaviour, 'Psychological Factors Determining Human Behaviour'

5 Psychology is as unnecessary as directions for using poison.
Karl Kraus

6 Psychology which explains everything
explains nothing,
and we are still in doubt.
Marianne Moore: Collected Poems, 'Marriage'

7 Idleness is the parent of all psychology.
Friedrich Nietzsche: Twilight of the Idols, 'Maxims and Missiles'

8 There is no psychology; there is only biography and autobiography.
Thomas Szasz: The Second Sin, 'Psychology'

PUBLIC

See also class, majority

1 *Vox populi, vox dei.*
The voice of the people is the voice of God.
Alcuin: Letter to Charlemagne

2 The great Unwashed.
Henry Peter Brougham: Attrib.

3 The people are the masters.
Edmund Burke: Speech on the Economical Reform (House of Commons, 11 Feb 1780)

4 The Public is an old woman. Let her maunder and mumble.
Thomas Carlyle: Journal, 1835

5 The public are usually more sensible than politicians or the press.
Kenneth Clarke: Speech at the Mansion House, 15 June 1994

6 The people would be just as noisy if they were going to see me hanged.
Oliver Cromwell: Referring to a cheering crowd.

7 Only constant repetition will finally succeed in imprinting an idea on the memory of the crowd.
Adolf Hitler: Mein Kampf, Ch. 6

8 The people long eagerly for just two things – bread and circuses.
Juvenal: Satires, X

9 The multitude is always in the wrong.
Earl of Roscommon: Essay on Translated Verse

10 Once the people begin to reason, all is lost.
Voltaire: Letter to Damilaville, 1 Apr 1766

11 Our supreme governors, the mob.
Horace Walpole: Letter to Sir Horace Mann, 7 Sept 1743

PUBLISHING

See also books

1 Publication is the male equivalent of childbirth.
Richard Acland: The Observer, 'Sayings of the Week', 19 May 1974

2 If I had been someone not very clever, I would have done an easier job like publishing. That's the easiest job I can think of.
A. J. Ayer: Remark, Sept 1994

3 As repressed sadists are supposed to become policemen or

butchers so those with irrational fear of life become publishers.
Cyril Connolly: Enemies of Promise, Ch. 3

4 My own motto is publish and be sued.
Richard Ingrams: Referring to his editorship of Private Eye. See Duke of WELLINGTON. BBC radio broadcast, 4 May 1977

5 Publish and be damned!
Duke of Wellington: On being offered the chance to avoid mention in the memoirs of Harriette Wilson by giving her money. Attrib.

PUNISHMENT

See also education, execution, imprisonment

1 And Cain said unto the Lord, My punishment is greater than I can bear.
Bible: Genesis: 4:12–13

2 Then the Lord rained upon Sodom and upon Gomorrah brimstone and fire from the Lord out of heaven.
Bible: Genesis: 19:24

3 He that spareth his rod hateth his son: but he that loveth him chasteneth him betimes.
Bible: Proverbs: 13:24

4 Love is a boy, by poets styl'd, Then spare the rod, and spoil the child.
Samuel Butler: Hudibras, Pt. II

5 Punishment is not for revenge, but to lessen crime and reform the criminal.
Elizabeth Fry: Biography of Distinguished Women (Sarah Josepha Hale)

6 The only thing I really mind about going to prison is the thought of Lord Longford coming to visit me.
Richard Ingrams: Attrib.

7 Corporal punishment is as humiliating for him who gives it as for him who receives it; it is ineffective besides. Neither shame nor physical pain have any other effect than a hardening one
Ellen Key: The Century of the Child, Ch. 8

8 The refined punishments of the spiritual mode are usually much more indecent and dangerous than a good smack.
D. H. Lawrence: Fantasia of the Unconscious, Ch. 4

9 Men are not hanged for stealing horses, but that horses may not be stolen.
George Saville: Political, Moral and Miscellaneous Thoughts and Reflections

10 Condemn the fault and not the actor of it?
William Shakespeare: Measure for Measure, II:2

11 Eating the bitter bread of banishment.
William Shakespeare: Richard II, III:1

12 Whipping and abuse are like laudanum: You have to double the dose as the sensibilities decline.
Harriet Beecher Stowe: Uncle Tom's Cabin, Ch. 20

13 I'm all for bringing back the birch, but only between consenting adults.

Gore Vidal: Said when asked by David Frost in a TV interview for his views about corporal punishment.

PUNS

See also humour

1 When I am dead, I hope it may be said:
'His sins were scarlet, but his books were read.'
Hilaire Belloc: Epigrams, 'On His Books'

2 Like Webster's Dictionary
We're Morocco bound.
Johnny Burke: Song, 'Road to Morocco' from the film The Road to Morocco

3 A man who could make so vile a pun would not scruple to pick a pocket.
John Dennis: The Gentleman's Magazine, 1781

4 Any stigma will do to beat a dogma.
Philip Guedalla: Attrib.

5 His death, which happen'd in his berth,
At forty-odd befell:
They went and told the sexton, and
The sexton toll'd the bell.
Thomas Hood: Faithless Sally Brown

6 Ben Battle was a soldier bold,
And used to war's alarms:
But a cannon-ball took off his legs,
So he laid down his arms!
Thomas Hood: Faithless Nelly Gray

7 It is a pistol let off at the ear; not a feather to tickle the intellect.

Charles Lamb: Referring to the nature of a pun. Last Essays of Elia, 'Popular Fallacies'

8 Thou canst not serve both cod and salmon.
Ada Beddington Leverson: Reply when offered a choice of fish at dinner. The Times, 7 Nov 1970

9 What's a thousand dollars? Mere chicken feed. A poultry matter.
Groucho Marx: The Cocoanuts

10 Contraceptives should be used on all conceivable occasions.
Spike Milligan

11 It has been said that a bride's attitude towards her betrothed can be summed up in three words: Aisle. Altar. Hymn.
Frank Muir: Upon My Word! (Frank Muir and Dennis Norden), 'A Jug of Wine'

12 You can lead a whore to culture but you can't make her think.
Dorothy Parker: Speech to American Horticultural Society

13 I tried to resist his overtures, but he plied me with symphonies, quartettes, chamber music and cantatas.
S. J. Perelman: Crazy Like a Fox, 'The Love Decoy'

14 Mother always told me my day was coming, but I never realized that I'd end up being the shortest knight of the year.
Gordon Richards: Referring to his diminutive size, on learning of his knighthood. Attrib.

15 That's right. 'Taint yours, and 'taint mine.

Mark Twain: Agreeing with a friend's comment that the money of a particular rich industrialist was 'tainted'. Attrib.

PURITANISM

See also prudery

1 A puritan's a person who pours righteous indignation into the wrong things.
G. K. Chesterton: Attrib.

2 To the Puritan all things are impure, as somebody says.
D. H. Lawrence: Etruscan Places, 'Cerveteri'

3 Puritanism – The haunting fear that someone, somewhere, may be happy.
H. L. Mencken: A Book of Burlesques

PURITY

1 I'm as pure as the driven slush.
Tallulah Bankhead: The Observer, 'Sayings of the Week', 24 Feb 1957

2 It is one of the superstitions of the human mind to have imagined that virginity could be a virtue.
Voltaire: Notebooks

3 I used to be Snow White…but I drifted.
Mae West: The Wit and Wisdom of Mae West (ed. J. Weintraub)

PURPOSE

See also motive

1 What is the use of a new-born child?
Benjamin Franklin: Response when asked the same question of a new invention. Life and Times of Benjamin Franklin (J. Parton), Pt. IV

2 A useless life is an early death.
Goethe: Iphigenie, I:2

3 The purpose of population is not ultimately peopling earth. It is to fill heaven.
Graham Leonard: Said during a debate on the Church and the Bomb. Speech, General Synod of the Church of England, 10 Feb 1983

4 If people want a sense of purpose they should get it from their archbishop. They should certainly not get it from their politicians.
Harold Macmillan: The Life of Politics (H. Fairlie)

Q

QUOTATIONS

See also misquotations

1 It is a good thing for an uneducated man to read books of quotations.
*Winston Churchill: My Early Life,
Ch. 9*

2 When a thing has been said and
said well, have no scruple. Take
it and copy it.
*Anatole France: The Routledge
Dictionary of Quotations (Robert
Andrews)*

3 Every quotation contributes
something to the stability or en-
largement of the language.
*Samuel Johnson: Dictionary of the
English Language*

4 If with the literate I am
Impelled to try an epigram
I never seek to take the credit
We all assume that Oscar said it.
Dorothy Parker: Oscar Wilde

5 It is gentlemanly to get one's
quotations very slightly wrong.
In that way one unprigs oneself
and allows the company to correct one.
*Lord Ribblesdale: The Light of
Common Day (Lady D. Cooper)*

6 The devil can cite Scripture for
his purpose.
*William Shakespeare: The
Merchant of Venice, I:3*

7 It's better to be quotable than to
be honest.
Tom Stoppard: The Guardian

8 The nicest thing about quotes is
that they give us a nodding acquaintance with the originator
which is often socially impres-
sive.
Kenneth Williams: Acid Drops

R

RACISM

See also equality, freedom, human rights, oppression

1 It is a great shock at the age of five or six to find that in a world of Gary Coopers you are the Indian.
James Baldwin: Gary Cooper, the US film actor, was best known for his roles as cowboy heroes in Westerns. Speech, Cambridge Union, 17 Feb 1965

2 To like an individual because he's black is just as insulting as to dislike him because he isn't white.
e. e. cummings: Attrib.

3 I suffer from an incurable disease – colour blindness.
Joost de Blank: Attrib.

4 I'm a coloured, one-eyed Jew.
Sammy Davis Jnr: When asked what his handicap was during a game of golf. Attrib.

5 When the white man came we had the land and they had the Bibles; now they have the land and we have the Bibles.
Dan George: Attrib.

6 All those who are not racially pure are mere chaff.
Adolf Hitler: Mein Kampf, Ch. 2

7 I want to be the white man's brother, not his brother-in-law.
Martin Luther King: New York Journal-American, 10 Sept 1962

8 When a white man in Africa by accident looks into the eyes of a native and sees the human being (which it is his chief preoccupa-tion to avoid), his sense of guilt, which he denies, fumes up in re-sentment and he brings down the whip.
Doris Lessing: The Grass is Singing, Ch. 8

9 A coloured man can tell, in five seconds dead, whether a white man likes him or not. If the white man *says* he does, he is in-stantly – and usually quite right-ly – mistrusted.
Colin MacInnes: England, Half English, 'A Short Guide for Jumbles'

10 It's just like when you've got some coffee that's too black, which means it's too strong. What do you do? You integrate it with cream, you make it weak… It used to wake you up, now it puts you to sleep.
Malcolm X: Referring to Black Power and the Civil Rights movement. Malcolm X Speaks, Ch. 14

11 The soil of our country is des-tined to be the scene of the fiercest fight and the sharpest struggles to rid our continent of the last vestiges of white minority rule.
Nelson Mandela: Speech, from prison, June 1980

12 One of the things that makes a Negro unpleasant to white folk is the fact that he suffers from their injustice. He is thus a standing rebuke to them.
H. L. Mencken: Notebooks, 'Minority Report'

231 REALISM

3 He's really awfully fond of coloured people. Well, he says himself, he wouldn't have white servants.
Dorothy Parker: Arrangements in Black and White

4 We don't want apartheid liberalized. We want it dismantled. You can't improve something that is intrinsically evil.
Archbishop Desmond Tutu: The Observer, 'Sayings of the Week', 10 Mar 1985

RAPE

Words such as 'beast', 'monster' and 'sex fiend' are commonly used to describe the rapist. Yet we rarely see the simple word 'man', which the rapist invariably is.
Cambridge Rape Crisis Centre: Out of Focus

Rape is a form of mass terrorism.
Susan Griffin: Women: a Feminist Perspective (ed. Jo Freeman)

All men are rapists.
Marilyn French: The Women's Room

If she doesn't want it she only has to keep her legs shut.
Judge David Wild: Cambridge, 1982

READING

See also books, fiction, literature, novels, poetry

Reading maketh a full man; conference a ready man; and writing an exact man.
Francis Bacon: Essays, 'Of Studies'

2 Reading is sometimes an ingenious device for avoiding thought.
Arthur Helps: Friends in Council

3 A man ought to read just as inclination leads him; for what he reads as a task will do him little good.
Samuel Johnson: Life of Johnson (J. Boswell), Vol. I

4 To read too many books is harmful.
Mao Tse-Tung: The New Yorker, 7 Mar 1977

5 People say that life is the thing, but I prefer reading.
Logan Pearsall Smith: Afterthoughts, 'Myself'

6 Reading is to the mind what exercise is to the body.
Richard Steele: The Tatler, 147

REALISM

1 Mr Lely, I desire you would use all your skill to paint my picture truly like me, and not flatter me at all; but remark all these roughnesses, pimples, warts, and everything as you see me, otherwise I will never pay a farthing for it.
Oliver Cromwell: The origin of the expression 'warts and all'. Anecdotes of Painting (Horace Walpole), Ch. 12

2 If at first you don't succeed, try, try again. Then quit. No use being a damn fool about it.
W. C. Fields

3 We must rediscover the distinc-

tion between hope and expectation.
Ivan Illich: Deschooling Society, Ch. 7

REALITY

1 For I see now that I am asleep that I dream when I am awake.
Pedro Calderón de la Barca: La Vida es Sueño, II

2 We live in a fantasy world, a world of illusion. The great task in life is to find reality.
Iris Murdoch: The Times, 15 Apr 1983

3 Things are entirely what they appear to be and *behind them…* there is nothing.
Jean-Paul Sartre: Nausea

4 And even the most solid of things, the most real, the best-loved and the well-known, are only hand-shadows on the wall. Empty space and points of light.
Jeanette Winterson: Sexing the Cherry

REASON

See also motive

1 Reason is itself a matter of faith. It is an act of faith to assert that our thoughts have any relation to reality at all.
G. K. Chesterton: Orthodoxy, Ch. 3

2 Fools give you reasons, wise men never try.
Oscar Hammerstein: South Pacific, 'Some Enchanted Evening'

3 Come now, let us reason together.
Lyndon B. Johnson: Attrib., often used

4 A man who does not lose his reason over certain things has none to lose.
Gotthold Ephraim Lessing: Emilia Galotti, IV:7

5 There is occasions and causes why and wherefore in all things.
William Shakespeare: Henry V, V:1

REBELLION

See also revolution

1 What is a rebel? A man who says no.
Albert Camus: The Rebel

2 No one can go on being a rebel too long without turning into an autocrat.
Lawrence Durrell: Balthazar, II

3 When the People contend for their Liberty, they seldom get anything by their Victory but new masters.
Lord Halifax: Political, Moral, and Miscellaneous Thoughts and Reflections

4 A little rebellion now and then is a good thing.
Thomas Jefferson: Letter to James Madison, 30 Jan 1787

5 A riot is at bottom the language of the unheard.
Martin Luther King: Chaos or Community, Ch. 4

REGRET

See also apologies, memory,

mourning, nostalgia, past,
sorrow

1 It is no use crying over spilt
milk.
Proverb

2 I say unto you, that likewise joy
shall be in heaven over one sin-
ner that repenteth, more than
over ninety and nine just persons, which need no repentance.
Bible: Luke: 15:7

3 Were it not better to forget
Than but remember and regret?
Letitia Landon: Despondency

4 Regret is an appalling waste of
energy; you can't build on it; it's
only good for wallowing in.
Katherine Mansfield: Attrib.

5 Maybe it would have been better if neither of us had been
born.
*Napoleon I: Said while looking at
the tomb of the philosopher Jean-
Jacques Rousseau, whose theories
had influenced the French
Revolution. The Story of
Civilization (W. Durant), Vol. II*

6 The follies which a man regrets
most in his life are those which
he didn't commit when he had
the opportunity.
*Helen Rowland: Reflections of a
Bachelor Girl*

7 But with the morning cool repentance came.
Walter Scott: Rob Roy, Ch. 12

RELIGION

See also belief, Christianity, faith

1 If I hungered, a single look at
the Prophet's face dispelled the
hunger. Before him all forgot
their griefs and pains.
*Ali: Describing Mohammed
(570–632). Chronique (Abu
Jafar Mohammed al-Tabari),
Pt. III, Ch. 46*

2 He was of the faith chiefly in the
sense that the church he cur-
rently did not attend was
Catholic.
*Kingsley Amis: One Fat
Englishman*

3 There is no salvation outside the
church.
*St Augustine of Hippo: De Bapt.,
IV*

4 The Jews and Arabs should sit
down and settle their differences
like good Christians.
Warren Austin: Attrib.

5 One cathedral is worth a hundred theologians capable of
proving the existence of God by
logic.
Julian Barnes: Staring at the Sun

6 INDIGESTION, n. A disease
which the patient and his friends
frequently mistake for deep religious conviction and concern
for the salvation of mankind.
*Ambrose Bierce: The Devil's
Dictionary*

7 Every day people are straying
away from the church and going
back to God. Really.
*Lenny Bruce: The Essential Lenny
Bruce (ed. J. Cohen), 'Religions
Inc.'*

8 This Ariyan Eightfold Path, that
is to say: Right view, right aim,
right speech, right action, right
living, right effort, right mind-
fulness, right contemplation.
*Buddha: Some Sayings of the
Buddha (F. L. Woodward)*

9 Man is by his constitution a religious animal.
Edmund Burke: Reflections on the Revolution in France

10 One religion is as true as another.
Robert Burton: Anatomy of Melancholy, Pt. III

11 It is a mockery to allow women to baptise. Even the Virgin Mary was not allowed this.
John Calvin: Institution de la religion Chrestienne

12 The idea that only a male can represent Christ at the altar is a most serious heresy.
George Carey: Reader's Digest, Apr 1991

13 Men will wrangle for religion; write for it; fight for it; anything but – live for it.
Charles Caleb Colton: Lacon, Vol. I

14 'Sensible men are all of the same religion.' 'And pray what is that?' inquired the prince. 'Sensible men never tell.'
Benjamin Disraeli: Endymion, Bk. I, Ch. 81

15 Christian Science explains all cause and effect as mental, not physical.
Mary Baker Eddy: Science and Health, with Key to the Scriptures

16 Science without religion is lame, religion without science is blind.
Albert Einstein: Out of My Later Years

17 The religions we call false were once true.
Ralph Waldo Emerson: Essays, 'Character'

18 There exists no politician in India daring enough to attempt to explain to the masses that cows can be eaten.
Indira Gandhi: The New York Review of Books, 'Indira's Coup' (Oriana Fallaci)

19 God has no religion.
Mahatma Gandhi: Attrib.

20 Decide for Christ.
Billy Graham: Slogan

21 I could always not deal with my problems by referring to God, my comfort…Religion was my protection against pain.
David Hare: The Sunday Times, 11 Feb 1990

22 The sedate, sober, silent, serious, sad-coloured sect.
Thomas Hood: Referring to the Quakers. The Doves and the Crows

23 To become a popular religion, it is only necessary for a superstition to enslave a philosophy.
Dean Inge: Outspoken Essays

24 Many people believe that they are attracted by God, or by Nature, when they are only repelled by man.
Dean Inge: More Lay Thoughts of a Dean

25 Here stand I. I can do no other God help me. Amen.
Martin Luther: Speech at the Diet of Worms, 18 Apr 1521

26 Religion…is the opium of the people.
Karl Marx: Criticism of the Hegelian Philosophy of Right, Introduction

27 Things have come to a pretty pass when religion is allowed to invade the sphere of private life.
Lord Melbourne: Attrib.

28 Man is quite insane. He wouldn't know how to create a maggot and he creates Gods by the dozen.
Michel de Montaigne: Essais, II

29 There is a very good saying that if triangles invented a god, they would make him three-sided.
Baron de Montesquieu: Lettres persanes

30 Our religion doesn't give women any human dignity.
Taslima Nasreen: The Times, 22 June 1994

31 The Christian resolution to find the world ugly and bad has made the world ugly and bad.
Friedrich Nietzsche: Die Fröhliche Wissenschaft

32 Religion has always been the wound, not the bandage.
Dennis Potter: The Observer, 'Sayings of the Week', 10 Apr 1994

33 If women in the priesthood has come as a result of women's liberation, then I think it is satanic.
William Pwaisiho: The Daily Telegraph, Aug 1988

34 Unlike Christianity, which preached a peace that it never achieved, Islam unashamedly came with a sword.
Steven Runciman: A History of the Crusades, 'The First Crusade'

35 Jesus loves me – this I know, For the Bible tells me so.
Susan Warner: The Love of Jesus

36 Religion is love; in no case is it logic.
Beatrice Webb: My Apprenticeship, Ch. 2

37 Why do born-again people so often make you wish they'd never been born the first time?
Katharine Whitehorn: The Observer, 20 May 1979

38 The Ethiopians say that their gods are snub-nosed and black, the Thracians that theirs have light blue eyes and red hair.
Xenophanes: Fragment 15

39 The only difference between a religion and a cult is the amount of real estate they own.
Frank Zappa: Interview

REMEDIES

See also doctors, medicine

1 Many medicines, few cures.
Proverb

2 Visitors' footfalls are like medicine; they heal the sick.
Bantu proverb

3 The remedy is worse than the disease.
Francis Bacon: Essays, 'Of Seditions and Troubles'

4 My father invented a cure for which there was no disease and unfortunately my mother caught it and died of it.
Victor Borge: In Concert

5 When a lot of remedies are suggested for a disease, that means it can't be cured.
Anton Chekhov: The Cherry Orchard, II

6 Men worry over the great number of diseases; doctors worry over the small number of remedies.
Pien Ch'iao

7 If you are too fond of new remedies, first you will not cure your

REPRESENTATION

patients; secondly, you will have
no patients to cure.

Astley Paston Cooper

8 What destroys one man preserves another.

Pierre Corneille: Cinna, II:1

9 Like cures like.

*Samuel Hahnemann: Motto for
homeopathy*

10 Extreme remedies are most appropriate for extreme diseases.

Hippocrates: Aphorisms, I

11 Poisons and medicine are oftentimes the same substance
given with different intents.

*Peter Mere Latham: General
Remarks on the Practice of
Medicine, Ch. 7*

12 The best of healers is good
cheer.

Pindar: Nemean Ode, IV

13 Our remedies oft in ourselves
do lie,
Which we ascribe to heaven.

*William Shakespeare: All's Well
That Ends Well, I:1*

14 Dr. Snow gave that blessed
Chloroform & the effect was
soothing, quieting & delightful
beyond measure.

*Victoria: Describing her labour.
Journal*

15 There is only one cure for grey
hair. It was invented by a
Frenchman. It is called the guillotine.

P. G. Wodehouse: The Old Reliable

REPRESENTATION

1 In Scotland there is no shadow
even of representation. There is
neither a representation of prop-

erty for the counties, nor of population for the towns.

*Charles James Fox: Parliamentary
History of England (W. Cobbett),
Vol. XXXIII*

2 Taxation without representation
is tyranny.

*James Otis: As 'No taxation
without representation' this became
the principal slogan of the
American Revolution. Attrib.*

3 No annihilation without
representation.

*Arnold Toynbee: Urging the need
for a greater British influence in the
UN 1947*

REPUTATION

See also fame, posterity

1 I hold it as certain, that no man
was ever written out of reputation but by himself.

*Richard Bentley: The Works of
Alexander Pope (W. Warburton),
Vol. IV*

2 Reputation is a bubble which
bursts when a man tries to blow
it up for himself.

Emma Carleton: Attrib.

3 Until you've lost your reputation, you never realize what a
burden it was or what freedom
really is.

*Margaret Mitchell: Gone with the
Wind*

4 Reputation, reputation, reputation! O, I have lost my reputation! I have lost the immortal
part of myself, and what remains
is bestial.

*William Shakespeare: Othello,
II:3*

5 My reputation grew with every failure.
George Bernard Shaw: Referring to his unsuccessful early novels.
Bernard Shaw (Hesketh Pearson)

RESEARCH

1 We vivisect the nightingale
To probe the secret of his note.
T. B. Aldrich

2 Research! A mere excuse for idleness; it has never achieved, and will never achieve any results of the slightest value.
Benjamin Jowett: Unforgotten Years (Logan Pearsall Smith)

3 The outcome of any serious research can only be to make two questions grow where only one grew before.
Thorstein Bunde Veblen: The Place of Science in Modern Civilization

RESPECT

See also courtesy, self-respect

1 Let them hate, so long as they fear.
Lucius Accius: Atreus, 'Seneca'

2 I hate victims who respect their executioners.
Jean-Paul Sartre: Altona

3 We owe respect to the living; to the dead we owe only truth.
Voltaire: Oeuvres, 'Première lettre sur Oedipe'

4 The old-fashioned respect for the young is fast dying out.
Oscar Wilde: The Importance of Being Earnest, I

RESPONSIBILITY

1 A bad workman always blames his tools.
Proverb

2 Each man the architect of his own fate.
Appius Caecus: De Civitate (Sallust), Bk. I

3 Perhaps it is better to be irresponsible and right than to be responsible and wrong.
Winston Churchill: Party Political Broadcast, London, 26 Aug 1950

4 Power without responsibility – the prerogative of the harlot throughout the ages.
Rudyard Kipling: Attrib.

5 Accuse not Nature, she hath done her part;
Do thou but thine.
John Milton: Paradise Lost, Bk. VIII

6 *We can believe what we choose. We are answerable for what we choose to believe.*
Cardinal Newman: Letter to Mrs Froude, 27 June 1848

7 You become responsible, forever, for what you have tamed. You are responsible for your rose.
Antoine de Saint-Exupéry: The Little Prince, Ch. 21

8 The House of Lords, an illusion to which I have never been able to subscribe – responsibility without power, the prerogative of the eunuch throughout the ages.
Tom Stoppard: Lord Malquist and Mr Moon, Pt. VI, Ch. 1

9 The buck stops here.

Harry S. Truman: Sign kept on his desk during his term as president. Presidential Anecdotes (P. Boller).

10 In dreams begins responsibility.
W. B. Yeats: Old Play, Epigraph, Responsibilities

REVENGE

1 Revenge is a dish that tastes better cold.
Proverb

2 Revenge is sweet.
Proverb

3 A man that studieth revenge keeps his own wounds green.
Francis Bacon: Essays, 'Of Revenge'

4 Perish the Universe, provided I have my revenge.
Cyrano de Bergerac: La Mort d'Agrippine, IV

5 No one delights more in vengeance than a woman.
Juvenal: Satires, XIII

6 Don't get mad, get even.
Joseph P. Kennedy: Conversations with Kennedy (B. Bradlee)

7 Revenge, at first though sweet, Bitter ere long back on itself recoils.
John Milton: Paradise Lost, Bk. IX

8 No more tears now; I will think upon revenge.
Mary Stuart: Remark on hearing of the murder (9 Mar 1566) of her secretary, David Riccio, by her husband, Lord Darnley

REVOLUTION

See also rebellion

1 Inferiors revolt in order that they may be equal and equals that they may be superior. Such is the state of mind which creates revolutions.
Aristotle: Politics, Bk. V

2 All modern revolutions have ended in a reinforcement of the power of the State.
Albert Camus: The Rebel

3 A revolution is not a bed of roses. A revolution is a struggle to the death between the future and the past.
Fidel Castro: Speech, Havana, Jan 1961 (2nd anniversary of the Cuban Revolution)

4 Many will call me an adventurer – and that I am, only one of a different sort: one of those who risks his skin to prove his platitudes.
Che Guevara: On leaving Cuba to join guerrillas in the Bolivian jungle. Last letter to his parents, 1965

5 What is wrong with a revolution is that it is natural. It is as natural as natural selection, as devastating as natural selection, and as horrible.
William Golding: The Observer, 'Sayings of the Year', 1974

6 Revolution is delightful in the preliminary stages. So long as it's a question of getting rid of the people at the top.
Aldous Huxley: Eyeless in Gaza

7 We are dancing on a volcano.

Comte de Salvandy: A remark made before the July Revolution in 1830.

8 To attempt to export revolution is nonsense.
Joseph Stalin: Remark, 1 Mar 1936, to Roy Howard (US newspaper owner)

9 Insurrection is an art, and like all arts it has its laws.
Leon Trotsky: History of the Russian Revolution, Pt. III, Ch. 6

10 The word 'revolution' is a word for which you kill, for which you die, for which you send the labouring masses to their death, but which does not possess any content.
Simone Weil: Oppression and Liberty, 'Reflections Concerning the Causes of Liberty and Social Oppression'

11 We invented the Revolution but we don't know how to run it.
Peter Weiss: MaratSade, 15

RIDICULE

See also satire

1 For what do we live, but to make sport for our neighbours, and laugh at them in our turn?
Jane Austen: Pride and Prejudice, Ch. 57

2 Few women care to be laughed at and men not at all, except for large sums of money.
Alan Ayckbourn: The Norman Conquests, Preface

3 It often happens, that he who endeavours to ridicule other people, especially in things of a serious nature, becomes himself a jest, and frequently to his great cost.
Giovanni Boccaccio: Decameron, 'Second Day'

4 Ridicule often checks what is absurd, and fully as often smothers that which is noble.
Walter Scott: Quentin Durward

RIGHT

1 This the grave of Mike O'Day
Who died maintaining his right of way.
His right was clear, his will was strong.
But he's just as dead as if he'd been wrong.
Anonymous: Epitaph

2 A child becomes an adult when he realizes that he has a right not only to be right but also to be wrong.
Thomas Szasz: The Second Sin

RIGHTEOUSNESS

See also good, integrity, morality, virtue

1 Righteous people terrify me…
Virtue is its own punishment.
Aneurin Bevan: Aneurin Bevan 1897–1945 (Michael Foot)

2 Ye must leave righteous ways behind, not to speak of un-righteous ways.
Buddha: Some Sayings of the Buddha (F. L. Woodward)

3 Live among men as if God beheld you; speak to God as if men were listening.
Seneca: Epistles

ROYALTY

See also monarchy

1 The personality conveyed by the utterances which are put into her mouth is that of a priggish schoolgirl, captain of the hockey team, a prefect, and a recent candidate for confirmation.
Lord Altrincham: Referring to Queen Elizabeth II. National and English Review, Aug 1958

2 Bloody hell, Ma'am, what's he doing here?
Elizabeth Andrews: Discovering an intruder sitting on Queen Elizabeth II's bed. Daily Mail, July 1982

3 There is no romance between us. He is here solely to exercise the horses.
Princess Anne: Shortly before her engagement to Captain Phillips. Attrib.

4 How different, how very different from the home life of our own dear Queen!
Anonymous: Remark about the character of Cleopatra as performed by Sarah Bernhardt. It refers to Queen Victoria.

5 Hark the herald angels sing Mrs Simpson's pinched our king.
Anonymous: Referring to the abdication of Edward VIII.

6 Speed, bonny boat, like a bird on the wing;
'Onward', the sailors cry;
Carry the lad that's born to be king
Over the sea to Skye.

H. E. Boulton: Referring to Bonnie Prince Charlie. 'Skye Boat Song'

7 Such grace had kings when the world began!
Robert Browning: Pippa Passes, Pt. I

8 Kings are naturally lovers of low company.
Edmund Burke: Speech on the Economical Reform (House of Commons, 11 Feb 1780)

9 I shall be an autocrat: that's my trade. And the good Lord will forgive me: that's his.
Catherine the Great: Attrib.

10 Retirement, for a monarch, is not a good idea.
Charles, Prince of Wales: Speech, 1974

11 Yes, until it became clear that the marriage had irretrievably broken down.
Charles, Prince of Wales: On being asked if he had been faithful to his wife. ITV programme Charles: The Private Man, The Public Role

12 Her Majesty is not a subject.
Benjamin Disraeli: Responding to Gladstone's taunt that Disraeli could make a joke out of any subject, including Queen Victoria. Attrib.

13 The courtiers who surrounded him have forgotten nothing and learnt nothing.
Charles-François Dumouriez: Referring to Louis XVIII. This remark is also attributed to the French statesman Talleyrand. Attrib.

14 Royalty must think the whole country always smells of fresh paint.

Elizabeth Dunn: The Sunday Times

15 I know I have the body of a weak and feeble woman, but I have the heart and stomach of a King, and of a King of England too.

Elizabeth I: Speech at Tilbury on the approach of the Spanish Armada

16 I will make you shorter by a head.

Elizabeth I: Sayings of Queen Elizabeth (Chamberlin)

17 I think that everyone will concede that – today of all days – I should begin by saying, 'My husband and I'.

Elizabeth II: On her silver-wedding. The phrase, 'My husband and I,' is mistakenly associated with her through the humorous idea that this is the way in which she begins all her speeches. Speech, Guildhall, 1972

18 1992 is not a year I shall look back on with undiluted pleasure. In the words of one of my more sympathetic correspondents, it has turned out to be an 'annus horribilis'.

Elizabeth II: Alluding to Annus Mirabilis, a poem by John Dryden.

19 A crown is merely a hat that lets the rain in.

Frederick the Great: Remark

20 I don't mind your being killed, but I object to your being taken prisoner.

Lord Kitchener: Said to the Prince of Wales (later Edward VIII) when he asked to go to the Front. Journal (Viscount Esher), 18 Dec 1914

21 When it comes to culture,

you'll find more on a month-old carton of yoghurt than between the ears of the Princess of Wales.

Richard Littlejohn: The Sun, 1993

22 Ah, if I were not king, I should lose my temper.

Louis XIV: Attrib.

23 Well, Mr Baldwin! this is a pretty kettle of fish!

Queen Mary: Referring to the abdication of Edward VIII. Life of Queen Mary (James Pope-Hennessy)

24 For God's sake, ma'am, let's have no more of that. If you get the English people into the way of making kings, you'll get them into the way of unmaking them.

Lord Melbourne: Advising Queen Victoria against granting Prince Albert the title of King Consort. Lord M. (Lord David Cecil)

25 The King has a way of making every man feel that he is enjoying his special favour, just as the London wives pray before the image of Our Lady by the Tower till each of them believes it is smiling upon her.

Thomas More: Referring to Henry VIII. Letter to Bishop John Fisher, 1518

26 I'm self-employed.

Prince Philip: Answering a query as to what nature of work he did. Attrib.

27 Not least among the qualities in a great King is a capacity to permit his ministers to serve him.

Cardinal Richelieu: Testament politique, Maxims

28 Kings and such like are just as funny as politicians.

Theodore Roosevelt: Mr Wilson's War (John Dos Passos), Ch. 1

29 Ay, every inch a king.
William Shakespeare: King Lear, IV:6

30 We are not amused!
Victoria: Attrib.

31 A merry monarch, scandalous and poor.
Earl of Rochester: Referring to Charles II. A Satire on King Charles II

32 The king is incompetent to govern in person. Throughout his reign he has been controlled and governed by others who have given him evil counsel.
John de Stratford: Referring to Edward II. Historiae Anglicanae Scriptores (Twysden)

33 I'd punch him in the snoot.
William Hale 'Big Bill' Thompson: His reaction if ever King George V were to come to Chicago. Attrib.

34 I go to therapy, and I'm very proud of that.
Duchess of York: The Times, 26 Aug 1993

RULES

1 The exception proves the rule.
Proverb

2 Rules and models destroy genius and art.

William Hazlitt: On Taste

3 The golden rule is that there are no golden rules.
George Bernard Shaw: Man and Superman, 'Maxims for Revolutionists'

RUTHLESSNESS

1 Would that the Roman people had but one neck!
Caligula: Life of Caligula (Suetonius), Ch. 30

2 I do not have to forgive my enemies, I have had them all shot.
Ramón Maria Narváez: Said on his deathbed, when asked by a priest if he forgave his enemies. Famous Last Words (B. Conrad)

3 3RD FISHERMAN. Master, I marvel how the fishes live in the sea. 1ST FISHERMAN. Why, as men do a-land – the great ones eat up the little ones.
William Shakespeare: Pericles, II:1

4 The world continues to offer glittering prizes to those who have stout hearts and sharp swords.
F. E. Smith: Speech, Glasgow University, 7 Nov 1923

5 It is not enough to succeed. Others must fail.
Gore Vidal: Antipanegyric for Tom Driberg (G. Irvine)

S

SATIRE

See also ridicule

1 It's hard not to write satire.
Juvenal: Satires, I

2 Satire should, like a polished
razor keen,
Wound with a touch that's
scarcely felt or seen.
*Lady Mary Wortley Montagu: To
the Imitator of the First Satire of
Horace, Bk. II*

3 Satire is a sort of glass, wherein
beholders do generally discover
everybody's face but their own.
*Jonathan Swift: The Battle of the
Books, 'Preface'*

SATISFACTION

See also contentment

1 I wasna fou, but just had plenty.
*Robert Burns: Death and Doctor
Hornbrook*

2 The reward of a thing well done
is to have done it.
*Ralph Waldo Emerson: Essays,
'New England Reformers'*

3 I can't get no satisfaction.
*Mick Jagger: 'Satisfaction' (With
Keith Richard)*

4 Open your eyes and look within.
Are you satisfied with the life
you're living?
Bob Marley: Exodus

SAYINGS

See also quotations

1 A platitude is simply a truth
repeated till people get tired of
hearing it.
Stanley Baldwin: Attrib.

2 The great writers of aphorisms
read as if they had all known
each other well.
*Elias Canetti: The Human
Province*

3 A proverb is much matter deco-
rated into few words.
*Thomas Fuller: The History of the
Worthies of England, Ch. 2*

4 A new maxim is often a brilliant
error.
*Chrétien Guillaume de
Lamoignon de Malesherbes:
Pensées et maximes*

5 A proverb is one man's wit and
all men's wisdom.
Lord John Russell: Attrib.

6 A truism is on that account
none the less true.
*Herbert Samuel: A Book of
Quotations*

SCEPTICISM

See also doubt

1 I am too much of a sceptic to
deny the possibility of anything.
*T. H. Huxley: Letter to Herbert
Spencer, 22 Mar 1886*

2 It is undesirable to believe a
proposition when there is no
ground whatever for supposing
it true.
Bertrand Russell: Sceptical Essays

3 She believed in nothing; only
her scepticism kept her from being an atheist.
Jean-Paul Sartre: Words

4 The temerity to believe in nothing.
Ivan Turgenev: Fathers and Sons, Ch. 14

SCIENCE

See also discovery, mathematics, nature, research

1 It is my intent to beget a good understanding between the chymists and the mechanical philosophers who have hitherto been too little acquainted with one another's learning.
Robert Boyle: The Sceptical Chymist

2 Science has nothing to be ashamed of, even in the ruins of Nagasaki.
Jacob Bronowski: Science and Human Values

3 When a distinguished but elderly scientist states that something is possible, he is almost certainly right. When he states that something is impossible, he is very probably wrong.
Arthur C. Clarke: Profiles of the Future

4 We have discovered the secret of life!
Francis Crick: Excitedly bursting into a Cambridge pub with James Watson to celebrate the fact that they had unravelled the structure of DNA. The Double Helix (J. D. Watson)

5 One never notices what has been done; one can only see what remains to be done.
Marie Curie: Letter to her brother, 18 Mar 1894

6 Every great advance in science has issued from a new audacity of imagination.
John Dewey: The Quest for Certainty, Ch. 11

7 Putting on the spectacles of science in expectation of finding the answer to everything looked at signifies inner blindness.
J. Frank Dobie: The Voice of Coyote, Introduction

8 The content of physics is the concern of physicists, its effect the concern of all men.
Friedrich Dürrenmatt: The Physicists

9 When you are courting a nice girl an hour seems like a second. When you sit on a red-hot cinder a second seems like an hour. That's relativity.
Albert Einstein: News Chronicle, 14 Mar 1949

10 God does not play dice.
Albert Einstein's objection to the quantum theory, in which physical events can only be known in terms of probabilities. It is sometimes quoted as 'God does not play dice with the Universe'. Albert Einstein, Creator and Rebel (B. Hoffman), Ch. 10

11 Everything should be made as simple as possible, but not simpler.
Albert Einstein: Attrib.

12 Physicists like to think that all you have to do is say, these are the conditions, now what happens next?
Richard Phillips Feynman: Chaos (James Gleick)

13 All the world is a laboratory to the inquiring mind.

*Martin H. Fischer: Fischerisms
(Howard Fabing and Ray Marr)*

14 A vacuum can only exist, I imagine, by the things which enclose it.
Zelda Fitzgerald: Journal, 1932

15 To some physicists chaos is a science of process rather than state, of becoming rather than being.
James Gleick: Chaos

16 Thus I saw that most men only care for science so far as they get a living by it, and that they worship even error when it affords them a subsistence.
Goethe: Conversations with Goethe (Johann Peter Eckermann)

17 MASTER: They split the atom by firing particles at it, at 5,500 miles a second.
BOY: Good heavens. And they only split it?
Will Hay: The Fourth Form at St Michael's

18 Science has 'explained' nothing; the more we know the more fantastic the world becomes and the profounder the surrounding darkness.
Aldous Huxley: Views Of Holland

19 The great tragedy of Science – the slaying of a beautiful hypothesis by an ugly fact.
T. H. Huxley: Collected Essays, 'Biogenesis and Abiogenesis'

20 Three quarks for Muster Mark!
*James Joyce: The word quark has since been adopted by physicists for hypothetical elementary particles.
Finnegans Wake*

21 We have genuflected before the god of science only to find that it has given us the atomic bomb, producing fears and anxieties that science can never mitigate.
Martin Luther King: Strength through Love, Ch. 13

22 Water is H_2O, hydrogen two parts, oxygen one,
but there is also a third thing, that makes it water
and nobody knows what that is.
D. H. Lawrence: Pansies, 'The Third Thing'

23 Science conducts us, step by step, through the whole range of creation, until we arrive, at length, at God.
Marguerite of Valois: Memoirs (1594–1600), Letter XII

24 Laboratorium est oratorium. The place where we do our scientific work is a place of prayer.
Joseph Needham: The Harvest of a Quiet Eye (A. L. Mackay)

25 Do you really believe that the sciences would ever have originated and grown if the way had not been prepared by magicians, alchemists, astrologers and witches whose promises and pretensions first had to create a thirst, a hunger, a taste for *hidden* and *forbidden* powers?
Friedrich Nietzsche: The Gay Science

26 Science must begin with myths, and with the criticism of myths.
Karl Popper: British Philosophy in the Mid-Century (ed. C. A. Mace)

27 Science may be described as the art of systematic over-simplification.

Karl Popper: Remark, Aug 1982

28 Science without conscience is the death of the soul.
François Rabelais

29 The people – could you patent the sun?
Jonas E. Salk: On being asked who owned the patent on his polio vaccine. Famous Men of Science (S. Bolton)

30 Science is always wrong. It never solves a problem without creating ten more.
George Bernard Shaw

31 Science is the great antidote to the poison of enthusiasm and superstition.
Adam Smith: The Wealth of Nations, Bk. V, Ch. 1

32 Fifty-five crystal spheres geared to God's crankshaft is my idea of a satisfying universe. I can't think of anything more trivial than quarks, quasars, big bangs and black holes.
Tom Stoppard: The Observer, 'Sayings of the Week', 22 May 1994

33 Discovery consists of seeing what everybody has seen and thinking what nobody has thought.
Albert Szent-Györgyi: The Scientist Speculates (I. J. Good)

34 Mystics always hope that science will some day overtake them.
Booth Tarkington: Looking Forward to the Great Adventure

35 Her own mother lived the latter years of her life in the horrible suspicion that electricity was dripping invisibly all over the house.
James Thurber: My Life and Hard Times, Ch. 2

36 Science robs men of wisdom and usually converts them into phantom beings loaded up with facts.
Miguel de Unamuno y Jugo: Essays and Soliloquies

37 Whenever science makes a discovery, the devil grabs it while the angels are debating the best way to use it.
Alan Valentine

38 Classical physics has been superseded by quantum theory: quantum theory is verified by experiments. Experiments must be described in terms of classical physics.
C. F. von Weizsäcker: Attrib.

39 The airplane stays up because it doesn't have the time to fall.
Orville Wright: Explaining the principles of powered flight. Attrib.

SCIENTISTS

1 The true men of action in our time, those who transform the world, are not the politicians and statesmen, but the scientists.
W. H. Auden: The Dyer's Hand

2 Scientists are treated like gods handing down new commandments.
Susan Howatch: The Observer, 8 May 1994

3 The physicists have known sin; and this is a knowledge which they cannot lose.
J. Robert Oppenheimer: Lecture, Massachusetts Institute of Technology, 25 Nov 1947

SEA

See also boats, navy

1 The voice of the sea speaks to
the soul.
*Kate Chopin: The Awakening,
Ch. 6*

2 We are as near to heaven by sea
as by land.
*Humphrey Gilbert: Remark made
shortly before he went down with
his ship* Squirrel. *A Book of
Anecdotes (D. George)*

3 When men come to like a sea-
life, they are not fit to live on
land.
*Samuel Johnson: Life of Johnson
(J. Boswell), Vol. II*

4 The snotgreen sea. The
scrotumtightening sea.
James Joyce: Ulysses

5 I must down to the seas again,
to the lonely sea and the sky,
And all I ask is a tall ship and a
star to steer her by,
And the wheel's kick and the
wind's song and the white sail's
shaking,
And a grey mist on the sea's face
and a grey dawn breaking.
*John Masefield: Often quoted
using 'sea' rather than 'seas', and
'I must go down' rather than 'I
must down'. Sea Fever*

6 A life on the ocean wave,
A home on the rolling deep.
*Epes Sargent: A Life on the Ocean
Wave*

7 O hear us when we cry to Thee
For those in peril on the sea.
*William Whiting: Eternal Father
Strong to Save*

SEASIDE

1 The King bathes, and with great
success; a machine follows the
Royal one into the sea, filled
with fiddlers, who play *God Save
the King* as his Majesty takes his
plunge.
*Fanny Burney: Referring to
George III at Weymouth. Diary,
8 July 1789*

2 The Walrus and the Carpenter
Were walking close at hand;
They wept like anything to see
Such quantities of sand:
'If this were only cleared away,'
They said, 'it* would *be grand!'
*Lewis Carroll: Through the
Looking-Glass, Ch. 4*

SEASONS

1 Four seasons fill the measure of
the year;
There are four seasons in the
mind of men.
John Keats: Four Seasons

2 No one thinks of winter when
the grass is green!
*Rudyard Kipling: A St Helena
Lullaby*

3 Winter is icumen in,
Lhude sing Goddamm,
Raineth drop and staineth slop
And how the wind doth ramm!
Sing: Goddamm.
Ezra Pound: Ancient Music

4 Spring has returned. The earth
is like a child that knows poems.
*Rainer Maria Rilke: Die Sonette
an Orpheus, I, 21*

5 If Winter comes, can Spring be
far behind?

Percy Bysshe Shelley: Ode to the West Wind

6 In the Spring a young man's fancy lightly turns to thoughts of love.
Alfred, Lord Tennyson: Locksley Hall

SECRECY

See also gossip

1 Only the nose knows
Where the nose goes
When the door close.
Muhammad Ali: When asked whether a boxer should have sex before a big fight. Remark, reported by Al Silverman

2 Stolen waters are sweet, and bread eaten in secret is pleasant.
Bible: Proverbs: 9:17

3 Mum's the word.
George Colman, the Younger: The Battle of Hexham, II:1

4 O fie miss, you must not kiss and tell.
William Congreve: Love for Love, II:10

5 Three may keep a secret, if two of them are dead.
Benjamin Franklin: Poor Richard's Almanack

6 Nobody tells me anything.
John Galsworthy: The Man of Property

SELF

1 Every man is his own worst enemy.
Proverb

2 God helps them that help themselves.
Proverb

3 He travels fastest who travels alone.
Proverb

4 I did it my way.
Paul Anka: Based on the French composition, 'Comme d'habitude'. My Way

5 Lord, deliver me from myself.
Thomas Browne: Religio Medici, Pt. II

6 I have always disliked myself at any given moment; the total of such moments is my life.
Cyril Connolly: Enemies of Promise, Ch. 18

7 But I do nothing upon myself, and yet I am mine own Executioner.
John Donne: Devotions, 12

8 We never remark any passion or principle in others, of which, in some degree or other, we may not find a parallel in ourselves.
David Hume: A Treatise of Human Nature

9 One should examine oneself for a very long time before thinking of condemning others.
Molière: Le Misanthrope, III:4

10 Self-love seems so often unrequited.
Anthony Powell: The Acceptance World

11 Self-sacrifice enables us to sacrifice Other people without blushing.
George Bernard Shaw: Man and Superman

12 I am always with myself, and it is I who am my tormentor.
Leo Tolstoy: Memoirs of a Madman

13 Do I contradict myself?

Very well then I contradict
myself,
(I am large, I contain multi-
tudes.)
Walt Whitman: Song of Myself, 51

SELF-CONFIDENCE

1 I know I'm not clever but I'm always right.
J. M. Barrie: Peter Pan

2 I wish I was as cocksure of anything as Tom Macaulay is of
everything.
*Lord Melbourne: Preface to Lord
Melbourne's Papers (Earl Cowper)*

3 Bring me no more reports; let
them fly all:
Till Birnam wood remove to
Dunsinane
I cannot taint with fear.
*William Shakespeare: Macbeth,
V:3*

4 'Tis an ill cook that cannot lick
his own fingers.
*William Shakespeare: Romeo and
Juliet, IV:2*

5 I am certain that we will win the
election with a good majority.
Not that I am ever over-
confident.
*Margaret Thatcher: Evening
Standard, 1987*

6 Speak up for yourself, or you'll
end up a rug.
Mae West: Attrib.

SELF-CONTROL

1 He that is slow to anger is better
than the mighty; and he that
ruleth his spirit than he that
taketh a city.
Bible: Proverbs: 16:32

2 The highest possible stage in
moral culture is when we recognize that we ought to control our
thoughts.
*Charles Darwin: Descent of Man,
Ch. 4*

3 When things are steep, remember to stay level-headed.
Horace: Odes, II

4 If you can keep your head when
all about you
Are losing theirs and blaming it
on you.
Rudyard Kipling: If

5 He that would govern others,
first should be
The master of himself.
*Philip Massinger: The Bondman,
I*

SELF-INTEREST

1 Every man for himself, and the
devil take the hindmost.
Proverb

2 The least pain in our little finger
gives us more concern and un-
easiness than the destruction of
millions of our fellow-beings.
*William Hazlitt: American
Literature, 'Dr Channing'*

3 It is difficult to love mankind
unless one has a reasonable private income and when one has a
reasonable private income one
has better things to do than loving mankind.
*Hugh Kingsmill: God's Apology
(R. Ingrams)*

4 Self-interest speaks all sorts of
tongues, and plays all sorts of
roles, even that of disinterested-
ness.

Duc de la Rochefoucauld:
Maximes, 39

SELFISHNESS

See also egotism

1 It's 'Damn you, Jack – I'm all
right!' with you chaps.
*David Bone: The Brassbounder,
Ch. 3*

2 The proud, the cold untroubled
heart of stone,
That never mused on sorrow but
its own.
*Thomas Campbell: Pleasures of
Hope, I*

SELF-KNOWLEDGE

1 Resolve to be thyself: and know,
that he
Who finds himself, loses his
misery.
Matthew Arnold: Self-Dependence

2 'I know myself,' he cried, 'but
that is all.'
*F. Scott Fitzgerald: This Side of
Paradise, Bk. II, Ch. 5*

3 I do not know myself, and God
forbid that I should.
*Goethe: Conversations with
Eckermann, 10 Apr 1829*

4 Know then thyself, presume not
God to scan.
*Alexander Pope: An Essay on
Man, II*

SELFLESSNESS

See also charity

1 Of gold she would not wear so
much as a seal-ring, choosing to
store her money in the stomachs
of the poor rather than to keep it
at her own disposal.
St Jerome: Letter CXXVII

2 The way to get things done is
not to mind who gets the credit
of doing them.
Benjamin Jowett: Attrib.

SELF-MADE MEN

1 I know he is, and he adores his
maker.
*Benjamin Disraeli: Replying to a
remark made in defence of John
Bright that he was a self-made
man. The Fine Art of Political Wit
(L. Harris)*

2 He was a self-made man who
owed his lack of success to
nobody.
Joseph Heller: Catch-22, Ch. 3

3 A self-made man is one who believes in luck and sends his son
to Oxford.
*Christina Stead: House of All
Nations, 'Credo'*

SELF-PRESERVATION

See also survival

1 Look after number one.
Proverb

2 He that fights and runs away
May live to fight another day.
Anonymous: Musarum Deliciae

3 There was only one catch and
that was Catch-22, which speci-
fied that a concern for one's own
safety in the face of dangers that
were real and immediate was the
process of a rational mind.
Joseph Heller: Catch-22, Ch. 5

4 The better part of valour is dis-

cretion; in the which better part
I have saved my life.
*William Shakespeare: Henry IV,
Part One, V:4*

5 *J'ai vécu.*
I survived.
*Abbé de Sieyès: Replying to an
enquiry concerning what he had
done during the Terror.
Dictionnaire Encyclopédique
(E. Guérard)*

6 He was gifted with the sly, sharp
instinct for self-preservation that
passes for wisdom among the
rich.
Evelyn Waugh: Scoop

SELF-RELIANCE

1 If you want a thing well done,
do it yourself.
Proverb

2 I am the cat that walks alone.
*Lord Beaverbrook: Beaverbrook
(A. J. P. Taylor)*

3 I thank God that I am endued
with such qualities that if I were
turned out of the Realm in my
petticoat I were able to live in
any place in Christome.
*Elizabeth I: Sayings of Queen
Elizabeth (Chamberlin)*

4 The greatest thing in the world
is to know how to be self-
sufficient.
Michel de Montaigne: Essais, I

5 I think it is about time we pulled
our fingers out…The rest of the
world most certainly does not
owe us a living.
*Prince Philip: Speech, London,
17 Oct 1961*

6 I'll never

Be such a gosling to obey in-
stinct, but stand
As if a man were author of
himself
And knew no other kin.
*William Shakespeare: Coriolanus,
V:3*

SELF-RESPECT

See also pride, respect

1 It is better to die on your feet
than to live on your knees.
*Dolores Ibarruri: Speech, Paris,
1936*

2 Self-respect – the secure feeling
that no one, as yet, is suspicious.
*H. L. Mencken: A Mencken
Chrestomathy*

3 And, above all things, never
think that you're not good
enough yourself. A man should
never think that. My belief is
that in life people will take you
very much at your own
reckoning.
*Anthony Trollope: The Small
House at Allington, Ch. 32*

4 When people do not respect us
we are sharply offended; yet
deep down in his heart no man
much respects himself.
Mark Twain: Notebooks

SENTIMENTALITY

See also emotion

1 They had been corrupted by
money, and he had been corrupted by sentiment. Sentiment
was the more dangerous, because you couldn't name its
price.

Graham Greene: The Heart of the Matter

2 Sentimentality is a superstructure covering brutality.
Carl Gustav Jung: Reflections

3 Sentimentality is only sentiment that rubs you up the wrong way.
W. Somerset Maugham: A Writer's Notebook

SERVICE

1 All English shop assistants are Miltonists. All Miltonists firmly believe that 'they serve who only stand and wait.'
George Mikes: How to be Inimitable

2 Small service is true service, while it lasts.
William Wordsworth: To a Child, Written in her Album

SERVILITY

See also flattery, humility

1 Fine words and an insinuating appearance are seldom associated with true virtue.
Confucius: Analects

2 I am well aware that I am the 'umblest person going…My mother is likewise a very 'umble person. We live in a numble abode.
Charles Dickens: Said by Uriah Heep. David Copperfield, Ch. 16

3 You know that nobody is strong-minded around a President…it is always: 'yes sir', 'no sir' (the 'no sir' comes when he asks whether you're dissatisfied).
George Edward Reedy: The White House (ed. R. Gordon Hoxie)

4 Whenever he met a great man he grovelled before him, and my-lorded him as only a free-born Briton can do.
William Makepeace Thackeray: Vanity Fair, Ch. 13

SEX

See also abstinence, adultery, contraception, debauchery, homosexuality, lust, marriage, virginity

1 Is sex dirty? Only if it's done right.
Woody Allen: All You've Ever Wanted to Know About Sex

2 Don't knock it, it's sex with someone you love.
Woody Allen: Referring to masturbation. Annie Hall

3 Sex between a man and a woman can be wonderful – provided you get between the right man and the right woman.
Woody Allen: Attrib.

4 I'll come and make love to you at five o'clock. If I'm late start without me.
Tallulah Bankhead: Somerset Maugham (E. Morgan)

5 Sexuality is the lyricism of the masses.
Charles Baudelaire: Journaux intimes, 93

6 If God had meant us to have group sex, I guess he'd have given us all more organs.
Malcolm Bradbury: Who Do You Think You Are?, 'A Very Hospitable Person'

7 Sex and the Single Girl
Helen Gurley Brown: Book title

8 He said it was artificial respiration but now I find I'm to have his child.

Anthony Burgess: Inside Mr. Enderby

9 It doesn't matter what you do in the bedroom as long as you don't do it in the street and frighten the horses.

Mrs Patrick Campbell: The Duchess of Jermyn Street (Daphne Fielding), Ch. 2

10 I said 10 years ago that in 10 years time it would be smart to be a virgin. Now everyone is back to virgins again.

Barbara Cartland: The Observer, 'Sayings of the Week', 12 July 1987

11 The doggie in front has suddenly gone blind, and the other one has very kindly offered to push him all the way to St Dunstan's.

Noël Coward: To a small child, who asked what two dogs were doing together in the street. St Dunstan's is a British institution for the blind. Two Hands Clapping (K. Tynan)

12 Ignorance of the necessity for sexual intercourse to the health and virtue of both man and woman, is the most fundamental error in medical and moral philosophy.

George Drysdale: The Elements of Social Science

13 No more about sex, it's too boring. Everyone's got one. Nastiness is a real stimulant though – but poor honest sex, like dying, should be a private matter.

Lawrence Durrell: Prospero's Cell, Ch. 1

14 When two individuals come together and leave their gender outside the bedroom door, then they make love. If they take it inside with them, they do something else, because society is in the room with them.

Andrea Dworkin: Intercourse

15 In an uncorrupted woman the sexual impulse does not manifest itself at all, but only love; and this love is the natural impulse of a woman to satisfy a man.

Johann Fichte: The Science of Rights

16 Well, what does it do this nine-inch penis? Where does it go?… Do I have a clitoris halfway up my stomach?

Carrie Fisher: Life, 1 May 1994

17 The members of our secret service have apparently spent so much time looking under the beds for Communists, they haven't had time to look in the bed.

Michael Foot: Referring to the Profumo affair. Attrib.

18 Personally I know nothing about sex because I've always been married.

Zsa Zsa Gabor: The Observer, 'Sayings of the Week', 16 Aug 1987

19 Ah, the sex thing. I'm glad that part of my life is over.

Greta Garbo: Attrib.

20 No sex is better than bad sex.

Germaine Greer: Attrib.

21 Masturbation is the thinking man's television.

Christopher Hampton: The Philanthropist

22 But did thee feel the earth move?
Ernest Hemingway: For Whom the Bell Tolls, Ch. 13

23 I am happy now that Charles calls on my bedchamber less frequently than of old. As it is, I now endure but two calls a week and when I hear his steps outside my door I lie down on my bed, close my eyes, open my legs and think of England.
Lady Alice Hillingdon: Often mistakenly attributed to Queen Victoria. Journal (1912)

24 People will insist...on treating the *mons Veneris* as though it were Mount Everest.
Aldous Huxley: Eyeless in Gaza, Ch. 30

25 'Bed,' as the Italian proverb succinctly puts it, 'is the poor man's opera.'
Aldous Huxley: Heaven and Hell

26 The zipless fuck is the purest thing there is. And it is rarer than the unicorn. And I have never had one.
Erica Jong: Fear of Flying

27 Sexual intercourse began
In nineteen sixty-three
(Which was rather late for me) –
Between the end of the
Chatterley ban
And the Beatles' first LP.
Philip Larkin: High Windows, 'Annus Mirabilis'

28 It's all this cold-hearted fucking that is death and idiocy.
D. H. Lawrence: Lady Chatterley's Lover, Ch. 14 (1928)

29 The trouble with Ian is that he gets off with women because he can't get on with them.
Rosamond Lehmann: Referring to Ian Fleming. The Life of Ian Fleming (J. Pearson)

30 He was into animal husbandry – until they caught him at it.
Tom Lehrer: An Evening Wasted with Tom Lehrer

31 You know the worst thing about oral sex? The view.
Maureen Lipman: Remark, 1990.

32 No sex without responsibility.
Lord Longford: The Observer, 'Sayings of the Week', 3 May 1954

33 Whoever named it necking was a poor judge of anatomy.
Groucho Marx: Attrib.

34 If sex is such a natural phenomenon, how come there are so many books on how to?
Bette Midler

35 Continental people have sex life; the English have hot-water bottles.
George Mikes: How to be an Alien

36 When she saw the sign 'Members Only' she thought of him.
Spike Milligan: Puckoon

37 Two minutes with Venus, two years with mercury.
J. Earle Moore: Alluding to the former use of mercury compounds in the treatment of syphilis. Aphorism

38 The orgasm has replaced the Cross as the focus of longing and the image of fulfilment.
Malcolm Muggeridge: The Most of Malcolm Muggeridge, 'Down with Sex'

39 It has to be admitted that we

English have sex on the brain, which is a very unsatisfactory place to have it.

Malcolm Muggeridge: The Observer, 'Sayings of the Decade', 1964

40 Tell him I've been too fucking busy – or vice versa.

Dorothy Parker: When asked why she had not delivered her copy on time. You Might As Well Live (J. Keats)

41 Someone asked Sophocles, 'How do you feel now about sex? Are you still able to have a woman?' He replied, 'Hush, man; most gladly indeed am I rid of it all, as though I had escaped from a mad and savage master.'

Plato: Republic Bk. I

42 MME LEROI. Love? I make it constantly but I never talk about it.

Marcel Proust: À La Recherche du temps perdu: Le Côté de Guermantes

43 Everything You Always Wanted to Know About Sex But Were Afraid to Ask.

David Reuben: Book title

44 The Christian view of sex is that it is, indeed, a form of holy communion.

John Robinson: Giving evidence in the prosecution of Penguin Books for publishing Lady Chatterly's Lover.

45 Love is two minutes fifty-two seconds of squishing noises. It shows your mind isn't clicking right.

Johnny Rotten: In the Daily Mirror in 1983 Rotten said that owing to a new-found technique, the time was now about five minutes. Attrib.

46 Love as a relation between men and women was ruined by the desire to make sure of the legitimacy of the children.

Bertrand Russell: Marriage and Morals

47 Your daughter and the Moor are now making the beast with two backs.

William Shakespeare: Othello, I:1

48 Lechery, lechery! Still wars and lechery! Nothing else holds fashion.

William Shakespeare: Troilus and Cressida, V:2

SEXES

See also marriage, men, women

1 There is more difference within the sexes than between them.

Ivy Compton-Burnett: Mother and Son

2 In the sex-war thoughtlessness is the weapon of the male, vindictiveness of the female.

Cyril Connolly: The Unquiet Grave

3 The reason that husbands and wives do not understand each other is because they belong to different sexes.

Dorothy Dix: News item

4 I don't think men and women were meant to live together. They are totally different animals.

Diana Dors: Remark, May 1988

5 Where young boys plan for what

they will achieve and attain,
young girls plan for whom they
will achieve and attain.
*Charlotte Perkins Gilman: Women
and Economics, Ch. 5*

6 Man has his will – but woman
has her way.
*Oliver Wendell Holmes: The
Autocrat of the Breakfast Table,
Prologue*

7 The silliest woman can manage
a clever man; but it needs a very
clever woman to manage a fool.
*Rudyard Kipling: Plain Tales from
the Hills, 'Three and – an Extra'*

8 The seldom female in a world of
males!
*Ruth Pitter: The Kitten's Eclogue,
IV*

9 Women have smaller brains
than men.
*Hojatolislam Rafsanjani: Remark,
July 1986*

10 I often want to cry. That is the
only advantage women have
over men – at least they can cry.
*Jean Rhys: Good Morning,
Midnight, Pt. II*

11 Woman's virtue is man's greatest invention.
Cornelia Otis Skinner: Attrib.

12 Man is a creature who lives not
upon bread alone, but principal-
ly by catchwords; and the little
rift between the sexes is aston-
ishingly widened by simply
teaching one set of catchwords
to the girls and another to the
boys.
*Robert Louis Stevenson:
Virginibus Puerisque*

13 Instead of this absurd division
into sexes they ought to class
people as static and dynamic.
*Evelyn Waugh: Decline and Fall,
Pt. III, Ch. 7*

14 All women become like their
mothers. That is their tragedy.
No man does. That's his.
*Oscar Wilde: The Importance of
Being Earnest, I*

15 Why are women…so much
more interesting to men than
men are to women?
*Virginia Woolf: A Room of One's
Own*

SHYNESS

1 I'm really a timid person – I was
beaten up by Quakers.
Woody Allen: Sleeper

2 A timid question will always receive a confident answer.
Lord Darling: Scintillae Juris

3 Shyness is just egotism out of its
depth.
*Penelope Keith: Remark, July
1988*

4 Had we but world enough, and
time,
This coyness, lady, were no
crime.
*Andrew Marvell: To His Coy
Mistress*

5 I have never known a *truly* mod-
est person to be the least bit shy.
*Elizabeth Taylor: The Bush,
'You'll Enjoy It When You Get
There'*

SIGNATURES

1 Never sign a valentine with
your own name.
*Charles Dickens: Said by Sam
Weller. Pickwick Papers, Ch. 33*

2 There, I guess King George will
be able to read that.
*John Hancock: Referring to his
signature, written in a bold hand,
on the US Declaration of
Independence. The American
Treasury (C. Fadiman)*

SILENCE

See also speech

1 A still tongue makes a wise
head.
Proverb

2 Speech is silver, silence is
golden.
Proverb

3 When you have nothing to say,
say nothing.
*Charles Caleb Colton: Lacon,
Vol. I*

4 For God's sake hold your
tongue and let me love.
John Donne: The Canonization

5 Silence is as full of potential wisdom and wit as the unhewn
marble of great sculpture.
*Aldous Huxley: Point Counter
Point*

6 Silence is the best tactic for him
who distrusts himself.
*Duc de la Rochefoucauld:
Maximes, 79*

7 Silence is the most perfect ex-
pression of scorn.
*George Bernard Shaw: Back to
Methuselah*

8 The cruellest lies are often told
in silence.
*Robert Louis Stevenson:
Virginibus Puerisque*

9 Whereof one cannot speak,
thereon one must remain silent.

*Ludwig Wittgenstein: Tractatus
Logico-Philosophicus, Ch. 7*

SIMILARITY

1 Birds of a feather flock together.
Proverb

2 Great minds think alike.
Proverb

3 Never mind, dear, we're all
made the same, though some
more than others.
Noël Coward: The Café de la Paix

4 I never knows the children. It's
just six of one and half-a-dozen
of the other.
*Frederick Marryat: The Pirate,
Ch. 4*

SIMPLICITY

1 'Excellent!' I cried. 'Elementary,' said he.
*Arthur Conan Doyle: Watson
talking to Sherlock Holmes;
Holmes's reply is often misquoted
as 'Elementary, my dear Watson'.
The Crooked Man*

2 O holy simplicity!
*John Huss: On noticing a peasant
adding a faggot to the pile at his
execution. Apophthegmata
(Zincgreff-Weidner), Pt. III*

3 A child of five would understand this.
Send somebody to fetch a child
of five.
Groucho Marx: Duck Soup

4 Entities should not be multi-
plied unnecessarily.
No more things should be pre-
sumed to exist than are absolutely necessary.

William of Ockham: 'Ockham's Razor'. Despite its attribution to William of Ockham, it was in fact a repetition of an ancient philosophical maxim.

5 Our life is frittered away by detail…Simplify, simplify.
Henry David Thoreau: Walden, 'Where I lived, and What I Lived For'

SIN

See also evil, vice

1 Old sins cast long shadows.
Proverb

2 All sin tends to be addictive, and the terminal point of addiction is what is called damnation.
W. H. Auden: A Certain World

3 He that is without sin among you, let him first cast a stone at her.
Bible: John: 8:7

4 We have erred, and strayed from thy ways like lost sheep.
The Book of Common Prayer: Morning Prayer, General Confession

5 I am not in the business of allotting sins.
George Carey: The Observer, 'Sayings of the Week', 22 May 1994

6 A private sin is not so prejudicial in the world as a public indecency.
Miguel de Cervantes: Don Quixote, Pt. II, Ch. 22

7 Sin brought death, and death will disappear with the disappearance of sin.
Mary Baker Eddy: Science and Health, with Key to the Scriptures

8 Fashions in sin change.
Lillian Hellman: Watch on the Rhine

9 There's nothing so artificial as sinning nowadays. I suppose it once was real.
D. H. Lawrence: St Mawr

10 People are no longer sinful, they are only immature or under privileged or frightened or, more particularly, sick.
Phyllis McGinley: The Province of the Heart, 'In Defense of Sin'

11 The only people who should really sin
Are the people who can sin with a grin.
Ogden Nash: I'm a Stranger Here Myself

12 I delight in sinning and hate to compose a mask for gossip.
Sulpicia: A Book of Women Poets (ed. Aliki and Willis Barnstone)

SINCERITY

See also frankness, honesty, integrity

1 What comes from the heart, goes to the heart.
Samuel Taylor Coleridge: Table Talk

2 Some of the worst men in the world are sincere and the more sincere they are the worse they are.
Lord Hailsham: The Observer, 'Sayings of the Week', 7 Jan 1968

3 A little sincerity is a dangerous thing, and a great deal of it is absolutely fatal.
Oscar Wilde: The Critic as Artist, Pt. 2

SLAVERY

See also oppression

1 Perhaps the master who had coupled with his slave saw his guilt in his wife's pale eyes in the morning. And the wife saw his children in the slave quarters.
James Baldwin: Nobody Knows my Name

2 From the beginning all were created equal by nature, slavery was introduced through the unjust oppression of worthless men, against the will of God; for, if God had wanted to create slaves, he would surely have decided at the beginning of the world who was to be slave and who master.
John Ball: Sermon, Blackheath, 1381

3 And Pharaoh said, Who is the Lord, that I should obey his voice to let Israel go?
Bible: Exodus: 5:2

4 The future is the only kind of property that the masters willingly concede to slaves.
Albert Camus: The Rebel

5 Of the surviving slaves, six thousand, whose masters could not be found, were exhibited on crosses set up like telegraph posts along the whole length of the Via Appia.
M. Cary: A History of Rome, 'The Slave War in Italy'

6 There they are cutting each other's throats, because one half of them prefer hiring their servants for life, and the other by the hour.
Thomas Carlyle: Referring to the American Civil War. Attrib.

SLEEP

See also bed

1 One hour's sleep before midnight, is worth two after.
Proverb

2 The beginning of health is sleep.
Irish proverb

3 Now I lay me down to sleep, I pray the Lord my soul to keep. If I should die before I wake, I pray the Lord my soul to take.
Anonymous: New England Primer, 1781

4 Laugh and the world laughs with you; snore and you sleep alone.
Anthony Burgess: Inside Mr. Enderby

5 Golden slumbers kiss your eyes, Smiles awake you when you rise.
Thomas Dekker: Patient Grissil, IV:2

6 Try thinking of love, or something.
Amor vincit insomnia.
Christopher Fry: A Sleep of Prisoners

7 He's a wicked man that comes after children when they won't go to bed and throws handfuls of sand in their eyes.
Ernst Hoffmann: The Sandman

8 The amount of sleep required by the average person is about five minutes more.
Max Kauffmann: Attrib.

9 O soft embalmer of the still midnight.
John Keats: To Sleep

10 Slepe is the nouryshment and food of a sucking child.
Thomas Phaer: The Boke of Chyldren

11 Our foster nurse of nature is repose.
William Shakespeare: King Lear, IV

12 Sleep's the only medicine that gives ease.
Sophocles: Philoctetes, 766

13 Sleep, Death's twin-brother, knows not Death,
Nor can I dream of thee as dead.
Alfred, Lord Tennyson: In Memoriam A.H.H., LXVIII

14 That sweet, deep sleep, so close to tranquil death.
Virgil: Aeneid, VI

SMALLNESS

See also triviality

1 The best things come in small parcels.
Proverb

2 It has long been an axiom of mine that the little things are infinitely the most important.
Arthur Conan Doyle: A Case of Identity

3 Small is beautiful.
E. F Schumacher: Title of book

4 Let us not take it for granted that life exists more fully in what is commonly thought big than in what is commonly thought small.
Virginia Woolf: The Common Reader

SMOKING

See also abstinence

1 It is better to be without a wife for a bit than without tobacco for an hour.
Proverb

2 The Elizabethan age might be better named the beginning of the smoking era.
J. M. Barrie: My Lady Nicotine

3 Certainly not – if you don't object if I'm sick.
Thomas Beecham: When asked whether he minded if someone smoked in a non-smoking compartment. Attrib.

4 Tobacco, divine, rare, super-excellent tobacco, which goes far beyond all their panaceas, potable gold, and philosopher's stones, a sovereign remedy to all diseases.
Robert Burton: Anatomy of Melancholy

5 Smokers, male and female, inject and excuse idleness in their lives every time they light a cigarette.
Colette: Earthly Paradise, 'Freedom'

6 It is quite a three-pipe problem.
Arthur Conan Doyle: The Red-Headed League

7 I have seen many a man turn his gold into smoke, but you are the first who has turned smoke into gold.
Elizabeth I: Speaking to Sir Walter Raleigh who brought the tobacco plant to England from America

8 Tobacco is a dirty weed. I like it.
It satisfies no normal need.
I like it.
It makes you thin, it makes you lean,

It takes the hair right off your bean.

It's the worst darn stuff I've ever seen.

I like it.

Graham Lee Hemminger: Penn State Froth, Nov 1915

9 A custom loathsome to the eye, hateful to the nose, harmful to the brain, dangerous to the lungs, and in the black, stinking fume thereof, nearest resembling the horrible Stygian smoke of the pit that is bottomless.

James I: A Counterblast to Tobacco

10 The tobacco business is a conspiracy against womanhood and manhood. It owes its origin to that scoundrel Sir Walter Raleigh, who was likewise the founder of American slavery.

John Harvey Kellogg: Tobacco

11 It is now proved beyond doubt that smoking is one of the leading causes of statistics.

Fletcher Knebel: Reader's Digest, Dec 1961

12 No matter what Aristotle and all philosophy may say, there's nothing like tobacco. 'Tis the passion of decent folk; he who lives without tobacco isn't worthy of living.

Molière: Don Juan, ou le festin de Pierre, I:1

13 This vice brings in one hundred million francs in taxes every year. I will certainly forbid it at once – as soon as you can name a virtue that brings in as much revenue.

Napoleon III: Reply when asked to ban smoking. Anekdotenschatz (H. Hoffmeister)

14 I have every sympathy with the American who was so horrified by what he had read of the effects of smoking that he gave up reading.

Henry G. Strauss: Quotations for Speakers and Writers (A. Andrews)

15 There are people who strictly deprive themselves of each and every eatable, drinkable and smokable which has in any way acquired a shady reputation. They pay this price for health. And health is all they get for it.

Mark Twain

16 Tobacco drieth the brain, dimmeth the sight, vitiateth the smell, hurteth the stomach, destroyeth the concoction, disturbeth the humors and spirits, corrupteth the breath, induceth a trembling of the limbs, exsiccateth the windpipe, lungs, and liver, annoyeth the milt, scorcheth the heart, and causeth the blood to be adjusted.

Tobias Venner: Via Recta ad Vitam Longam

17 A cigarette is the perfect type of a perfect pleasure. It is exquisite, and it leaves one unsatisfied. What more can one want?

Oscar Wilde: The Picture of Dorian Gray, Ch. 6

SNOBBERY

See also aristocracy, class, one-upmanship

1 In our way we were both snobs, and no snob welcomes another who has risen with him.

SOCIALISM

Cecil Beaton: Referring to the writer Evelyn Waugh. Attrib.

2 His hatred of snobs was a derivative of his snobbishness, but made the simpletons (in other words, everyone) believe that he was immune from snobbishness.
Marcel Proust: A la Recherche du temps perdu: Le Côté de Guermantes

3 He who meanly admires mean things is a Snob.
William Makepeace Thackeray: The Book of Snobs, Ch. 2

4 Never speak disrespectfully of Society, Algernon. Only people who can't get into it do that.
Oscar Wilde: The Importance of Being Earnest, III

SOCIALISM

See also Communism, Marxism

1 The language of priorities is the religion of Socialism.
Aneurin Bevan: Aneurin Bevan (Vincent Brome), Ch. 1

2 Socialism with a human face must function again for a new generation. We have lived in the darkness for long enough.
Alexander Dubček: Speech, Wenceslas Square, Prague, 24 Nov 1989

3 There is nothing in Socialism that a little age or a little money will not cure.
Will Durant: Attrib.

4 Socialism can only arrive by bicycle.
José Antonio Viera Gallo: Energy and Equity (Ivan Illich)

5 The essence of perestroika lies in the fact that *it unites socialism with democracy* and revives the feminist concept of socialist construction both in theory and in practice.
Mikhail Gorbachov: Perestroika

6 Under socialism *all* will govern in turn and will soon become accustomed to no one governing.
Lenin: The State and Revolution, Ch. 6

7 In so far as socialism means anything, it must be about the wider distribution of smoked salmon and caviar.
Richard Marsh: Remark, Oct 1976

8 To the ordinary working man, the sort you would meet in any pub on Saturday night, Socialism does not mean much more than better wages and shorter hours and nobody bossing you about.
George Orwell: The Road to Wigan Pier, Ch. 11

9 I am a socialist – and I only wish the Labour Party was.
Donald Soper: Any Questions (radio programme), 11 May 1979

10 State socialism is totally alien to the British character.
Margaret Thatcher: The Times, 1983

SOCIETY

See also mankind

1 A characteristic of Thatcherism is a reversion to the idea of nature, irreparable in its forces. Poverty and sickness are seen as part of an order.
Howard Barker: The Times, 3 Jan 1990

2 Man was formed for society.
*William Blackstone:
Commentaries on the Laws of
England, Introduction*

3 Society, being codified by man,
decrees that woman is inferior:
she can do away with this inferiority only by destroying the
male's superiority.
*Simone de Beauvoir: Le Deuxième
Sexe (The Second Sex)*

4 My ideal is a society full of responsible men and women who
show solidarity to those who
can't keep up.
*Jacques Delors: The Independent,
22 June 1994*

5 No man is an Island, entire of it-
self; every man is a piece of the
Continent, a part of the main.
John Donne: Devotions, 17

6 Problem children tend to grow
up into problem adults and
problem adults tend to produce
more problem children.
*David Farrington: The Times,
19 May 1994*

7 The permissive society has been
allowed to become a dirty
phrase. A better phrase is the
civilized society.
*Roy Jenkins: Speech, Abingdon,
19 July 1969*

8 If a free society cannot help the
many who are poor, it cannot
save the few who are rich.
*John Fitzgerald Kennedy: Speech,
20 Jan 1961*

9 Society is no comfort
To one not sociable.
*William Shakespeare: Cymbeline,
IV:2*

10 Man is a social animal.
Benedict Spinoza: Ethics

SOLDIERS

See also army, officers, war

1 It's Tommy this, an' Tommy
that, an' 'Chuck him out, the
brute!'
But it's 'Saviour of 'is country'
when the guns begin to shoot.
Rudyard Kipling: Tommy

2 They're changing guard at
Buckingham Palace.
*A. A. Milne: When We Were Very
Young, 'Buckingham Palace'*

3 Then was seen with what a
strength and majesty the British
soldier fights.
*William Napier: History of the
War in the Peninsula Bk. XII,
Ch. 6*

4 The soldier's body becomes a
stock of accessories that are not
his property.
*Antoine de Saint-Exupéry: Flight
To Arras*

5 Soldiers are citizens of death's
grey land,
Drawing no dividend from
time's tomorrows.
Siegfried Sassoon: Dreamers

6 I never expect a soldier to think.
*George Bernard Shaw: The
Devil's Disciple, III*

7 They're overpaid, overfed, over-
sexed and over here.
*Tommy Trinder: Referring to the
G.I.s in Britain during World War
II. Attrib.*

SOLITUDE

See also loneliness

1 Alone, alone, all, all alone,
Alone on a wide wide sea!
And never a saint took pity on

SORROW

My soul in agony.
Samuel Taylor Coleridge: The Rime of the Ancient Mariner, IV

2 Solitude is a torment which is not threatened in *hell* itselfe.
John Donne: Awakenings (Oliver W. Sacks)

3 One of the pleasantest things in the world is going on a journey; but I like to go by myself.
William Hazlitt: On Going a Journey

4 It is a fine thing to be out on the hills alone. A man can hardly be a beast or a fool alone on a great mountain.
Francis Kilvert: Diary, 29 May 1871

5 I want to be a movement
But there's no one on my side.
Adrian Mitchell: Loose Leaf Poem

6 A man must keep a little back shop where he can be himself without reserve. In solitude alone can he know true freedom.
Michel de Montaigne: Essais, I

7 Solitude is the playfield of Satan.
Vladimir Nabokov: Pale Fire

8 I never found the companion that was so companionable as solitude.
Henry David Thoreau: Walden, 'Solitude'

SORROW

See also despair, melancholy, mourning, regret

1 My eye cried and woke me.
The night was pain.
Al-Khansa: 'The Night'

2 Every tear from every eye

Becomes a babe in Eternity.
William Blake: Auguries of Innocence

3 Grief and constant anxiety kill nearly as many women as men die on the battlefield.
Mary Chesnut: Diary from Dixie, 9 June 1862

4 One often calms one's grief by recounting it.
Pierre Corneille: Polyeucte, I:3

5 Tears were to me what glass beads are to African traders.
Quentin Crisp: The Naked Civil Servant

6 There is no greater sorrow than to recall a time of happiness when in misery.
Dante: Divine Comedy, Inferno, V

7 A moment of time may make us unhappy for ever.
John Gay: The Beggar's Opera

8 Sadness is almost never anything but a form of fatigue.
André Gide: Journals, 1922

9 A woman's heart always has a burned name.
Louise Labé: Oeuvres, Sonnet II

10 Tears such as angels weep, burst forth.
John Milton: Paradise Lost, Bk. I

11 Line after line my gushing eyes o'erflow,
Led through a sad variety of woe.
Alexander Pope: Eloisa to Abelard

12 As soon as one is unhappy one becomes moral.
Marcel Proust: À La Recherche du temps perdu: À l'ombre des jeunes filles en fleurs

13 It is such a secret place, the land of tears.

Antoine de Saint-Exupéry: The Little Prince, Ch. 7

14 When sorrows come, they come not single spies,
But in battalions.
William Shakespeare: Hamlet, IV:5

15 'Tis held that sorrow makes us wise.
Alfred, Lord Tennyson: In Memoriam A.H.H., CXIII

SOUL

1 The eyes are the window of the soul.
Proverb

2 Man has no Body distinct from his Soul; for that called Body is a portion of Soul discerned by the five Senses, the chief inlets of Soul in this age.
William Blake: The Marriage of Heaven and Hell, 'The Voice of the Devil'

3 In the real dark night of the soul it is always three o'clock in the morning.
F. Scott Fitzgerald: See ST JOHN OF THE CROSS. The Crack-Up

4 The dark night of the soul.
St John of the Cross: See also F. SCOTT FITZGERALD. English translation of Noche obscura del alma, the title of a poem.

5 Fair seed-time had my soul, and I grew up
Fostered alike by beauty and by fear.
William Wordsworth: The Prelude, I

SPACE

See also exploration, moon, science

1 Space...is big. Really big. You just won't believe how vastly hugely mindbogglingly big it is. I mean you may think it's a long way down the road to the chemist, but that's just peanuts to space.
Douglas Adams: The Hitch Hiker's Guide to the Galaxy, Ch. 8

2 That's one small step for man, one giant leap for mankind.
Neil Armstrong: Said on stepping onto the moon. In his autobiography Armstrong claimed that he had said, 'small step for a man...', but that the radio transmission had distorted his words. Remark, 21 July 1969

3 Outer space is no place for a person of breeding.
Violet Bonham Carter: The New Yorker

4 The Earth is just too small and fragile a basket for the human race to keep all its eggs in.
Robert Heinlein: Speech

5 Space isn't remote at all. It's only an hour's drive away if your car could go straight upwards.
Fred Hoyle: The Observer, 9 Sept 1979

6 Space is almost infinite. As a matter of fact we think it *is* infinite.
Dan Quayle: The Sunday Times, 31 Dec 1989

7 Space is out of this world.
Helen Sharman: Remark, May 1991

SPEECH

See also silence, verbosity, words

1 Speak when you are spoken to.
Proverb

2 No, Sir, because I have time to think before I speak, and don't ask impertinent questions.
Erasmus Darwin: Reply when asked whether he found his stammer inconvenient.
Reminiscences of My Father's Everyday Life (Sir Francis Darwin)

3 The true use of speech is not so much to express our wants as to conceal them.
Oliver Goldsmith: Essays, 'The Use of Language'

4 Talking and eloquence are not the same: to speak, and to speak well, are two things.
Ben Jonson: Timber, or Discoveries made upon Men and Matter

5 The thoughtless are rarely wordless.
Howard W. Newton: Attrib.

6 The most precious things in speech are pauses.
Ralph Richardson: Attrib.

7 Words may be false and full of art,
Sighs are the natural language of the heart.
Thomas Shadwell: Psyche, III

SPEECHES

1 I take the view, and always have done, that if you cannot say what you have to say in twenty minutes, you should go away and write a book about it.
Lord Brabazon of Tara: Attrib.

2 Call that a maiden speech? I call it a brazen hussy of a speech.
Winston Churchill: To A. P. Herbert. Immortal Jester (L. Frewin)

3 I dreamt that I was making a speech in the House. I woke up, and by Jove I was!
Duke of Devonshire: Thought and Adventures (W. S. Churchill)

4 Don't quote Latin; say what you have to say, and then sit down.
Duke of Wellington: Advice to a new Member of Parliament. Attrib.

SPONTANEITY

See also impetuosity

1 Spontaneity is only a term for man's ignorance of the gods.
Samuel Butler: Erewhon, Ch. 25

2 L'acte gratuite.
The unmotivated action.
André Gide: Les Caves du Vatican

3 Nothing prevents us from being natural so much as the desire to appear so.
Duc de la Rochefoucauld: Maximes, 431

SPORT AND GAMES

See also cricket, football, horses, hunting

1 Anyone for tennis?
Anonymous

2 The game isn't over till it's over.
Yogi Berra: Attrib.

3 Life's too short for chess.
Henry James Byron: Our Boys, I

4 This government says it intends to drive hooliganism out of sport – yet it appoints a hooligan to oversee it.

Richard Course: Referring to Minister of Sport, Dick Tracey. Speech, 1986

5 There is plenty of time to win this game, and to thrash the Spaniards too.

Francis Drake: Referring to the sighting of the Armada during a game of bowls, 20 July 1588. Attrib.

6 I am sorry I have not learned to play at cards. It is very useful in life: it generates kindness and consolidates society.

Samuel Johnson: Tour to the Hebrides (J. Boswell)

7 Man is a gaming animal. He must always be trying to get the better in something or other.

Charles Lamb: Essays of Elia, 'Mrs Battle's Opinions on Whist'

8 O, he flies through the air with the greatest of ease,
This daring young man on the flying trapeze.

George Leybourne: The Man on the Flying Trapeze

9 Ayrton and I shared some of the most exciting races ever staged. When a truly great driver and a great champion loses his life, there is a very big void left behind.

Nigel Mansell: Referring to the Brazilian racing driver Ayrton Senna (1960–94). The Independent, 3 May 1994

10 I didn't take drugs and above all I did not let down those who love me.

Diego Maradona: Having been expelled from the 1994 World Cup for taking drugs. The Independent, 1 July 1994

11 I'm playing as well as I ever have in my career. It's just hard to get out of bed in the morning.

Martina Navratilova: The Guardian, 30 June 1993

12 Serious sport has nothing to do with fair play. It is bound up with hatred, jealousy, boastfulness, disregard of all rules and sadistic pleasure in witnessing violence; in other words it is war minus the shooting.

George Orwell: The Sporting Spirit

13 Gamesmanship or The Art of Winning Games Without Actually Cheating.

Stephen Potter: Book title

14 Show me a good and gracious loser and I'll show you a failure.

Knute Rockne: Attrib.

15 The cars are very fast and difficult to drive. It's going to be a season with lots of accidents and I'll risk saying we'll be lucky if something really serious doesn't happen.

Ayrton Senna: The Times, 3 May 1994

STATE

See also democracy, government

1 So long as the state exists there is no freedom. When there is freedom there will be no state.

Lenin: The State and Revolution, Ch. 5

2 In a free society the state does not administer the affairs of men. It administers justice among men who conduct their own affairs.

Walter Lippman: An Enquiry into the Principles of a Good Society

3 The worth of a State in the long run is the worth of the individuals composing it.
John Stuart Mill: On Liberty, Ch. 5

4 The state is an instrument in the hands of the ruling class for suppressing the resistance of its class enemies.
Joseph Stalin: Foundations of Leninism

STATELY HOMES

See also architecture, aristocracy, houses

1 An extraordinary aspect of running a stately home is that much of its success depends, not on how many Van Dycks you have, but how many loos. No amount of beautiful objects can compensate a visitor who is kept queuing in the cold.
Duchess of Bedford: Nicole Nobody

2 Now Spring, sweet laxative of Georgian strains,
Quickens the ink in literary veins,
The Stately Homes of England ope their doors
To piping Nancy-boys and Crashing Bores.
Roy Campbell: The Georgiad

3 The Stately Homes of England
How beautiful they stand,
To prove the upper classes
Have still the upper hand.
Noël Coward: Operette, 'The Stately Homes of England'

4 The stately homes of England,
How beautiful they stand!
Amidst their tall ancestral trees,
O'er all the pleasant land.
Felicia Dorothea Hemans: The Homes of England

5 Those comfortably padded lunatic asylums which are known, euphemistically, as the stately homes of England.
Virginia Woolf: The Common Reader, 'Lady Dorothy Nevill'

STATISTICS

1 A witty statesman said, you might prove anything by figures.
Thomas Carlyle: Critical and Miscellaneous Essays, 'Chartism'

2 There are three kinds of lies: lies, damned lies and statistics.
Benjamin Disraeli: Autobiography (Mark Twain)

3 We are just statistics, born to consume resources.
Horace: Epistles, I

4 He uses statistics as a drunken man uses lamp-posts – for support rather than illumination.
Andrew Lang: Treasury of Humorous Quotations

5 You cannot feed the hungry on statistics.
David Lloyd George: Advocating Tariff Reform. Speech, 1904

6 Statistics will prove anything, even the truth.
Noël Moynihan: Attrib.

7 To understand God's thoughts we must study statistics, for these are the measure of his purpose.
Florence Nightingale: Life...of Francis Galton (K. Pearson), Vol. II, Ch. 13

8 Facts speak louder than statistics.

Geoffrey Streatfield: The Observer, 'Sayings of the Week', 19 Mar 1950

STRIKES

1 The rights and interests of the laboring man will be protected and cared for, not by the labor agitators, but by the Christian men to whom God in His infinite wisdom has given control of the property interests of the country.
George Baer: Written during the Pennsylvania miners' strike. Letter to the press, Oct 1902

2 Not a penny off the pay; not a minute on the day.
A. J. Cook: Slogan used in the miners' strike, 1926

3 It is difficult to go on strike if there is no work in the first place.
Lord George-Brown: The Observer, 24 Feb 1980

STUBBORNNESS

See also determination

1 You can lead a horse to the water, but you can't make him drink.
Proverb

2 None so blind as those who won't see.
Proverb

3 Obstinate people can be divided into the opinionated, the ignorant, and the boorish.
Aristotle: Nicomachean Ethics, Bk. VII

4 'Tis known by the name of per-

severance in a good cause, – and of obstinacy in a bad one.
Laurence Sterne: Tristram Shandy

STUPIDITY

See also foolishness, ignorance

1 His mind is open; yes, it is so open that nothing is retained; ideas simply pass through him.
F. H. Bradley: Attrib.

2 He is not only dull in himself, but the cause of dullness in others.
Samuel Foote: Parody of a line from Shakespeare's Henry IV, Part Two. Life of Johnson (J. Boswell)

3 Jerry Ford is so dumb that he can't fart and chew gum at the same time.
Lyndon B. Johnson: Sometimes quoted as '...can't walk and chew gum'. A Ford, Not a Lincoln (R. Reeves), Ch. 1

4 That fellow seems to me to possess but one idea, and that is a wrong one.
Samuel Johnson: Life of Johnson (J. Boswell), Vol. II

5 She looks like a million dollars, but she only knows a hundred and twenty words and she's only got two ideas in her head. The other one's hats.
Eric Linklater: Juan in America, Pt. II, Ch. 5

6 You've got the brain of a four-year-old boy, and I bet he was glad to get rid of it.
Groucho Marx: Horse Feathers

7 Human Stupidity consists in having lots of ideas, but stupid ones.
Henry de Montherlant: Notebooks

8 I've examined your son's head,
Mr Glum, and there's nothing
there.
*Frank Muir: Take It from Here
(Frank Muir and Dennis
Norden), 1957*

9 You beat your pate, and fancy
wit will come;
Knock as you please, there's
nobody at home.
Alexander Pope: Epigram

10 There is no sin except stu-
pidity.
*Oscar Wilde: The Critic as Artist,
Pt. 2*

SUBJECTIVITY

See also objectivity, prejudice

1 She was one of the people who
say, 'I don't know anything
about music really, but I know
what I like'.
*Max Beerbohm: Zuleika Dobson,
Ch. 16*

2 He who knows only his own side
of the case knows little of that.
*John Stuart Mill: On Liberty,
Ch. 2*

3 To observations which ourselves
we make
We grow more partial for th' observer's sake
Alexander Pope: Moral Essays, I

4 Partisanship is our great curse.
We too readily assume that
everything has two sides and
that it is our duty to be on one or
the other.
*James Harvey Robinson: The
Mind in the Making*

SUCCESS

See also achievement, failure, victory

1 Nothing succeeds like success.
Proverb

2 'Tis not in mortals to command
success,
But we'll do more, Sempronius;
we'll deserve it.
Joseph Addison: Cato, I:2

3 The penalty of success is to be
bored by people who used to
snub you.
*Nancy Astor: Sunday Express, 12
Jan 1956*

4 A woman who is loved always
has success.
Vicki Baum: Grand Hotel

5 All I think about is winning that
bleedin' title.
Frank Bruno: Remark, Jan 1989

6 The only infallible criterion of
wisdom to vulgar minds –
success.
*Edmund Burke: Letter to a
Member of the National Assembly*

7 Success is counted sweetest
By those who ne'er succeed.
*Emily Dickinson: Success is
Counted Sweetest*

8 Success is relative. It is what we
can make of the mess we have
made of things.
T. S. Eliot: The Family Reunion

9 There are two reasons why I am
successful in show business and
I am standing on both of them.
Betty Grable: Attrib.

10 The shortest and best way to
make your fortune is to let people see clearly that it is in their
interests to promote yours.

Jean de La Bruyère: Les Caractères

11 Powerful men often succeed through the help of their wives. Powerful women only succeed in spite of their husbands.

Linda Lee-Potter: Daily Mail, 16 May 1984

12 Sweet Smell of Success.

Ernest Lehman: Novel and film title

13 We in this industry know that behind every successful screenwriter stands a woman. And behind stands his wife.

Groucho Marx: Attrib.

14 Nothing fails like success; nothing is so defeated as yesterday's triumphant Cause.

Phyllis McGinley: The Province of the Heart, 'How to Get Along with Men'

15 As is the case in all branches of art, success depends in a very large measure upon individual initiative and exertion, and cannot be achieved except by dint of hard work.

Anna Pavlova: Pavlova: A Biography (ed. A. H. Franks), 'Pages of My Life'

16 No pain, no palm; no thorns, no throne; no gall, no glory; no cross, no crown.

William Penn: No Cross, No Crown

17 The only place where success comes before work is a dictionary.

Vidal Sassoon: Quoting one of his teachers in a BBC radio broadcast

18 There are no gains without pains.

Adlai Stevenson: Speech, Chicago, 26 July 1952

19 Success? Ah yes, the first three-piece suit, first lawsuit.

Robin Williams: Playboy, 1979

SUICIDE

See also death

1 I was suicidal, and would have killed myself, but I was in analysis with a strict Freudian, and if you kill yourself they make you pay for the lessons you miss.

Woody Allen: Halliwell's Filmgoers' and Video Viewers' Companion

2 To run away from trouble is a form of cowardice and, while it is true that the suicide braves death, he does it not for some noble object but to escape some ill.

Aristotle: Nicomachean Ethics, 3

3 There is but one truly serious philosophical problem, and that is suicide. Judging whether life is, or is not worth living amounts to answering the fundamental question of philosophy.

Albert Camus: The Myth of Sisyphus

4 To attempt suicide is a criminal offense. Any man who, of his own will, tries to escape the treadmill to which the rest of us feel chained incites our envy, and therefore our fury. We do not suffer him to go unpunished.

Alexander Chase: Perspectives

5 Suicide is the worst form of murder, because it leaves no opportunity for repentance.

*John Churton Collins: Life and
Memoirs of John Churton Collins
(L. C. Collins), Appendix VII*

6 There are many who dare not
kill themselves for fear of what
the neighbours might say.
*Cyril Connolly: The Unquiet
Grave*

7 My work is done. Why wait?
George Eastman: His suicide note

8 The prevalence of suicide is a
test of height in civilization; it
means that the population is
winding up its nervous and intellectual system to the utmost
point of tension and that sometimes it snaps.
Havelock Ellis

9 I take it that no man is educated
who has never dallied with the
thought of suicide.
William James

10 Razors pain you
Rivers are damp;
Acids stain you;
And drugs cause cramp.
Guns aren't lawful;
Nooses give;
Gas smells awful;
You might as well live.
*Dorothy Parker: Enough Rope,
'Resumé'*

11 Amid the miseries of our life
on earth, suicide is God's best
gift to man.
*Pliny the Elder: Natural History,
II*

12 Next week, or next month, or
next year I'll kill myself. But I
might as well last out my
month's rent, which has been
paid up, and my credit for
breakfast in the morning.
*Jean Rhys: Good Morning,
Midnight, Pt. II*

13 It is against the law to commit
suicide in this man's town...al-
though what the law can do to a
guy who commits suicide I am
never able to figure out.
Damon Runyon: Guys and Dolls

14 I am the only man in the world
who cannot commit suicide.
Rev. Chad Varah: Attrib.

15 Never murder a man who is
committing suicide.
*Woodrow Wilson: Mr Wilson's
War (John Dos Passos), Pt. II,
Ch. 10*

SUMMONS

1 Mr Watson, come here; I want
you.
*Alexander Graham Bell: The first
telephone conversation, 10 Mar
1876, in Boston. Attrib.*

2 Dauntless the slug-horn to my
lips I set,
And blew. *Childe Roland to the
Dark Tower came.*
*Robert Browning: Childe Roland
to the Dark Tower Came, XXXIV*

SUN

See also weather

1 The night has a thousand eyes,
And the day but one;
Yet the light of the bright world
dies
With the dying sun.
Francis William Bourdillon: Light

2 Busy old fool, unruly Sun,
Why dost thou thus,
Through windows and through
curtains call on us?

John Donne: The Sun Rising

3 I have a horror of sunsets, they're so romantic, so operatic.
Marcel Proust: A La Recherche du temps perdu: Sodome et Gomorrhe

SUPERIORITY

See also equality, one-upmanship, snobbery

1 The superior man is satisfied and composed; the mean man is always full of distress.
Confucius: Analects

2 Though I've belted you an' flayed you,
By the livin' Gawd that made you,
You're a better man than I am, Gunga Din!
Rudyard Kipling: Gunga Din

3 I teach you the Superman. Man is something that is to be surpassed.
Friedrich Nietzsche: Thus Spake Zarathustra

4 My parents just didn't have that sense of innate superiority that the successful parents had.
Michael Palin: The Times, 24 Feb 1990

5 'I believe I take precedence,' he said coldly; 'you are merely the club Bore: I am the club Liar.'
Saki: A Defensive Diamond

6 In the Country of the Blind the One-eyed Man is King.
H. G. Wells: The Country of the Blind

SUPERNATURAL

See also fairies

1 From ghoulies and ghosties and long-leggety beasties
And things that go bump in the night,
Good Lord, deliver us!
Anonymous: Cornish prayer

2 Open Sesame!
The Arabian Nights: The History of Ali Baba

3 Thou shalt not suffer a witch to live.
Bible: Exodus: 22:18

4 That old black magic has me in its spell.
Johnny Mercer: That Old Black Magic

5 There are more things in heaven and earth, Horatio,
Than are dreamt of in your philosophy.
William Shakespeare: Hamlet, I:5

SUPERSTITION

See also luck

1 Of course I don't believe in it. But I understand that it brings you luck whether you believe in it or not.
Niels Bohr: When asked why he had a horseshoe on his wall. Attrib.

2 Superstition is the religion of feeble minds.
Edmund Burke: Reflections on the Revolution in France

3 Superstition is the poetry of life.
Goethe: Sprüche in Prosa, III

4 Superstition sets the whole world in flames; philosophy quenches them.
Voltaire: Dictionnaire philosophique, 'Superstition'

SUPPORT

See also loyalty

1 Either back us or sack us.
James Callaghan: Speech, Labour Party Conference, Brighton, 5 Oct 1977

2 What I want is men who will support me when I am in the wrong.
Lord Melbourne: Replying to someone who said he would support Melbourne as long as he was in the right. Lord M. (Lord David Cecil)

3 And so, tonight – to you, the great silent majority of my fellow Americans – I ask for your support.
Richard Milhous Nixon: On a plan for peace in Vietnam. Broadcast address, 3 Nov 1969

SURVIVAL

See also evolution, self-preservation

1 I haven't asked you to make me young again. All I want is to go on getting older.
Konrad Adenauer: Replying to his doctor. Attrib.

2 It isn't important to come out on top; what matters is to come out alive.
Bertolt Brecht: Jungle of Cities

3 People are inexterminable – like flies and bed-bugs. There will always be some that survive in cracks and crevices – that's us.
Robert Frost: The Observer, 29 Mar 1959

4 The perpetual struggle for room and food.
Thomas Robert Malthus: Essays on the Principle of Population

5 Survival of the fittest.
Herbert Spencer: Principles of Biology, Pt. III, Ch. 12

6 One can survive everything nowadays, except death.
Oscar Wilde: A Woman of No Importance, I

SYMPATHY

See also comfort

1 Sympathy – for all these people, for being foreigners – lay over the gathering like a woolly blanket; and no one was enjoying it at all.
Malcolm Bradbury: Eating People is Wrong, Ch. 2

2 To be sympathetic without discrimination is so very debilitating.
Ronald Firbank: Vainglory

3 She was a machine-gun riddling her hostess with sympathy.
Aldous Huxley: Mortal Coils, 'The Gioconda Smile'

4 To show pity is felt as a sign of contempt because one has clearly ceased to be an object of fear as soon as one is pitied.
Friedrich Nietzsche: The Wanderer and His Shadow

5 I can sympathize with everything, except suffering.
Oscar Wilde: The Picture of Dorian Gray, Ch. 3

T

TACT

See also diplomacy

1 One shouldn't talk of halters in the hanged man's house.
Miguel de Cervantes: Don Quixote, Pt. I, Ch. 25

2 Tact consists in knowing how far we may go too far.
Jean Cocteau: In Treasury of Humorous Quotations

3 My advice was delicately poised between the cliché and the indiscretion.
Robert Runcie: Comment to the press concerning his advice to the Prince of Wales and Lady Diana Spencer on their approaching wedding, 13 July 1981

TALENT

See also genius

1 The English instinctively admire any man who has no talent and is modest about it.
James Agate: Attrib.

2 Whom the gods wish to destroy they first call promising.
Cyril Connolly: Enemies of Promise, Ch. 3

3 Middle age snuffs out more talent than even wars or sudden deaths do.
Richard Hughes: The Fox in the Attic

4 It's not enough to be Hungarian, you must have talent too.
Alexander Korda: Alexander Korda (K. Kulik)

TASTE

See also individuality

1 Between friends differences in taste or opinions are irritating in direct proportion to their triviality.
W. H. Auden: The Dyer's Hand

2 Good taste is better than bad taste, but bad taste is better than no taste.
Arnold Bennett: The Observer, 'Sayings of the Week', 24 Aug 1930

3 What is food to one man is bitter poison to others.
Lucretius: On the Nature of the Universe, IV

4 The kind of people who always go on about whether a thing is in good taste invariably have very bad taste.
Joe Orton: Attrib.

5 The play, I remember, pleas'd not the million; 'twas caviare to the general.
William Shakespeare: Hamlet, II:2

6 Do not do unto others as you would they should do unto you. Their tastes may not be the same.
George Bernard Shaw: Man and Superman, 'Maxims for Revolutionists'

TAXATION

1 Neither will it be, that a people overlaid with taxes should ever become valiant and martial.

John Aubrey: Essays, 'Of the True Greatness of Kingdoms'

2 The hardest thing in the world to understand is income tax.

Albert Einstein: Attrib.

3 In this world nothing is certain but death and taxes.

Benjamin Franklin: Letter to Jean-Baptiste Leroy, 13 Nov 1789

4 Sir, I now pay you this exorbitant charge, but I must ask you to explain to her Majesty that she must not in future look upon me as a source of income.

Charles Kemble: On being obliged to hand over his income tax to the tax collector. Humour in the Theatre (J. Aye)

5 The avoidance of taxes is the only pursuit that still carries any reward.

John Maynard Keynes: Attrib.

6 It is ironic that the wife who made Britain great again, and who is the leader of the Western World, has to get her husband to sign her tax form.

Jacqui Lait: Referring to Margaret Thatcher. Speech, Oct 1987

7 There is no art which one government sooner learns of another than that of draining money from the pockets of the people.

Adam Smith: The Wealth of Nations

8 For God's sake, madam, don't say that in England for if you do, they will surely tax it.

Jonathan Swift: Responding to Lady Carteret's admiration for the quality of the air in Ireland. Lives of the Wits (H. Pearson)

TECHNOLOGY

See also science

1 Give me a firm place to stand, and I will move the earth.

Archimedes: On the Lever

2 Man is a tool-using animal.

Thomas Carlyle: Sartor Resartus, Bk. I, Ch. 5

3 Any sufficiently advanced technology is indistinguishable from magic.

Arthur C. Clarke: The Lost Worlds of 2001

4 Man is a tool-making animal.

Benjamin Franklin: Life of Johnson (J. Boswell), 7 Apr 1778

5 One machine can do the work of fifty ordinary men. No machine can do the work of one extraordinary man.

Elbert Hubbard: Roycroft Dictionary and Book of Epigrams

6 The new electronic interdependence recreates the world in the image of a global village.

Marshall McLuhan: The Gutenberg Galaxy

7 No man...who has wrestled with a self-adjusting card table can ever quite be the man he once was.

James Thurber: Let Your Mind Alone, 'Sex ex Machina'

8 I see no reason to suppose that these machines will ever force themselves into general use.

Duke of Wellington: Referring to steam locomotives. Geoffrey Madan's Notebooks (J. Gere)

TELEVISION

See also media, journalism

TEMPTATION

1 That's the sixty-four thousand dollar question.
Anonymous: Title of US TV quizzes

2 Some television programs are so much chewing gum for the eyes.
John Mason Brown: Interview, 28 July 1955

3 Television is for appearing on, not looking at.
Noël Coward: Attrib.

4 TV…is our latest medium – we call it a medium because nothing's well done.
Ace Goodman: Letter to Groucho Marx, 1954. The Groucho Letters

5 Television won't matter in your lifetime or mine.
Rex Lambert: The Listener

TEMPTATION

1 Forbidden fruit is sweet.
Proverb

2 If you can't be good, be careful.
Proverb

3 I am not over-fond of resisting temptation.
William Beckford: Vathek

4 'You oughtn't to yield to temptation.'
'Well, somebody must, or the thing becomes absurd.'
Anthony Hope: The Dolly Dialogues

5 I never resist temptation because I have found that things that are bad for me never tempt me.
George Bernard Shaw: The Apple Cart

6 I can resist everything except temptation.

Oscar Wilde: Lady Windermere's Fan, I

THEATRE

See also acting, actors, criticism, literature, plays

1 The reason why Absurdist plays take place in No Man's Land with only two characters is primarily financial.
Arthur Adamov: Said at the Edinburgh International Drama Conference, 13 Sept 1963

2 It's one of the tragic ironies of the theatre that only one man in it can count on steady work – the night watchman.
Tallulah Bankhead: Tallulah, Ch. 1

3 Tragedy is if I cut my finger. Comedy is if I walk into an open sewer and die.
Mel Brooks: New Yorker, 30 Oct 1978

4 All tragedies are finish'd by a death,
All comedies are ended by a marriage.
Lord Byron: Don Juan, III

5 You know, I go to the theatre to be entertained…I don't want to see plays about rape, sodomy and drug addiction…I can get all that at home.
Peter Cook: The Observer, caption to cartoon, 8 July 1962

6 Don't put your daughter on the stage, Mrs Worthington.
Noël Coward: Song title

7 Drama never changed anybody's mind about anything.
David Mamet: The Times, 15 Sept 1993

8 I depict men as they ought to be, but Euripides portrays them as they are.
Sophocles: Poetics (Aristotle)

9 The bad end unhappily, the good unluckily. That is what tragedy means.
Tom Stoppard: Rosencrantz and Guildenstern Are Dead, II

THEFT

See also crime

1 The fault is great in man or woman
Who steals a goose from off a common;
But what can plead that man's excuse
Who steals a common from a goose?
Anonymous: The Tickler Magazine, 1 Feb 1821

2 Stolen sweets are best.
Colley Cibber: The Rival Fools, I

3 Travel light and you can sing in the robber's face.
Juvenal: Satires, X

THEORY

See also ideas

1 A thing may look specious in theory, and yet be ruinous in practice; and a thing may look evil in theory, and yet be in practice excellent.
Edmund Burke: Impeachment of Warren Hastings, 19 Feb 1788

2 A theory can be proved by experiment; but no path leads from experiment to the birth of a theory.
Albert Einstein: The Sunday Times, 18 July 1976

3 Dear friend, theory is all grey, And the golden tree of life is green.
Goethe: Faust, Pt. I

4 You know very well that unless you're a scientist, it's much more important for a theory to be shapely, than for it to be true.
Christopher Hampton: The Philanthropist, I

5 A first rate theory predicts; a second rate theory forbids, and third rate theory explains after the event.
A. I. Kitaigorodskii: Harvest of a Quiet Eye

6 Practice should always be based upon a sound knowledge of theory.
Leonardo da Vinci: The Notebook of Leonardo da Vinci (Edward MacCurdy)

7 It is a good morning exercise for a research scientist to discard a pet hypothesis every day before breakfast. It keeps him young.
Konrad Lorenz: On Aggression, Ch. 2

8 In making theories always keep a window open so that you can throw one out if necessary.
Béla Schick: Aphorisms and Facetiae of Béla Schick (I. J. Wolf)

THINKING

See also intellect, intelligence, mind, philosophy

1 Cogito, ergo sum.
I think, therefore I am.
René Descartes: Le Discours de la méthode

2 The most fluent talkers or most plausible reasoners are not always the justest thinkers.
William Hazlitt: On Prejudice

3 Most of one's life…is one prolonged effort to prevent oneself thinking.
Aldous Huxley: Mortal Coils, 'Green Tunnels'

4 Meditation is not a means to an end. It is both the means and the end.
Jiddu Krishnamurti: The Penguin Krishnamurti Reader

5 His thoughts, few that they were, lay silent in the privacy of his head.
Spike Milligan: Puckoon, Ch. 1

6 Many people would sooner die than think. In fact they do.
Bertrand Russell: Thinking About Thinking (A. Flew)

7 There is nothing either good or bad, but thinking makes it so.
William Shakespeare: Hamlet, II:2

8 In order to draw a limit to thinking, we should have to be able to think both sides of this limit.
Ludwig Wittgenstein: Tractatus Logico-Philosophicus, Preface

THRIFT

See also extravagance, money

1 A penny saved is a penny earned.
Proverb

2 Penny wise, pound foolish.
Proverb

3 I knew once a very covetous, sordid fellow, who used to say, 'Take care of the pence, for the pounds will take care of themselves.'
Earl of Chesterfield: Possibly referring to William Lowndes. Letter to his son, 6 Nov 1747

4 Thrift has nearly killed her on several occasions, through the agency of old sausages, slow-punctured tyres, rusty blades.
Margaret Drabble: The Radiant Way

5 Everybody is always in favour of general economy and particular expenditure.
Anthony Eden: The Observer, 'Sayings of the Week', 17 June 1956

6 Economy is going without something you do want in case you should, some day, want something you probably won't want.
Anthony Hope: The Dolly Dialogues

TIME

See also eternity, future, life, past, present, transience

1 An hour in the morning is worth two in the evening.
Proverb

2 There are only twenty-four hours in the day.
Proverb

3 Time and tide wait for no man.
Proverb

4 Time will tell.
Proverb

5 Except Time all other things are created. Time is the creator; and Time has no limit, neither top nor bottom.
The Persian Rivayat

6 To choose time is to save time.
Francis Bacon: Essays, 'Of Dispatch'

7 We should count time by heart-throbs.
Philip James Bailey: Festus

8 I believe the twenty-four hour day has come to stay.
Max Beerbohm: A Christmas Garland, 'Perkins and Mankind'

9 Time is a great teacher, but unfortunately it kills all its pupils.
Hector Berlioz: Almanach des lettres françaises

10 Men talk of killing time, while time quietly kills them.
Dion Boucicault: London Assurance, II:1

11 Time is a physician that heals every grief.
Diphilius

12 Time present and time past
Are both perhaps present in time future
And time future contained in time past.
T. S. Eliot: Four Quartets

13 Dost thou love life? Then do not squander time, for that's the stuff life is made of.
Benjamin Franklin: Poor Richard's Almanack

14 The fundamental things apply
As time goes by.
Herman Hupfeld: From the film Casablanca. As Time Goes By

15 The now, the here, through which all future plunges to the past.
James Joyce: Ulysses

16 O aching time! O moments big as years!
John Keats: Hyperion, I

17 We must use time as a tool, not as a couch.
John Fitzgerald Kennedy: The Observer, 'Sayings of the Week', 10 Dec 1961

18 The Future is something which everyone reaches at the rate of sixty minutes an hour, whatever he does, whoever he is.
C. S. Lewis: The Screwtape Letters

19 Time wounds all heels.
Groucho Marx: Attrib.

20 It is only time that weighs upon our hands.
It is only time, and that is not material.
Sylvia Plath: Winter Trees, 'The Three Women'

21 Distances are only the relation of space to time and vary with that relation.
Marcel Proust: A La Recherche du temps perdu, Sodome et Gomorrhe

22 If you want to know the time, Ask a Policeman.
E. W. Rogers: Ask a P'liceman

23 They do that to pass the time, nothing more. But Time is too large, it refuses to let itself be filled up.
Jean-Paul Sartre: Nausea

24 Ah! the clock is always slow;
It is later than you think.
Robert William Service: It is Later than You Think

25 Th' inaudible and noiseless foot of Time.
William Shakespeare: All's Well that Ends Well, V:3

26 Like as the waves make towards the pebbled shore,
So do our minutes hasten to their end.

William Shakespeare: Sonnet 60

Time hath, my lord, a wallet at his back,
Wherein he puts alms for oblivion,
A great-siz'd monster of ingratitudes.
William Shakespeare: Troilus and Cressida, III:3

3 In reality, killing time
is only the name for another of the multifarious ways
by which Time kills us.
Osbert Sitwell: Milordo Inglese

Time is but the stream I go a-fishing in.
Henry David Thoreau: Walden, 'Where I Lived, and What I Lived For'

But meanwhile it is flying, irretrievable time is flying.
Virgil: Georgics, Bk. III

The Hopi, an Indian tribe, have a language as sophisticated as ours, but no tenses for past, present and future. The division does not exist. What does this say about time?
Jeanette Winterson: Sexing the Cherry

The bell strikes one. We take no note of time
But from its loss.
Edward Young: Night Thoughts

TITLES

See also aristocracy, courtesy, nobility

Madam I may not call you; mistress I am ashamed to call you; and so I know not what to call you; but howsoever, I thank you.
Elizabeth I: Writing to the wife of the Archbishop of Canterbury, expressing her disapproval of married clergy. Brief View of the State of the Church (Harington)

2 Pooh-Bah (Lord High Everything Else).
W. S. Gilbert: The Mikado, Dramatis Personae

3 When I want a peerage, I shall buy one like an honest man.
Lord Northcliffe: Attrib.

4 Call me madame.
Frances Perkins: Deciding the term of address she would prefer when made the first woman to hold a cabinet office in America. Familiar Quotations (J. Bartlett)

5 A person seeking a quiet life is greatly helped by not having a title.
Captain Mark Phillips: Attrib.

6 Members rise from CMG (known sometimes in Whitehall as 'Call me God') to the KCMG ('Kindly Call me God') to...The GCMG ('God Calls me God').
Anthony Sampson: Anatomy of Britain, Ch. 18

TOLERANCE

1 There is, however, a limit at which forbearance ceases to be a virtue.
Edmund Burke: Observations on a Publication, 'The Present State of the Nation'

2 No party has a monopoly over what is right.
Mikhail Gorbachev: Speech, Mar 1986

3 If you cannot mould yourself as you would wish, how can you

expect other people to be entirely to your liking?
Thomas à Kempis: The Imitation of Christ, I

4 We must respect the other fellow's religion, but only in the sense and to the extent that we respect his theory that his wife is beautiful and his children smart.
H. L. Mencken: Notebooks, 'Minority Report'

5 Steven's mind was so tolerant that he could have attended a lynching every day without becoming critical.
Thorne Smith: The Jovial Ghosts, Ch. 11

TRANSIENCE

See also life, mortality, time

1 Sic transit gloria mundi
So passes the glory of the world.
Anonymous: Referring to the large number of ruined castles in England, Normandy, and Anjou, which had been demolished after the rebellion (1173–74) against Henry II. Histoire de Guillaume le Maréchal

2 They are not long, the days of wine and roses.
Ernest Dowson: Vitae Summa Brevis Spem Nos Vetat Incohare Longam

3 Gone With the Wind.
Margaret Mitchell: From the poem Non Sum Qualis Eram (Ernest Dowson): 'I have forgot much, Cynara! Gone with the wind…' Book title

4 Our little systems have their day;

They have their day and cease to be.
Alfred, Lord Tennyson: In Memoriam A.H.H., Prologue

TRANSLATION

1 The original is unfaithful to the translation.
Jorge Luis Borges: Referring to Henley's translation of Beckford's Vathek. Sobre el 'Vathek' de William Beckford

2 Translations (like wives) are seldom faithful if they are in the least attractive.
Roy Campbell: Poetry Review

3 Poetry is what gets lost in translation.
Robert Frost: Attrib.

4 An idea does not pass from one language to another without change.
Miguel de Unamuno y Jugo: The Tragic Sense of Life

5 Humour is the first of the gifts to perish in a foreign tongue.
Virginia Woolf: The Common Reader

TRAVEL

See also boats, flying

1 Travel broadens the mind.
Proverb

2 Is your journey really necessary?
Anonymous: British wartime slogan

3 If It's Tuesday, This Must be Belgium.
Anonymous: Title of film about U tourists in Europe

4 I have recently been all round

the world and have formed a very poor opinion of it.
Thomas Beecham: Speech at the Savoy. The News Review, 22 Aug 1946

Before the Roman came to Rye or out to Severn strode,
The rolling English drunkard made the rolling English road.
G. K. Chesterton: The Rolling English Road

The only way to be sure of catching a train is to miss the one before it.
G. K. Chesterton: Vacances à tous prix, 'Le Supplice de l'heure' (P. Daninos)

Travelling is almost like talking with men of other centuries.
René Descartes: Le Discours de la méthode

How does it feel
To be without a home
Like a complete unknown
Like a rolling stone?
Bob Dylan: Like a Rolling Stone

Follow the Yellow Brick Road.
E. Y. Harburg: The Wizard of Oz, Song title

Much have I travell'd in the realms of gold,
And many goodly states and kingdoms seen.
John Keats: On first looking into Chapman's Homer

Of all noxious animals, too, the most noxious is a tourist. And of all tourists the most vulgar, ill-bred, offensive and loathsome is the British tourist.
Francis Kilvert: Diary, 5 Apr 1870

Oh, mister porter, what shall I

I wanted to go to Birmingham, but they've carried me on to Crewe.
Marie Lloyd: Oh, Mister Porter

13 The great and recurrent question about abroad is, is it worth getting there?
Rose Macaulay: Attrib.

14 Whenever I prepare for a journey I prepare as though for death. Should I never return, all is in order. This is what life has taught me.
Katherine Mansfield: The Journal of Katherine Mansfield, 1922

15 The car has become the carapace, the protective and aggressive shell, of urban and suburban man.
Marshall McLuhan: Understanding Media, Ch. 22

16 Rush hour: that hour when traffic is almost at a standstill.
J. B. Morton: Morton's Folly

17 It is the overtakers who keep the undertakers busy.
William Ewart Pitts: The Observer, 'Sayings of the Week', 22 Dec 1963

18 A trip to the moon on gossamer wings.
Cole Porter: Jubilee, 'Just One of Those Things'

19 In the middle ages people were tourists because of their religion, whereas now they are tourists because tourism is their religion.
Robert Runcie: The Observer, 'Sayings of the Week', 11 Dec 1988

20 All I seek, the heaven above And the road below me.
Robert Louis Stevenson: Songs of Travel, 'The Vagabond'

21 Travel is glamorous only in retrospect.
Paul Theroux: The Observer, 'Sayings of the Week', 7 Oct 1979

22 He travelled in order to come home.
William Trevor: Matilda's England

23 If you ever plan to motor west, Travel my way, take the highway, that's the best,
Get your kicks on Route 66.
Bobby Troup: Route 66

24 Commuter – one who spends his life
In riding to and from his wife;
A man who shaves and takes a train,
And then rides back to shave again.
Elwyn Brooks White: The Commuter

TREASON

See also betrayal

1 Please to remember the Fifth of November,
Gunpowder Treason and Plot.
We know no reason why gunpowder treason
Should ever be forgot.
Anonymous: Traditional

2 Treason doth never prosper: what's the reason?
For if it prosper, none dare call it treason.
John Harington: Epigrams, 'Of Treason'

3 Germany calling, Germany calling.
'Lord Haw-Haw': Radio broadcasts to Britain, during World War II

4 Any service rendered to the temporal king to the prejudice of the eternal king is, without doubt, an act of treachery.
Stephen Langton: Letter to the barons of England, 1207

5 Three Judases, each one thrice worse than Judas!
William Shakespeare: Richard II, III:2

TREES

See also countryside, nature

1 But of the tree of the knowledge of good and evil, thou shalt not eat of it: for in the day that thou eatest thereof thou shalt surely die.
Bible: Genesis: 2:17

2 O leave this barren spot to me! Spare, woodman, spare the beechen tree.
Thomas Campbell: The Beech-Tree's Petition

3 I'm replacing some of the timber used up by my books. Books are just trees with squiggles on them.
Hammond Innes: Interview in Radio Times, 18 Aug 1984

4 Poems are made by fools like me,
But only God can make a tree.
Alfred Joyce Kilmer: Trees

5 Woodman, spare that tree! Touch not a single bough! In youth it sheltered me, And I'll protect it now.
George Pope Morris: Woodman, Spare That Tree

6 The difference between a gun and a tree is a difference of

,79   **TRUTH**

tempo. The tree explodes every
spring.
Ezra Pound: Criterion, July 1937

TRIVIALITY

Nothing matters very much,
and very few things matter at all.
Arthur Balfour: Attrib.

A Storm in a Teacup.
W. B. Bernard: Play title

Little things affect little minds.
*Benjamin Disraeli: Sybil, Bk. III,
Ch. 2*

You know my method. It is
founded upon the observance of
trifles.
*Arthur Conan Doyle: The
Boscombe Valley Mystery*

Depend upon it, there is
nothing so unnatural as the
commonplace.
*Arthur Conan Doyle: A Case of
Identity*

Little minds are interested in
the extraordinary; great minds
in the commonplace.
*Elbert Hubbard: Roycroft
Dictionary and Book of Epigrams*

To suckle fools and chronicle
small beer.
*William Shakespeare: Othello,
II:1*

TRUST

See also faith, mistrust

Trust ye not in a friend, put ye
not confidence in a guide: keep
the doors of thy mouth from her
that lieth in thy bosom.
Bible: Micah: 7:5

We are inclined to believe those

whom we do not know because
they have never deceived us.
Samuel Johnson: The Idler

3 Never trust a husband too far,
nor a bachelor too near.
*Helen Rowland: The Rubaiyat of a
Bachelor*

4 Would you buy a second-hand
car from this man?
*Mort Sahl: Referring to President
Nixon. Attrib.*

TRUTH

*See also facts, frankness, honesty,
sincerity*

1 Many a true word is spoken in
jest.
Proverb

2 Truth will out.
Proverb

3 The truth that makes men free
is for the most part the truth
which men prefer not to hear.
*Herbert Sebastian Agar: A Time
for Greatness*

4 Plato is dear to me, but dearer
still is truth.
Aristotle: Attrib.

5 Truth sits upon the lips of dying
men.
*Matthew Arnold: Sohrab and
Rustum*

6 And ye shall know the truth,
and the truth shall make you
free.
Bible: John: 8:32

7 A truth that's told with bad in-
tent
Beats all the lies you can invent.
*William Blake: Auguries of
Innocence*

8 To treat your facts with imagi-

nation is one thing, to imagine your facts is another.
John Burroughs: The Heart of Burroughs Journals

9 Some men love truth so much that they seem to be in continual fear lest she should catch a cold on overexposure.
Samuel Butler: Notebooks

10 Agree to a short armistice with truth.
Lord Byron: Don Juan, III

11 'Tis strange – but true; for truth is always strange;
Stranger than fiction: if it could be told,
How much would novels gain by the exchange!
Lord Byron: Don Juan, XIV

12 You can only find truth with logic if you have already found truth without it.
G. K. Chesterton: The Man who was Orthodox

13 I tore myself away from the safe comfort of certainties through my love for truth; and truth rewarded me.
Simone de Beauvoir: All Said and Done

14 I do not want to use the word 'true'. There are only opinions, some of which are preferable to others. One cannot say: 'Ah. If it is just a matter of preference to hell with it'…One can die for an opinion which is only preferable.
Umberto Eco: Index on Censorship, Vol. 23, May/June 1994

15 If nobody is telling the truth then the lies they are telling are no longer lies but the norm is the truth.
Stephen Fry: The Liar

16 True and False are attributes of speech, not of things. And where speech is not, there is neither Truth nor Falsehood.
Thomas Hobbes: Leviathan, Pt. I, Ch. 4

17 'Beauty is truth, truth beauty,' – that is all
Ye know on earth, and all ye need to know.
John Keats: Ode on a Grecian Urn

18 It is hard to believe that a man is telling the truth when you know that you would lie if you were in his place.
H. L. Mencken

19 No one wants the truth if it is inconvenient.
Arthur Miller: The Observer, 'Sayings of the Week', 8 Jan 1989

20 There can be no whitewash at the White House.
Richard Milhous Nixon: Referring to the Watergate scandal. The Observer, 'Sayings of the Week', 30 Dec 1973

21 Truth telling is not compatible with the defence of the realm.
George Bernard Shaw: Heartbreak House

22 My way of joking is to tell the truth. It's the funniest joke in the world.
George Bernard Shaw: John Bull's Other Island, II

23 There are no whole truths; all truths are half-truths. It is trying to treat them as whole truths that plays the devil.
A. N. Whitehead: Dialogues, 16

24 Truth is on the march; nothing can stop it now.

Émile Zola: Referring to the Dreyfus scandal. Attrib.

TYRANNY

See also authoritarianism, oppression

Churchill on top of the wave has in him the stuff of which tyrants are made.
Lord Beaverbrook: Politicians and the War

To tell the truth, Napoleon is a dangerous man in a free country. He seems to me to have the makings of a tyrant.
Lucien Bonaparte: Letter to Joseph Bonaparte, 1790

Nature has left this tincture in the blood,
That all men would be tyrants if they could.
Daniel Defoe: The Kentish Petition, Addenda

'Twixt kings and tyrants there's this difference known;
Kings seek their subjects' good: tyrants their own.
Robert Herrick: Hesperides, 'Kings and Tyrants'

5 So long as men worship the Caesars and Napoleons, Caesars and Napoleons will arise to make them miserable.
Aldous Huxley: Ends and Means

6 It is better that a man should tyrannize over his bank balance than over his fellow citizens.
John Maynard Keynes: The General Theory of Employment, Interest and Money, Bk. VI, Ch. 24

7 Where laws end, tyranny begins.
William Pitt the Elder: Referring to John Wilkes, an 18th century journalist and radical politician, regarded as a champion of liberty. Speech, House of Lords, 9 Jan 1770

8 The only tyrannies from which men, women and children are suffering in real life are the tyrannies of minorities.
Theodore Roosevelt: Speech, 22 Mar 1912

U

UNCERTAINTY

See also doubt, indecision

1 If ifs and ans were pots and pans, there'd be no trade for tinkers.
Proverb

2 I have known uncertainty: a state unknown to the Greeks.
Jorge Luis Borges: Ficciones, 'The Babylonian Lottery'

3 Of course not. After all, I may be wrong.
Bertrand Russell: On being asked whether he would be prepared to die for his beliefs. Attrib.

UNDERSTANDING

See also intelligence, wisdom

1 It is good to know what a man is, and also what the world takes him for. But you do not understand him until you have learnt how he understands himself.
F. H. Bradley: Aphorisms

2 The people may be made to follow a course of action, but they may not be made to understand it.
Confucius: Analects

3 Only one man ever understood me...And he didn't understand me.
Hegel: Said on his deathbed. Famous Last Words (B. Conrad)

4 Perfect understanding will sometimes almost extinguish pleasure.
A. E. Housman: The Name and Nature of Poetry

5 Thought must be divided against itself before it can come to any knowledge of itself.
Aldous Huxley: Do What You Will

6 She did her work with the thoroughness of a mind that reveres details and never quite understands them.
Sinclair Lewis: Babbitt, Ch. 18

7 I used to tell my husband that, if he could make *me* understand something, it would be clear to all the other people in the country.
Eleanor Roosevelt: Newspaper column, 'My Day', 12 Feb 1947

UNEMPLOYMENT

See also work

1 We must do more than attack the scourge of unemployment. We should also get rid of dead-end, low-paid work with no prospects.
Tony Blair: The Independent, 14 June 1994

2 Giz a job, I could do that.
Alan Bleasdale: Said by his character Yosser Hughes. Boys From the Blackstuff

3 When a great many people are unable to find work, unemployment results.
Calvin Coolidge: City Editor

4 My father did not wait around...he got on his bike and went out looking for work.
Norman Tebbit: Speech, Conservative Party conference, 1981

5 It's a recession when your neighbour loses his job; it's a depression when you lose your own.
Harry S. Truman: The Observer, 'Sayings of the Week', 6 Apr 1958

6 Something must be done.
Duke of Windsor: Said while visiting areas of high unemployment in South Wales during the 1930s. Attrib.

UNITY

1 A chain is no stronger than its weakest link.
Proverb

2 United we stand, divided we fall.
Proverb

3 That typically English characteristic for which there is no English name – *esprit de corps*.
Frank Ezra Adcock: Presidential address

4 And the whole earth was of one language, and of one speech.
Bible: Genesis: 11:1

5 All for one, and one for all.
Alexandre Dumas, père: The Three Musketeers

6 We must indeed all hang together, or most assuredly, we shall all hang separately.
Benjamin Franklin: Remark on signing the Declaration of Independence, 4 July 1776

7 No human relation gives one possession in another – every two souls are absolutely different. In friendship or in love, the two side by side raise hands together to find what one cannot reach alone.

Kahlil Gibran: Beloved Prophet (ed. Virginia Hilu)

UNIVERSE

See also moon, space, sun, world

1 Had I been present at the Creation, I would have given some useful hints for the better ordering of the universe.
Alfonso the Wise: Referring to the complicated Ptolemaic model of the universe. Often quoted as, 'Had I been consulted I would have recommended something simpler'. Attrib.

2 The visible universe was an illusion or, more precisely, a sophism. Mirrors and fatherhood are abominable because they multiply it and extend it.
Jorge Luis Borges: Ficciones, 'Tlön, Uqbar, Orbis Tertius'

3 In this unbelievable universe in which we live there are no absolutes. Even parallel lines, reaching into infinity, meet somewhere yonder.
Pearl Buck: A Bridge for Passing

4 I don't pretend to understand the Universe – it's a great deal bigger than I am.
Thomas Carlyle: Attrib.

5 I am very interested in the Universe – I am specializing in the universe and all that surrounds it.
Peter Cook: Beyond the Fringe

6 Listen; there's a hell of a good universe next door: let's go.
e. e. cummings: Pity this Busy Monster, Mankind

7 My own suspicion is that the universe is not only queerer than

we suppose, but queerer than we *can* suppose.

J. B. S. Haldane: Possible Worlds, 'On Being the Right Size'

8 The universe is not hostile, nor yet is it friendly. It is simply indifferent.

John Haynes Holmes: A Sensible Man's View of Religion

9 The universe begins to look more like a great thought than like a great machine.

James Jeans: The Mysterious Universe

10 Out of all possible universes, the only one which can exist, in the sense that it can be known, is simply the one which satisfies the narrow conditions necessary for the development of intelligent life.

Bernard Lovell: In the Centre of Immensities

11 My theology, briefly, is that the universe was dictated but not signed.

Christopher Morley: Attrib.

V

VERBOSITY

See also speeches, writing

1 A sophistical rhetorician inebriated with the exuberance of his own verbosity.
Benjamin Disraeli: Referring to the Liberal statesman Gladstone. Speech, 27 July 1878

2 But far more numerous was the Herd of such,
Who think too little, and who talk too much.
John Dryden: Absalom and Achitophel, I

VICE

See also crime, evil, sin, virtue and vice

1 We make ourselves a ladder out of our vices if we trample the vices themselves underfoot.
St Augustine of Hippo: Sermons, Bk. III, 'De Ascensione'

2 Often the fear of one evil leads us into a worse.
Nicolas Boileau: L'Art poétique, I

3 Vice is its own reward.
Quentin Crisp: The Naked Civil Servant

4 It is the restrictions placed on vice by our social code which makes its pursuit so peculiarly agreeable.
Kenneth Grahame: Pagan Papers

5 Vice is waste of life. Poverty, obedience and celibacy are the canonical vices.
George Bernard Shaw: Man and Superman

6 Wrongdoing can only be avoided if those who are not wronged feel the same indignation at it as those who are.
Solon: Greek Wit (F. Paley)

7 Whenever I'm caught between two evils, I take the one I've never tried.
Mae West: Attrib.

VICTORY

See also war

1 Veni, vidi, vici.
I came, I saw, I conquered.
Julius Caesar: The Twelve Caesars (Suetonius)

2 I came, I saw, God conquered.
Charles V: Echoing Caesar's 'veni, vidi, vici'. Remark after the Battle of Mühlberg, 23 Apr 1547

3 Victory at all costs, victory in spite of all terror, victory however long and hard the road may be; for without victory there is no survival.
Winston Churchill: Speech, House of Commons, 13 May 1940

4 We triumph without glory when we conquer without danger.
Pierre Corneille: Le Cid, II:2

5 The most important thing in the Olympic Games is not winning but taking part...The essential thing in life is not conquering but fighting well.
Pierre de Coubertin: Speech, Banquet for Officials of the Olympic Games, London, 24 July 1908

6 A game which a sharper once

played with a dupe, entitled
'Heads I win, tails you lose.'
*John Wilson Croker: Croker
Papers*

7 The happy state of getting the
victor's palm without the dust of
racing.
Horace: Epistles, I

8 They talk about who won and
who lost. Human reason won.
Mankind won.
*Nikita Khrushchev: Referring to
the Cuban missiles crisis. The
Observer, 'Sayings of the Week',
11 Nov 1962*

9 Winning isn't everything, but
wanting to win is.
Vince Lombardi

10 See, the conquering hero
comes!
Sound the trumpets, beat the
drums!
*Thomas Morell: The libretto for
Handel's oratorio. Joshua, Pt. III*

11 Such another victory and we
are ruined.
*Pyrrhus: Commenting upon the
costliness of his victory at the Battle
of Asculum (279 BC). Life of
Pyrrhus (Plutarch)*

12 The earth is still bursting with
the dead bodies of the victors.
*George Bernard Shaw:
Heartbreak House, Preface*

13 It was easier to conquer it than
to know what to do with it.
*Horace Walpole: Referring to the
East. Letter to Sir Horace Mann,
27 Mar 1772*

14 I always say that, next to a battle lost, the greatest misery is a
battle gained.
*Duke of Wellington: Diary
(Frances, Lady Shelley)*

See also cruelty

1 You know I hate fighting. If I
knew how to make a living some
other way, I would.
*Muhammad Ali: The Observer,
'Sayings of the Week', 21 Nov
1971*

2 I would be quite happy for men
to hit women if there was a law
saying that women could carry
guns. Because then, if a man hit
you, you could shoot him.
Jo Brand: Q, June 1994

3 A bit of shooting takes your
mind off your troubles – it
makes you forget the cost of
living.
Brendan Behan: The Hostage

4 Violence is the repartee of the
illiterate.
Alan Brien: Punch, 7 Feb 1973

5 It is better to be violent, if there
is violence in our hearts, than to
put on the cloak of non-violence
to cover impotence.
*Mahatma Gandhi: Non-Violence
in Peace and War*

6 Brute force, the law of violence,
rules to a great extent in the
poor man's domicile; and
woman is little more than his
drudge.
*Sarah Moore Grimké: Letter from
Brookline, Sept 1837*

7 It's possible to disagree with
someone about the ethics of
non-violence without wanting to
kick his face in.
*Christopher Hampton: Treats,
Sc. I*

8 We are effectively destroying

ourselves by violence masquerading as love.
R. D. Laing: The Politics of Experience, Ch. 13

Today violence is the rhetoric of the period.
José Ortega y Gasset: The Revolt of the Masses

10 If you strike a child, take care that you strike it in anger, even at the risk of maiming it for life. A blow in cold blood neither can nor should be forgiven.
George Bernard Shaw: Man and Superman, 'Maxims for Revolutionists'

11 Blows are fitter for beasts than for rational creatures.
Hannah Woolley: The Gentlewoman's Companion

VIRGINITY

The error of Jovian consisted in holding virginity not to be preferable to marriage. This error is refuted above all by the example of Christ Who both chose a virgin for His mother and remained Himself a virgin.
St Thomas Aquinas: Summa Theologica

Yet I can't imagine a man sticking around much after two or three months if you hadn't slept together.
Sacha Cowlam: Out of the Doll's House (Angela Holdsworth)

Are there still virgins? One is tempted to answer no. There are only girls who have not yet crossed the line, because they want to preserve their market value.

Françoise Giroud: Coronet, Nov 1960

4 It is one of the superstitions of the human mind to have imagined that virginity could be a virtue.
Voltaire: Notebooks

5 I used to be Snow White...but I drifted.
Mae West: The Wit and Wisdom of Mae West (ed. J. Weintraub)

VIRTUE

See also good, morality, purity, righteousness, virtue and vice

1 Virtue is like a rich stone, best plain set.
Francis Bacon: Essays, 'Of Beauty'

2 Finally, brethren, whatsoever things are true, whatsoever things are honest, whatsoever things are just, whatsoever things are pure, whatsoever things are lovely, whatsoever things are of good report; if there be any virtue; and if there be any praise, think on these things.
Bible: Philippians: 4:8

3 Whenever there are tremendous virtues it's a sure sign something's wrong.
Bertolt Brecht: Mother Courage

4 Virtue consisted in avoiding scandal and venereal disease.
Robert Cecil: Life in Edwardian England

5 The greatest offence against virtue is to speak ill of it.
William Hazlitt: On Cant and Hypocrisy

6 Most men admire

Virtue, who follow not her lore.
*John Milton: Paradise Regained,
Bk. I*

7 Most good women are hidden
treasures who are only safe because nobody looks for them.
*Dorothy Parker: The New York
Times, Obituary, 8 June 1967*

8 Woman's virtue is man's greatest invention.
Cornelia Otis Skinner: Attrib.

VIRTUE AND VICE

See also good and evil

1 Good girls go to heaven, bad
girls go everywhere.
*Helen Gurley Brown:
Cosmopolitan*

2 It is the function of vice to keep
virtue within reasonable
bounds.
Samuel Butler: Notebooks

3 Our virtues and vices couple
with one another, and get children that resemble both their
parents.
*Lord Halifax: Political, Moral and
Miscellaneous Thoughts and
Reflections*

4 Most usually our virtues are
only vices in disguise.
*Duc de la Rochefoucauld:
Maximes, added to the 4th edition*

VULGARITY

1 You gotta have a swine to show
you where the truffles are.
*Edward Albee: Who's Afraid of
Virginia Woolf?, I*

2 The aristocratic pleasure of dis-
pleasing is not the only delight
that bad taste can yield. One can
love a certain kind of vulgarity
for its own sake.
*Aldous Huxley: Vulgarity in
Literature, Ch. 4*

3 That fellow would vulgarize the
day of judgment.
*Douglas William Jerrold: Wit and
Opinions of Douglas Jerrold, 'A
Comic Author'*

4 It is disgusting to pick your
teeth. What is vulgar is to use a
gold toothpick.
*Louis Kronenberger: The Cat and
the Horse*

5 I can't stand a naked light bulb,
any more than I can a rude remark or a vulgar action.
*Tennessee Williams: A Streetcar
Named Desire, II:3*

W

WAR

See also army, Cold War, navy, nuclear weapons, soldiers, weapons, World War I, World War II

1 *Flavit deus et dissipati sunt.*
God blew and they were scattered.
Anonymous: Inscription on the medallion minted to commemorate the defeat of the Spanish Armada.

2 The region is undergoing ethnic cleansing.
Anonymous: Referring to Bosnia-Hercegovina.

3 Your country needs YOU.
Anonymous: British recruiting poster featuring Lord Kitchener

4 It became necessary to destroy the town of Ben Tre to save it.
Anonymous: Said by a US Major in Vietnam. The Observer, 'Sayings of the Week', 11 Feb 1968

5 To save your world you asked this man to die:
Would this man, could he see you now, ask why?
W. H. Auden: Epitaph for an Unknown Soldier

6 The only defence is in offence, which means that you have to kill more women and children more quickly than the enemy if you want to save yourselves.
Stanley Baldwin: Speech, Nov 1932

7 If there is ever another war in Europe, it will come out of some damned silly thing in the Balkans.
Bismarck: Remark to Ballen, shortly before Bismarck's death.

8 *C'est magnifique, mais ce n'est pas la guerre.*
It is magnificent, but it is not war.
Pierre Bosquet: Referring to the Charge of the Light Brigade at the Battle of Balaclava, 25 Oct 1854. Attrib.

9 What they could do with round here is a good war.
Bertolt Brecht: Mother Courage, I

10 If I should die, think only this of me:
That there's some corner of a foreign field
That is forever England.
Rupert Brooke: The Soldier

11 I will draw a line in the sand.
George Bush: Referring to the defence of Saudi Arabia by US forces following the Iraqi invasion of Kuwait (1990). Speech, 1990

12 The war wasn't fought about democracy in Kuwait.
George Bush: Referring to the Gulf War (1991). The Observer, 14 July 1991

13 Carthage must be destroyed.
Cato the Elder: Life of Cato (Plutarch)

14 War is the continuation of politics by other means.
Karl von Clausewitz: The usual misquotation of 'War is nothing but a continuation of politics with the admixture of other means'. Vom Kriege

15 My home policy? I wage war.
My foreign policy? I wage war.
Always, everywhere, I wage
war…And I shall continue to
wage war until the last quarter of
an hour.
*Georges Clemenceau: Speech,
Chamber of Deputies, 8 Mar 1918.*

16 Come on, you sons of bitches!
Do you want to live for ever?
*Dan Daly: Remark during Allied
resistance at Belleau Wood, June
1918. See also* FREDERICK THE
GREAT. *Attrib.*

17 France has lost a battle, but
France has not lost the war!
*Charles de Gaulle: Proclamation,
18 June 1940*

18 We are not at war with Egypt.
We are in an armed conflict.
*Anthony Eden: Speech, House of
Commons, 4 Nov 1956*

19 There is nothing that war has
ever achieved that we could not
better achieve without it.
*Havelock Ellis: The Philosophy of
Conflict*

20 My centre is giving way, my
right is in retreat; situation
excellent. I shall attack.
*Marshal Foch: Message sent
during the second Battle of the
Marne, 1918. Biography of Foch
(Aston), Ch. 13*

21 Praise the Lord and pass the
ammunition!
*Howell Maurice Forgy: Remark
made during the Japanese attack
on Pearl Harbor, 7 Dec 1941.
Attrib. in The Los Angeles Times*

22 I got there fustest with the
mostest.
*Nathan Bedford Forrest: Popular
misquotation of his explanation of
his success in capturing
Murfreesboro; his actual words
were, 'I just took the short cut and
got there first with the most men.'
A Civil War Treasury (B. Botkin).*

23 Rascals, would you live for
ever?
*Frederick the Great: Addressed to
reluctant soldiers at the Battle of
Kolin, 18 June 1757. See also
DALY.*

24 You've got to forget about this
civilian. Whenever you drop
bombs, you're going to hit
civilians.
*Barry Goldwater: Speech, New
York, 23 Jan 1967*

25 In starting and waging a war it
is not right that matters, but
victory.
*Adolf Hitler: The Rise and Fall of
the Third Reich (W. L. Shirer),
Ch. 16*

26 Older men declare war. But it
is youth that must fight and die.
*Herbert Hoover: Speech,
Republican National Convention,
Chicago, 27 June 1944*

27 The mother of battles will
be our battle of victory and
martyrdom.
*Saddam Hussein: Referring to the
imminent Gulf War. Speech, 1991*

28 War should belong to the tragic
past, to history: it should find no
place on humanity's agenda for
the future.
John Paul II: Speech, 1982

29 The first casualty when war
comes is truth.
*Hiram Warren Johnson: Speech,
U.S. Senate, 1917*

30 Our scientific power has out-run our spiritual power. We have guided missiles and misguided men.

Martin Luther King: Strength to Love

31 The conventional army loses if it does not win. The guerrilla wins if he does not lose.

Henry Kissinger: Foreign Affairs, XIII (Jan 1969), 'The Vietnam Negotiations'

32 Where do all the women who have watched so carefully over the lives of their beloved ones get the heroism to send them to face the canon?

Käthe Kollwitz: Diary entry, 27 Aug 1914

33 It is well that war is so terrible; else we would grow too fond of it.

Robert E. Lee: Speaking to another general during the Battle of Fredericksburg. The American Treasury (C. Fadiman)

34 This war, like the next war, is a war to end war.

David Lloyd George: Referring to the popular opinion that World War I would be the last major war.

35 War will never cease until babies begin to come into the world with larger cerebrums and smaller adrenal glands.

H. L. Mencken: Notebooks, 'Minority Report'

36 Any fool can be brave on a battle field when it's be brave or else be killed.

Margaret Mitchell: Gone with the Wind

37 An empire founded by war has to maintain itself by war.

Baron de Montesquieu: Considérations sur les causes de la grandeur et de la décadence des romains, Ch. 8

38 It's the most beautiful battle-field I've ever seen.

Napoleon I: Referring to carnage on the field of Borodino, near Moscow, after the battle (7 Sept 1812). Attrib

39 War is war. The only good human being is a dead one.

George Orwell: Animal Farm, Ch. 4

40 If sunbeams were weapons of war, we would have had solar energy long ago.

George Porter: The Observer, 'Sayings of the Week', 26 Aug 1973

41 Don't fire until you see the whites of their eyes.

William Prescott: Command given at the Battle of Bunker Hill

42 War is, after all, the universal perversion. We are all tainted: if we cannot experience our perversion at first hand we spend our time reading war stories, the pornography of war; or seeing war films, the blue films of war; or titillating our senses with the imagination of great deeds, the masturbation of war.

John Rae: The Custard Boys, Ch. 6

43 As a woman I can't go to war, and I refuse to send anyone else.

Jeannette Rankin: Jeannette Rankin: First Lady in Congress, Prologue

44 All Quiet on the Western Front.

Erich Maria Remarque: Title of novel

45 More than an end to war, we want an end to the beginnings of all wars.
Franklin D. Roosevelt: Speech broadcast on the day after his death (13 Apr 1945)

46 I discovered to my amazement that average men and women were delighted at the prospect of war. I had fondly imagined that most pacifists contended, that wars were forced upon a reluctant population by despotic and Machiavellian governments.
Bertrand Russell: The Autobiography of Bertrand Russell

47 They dashed on towards that *thin red line tipped with steel.*
William Howard Russell: Description of the Russian charge against the British at the Battle of Balaclava, 1854. The British Expedition to the Crimea

48 If I were fierce and bald and short of breath,
I'd live with scarlet Majors at the Base,
And speed glum heroes up the line to death.
Siegfried Sassoon: Base Details

49 Wars come because not enough people are sufficiently afraid.
Hugh Schonfield: The News Review, 26 Feb 1948

50 The Cavaliers (wrong but Wromantic) and the Roundheads (Right but Repulsive).
W. C. Sellar: 1066 And All That

51 Everyone is always talking about our defense effort in terms of defending women and children, but no one ever asks the women and children what they think.
Patricia Schroeder: American Political Women

52 Cry 'Havoc!' and let slip the dogs of war.
William Shakespeare: Julius Caesar, III:1

53 The British soldier can stand up to anything except the British War Office.
George Bernard Shaw: The Devil's Disciple, II

54 I am tired and sick of war. Its glory is all moonshine…War is hell.
William Sherman: Attrib. in address, Michigan Military Academy, 19 June 1879

55 To win in Vietnam, we will have to exterminate a nation.
Benjamin Spock: Dr Spock on Vietnam, Ch.7

56 That's what you are. That's what you all are. All of you young people who served in the war. You are a lost generation.
Gertrude Stein: A Moveable Feast (E. Hemingway)

57 War is capitalism with the gloves off.
Tom Stoppard: Travesties

58 They make a wilderness and call it peace.
Tacitus: Agricola, 30

59 The military don't start wars. The politicians start wars.
William Westmorland: Attrib.

60 As long as war is regarded as wicked, it will always have its fascination. When it is looked upon as vulgar, it will cease to be popular.

Oscar Wilde: The Critic as Artist,
Pt. 2

61 It takes only one gramme of
explosive to kill a man, so why
waste five tons?
*Solly Zuckerman: From Apes to
War Lords*

WAR AND PEACE

See also peace

1 Since wars begin in the minds of
men, it is in the minds of men
that the defences of peace must
be constructed.
*Anonymous: Constitution of
UNESCO*

2 The Israelis are now what we
call the 'enemy-friends.
*Anonymous adviser to the
Palestinian leader Yasser Arafat.:
The Independent, 5 July 1994*

3 In war, resolution; in defeat, de-
fiance; in victory, magnanimity;
in peace, goodwill.
*Winston Churchill: Epigram used
by Sir Edward Marsh after World
War II; used as 'a moral of the
work' in Churchill's book. The
Second World War*

4 My pacifism is not based on any
intellectual theory but on a deep
antipathy to every form of cruelty and hatred.
*Albert Einstein: Said on the
outbreak of World War I. Attrib.*

5 There never was a good war or a
bad peace.
*Benjamin Franklin: Letter to
Josiah Quincy, 11 Sept 1783*

6 Peace hath her victories
No less renowned than war.
*John Milton: Sonnet: 'To the Lord
General Cromwell, May 1652'*

7 Peace is not only better than
war, but infinitely more
arduous.
*George Bernard Shaw:
Heartbreak House (Preface)*

WATER

See also drinks

1 Well, the principle seems the
same. The water still keeps
falling over.
*Winston Churchill: When asked
whether the Niagara Falls looked
the same as when he first saw them.
Closing the Ring, Ch. 5*

2 Water, water, every where,
And all the boards did shrink;
Water, water, every where,
Nor any drop to drink.
*Samuel Taylor Coleridge: The
Rime of the Ancient Mariner, II*

3 Instead of drinking Coca Colas,
turn on the tap and drink what
the good Lord gave us.
Edwina Currie: Speech, Nov 1988

4 Fish fuck in it.
*W. C. Fields: His reason for not
drinking water. Attrib.*

5 The biggest waste of water in
the country by far. You spend
half a pint and flush two gallons.
Prince Philip: Speech, 1965

6 Human beings were invented by
water as a device for transport-
ing itself from one place to another.
*Tom Robbins: Another Roadside
Attraction*

WEAKNESS

1 The weakest goes to the wall.
Proverb

WEALTH

WEALTH

2 Oh, your precious 'lame ducks'!
John Galsworthy: The Man of Property, Pt. II, Ch. 12

3 A sheep in sheep's clothing.
Edmund Gosse: Referring to T. Sturge Moore. Sometimes attributed to Winston Churchill, referring to Clement Attlee. Under the Bridge (Ferris Greenslet), Ch. 12

4 Frailty, thy name is woman!
William Shakespeare: Hamlet, I:2

WEALTH

See also capitalism, commercialism, extravagance, materialism, money

1 The best things in life are free.
Proverb

2 You can't take it with you when you go.
Proverb

3 A man who has a million dollars is as well off as if he were rich.
John Jacob Astor: Attrib.

4 It is easier for a camel to go through the eye of a needle, than for a rich man to enter into the kingdom of God.
Bible: Matthew: 19:24

5 Maidens, like moths, are ever caught by glare,
And Mammon wins his way where Seraphs might despair.
Lord Byron: British poet. Childe Harold's Pilgrimage, I

6 Nothing melts a Woman's Heart like gold.
Susannah Centlivre: The Basset-Table, IV

7 The rich are the scum of the earth in every country.
G. K. Chesterton: The Flying Inn

8 Poor Little Rich Girl.
Noël Coward: Song title

9 Riches have wings, and grandeur is a dream.
William Cowper: The Task

10 The meek shall inherit the earth but not the mineral rights.
J. Paul Getty: Attrib.

11 The rich hate signing cheques. Hence the success of credit cards.
Graham Greene: Dr. Fischer of Geneva

12 Wealth covers sin – the poor Are naked as a pin.
Kassia: Women Poets of the World (eds Joanna Bankier and Deirdre Lashgari)

13 Those in the cheaper seats clap. The rest of you rattle your jewellery.
John Lennon: Remark, Royal Variety Performance, 15 Nov 1963

14 They gave me star treatment because I was making a lot of money. But I was just as good when I was poor.
Bob Marley: The Radio Times, 18 Sept 1981

15 I am rich beyond the dreams of avarice.
Edward Moore: The Gamester, II

16 God shows his contempt for wealth by the kind of person he selects to receive it.
Austin O'Malley

17 Who Wants to Be a Millionaire?
Cole Porter: Who Wants to be a Millionaire?, song title

18 I am a millionaire. That is my religion.

George Bernard Shaw: Major Barbara

19 With the great part of rich people, the chief employment of riches consists in the parade of riches.

Adam Smith: The Wealth of Nations

20 It is the wretchedness of being rich that you have to live with rich people.

Logan Pearsall Smith: Afterthoughts, 'In the World'

WEAPONS

See also nuclear weapons, power politics, war

1 It was very successful, but it fell on the wrong planet.

Wernher von Braun: Referring to the first V2 rocket to hit London during World War II. Attrib.

2 We may find in the long run that tinned food is a deadlier weapon than the machine-gun.

George Orwell: The Road to Wigan Pier, Ch. 6

3 Arms control so easily becomes an incantation rather than policy.

Richard Perle: Remark, Mar 1987

4 Today we have naming of parts. Yesterday,
We had daily cleaning. And tomorrow morning
We shall have what to do after firing. But today,
Today we have naming of parts.

Henry Reed: Naming of Parts

5 But bombs *are* unbelievable until they actually fall.

Patrick White: Riders in the Chariot, I:4

WEATHER

See also sun

1 Red sky at night, shepherd's delight; red sky in the morning, shepherd's warning.

Proverb

2 St. Swithin's Day, if thou dost rain, for forty days it will remain; St. Swithin's Day, if thou be fair, for forty days 'twill rain no more.

Proverb

3 What dreadful hot weather we have! It keeps me in a continual state of inelegance.

Jane Austen: Letter, 18 Sept 1796

4 This is a London particular...A fog, miss.

Charles Dickens: Bleak House, Ch. 3

5 I'm singing in the rain, just singing in the rain;
What a wonderful feeling, I'm happy again.

Arthur Freed: From the musical, Hollywood Revue of 1929. Singing in the Rain

6 When two Englishmen meet, their first talk is of the weather.

Samuel Johnson: The Idler

7 Who has seen the wind?
Neither you nor I:
But when the trees bow down their heads,
The wind is passing by.

Christina Rossetti: Who Has Seen the Wind?

8 So foul and fair a day I have not seen.

William Shakespeare: Macbeth, I:3

9 I wield the flail of the lashing hail,

And whiten the green plains
under,
And then again I dissolve it in
rain,
And laugh as I pass in thunder.
Percy Bysshe Shelley: The Cloud

10 It was the wrong kind of snow.
*Terry Worrall: Explaining why
British Rail's anti-snow measures
had not worked. The Observer,
17 Feb 1991*

WISDOM

See also intelligence, knowledge,
prudence

1 It is easy to be wise after the
event.
Proverb

2 Wisdom reacheth from one end
to another mightily: and sweetly
doth she order all things.
Bible: Wisdom: 8:1

3 Can Wisdom be put in a silver
rod,
Or love in a golden bowl?
*William Blake: The Book of Thel,
'Thel's Motto'*

4 Be wiser than other people if
you can, but do not tell them so.
*Earl of Chesterfield: Letter to his
son, 19 Nov 1745*

5 A sadder and a wiser man,
He rose the morrow morn.
*Samuel Taylor Coleridge: The
Rime of the Ancient Mariner, VII*

6 Knowledge dwells
In heads replete with thoughts
of other men;
Wisdom in minds attentive to
their own.
William Cowper: The Task

7 Some are weather-wise, some
are otherwise.
*Benjamin Franklin: Poor
Richard's Almanack*

8 Vain wisdom all, and false philosophy.
John Milton: Paradise Lost, Bk. II

9 There is more wisdom in your
body than in your deepest philosophy.
*Friedrich Nietzsche: Human, All
Too Human, Pt. II*

10 Thou speakest wiser than thou
art ware of.
*William Shakespeare: As You Like
It, II:4*

11 Possibly no wiser, My Lord,
but far better informed.
*F. E. Smith: To judge who
complained that he had listened to
Smith's argument but was still
none the wiser. Life of F. E. Smith
(Birkenhead)*

12 It is never wise to try to appear
to be more clever than you are.
It is sometimes wise to appear
slightly less so.
*William Whitelaw: The Observer,
'Sayings of the Year', 1975*

WISDOM AND FOOLISHNESS

1 A wise man makes his own decisions, an ignorant man follows
the public opinion.
Chinese proverb

2 For ye suffer fools gladly, seeing
ye yourselves are wise.
Bible: II Corinthians: 11:19

3 A fool sees not the same tree
that a wise man sees.
*William Blake: The Marriage of
Heaven and Hell, 'Proverbs of
Hell'*

4 Many have been the wise
speeches of fools, though not so

many as the foolish speeches of wise men.
Thomas Fuller: The Holy State and the Profane State

WOMAN'S ROLE

See also feminism, sexes, women

1 God could not be everywhere and therefore he made mothers.
Jewish proverb

2 What they say of us is that we have a peaceful time
Living at home, while they do the fighting in war.
How wrong they are! I would very much rather stand
Three times in the front of battle than bear one child.
Euripides: Medea, 248

3 Mother is the dead heart of the family, spending father's earnings on consumer goods to enhance the environment in which he eats, sleeps and watches the television.
Germaine Greer: The Female Eunuch

4 These are rare attainments for a damsel, but pray tell me, can she spin?
James I: On being introduced to a young girl proficient in Latin, Greek, and Hebrew. Attrib.

5 Women exist in the main solely for the propagation of the species.
Arthur Schopenhauer

6 Vain man is apt to think we were merely intended for the world's propagation and to keep its humane inhabitants sweet and clean; but, by their leaves, had we the same literature he would

find our brains as fruitful as our bodies.
Hannah Woolley: Gentlewoman's Companion, 1675

WOMEN

See also feminism, sexes

1 A man of straw is worth a woman of gold.
Proverb

2 A woman's work is never done.
Proverb

3 The hand that rocks the cradle rules the world.
Proverb

4 Old-fashioned ways which no longer apply to changed conditions are a snare in which the feet of women have always become readily entangled.
Jane Addams: In Newer Ideals of Peace, 'Utilization of Women in City Government'

5 Votes for Women.
Anonymous: Slogan

6 A woman, especially if she have the misfortune of knowing anything, should conceal it as well as she can.
Jane Austen: Northanger Abbey, Ch. 14

7 One is not born a woman, one becomes one.
Simone de Beauvoir: Le Deuxième Sexe (trans. The Second Sex)

8 It is in great part the anxiety of being a woman that devastates the feminine body.
Simone de Beauvoir: Womansize (Kim Chernin)

9 Intimacies between women often go backwards, beginning in

revelations and ending in small talk without loss of esteem.

Elizabeth Bowen: The Death of the Heart

10 Brigands demand your money or your life; women require both.

Samuel Butler: Attrib.

11 Women are much more like each other than men: they have, in truth, but two passions, vanity and love; these are their universal characteristics.

Earl of Chesterfield: Letter to his son, 19 Dec 1749

12 Certain women should be struck regularly, like gongs.

Noël Coward: Private Lives

13 Women never have young minds. They are born three thousand years old.

Shelagh Delaney: A Taste of Honey, I:1

14 It is only the women whose eyes have been washed clear with tears who get the broad vision that makes them little sisters to all the world.

Dorothy Dix: Dorothy Dix, Her Book, Introduction

15 There are only three things to be done with a woman. You can love her, you can suffer for her, or you can turn her into literature.

Lawrence Durrell: Justine

16 I'm not denyin' the women are foolish: God Almighty made 'em to match the men.

George Eliot: Adam Bede, Ch. 53

17 When a woman behaves like a man, why doesn't she behave like a nice man?

Edith Evans: The Observer, 'Sayings of the Week', 30 Sept 1956

18 Women are equal because they are not different any more.

Erich Fromm: The Art of Loving

19 How, like a moth, the simple maid
Still plays about the flame!

John Gay: The Beggar's Opera

20 You have to admit that most women who have done something with their lives have been disliked by almost everyone.

Françoise Gilot: Remark, Oct 1987

21 I know you do not make the laws but I also know that you are the wives and mothers, the sisters and daughters of those who do.

Angelina Grimké: The Anti-Slavery Examiner (Sep 1836), 'Appeal to the Christian Women of the South'

22 My mother said it was simple to keep a man, you must be a maid in the living room, a cook in the kitchen and a whore in the bedroom. I said I'd hire the other two and take care of the bedroom bit.

Jerry Hall: Remark, Oct 1985

23 If men knew how women pass their time when they are alone, they'd never marry.

O. Henry: The Four Million Memoirs of a Yellow Dog

24 For the female of the species is more deadly than the male.

Rudyard Kipling: The Female of the Species

25 Women run to extremes; they

are either better or worse than men.

Jean de La Bruyère: Les Caractères

26 How lucky we are that women defend themselves so poorly! We should, otherwise, be no more to them than timid slaves.

Pierre Choderlos de Laclos: Les Liaisons dangereuses, Letter 4

27 I see some rats have got in; let them squeal, it doesn't matter.

David Lloyd George: Said when suffragettes interrupted a meeting. The Faber Book of English History in Verse (Kenneth Baker)

28 So this gentleman said a girl with brains ought to do something else with them besides think.

Anita Loos: Gentlemen Prefer Blondes, Ch. 1

29 The Professor of Gynaecology began his course of lectures as follows: Gentlemen, woman is an animal that micturates once a day, defecates once a month, menstruates once a month, parturates once a year and copulates whenever she has the opportunity.

W. Somerset Maugham: A Writer's Notebook

30 I shrug my shoulders in despair at women who moan at the lack of opportunities and then take two weeks off as a result of falling out with their boyfriends.

Sophie Mirman: On receiving the Business Woman of the Year Award.

31 Women would rather be right than reasonable.

Ogden Nash: Frailty, Thy Name Is a Misnomer

32 When a woman becomes a scholar there is usually something wrong with her sexual organs.

Friedrich Nietzsche: Bartlett's Unfamiliar Quotations (Leonard Louis Levinson)

33 There are already so many women in the world! Why then...was I born a woman, to be scorned by men in words and deeds?

Isotta Nogarola: Letter to Guarino Veronese

34 So greatly did she care for freedom that she died for it. So dearly did she love women that she offered her life as their ransom. That is the verdict given at the great Inquest of the Nation on the death of Emily Wilding Davison.

Christabel Pankhurst: Emily Davison threw herself under the King's horse in protest at the imprisoning of suffragettes. The Suffragette, 13 June 1913

35 There are two kinds of women – goddesses and doormats.

Pablo Picasso: Attrib.

36 O tiger's heart wrapp'd in a woman's hide!

William Shakespeare: Henry VI, Part Three, I:4

37 Womanhood is the great fact in her life; wifehood and motherhood are but incidental relations.

Elizabeth Stanton: History of Woman Suffrage (with Susan B. Anthony and Mathilda Gage), Vol. I

WONDER

38 I've got a woman's ability to
stick to a job and get on with it
when everyone else walks off
and leaves it.
*Margaret Thatcher: The Observer,
'Sayings of the Week', 16 Feb
1975*

39 I am a source of satisfaction to
him, a nurse, a piece of furniture, a *woman* – nothing more.
*Sophie Tolstoy: A Diary of
Tolstoy's Wife, 1860–1891*

40 Scarce, sir. Mighty scarce.
*Mark Twain: Responding to the
question 'In a world without
women what would men become?'
Attrib.*

41 I would venture to guess that
Anon, who wrote so many po-
ems without signing them, was
often a woman.
*Virginia Woolf: A Room of One's
Own*

42 Women have served all these
centuries as looking-glasses pos-
sessing the magic and delicious
power of reflecting the figure of
man at twice its natural size.
*Virginia Woolf: A Room of One's
Own*

WONDER

See also admiration, curiosity

1 To see a World in a grain of
sand,
And a Heaven in a wild flower,
Hold Infinity in the palm of your
hand,
And Eternity in an hour.
*William Blake: Auguries of
Innocence*

2 Two things fill the mind with
ever new and increasing wonder

and awe, the more often and the
more seriously reflection concentrates upon them: the starry
heaven above me and the moral
law within me.
*Immanuel Kant: Critique of
Practical Reason, Conclusion*

WORDS

See also language, speech, verbosity

1 In the beginning was the Word,
and the Word was with God,
and the Word was God.
Bible: John: 1:1

2 Actions speak louder than
words.
Proverb

3 He said true things, but called
them by wrong names.
*Robert Browning: Bishop
Blougram's Apology*

4 Until we learn the use of living
words we shall continue to be
waxworks inhabited by gramo-
phones.
*Walter De La Mare: The
Observer, 'Sayings of the Week',
12 May 1929*

5 When there is no explanation,
they give it a name, which immediately explains everything.
*Martin H. Fischer: Fischerisms
(Howard Fabing and Ray Marr)*

6 It was in the barbarous, gothic
times when words had a meaning; in those days, writers ex-
pressed thoughts.
*Anatole France: The Literary Life,
'M. Charles Morice'*

7 Thanks to words, we have been
able to rise above the brutes;
and thanks to words, we have of-

ten sunk to the level of the demons.
Aldous Huxley: Adonis and the Alphabet

8 I am a Bear of Very Little Brain, and long words Bother me.
A. A. Milne: Winnie-the-Pooh, Ch. 4

9 My father still reads the dictionary every day. He says your life depends on your power to master words.
Arthur Scargill: The Sunday Times, 10 Jan 1982

10 There is a Southern proverb – fine words butter no parsnips.
Walter Scott: The Legend of Montrose, Ch. 3

11 My words fly up, my thoughts remain below:
Words without thoughts never to heaven go.
William Shakespeare: Hamlet, III:3

12 Man does not live by words alone, despite the fact that sometimes he has to eat them.
Adlai Stevenson: Attrib.

13 No, my dear, it is *I* who am surprised; you are merely astonished.
Noah Webster: Responding to his wife's comment that she had been surprised to find him embracing their maid. Attrib.

WORK

See also effort, unemployment

1 All work and no play makes Jack a dull boy.
Proverb

2 No bees, no honey; no work, no money.
Proverb

3 There is dignity in work only when it is work freely accepted.
Albert Camus: Notebooks, 1935–42

4 Work is much more fun than fun.
Noël Coward: The Observer, 'Sayings of the Week', 21 June 1963

5 By working faithfully eight hours a day you may eventually get to be a boss and work twelve hours a day.
Robert Frost: Attrib.

6 Employment is nature's physician, and is essential to human happiness.
Galen

7 When work is a pleasure, life is a joy! When work is a duty, life is slavery.
Maxim Gorky: The Lower Depths

8 Horny-handed sons of toil.
Denis Kearney: Speech, San Francisco, c. 1878

9 Life is too short to do anything for oneself that one can pay others to do for one.
W. Somerset Maugham: The Summing Up

10 Work expands so as to fill the time available for its completion.
Cyril Northcote Parkinson: Parkinson's Law, Ch. 1

11 In a hierarchy every employee tends to rise to his level of incompetence.
Laurence J. Peter: Peter Principle, Ch. 1

12 They say hard work never hurt anybody, but I figure why take the chance.

Ronald Reagan: Attrib.

13 Pennies do not come from heaven. They have to be earned here on earth.
Margaret Thatcher: The Sunday Telegraph, 1982

14 I should have worked just long enough to discover that I didn't like it.
Paul Theroux: The Observer Magazine, 1 Apr 1979

15 Work banishes those three great evils, boredom, vice, and poverty.
Voltaire: Candide, Ch. 30

16 How doth the little busy bee
Improve each shining hour,
And gather honey all the day
From every opening flower!
Isaac Watts: Divine Songs for Children, 'Against Idleness and Mischief'

17 Work is the curse of the drinking classes.
Oscar Wilde: Attrib.

WORLD

1 For the world, I count it not an inn, but an hospital, and a place, not to live, but to die in.
Thomas Browne: Religio Medici, Pt. II

2 As I walked through the wilderness of this world.
John Bunyan: The Pilgrim's Progress, Pt. I

3 Sell a country! Why not sell the air, the great sea, as well as the earth? Did not the Great Spirit make them all for the use of his children?

Tecumseh: Protesting to Governor W. H. Harrison over the breach of the Treaty of Greenville, 1810.

WORLD WAR I

1 Belgium put the kibosh on the Kaiser,
Europe took a stick and made him sore;
And if Turkey makes a stand
She'll get ghurka'd and japanned,
And it won't be Hoch the Kaiser any more.
Anonymous: Song of World War I

2 Six million young men lie in premature graves, and four old men sit in Paris partitioning the earth.
Anonymous: New York Nation, 1919

3 What did you do in the Great War, Daddy?
British Recruiting Poster

4 This is not peace: it is an armistice for twenty years.
Marshal Foch: Attrib.

5 Please God – let there be victory, before the Americans arrive.
Douglas Haig: Diary, 1917

6 If any question why we died,
Tell them because our fathers lied.
Rudyard Kipling: Epitaphs of War

7 I cannot get any sense of an enemy – only of a disaster.
D. H. Lawrence: Letter to Edward Marsh, Oct 1914

8 What passing-bells for these who die as cattle?
Only the monstrous anger of the guns,

Only the stuttering rifles' rapid
rattle
Can patter out their hasty
orisons.

*Wilfred Owen: Anthem for
Doomed Youth*

9 Man, it seemed, had been created to jab the life out of Germans.

*Siegfried Sassoon: Memoirs of an
Infantry Officer, Pt. I, Ch. 1*

10 You will be home before the
leaves have fallen from the trees.

*Wilhelm II: Said to troops leaving
for the Front, Aug 1914. August
1914 (Barbara Tuchman), Ch. 9*

11 My message today was a message of death for your young
men. How strange it seems to
applaud that.

*Woodrow Wilson: Remark after his
speech to Congress asking for a
declaration of war, Apr 1917*

WORLD WAR II

See also Nazism
    Hitler
    Has only got one ball!
    Goering
    Has two, but very small!
    Himmler
    Has something similar,
    But poor old Goebbels
    Has no balls at all!

*Anonymous: World War II song (to
the tune of 'Colonel Bogey')*

This morning the British Ambassador in Berlin handed the
German Government a final
note stating that, unless we
heard from them by eleven
o'clock that they were prepared
at once to withdraw their troops
from Poland, a state of war
would exist between us. I have to
tell you that no such undertaking has been received, and that
consequently this country is at
war with Germany.

*Neville Chamberlain: Radio
broadcast from Downing Street,
London, 3 Sept 1939*

3 If we can stand up to Hitler, all
Europe may be free and the life
of the world may move forward
into broad, sunlit uplands.

*Winston Churchill: Speech, House
of Commons, 18 June 1940*

4 We shall not flag or fail. We shall
fight in France, we shall fight on
the seas and oceans, we shall
fight with growing confidence
and growing strength in the air,
we shall defend our island,
whatever the cost may be, we
shall fight on the beaches, we
shall fight on the landing
grounds, we shall fight in the
fields and in the streets, we shall
fight in the hills; we shall never
surrender.

*Winston Churchill: Speech, House
of Commons, 4 June 1940*

5 The battle of Britain is about to
begin.

*Winston Churchill: Speech, House
of Commons, 18 June 1940*

6 Never in the field of human
conflict was so much owed by so
many to so few.

*Winston Churchill: Referring to
the Battle of Britain pilots. Speech,
House of Commons, 20 Aug 1940*

7 This whipped jackal ... is frisk-
ing up by the side of the German
tiger.

Winston Churchill: Referring to the Italian dictator, Mussolini. Speech, House of Commons, Apr 1941

8 Before Alamein we never had a victory. After Alamein we never had a defeat.

Winston Churchill: The Hinge of Fate, Ch. 33

9 Now we can look the East End in the face.

Elizabeth the Queen Mother: Surveying the damage caused to Buckingham Palace by a bomb during the Blitz in World War II. Attrib.

10 They entered the war to prevent us from going into the East, not to have the East come to the Atlantic.

Hermann Goering: Referring to the war aims of the British in World War II. Nuremberg Diary (G. M. Gilbert).

11 The little ships, the unforgotten Homeric catalogue of *Mary Jane* and *Peggy IV*, of *Folkestone Belle, Boy Billy*, and *Ethel Maud*, of *Lady Haig* and *Skylark*...the little ships of England brought the Army home.

Philip Guedalla: Referring to the evacuation of Dunkirk. Mr. Churchill

12 The war situation has developed not necessarily to Japan's advantage.

Hirohito: Announcing Japan's surrender, 15 Aug 1945

13 Before us stands the last problem that must be solved and will be solved. It is the last territorial claim which I have to make in Europe, but it is the claim from which I will not recede.

Adolf Hitler: Referring to the Sudetenland (Czechoslovakia). Speech, Berlin, 26 Sept 1938

14 Well, he seemed such a nice old gentleman, I thought I would give him my autograph as a souvenir.

Adolf Hitler: Referring to Neville Chamberlain and the Munich agreement. Attrib.

15 To make a union with Great Britain would be fusion with a corpse.

Marshal Pétain: On hearing Churchill's suggestion for an Anglo-French union, 1940. Their Finest Hour (Winston S. Churchill), Ch. 10

16 The best immediate defence of the United States is the success of Great Britain defending itself.

Franklin D. Roosevelt: At press conference, 17 Dec 1940. Their Finest Hour (Winston S. Churchill), Ch. 28

17 A date that will live in infamy.

Franklin D. Roosevelt: Referring to 7 Dec 1941, when Japan attacked Pearl Harbor. Message to Congress, 8 Dec 1941

18 We have finished the job, what shall we do with the tools?

Haile Selassie: Telegram sent to Winston Churchill, mimicking his 'Give us the tools, and we will finish the job'. Ambrosia and Small Beer, Ch. 4 (Edward Marsh)

19 If we see that Germany is winning the war we ought to help Russia, and if Russia is winning we ought to help Germany, and in that way let them kill as many as possible.

Harry S. Truman: The New York Times, 24 July 1941, when Russia was invaded by Germany.

20 I fear we have only awakened a sleeping giant, and his reaction will be terrible.

Isoroku Yamamoto: Said after the Japanese attack on Pearl Harbor, 1941.

WORLD-WEARINESS

1 Bankrupt of Life, yet Prodigal of Ease.
John Dryden: Absalom and Achitophel, I

2 Death is a delightful hiding-place for weary men.
Herodotus: Histories, VII, 46

3 Stop the World, I Want to Get Off.
Anthony Newley: With Leslie Bricusse. Title of musical

4 How weary, stale, flat, and unprofitable,
Seem to me all the uses of this world!
William Shakespeare: Hamlet, I:2

5 Death is not the greatest of ills; it is worse to want to die, and not be able to.
Sophocles: Electra, 1007

WORRY

See also misfortune

1 A trouble shared is a trouble halved.
Proverb

2 Don't meet troubles half-way.
Proverb

3 Every little yielding to anxiety is

a step away from the natural heart of man.
Japanese proverb

4 'Life's too short for worrying.'
'Yes, that's what worries me.'
Anonymous

5 When I look back on all these worries I remember the story of the old man who said on his deathbed that he had had a lot of trouble in his life, most of which had never happened.
Winston Churchill: Their Finest Hour

6 Worry affects circulation, the heart and the glands, the whole nervous sytem, and profoundly affects the heart. I have never known a man who died from overwork, but many who died from doubt.
Charles H. Mayo: Bartlett's Unfamiliar Quotations (Leonard Louis Levinson)

7 Care
Sat on his faded cheek.
John Milton: Paradise Lost, Bk. I

WRITERS

See also criticism, poets

1 Writers, like teeth, are divided into incisors and grinders.
Walter Bagehot: Estimates of some Englishmen and Scotchmen, 'The First Edinburgh Reviewers'

2 The idea that it is necessary to go to a university in order to become a successful writer, or even a man or woman of letters (which is by no means the same thing), is one of those phantasies that surround authorship.

Vera Brittain: On Being an Author, Ch. 2

3 I believe the souls of five hundred Sir Isaac Newtons would go to the making up of a Shakespeare or a Milton.
Samuel Taylor Coleridge: Letter to Thomas Poole, 23 Mar 1801

4 A great writer creates a world of his own and his readers are proud to live in it. A lesser writer may entice them in for a moment, but soon he will watch them filing out.
Cyril Connolly: Enemies of Promise, Ch. 1

5 The reciprocal civility of authors is one of the most risible scenes in the farce of life.
Samuel Johnson: Life of Sir Thomas Browne

6 Authors are easy to get on with – if you're fond of children.
Michael Joseph: The Observer, 1949

7 There is a vanity and a paranoia about writers – which makes excellent dramatic material – but which also makes me question the nature of writing.
David Lodge: The Times Educational Supplement, 18 May 1990

8 Our principal writers have nearly all been fortunate in escaping regular education.
Hugh MacDiarmid: The Observer, 'Sayings of the Week', 29 Mar 1953

9 A list of authors who have made themselves most beloved and therefore, most comfortable financially, shows that it is our na-tional joy to mistake for the first-rate, the fecund rate.
Dorothy Parker: Wit's End (R. E. Drennan)

10 Everybody writes a book too many.
Mordecai Richler: The Observer, 'Sayings of the Week', 9 Jan 1985

11 When I was a little boy they called me a liar but now that I am a grown up they call me a writer.
Isaac Bashevis Singer: Remark, July 1983

12 I think it's good for a writer to think he's dying; he works harder.
Tennessee Williams: The Observer, 'Sayings of the Week', 31 Oct 1976

13 Literature is strewn with the wreckage of men who have minded beyond reason the opinions of others.
Virginia Woolf: A Room of One's Own

14 It's not a writer's business to hold opinions.
W. B. Yeats: Speaking to playwright, Denis Johnston. The Guardian, 5 May 1977

WRITING

See also books, criticism, fiction, literature, poetry

1 Every book must be chewed to get out its juice.
Chinese proverb

2 Most people enjoy the sight of their own handwriting as they enjoy the smell of their own farts.

W. H. Auden: *The Dyer's Hand*, 'Writing'

It is all very well to be able to write books, but can you waggle your ears?
J. M. Barrie: *Speaking to H. G. Wells.* Barrie: *The Story of A Genius (J. A. Hamerton)*

From this it is clear how much more cruel the pen is than the sword.
Robert Burton: *Anatomy of Melancholy*, Pt. I

That's not writing, that's typing.
Truman Capote: *Referring to the writer Jack Kerouac. Attrib.*

Better to write for yourself and have no public, than write for the public and have no self.
Cyril Connolly: *Turnstile One (ed. V. S. Pritchett)*

Another damned, thick, square book! Always scribble, scribble, scribble! Eh! Mr Gibbon?
William, Duke of Gloucester: *Addressing Edward Gibbon, author of the six-volume* The History of the Decline and Fall of the Roman Empire. *Literary Memorials (Best)*

You must write for children in the same way as you do for adults, only better.
Maxim Gorky: *Attrib.*

I cannot write as well as some people; my talent is in coming up with good stories about lawyers. That is what I am good at.
John Grisham: *The Independent on Sunday, 5 June 1994*

I wasn't born until I started to write.

David Hare: *The Sunday Times, 11 Feb 1990*

11 Read over your compositions, and where ever you meet with a passage which you think is particularly fine, strike it out.
Samuel Johnson: *Recalling the advice of a college tutor. Life of Johnson (J. Boswell), Vol. II*

12 Clear writers, like clear fountains, do not seem so deep as they are; the turbid look the most profound.
Walter Savage Landor: *Imaginary Conversations, 'Southey and Porson'*

13 I like to write when I feel spiteful: it's like having a good sneeze.
D. H. Lawrence: *Letter to Lady Cynthia Asquith, Nov 1913*

14 There is an impression abroad that everyone has it in him to write one book; but if by this is implied a good book the impression is false.
W. Somerset Maugham: *The Summing Up*

15 When you steal from one author, it's plagiarism; if you steal from many, it's research.
Wilson Mizner: *Attrib.*

16 Writing is like getting married. One should never commit oneself until one is amazed at one's luck.
Iris Murdoch: *The Black Prince, 'Bradley Pearson's Foreword'*

17 One always writes comedy at the moment of deepest hysteria.
V. S. Naipaul: *The Observer, 'Sayings of the Week', 1 May 1994*

18 Make 'em laugh; make 'em cry; make 'em wait.
Charles Reade: Advice to an aspiring writer. Attrib.

19 No, this right hand shall work it all off.
Walter Scott: Refusing offers of help following his bankruptcy in 1826. Century of Anecdote (J. Timbs)

20 Whatever sentence will bear to be read twice, we may be sure was thought twice.
Henry David Thoreau: Journal, 1842

21 Praise and blame are much the same for the writer. One is better for your vanity, but neither gets you much further with your work.
Jeanette Winterson: The Guardian, 18 June 1994

YOUTH

See also age, children

1 A stage between infancy and adultery.
Anonymous

2 Youth is something very new: twenty years ago no one mentioned it.
Coco Chanel: Coco Chanel, Her Life, Her Secrets (Marcel Haedrich)

3 The young always have the same problem – how to rebel and conform at the same time. They have now solved this by defying their parents and copying one another.
Quentin Crisp: The Naked Civil Servant

4 Almost everything that is great has been done by youth.
Benjamin Disraeli: Coningsby, Bk. III, Ch. 1

5 I never dared to be radical when young, for fear it would make me conservative when old.
Robert Frost: Precaution

6 Les enfants terribles.
The embarrassing young.
Paul Gavarni: Title of a series of prints

7 No young man believes he shall ever die.
William Hazlitt: The Monthly Magazine, Mar 1827

8 It is the malady of our age that the young are so busy teaching us that they have no time left to learn.
Eric Hoffer

9 Youth is a malady of which one becomes cured a little every day.
Benito Mussolini: Said on his 50th birthday.

10 One starts to get young at the age of sixty and then it is too late.
Pablo Picasso: The Sunday Times, 20 Oct 1963

11 He whom the gods love dies young, while he has his strength and senses and wits.
Plautus: Bacchides, IV:8

12 My salad days,
When I was green in judgment, cold in blood,
To say as I said then!
William Shakespeare: Antony and Cleopatra, I:5

13 Live as long as you may, the first twenty years are the longest half of your life.
Robert Southey: The Doctor

14 Proficiency at billiards is proof of a misspent youth.
Herbert Spencer: Attrib.

15 I looked younger than 26. I looked 17, and I had acne, and that doesn't help instil confidence in seasoned film crews.
Steven Spielberg: New Yorker, 1994

16 Young people ought not to be idle. It is very bad for them.
Margaret Thatcher: The Times, 1984

17 'Smart Juniors,' said Polly to himself, 'full of Smart Juniosity. The Shoveacious Cult.'
H. G. Wells: The History of Mr Polly, Pt. III

KEYWORD INDEX

Let's talk sense to the A. people
ENDURANCE, 6

spiteful to me in the A. press
NEWSPAPERS, 7

We are all A. at puberty
NATIONALITY, 5

whereby A. girls turn into A. women
CAPITALISM, 4

Americans majority of my fellow A.
SUPPORT, 1

amused We are not a.
ROYALTY, 30

analysis in a. with a strict Freudian
SUICIDE, 1

anatomy A. is destiny
DESTINY, 5

he has studied a.
MARRIAGE, 9

animal He was into a. husbandry
SEX, 3

Whenever you observe an a. closely
ANIMALS, 7

annihilation No a.
REPRESENTATION, 3

annus an 'a. horribilis'
ROYALTY, 18

answer A timid question...a confident a.
SHYNESS, 2

more than the wisest man can a.
EXAMINATIONS, 1

anticipation the intelligent a. of facts
JOURNALISM, 8

anxiety Every little yielding to a.
WORRY, 3

the Age of A.
NEUROSIS, 2

the a. of being a woman
WOMEN, 9

anxious piles to give him an A. Expression
DOCTORS, 3

apartheid We don't want a. liberalized
RACISM, 14

apathy sheer a. and boredom
DISCOVERY, 4

ape How like us is that ugly brute, the a.
EVOLUTION, 4

Is man an a. or an angel
EVOLUTION, 3

The exception is a naked a.
MANKIND, 16

aphrodisiac Fame is a powerful a.
FAME, 7

Power is the ultimate a.
POWER, 7

Apostles Christ called as his A. only men
MEN, 5

appetite a. may sicken and so die
MUSIC, 18

the desire of satisfying a voracious a.
LUST, 2

approve They that a....call it opinion
OPINIONS, 4

Arabia All the perfumes of A.
GUILT, 6

archaeologist An a. is the best husband
MARRIAGE, 20

architect a. of his own fate
RESPONSIBILITY, 2

argument work of art must start an a.
ART, 19

armed We should be a.
FEMINISM, 6

armour Conceit is the finest a.
CONCEIT, 4

arrest My father didn't create you to a. me
POLICE, 6

arrested Christ...have been a.
OPPRESSION, 3

arrow a....feels the attraction of earth
AMBITION, 9

I shot an a. into the air
CHANCE, 2

artistic There never was an a. period
PHILISTINISM, 4

aspect Meet in her a.
BEAUTY, 7

ass An unlettered king is a crowned a.
MONARCHY, 1

the law is a a.
LAW, 4

astonishment Dear Sir, Your a.'s odd
EXISTENCE, 1

asylums lunatic a....the stately homes
STATELY HOMES, 1

Athens A. holds sway over all Greece
INFLUENCE, 4

atom The a. bomb is a paper tiger
NUCLEAR WEAPONS, 9

There is no evil in the a.
NUCLEAR WEAPONS, 13

They split the a.
SCIENCE, 17

atone a. for the sins of your fathers
INJUSTICE, 6

better

attractive if they are in the least a.
TRANSLATION, 1
author a. who speaks about his own books
EGOTISM, 2
authority a top hat to give him A.
DOCTORS, 3
No morality can be founded on a.
MORALITY, 1
place him in a.
CHARACTER, 1
autograph give him my a.
WORLD WAR II, 14
avarice rich beyond the dreams of a.
WEALTH, 15
bachelor Never trust...a b. too near
TRUST, 3
back Either b. us or sack us
SUPPORT, 1
bad A truth that's told with b. intent
TRUTH, 7
B. girls don't have the time
DIARIES, 1
b. taste is better than no taste
TASTE, 2
Defend the b. against the worse
DECLINE, 2
nothing either good or b.
THINKING, 7
resolved to do something b.
DECISION, 3
balance The b. of power
POWER, 14
baldness premature b.
AGE, 17
Balkans silly thing in the B.
WAR, 7
ballot b. is stronger than the bullet
DEMOCRACY, 7
banality b. of evil
EVIL, 2
bandage Religion...the wound, not the b.
RELIGION, 32
Basingstoke hidden meaning – like B.
PLACES, 7
bastards politicians are not b.
POLITICIANS, 14
that'll hold the little b.
CHILDREN, 12
bat They came to see me b.
CRICKET, 3

bath B....once a week
CLEANNESS, 2
bathes The King b.
SEASIDE, 1
bathing a large b. machine
BOATS, 2
bats b. in the belfry
MADNESS, 15
battlefield the most beautiful b.
WAR, 38
we survive...as on a b.
OLD AGE, 30
beards beware of long arguments and long b.
BREVITY, 5
beast b. of the earth
ANIMALS, 3
hardly be a b. or a fool alone
SOLITUDE, 4
the b. with two backs
SEX, 47
the mark...of the b.
DEVIL, 3
beautiful food is, actually, very b.
FOOD, 13
The good is the b.
GOOD, 5
bee How doth the little busy b.
WORK, 16
Beethoven Roll Over B.
POPULAR MUSIC, 3
beg forbidden to b.
POVERTY, 8
beginnings end to the b. of all wars
WAR, 45
mighty things from small b.
NATURE, 4
believe b. those whom we do not know
TRUST, 2
b....or not
SUPERSTITION, 1
undesirable to b. a proposition
SCEPTICISM, 2
We can b. what we choose
RESPONSIBILITY, 6
best all that's b. of dark and bright
BEAUTY, 1
as in the b. it is
MURDER, 6
Stolen sweets are b.
THEFT, 2
the b. of possible worlds
OPTIMISM, 9, 15
The b. things in life
WEALTH, 1
better b. to marry than to burn
MARRIAGE, 13
for b. for worse
MARRIAGE, 14
We have seen b. days
NOSTALGIA, 9

bewildered I was b. once
CONFUSION, 2

Bible the B. tells me so
RELIGION, 35

Bibles they have the land and we
have the B.
RACISM, 5

big A b. man has no time FAME, 5

A government…b. enough
GOVERNMENT, 7

B. Brother is watching you
AUTHORITARIANISM, 5

The b. print giveth BUSINESS, 15

birthday a woman's b. AGE, 19

bishop Make him a b., and you
will silence him CLERGY, 1

the symbol of a b. is a crook
CLERGY, 3

bites when a man b. a dog that is
news MEDIA, 2

black coffee that's too b.
RACISM, 10

looking for a b. hat METAPHYSICS, 1

That old b. magic
SUPERNATURAL, 4

blasphemies All great truths begin
as b. NOVELTY, 5

blessed B. are the meek
HUMILITY, 1

B. is the man who expects nothing
EXPECTATION, 3

blind A b. man in a dark room
METAPHYSICS, 1

b. as those who won't see
STUBBORNNESS, 2

Country of the B. SUPERIORITY, 1

union of a deaf man to a b. woman
MARRIAGE, 21

block every b. of stone FAME, 4

blocks unravel people's mental b.
PHILOSOPHY, 3

blood B. is thicker FAMILY, 1

b., toil, tears and sweat EFFORT, 3

thy brother's b. crieth unto me
MURDER, 1

without shedding of b. is no
remission EXECUTION, 1

bloodiness b. of family life
FAMILY, 13

blow A b. in cold blood
VIOLENCE, 10

Another year! – another deadly b.
DEFEAT, 9

blunders b. usually do more to
shape history MISTAKES, 10

blush b. to find it fame GOOD, 6

bodies our dead b. must tell the
tale EXPLORATION, 3

Our minds are lazier than our b.
MIND, 10

You may house their b. but not
their souls CHILDREN, 15

body a sound mind in a sound b.
HEALTH AND HEALTHY LIVING, 4

b. of a weak and feeble woman
ROYALTY, 5

fear made manifest on the b.
DISEASE, 7

Man has no B. distinct from his
Soul SOUL, 2

My b. is a floating weed
LONELINESS, 3

the human b. is sacred
MANKIND, 26

the human psyche lives…with the
b. PSYCHOLOGY, 4

There is more wisdom in your b.
WISDOM, 9

Why be given a b. if you…keep it
shut up NAKEDNESS, 3

Bognor Bugger B. LAST WORDS, 15

bomb Ban the b.
NUCLEAR WEAPONS, 1

god of science…has given us the
atomic b. SCIENCE, 21

bombs b. are unbelievable
WEAPONS, 7

drop b.…hit civilians WAR, 24

test the Russians, not the b.
NUCLEAR WEAPONS, 6

book any b. should be banned
CENSORSHIP, 1

You can't tell a b. APPEARANCES, 5

boot b. stamping on a human face
OPPRESSION, 5

bore Every hero becomes a b.
HEROISM, 4

you are...the club B.
SUPERIORITY, 5

bored aged diplomats to be b.
DIPLOMACY, 1

Punctuality is the virtue of the b.
PROMPTNESS, 4

born better if neither of us had
been b.
REGRET, 5

B. under one law
HUMAN CONDITION, 3

One is not b. a woman WOMEN, 7

Some are b. great GREATNESS, 6

Some men are b. mediocre
MEDIOCRITY, 3

sucker b. every minute
GULLIBILITY, 1

boss get to be a b.
WORK, 5

bottles people as with...b.
CHARACTER, 5

bourgeois B....is an epithet
CLASS, 8

How beastly the b. is MEN, 6

bovine The cow is of the b. ilk
ANIMALS, 11

bowl love in a golden b. WISDOM, 5

see me bat not to see you b.
CRICKET, 3

boy A thing of duty is a b. for ever
POLICE, 4

Love is a b. PUNISHMENT, 4

Mad about the b. LOVE, 20

When I was a little b. they called
me a liar WRITERS, 11

boys B. are capital fellows
CHILDREN, 23

b. plan for what...girls plan for
whom SEXES, 5

brain for mind that we are
searching the b. MIND, 12

Let schoolmasters puzzle their b.
ALCOHOL, 14

The b. is the organ of longevity
LONGEVITY, 6

the reflection of the structure of
the b. MIND, 3

Tobacco drieth the b. SMOKING, 16

You've got the b. of a four-year-
old boy STUPIDITY, 6

brains a girl with b. WOMEN, 28

many b. and many hands are
needed DISCOVERY, 7

our b. as fruitful as our bodies
WOMAN'S ROLE, 6

What good are b. to a man
INTELLIGENCE, 7

bread b. and circuses PUBLIC, 8

b. eaten in secret is pleasant
SECRECY, 2

cast thy b. upon the waters
OPPORTUNITY, 7

that b. should be so dear
POVERTY, 12

breath blow hot and cold with the
same b. INDECISION, 1

bridge Like a b. over troubled
water COMFORT, 3

over the B. of Sighs into eternity
DEATH, 25

Britain battle of B. is about to
begin WORLD WAR II, 5

B. could say that she supported
DIPLOMACY, 13

To make a union with Great B.
WORLD WAR II, 15

British B. loathe the middle-aged
AGE, 37

but we are B. – thank God
HOMOSEXUALITY, 8

socialism...alien to the B.
character SOCIALISM, 10

the most vulgar...is the B. tourist
TRAVEL, 11

Briton as only a free-born B. can
do SERVILITY, 4

broken Laws were made to be b.
LAW, 11

marriage had irretrievably b. down
ROYALTY, 11

peace has b. out PEACE, 5

brothels b. with bricks of Religion
HYPOCRISY, 2

brother am I my b.'s keeper
MURDER, 1

Big B. is watching you
AUTHORITARIANISM, 5

I want to be the white man's b.
RACISM, 2

the mote that is in thy b.'s eye
JUDGMENT, 2

brutality industry without art is b.
ART, 16

superstructure covering b.
SENTIMENTALITY, 1

brute B. force...rules VIOLENCE, 6

brutes rise above the b. WORDS, 7

bubbles With beaded b. winking at
the brim ALCOHOL, 18

buck The b. stops here
RESPONSIBILITY, 9

Buckingham Palace changing
guard at B. SOLDIERS, 2

budget b. is a method of worrying
ECONOMICS, 2

bullet ballot is stronger than the b.
DEMOCRACY, 7

Every b. has its billet DESTINY, 12

bump And things that go b. in the
night SUPERNATURAL, 1

don't b. into the furniture
ACTING, 5

bunk History is more or less b.
HISTORY, 8

burn better to marry than to b.
MARRIAGE, 13

burned A woman's heart always
has a b. mark SORROW, 9

Whenever books are b.
CENSORSHIP, 3

burr kind of b.; I shall stick
PERSISTENCE, 6

busy How doth the little b. bee
WORK, 16

too fucking b. – or vice versa
SEX, 40

butterfly a man dreaming I was a b.
DREAMS, 2

Caesar I come to bury C. EVIL, 8

Caesars men worship the C. and
Napoleons TYRANNY, 5

cage Marriage is like a c.
MARRIAGE, 36

Nor iron bars a c.
IMPRISONMENT, 4

robin redbreast in a c.
IMPRISONMENT, 1

caged We think c. birds sing
IMPRISONMENT, 5

cake Let them eat c. HUNGER, 7

came I c., I saw, God conquered
VICTORY, 2

I c., I saw, I conquered VICTORY, 1

camel easier for a c. WEALTH, 4

camera I am a c. OBJECTIVITY, 1

The c. cannot lie PHOTOGRAPHY, 1

Canada what street C. is on
PLACES, 3

candle blow out your c. ATHEISM, 3

little c. throws his beams GOOD, 7

capitalist C. production
MARXISM, 5

capitulate I will not c.
DETERMINATION, 2

captains C. of industry
LEADERSHIP, 3

captive Beauty stands...Led c.
BEAUTY, 17

car The c. has become the
carapace TRAVEL, 15

carbuncle Like a c. on the face
ARCHITECTURE, 2

care age is full of c. AGE, 34

C. Sat on his faded cheek
WORRY, 7

c. for the opinion of those we don't
c. for CONCEIT, 3

Take c. of the pence THRIFT, 3

The first C. in building of Cities
ENVIRONMENT, 1

what is past my help is past my c.
INDIFFERENCE, 1

cargo With a c. of ivory BOATS, 6

carpe C. diem PRESENT, 3

Carthage C. must be destroyed
WAR, 13

cash only the poor who pay c.
MONEY, 10

cassowary If I were a c.
CLERGY, 5

cast c. thy bread upon the waters
OPPORTUNITY, 7

let him first c. a stone SIN, 3

set my life upon a c. CHANCE, 4

The die is c. IRREVOCABILITY, 3

castle builds a c. in the air
PSYCHIATRY, 17

The house of every one is to him as
his c. PRIVACY, 1

castles C. in the air DREAMS, 3

casualty except the c. list of the
World War MURDER, 2

cat A c. may look EQUALITY, 1

c. is a diagram CATS, 7

I am the c. that walks alone
SELF-RELIANCE, 2

I'll bell the c. COURAGE, 4

When I play with my c. CATS, 3

catch only one c. and that was
Catch-22 SELF-PRESERVATION, 3

catchwords Man is a creature who
lives…by c. SEXES, 12

cathedral c. is worth a hundred
theologians RELIGION, 5

cattle Actors should be treated like
c. ACTORS, 3

caves be c.…in which his shadow
will be shown GOD, 11

pleasure-dome with c. of ice
PLEASURE, 5

caviare c. to the general TASTE, 3

celibacy c. is…a muddy horsepond MARRIAGE, 40

cells These little grey c.
INTELLECT, 1

celluloid expensive habit…is c. not
heroin CINEMA, 14

certainties begin with c.
CERTAINTY, 1

His doubts are better than…c.
DOUBT, 1

the safe comfort of c. TRUTH, 3

chaff not racially pure are mere c.
RACISM, 6

chain A c. is no stronger UNITY, 1

the flesh to feel the c.
IMPRISONMENT, 2

chains It's often safer to be in c.
FREEDOM, 10

Man…everywhere he is in c.
FREEDOM, 20

nothing to lose but their c.
MARXISM, 3

chair the age of the editorial c.
PSYCHIATRY, 12

champion great c. loses his life
SPORT AND GAMES, 9

changed All c., c. utterly
BEAUTY, 21

Channel crossing the C. BOATS, 2

chaos is a science of process
SCIENCE, 15

chapels c. had been churches
ACTION, 7

chapter of accidents
MISFORTUNE, 4

cheap flesh and blood so c.
POVERTY, 12

Pile it high, sell it c. BUSINESS, 3

check C. enclosed MONEY, 18

dreadful is the c. IMPRISONMENT, 2

chemical c. barrage…against the
fabric of life ECOLOGY, 1

cheques The rich hate signing c.
WEALTH, 1

child c. becomes an adult RIGHT, 2

If you strike a c. VIOLENCE, 10

nobody's c. LONELINESS, 1

One stops being a c. DISILLUSION, 1

spoil the c. PUNISHMENT, 4

than bear one c. WOMAN'S ROLE, 3

to influence the character of a c.
INFLUENCE, 2

What is the use of a new-born c.
PURPOSE, 1

childbirth Death and taxes and c.
EXPEDIENCY, 1

the male equivalent of c.
PUBLISHING, 1

childish Sweet c. days
NOSTALGIA, 10

childishness second c. OLD AGE, 27

chloroform that blessed c.
REMEDIES, 14

choose We can believe what we c.
RESPONSIBILITY, 6

Christ C. called as his Apostles
only men MEN, 5
C....would quite likely have been
arrested OPPRESSION, 3
male can represent C. RELIGION, 12
We're more popular than Jesus C.
POPULARITY, 5

Christian A C....feels Repentance
HYPOCRISY, 1
C. presence...Disney Theme Park
COMMERCIALISM, 1
C. Science will cure imaginary
diseases MEDICINE, 4

chronologie according to our C.
CREATION, 9

churches chapels had been c.
ACTION, 7

cigar It is like a c. LOVE, 50
Sometimes a c. PSYCHIATRY, 7

cigarette A c. is...a perfect
pleasure SMOKING, 17

circle wheel is come full c.
DESTINY, 10

circulation Worry affects c.
WORRY, 6

circumstance no c....is too minute
PHILOSOPHERS, 3

circumstances to face straitened c.
at home POVERTY, 14

circuses bread and c. PUBLIC, 8

citizen c. of the world
NATIONALITY, 4

clattering in charge of the c. train
JOURNALISM, 3

clear His right was c., his will was
strong RIGHT, 1
make *me* understand...it would be
c. UNDERSTANDING, 7

Cleopatra Had C.'s nose been
shorter APPEARANCE, 13

clever It's c., but is it art ART, 10
never wise to try to appear...more
c. WISDOM, 12
not c. but I'm always right
SELF-CONFIDENCE, 1
To be c. enough to get...money
MATERIALISM, 4

closed Mankind is a c. society
MANKIND, 19

closer c. to the ground as children
CHILDREN, 7

closets Out of the c.
HOMOSEXUALITY, 1

cloud Every c. has a silver lining
OPTIMISM, 6
no silver linings without a c.
OPTIMISM, 10

club Mankind is a c. MANKIND, 9

coal best sun...made of Newcastle
c. BUSINESS, 18

Coca Colas Instead of drinking C.
WATER, 3

cocaine C. is God's way of saying
DRUGS, 4

codfish Unlike the male c.
ARISTOCRACY, 10

coffee c. that's too black
RACISM, 10

cogito C., ergo sum THINKING, 1

cold blow hot and c. with the same
breath INDECISION, 1
Feed a c. ILLNESS, 1
I beg c. comfort COMFORT, 2
she should catch a c. on
overexposure TRUTH, 9

collections those mutilators of c.
BOOKS, 14

colour an incurable disease – c.
blindness RACISM, 3

comedies c. are ended by a
marriage THEATRE, 4

comedy c. at the moment of
deepest hysteria WRITING, 17
C. is if I walk into an open sewer
and die THEATRE, 3
C. is medicine MEDICINE, 7

Sell a c. WORLD, 3
The past is a foreign c. PAST, 4
The soil of our c. RACISM, 11
The undiscover'd c. AFTERLIFE, 6
This isn't going to be a good c. EQUALITY, 12
we can die but once to serve our c. PATRIOTISM, 1
Your c. needs YOU WAR, 3

courting When you are c. a nice girl SCIENCE, 9

craftsmanship Skill without imagination is c. ART, 17

crankshaft spheres geared to God's c. SCIENCE, 32

create c. a world CINEMA, 2
My father didn't c. you to arrest me POLICE, 1

credit not to mind who gets the c. SELFLESSNESS, 2

credulity from c. to scepticism MIND, 6

creeds Vain are the thousand c. BELIEF, 3

crimes Catholics and Communists have committed great c. COMMITMENT, 4
Oh liberty!...What c. are committed in thy name EXECUTION, 9

crook symbol of a bishop is a c. CLERGY, 3

cross The orgasm has replaced the c. SEX, 38

crow sun had risen to hear him c. ARROGANCE, 2

cry I often want to c. SEXES, 10
make 'em c. WRITING, 18
women...can c. SEXES, 10

crying It is no use c. REGRET, 1

cult difference between a religion and a c. RELIGION, 39
What's a c. MINORITY, 1

cup personality of a paper c. PLACES, 4

cure a c. for which there was no disease REMEDIES, 4

C. the disease DISEASE, 4
death is the c. of all diseases DEATH, 13
Difficult as it may be to c. KILLING, 1
Show me a sane man and I will c. him MADNESS, 10
'There is no c. for this disease.' DOCTORS, 4

curiosities How these c. would be quite forgot GOSSIP, 7

curse Work is the c. of the drinking classes WORK, 17

customer The c. is always right BUSINESS, 14

cutting busy driving cabs and c. hair GOVERNMENT, 5

dad They fuck you up, your mum and d. FAMILY, 10

Daily Telegraph letters page of the D. HOMOSEXUALITY, 9

damned Life is just one d. thing after another LIFE, 20
Publish and be d. PUBLISHING, 5
The public be d. CAPITALISM, 12

dangerous A little learning is a d. thing KNOWLEDGE, 15
If a little knowledge is d. KNOWLEDGE, 10

dares Who d., wins COURAGE, 2

dark A blind man in a d. room METAPHYSICS, 1
The d. night of the soul SOUL, 4

dawn a grey d. breaking SEA, 5

days d. of wine and roses TRANSIENCE, 2
Sweet childish d. NOSTALGIA, 10

dead Better red than d. NUCLEAR WEAPONS, 1
Mother is the d. heart WOMAN'S ROLE, 1
The novel being d. NOVELS, 1
The past is the only d. thing PAST, 1
to the d. we owe only truth RESPECT, 2

e survive amongst the d. and the
ying OLD AGE, 30

eaf union of a d. man to a blind
oman MARRIAGE, 21

efence d. of the United States
WORLD WAR II, 16

he only d. is in offence WAR, 6
ruth telling...d. of the realm
TRUTH, 21

efend I will d....your right to say
FREEDOM, 25

elight Energy is Eternal D.
EFFORT, 2

ery temple of d. MELANCHOLY, 2

eliver me from myself SELF, 5

enmark rotten in the state of D.
CORRUPTION, 7

entopedology D. is the science of
pening your mouth MISTAKES, 7

eserve I have arthritis, and I
on't d. that either MERIT, 2

eserves the government it d.
GOVERNMENT, 10

esiring d. the things they fear
PESSIMISM, 5

espond name of the slough was
DESPAIR, 1

estroy necessary to d. the town
WAR, 4

ught to d. institutions
INDIFFERENCE, 4

ey shall not hurt nor d. PEACE, 2

hom God wishes to d.
MADNESS, 6

hom the gods wish to
TALENT, 2

estroyer I am become death,
of worlds NUCLEAR WEAPONS, 10

estroying simplifying something
d. CIVILIZATION, 2

eterrent the d. is a phallic symbol
NUCLEAR WEAPONS, 14

amonds D. Are A Girl's Best
riend MATERIALISM, 3

give him d. back MATERIALISM, 10

ctated universe was d. but not
gned UNIVERSE, 11

dictionary The responsibility of a
d. LEXICOGRAPHY, 2

die better to d. on your feet
SELF-RESPECT, 1

either do, or d. ACTION, 2

it is worse to want to d.
WORLD-WEARINESS, 5

Let us do or d. ACTION, 4

live for ever or d. IMMORTALITY, 2

Never say d. PERSISTENCE, 1

No young man believes he shall
ever d. YOUTH, 7

one may d. without ever laughing
LAUGHTER, 3

people would sooner d. than think
THINKING, 6

something that he would d. for
IDEALISM, 2

we can d. but once PATRIOTISM, 1

We must love one another or d.
LOVE, 8

you asked this man to d. WAR, 5

died A piece of each of us d. at that
moment ASSASSINATION, 4

never been the same since God d.
GOD, 10

dies a young person, who...
HUMAN NATURE, 1

marries or d. HUMAN NATURE, 1

because a man d. for it
MARTYRDOM, 4

difference Because there is no d.
LIFE AND DEATH, 11

more d. within the sexes SEXES, 1

difficulty d. for every solution
BUREAUCRACY, 2

dignity a paunch to give him D.
DOCTORS, 3

d. and rights HUMAN RIGHTS, 1

Official d. DIPLOMACY, 8

dim My eyes are d. BLINDNESS, 1

diplomat A d....always remembers
AGE, 19

director Theatre d.: a person
ACTING, 1

want to be a d. CINEMA, 13

dirt the d. doesn't get any worse
HOUSEWORK, 1

disbelief

Throw d. enough GOSSIP, 4
disbelief willing suspension of d.
POETRY, 9
discovered We have d. the secret
of life DISCOVERY, 4
discretion better part of valour is
d. SELF-PRESERVATION, 4
disinterested D. intellectual
curiosity CURIOSITY, 5
dissipated still keep looking so d.
DEBAUCHERY, 1
distances D. are only the relation
of space to time TIME, 21
distress All pray in their d.
PRAYER, 2
the mean man is always full of d.
SUPERIORITY, 1
disturb What isn't part of ourselves
doesn't d. us HATE, 3
diversity biological and cultural
d....threatened ECOLOGY, 2
divide D. and rule POWER, 1
divided Obstinate people can be d.
STUBBORNNESS, 3
divine The d. _right_ of husbands
FEMINISM, 8
The Hand that made us is d.
CREATION, 1
The right d. of kings to govern
wrong MONARCHY, 7
To err is human, to forgive, d.
MISTAKES, 8
divorce D.? Never MARRIAGE, 53
doctor a man who drinks more
than his own d. DRUNKENNESS, 3
If you are too smart to pay the d.
ILLNESS, 2
I told my d. I get very tired...on a
diet FOOD, 2
People pay the d. for his trouble
KINDNESS, 4
doors the d. of perception were
cleansed PERCEPTION, 1
double-crossing You dirty d. rat
MISQUOTATIONS, 1
doubts end in d. CERTAINTY, 1

His d. are better than...certainties
DOUBT, 1
dreadful d. is the check
IMPRISONMENT, 2
Other people are quite d.
MISANTHROPY, 1
dream I d. when I am awake
REALITY, 1
I have a d. EQUALITY, 10
life is a d. LIFE, 19
dreamt d. of in your philosophy
SUPERNATURAL, 5
drinking D....and making love
MANKIND, 3
resolve to give up smoking, d. and
loving ABSTINENCE, 2
dripping Constant d. hollows out a
stone PERSISTENCE, 6
electricity was d. invisibly
SCIENCE, 35
drop Nor any d. to drink WATER, 2
drowning A d. man HOPE, 1
drunken He uses statistics as a d.
man STATISTICS, 4
What shall we do with the d. sailor
DRUNKENNESS, 10
duck looks like a d. COMMUNISM, 1
ducks your precious 'lame d.'
WEAKNESS, 2
dull a very d. Play MARRIAGE, 22
dunces the d. are all in
confederacy GENIUS, 2
dust raised a d. COMPLAINTS, 1
this quintessence of d.
MANKIND, 2
dying good for a writer to think
he's d. WRITERS, 7
sex, like d., should be a private
matter SEX, 11
Truth sits upon the lips of d. men
TRUTH, 1
dynamic class people as static and
d. SEXES, 1
ear a pistol let off at the e. PUNS, 1
the e. begins to hear
IMPRISONMENT, 2

arly A useless life is an e. death
PURPOSE, 2

ood die e. GOOD AND EVIL, 2

ou have to get up e. BED, 3

ars can you waggle your e.
WRITING, 3

omans, countrymen, lend me
your e. EVIL, 8

arth But did thee feel the e. move
SEX, 22

. is just too small SPACE, 4

will move the e. TECHNOLOGY, 1

ore things in heaven and e.
SUPERNATURAL, 5

paceship, E. ENVIRONMENT, 3

ae e. is free HUMAN RIGHTS, 1

he meek do not inherit the e.
HUMILITY, 1

asier E. said than done ACTION, 1

ast look the E. End in the face
WORLD WAR II, 9

at e. to live, not live to e.
FOOD, 11

reat ones e. up the little ones
RUTHLESSNESS, 3

ome hae meat, and canna e.
FOOD, 4

ats e., sleeps and watches the
elevision WOMAN'S ROLE, 3

iendly terms with the victims...
e e. HYPOCRISY, 3

e that e. till he is sick GREED, 1

den a garden eastward in E.
GARDENS, 2

dge on the e. of a new frontier
BEGINNING, 7

ggs all your e. in one basket
CAUTION, 2

derly see it as an e. lady
CHURCH, 2

hen a distinguished but e.
ientist states SCIENCE, 3

ection charity at e. time
OPPRESSION, 4

e will win the e.
SELF-CONFIDENCE, 5

electricity e. was dripping invisibly
SCIENCE, 35

elementary 'E.,' said he
MISQUOTATIONS, 8

elephant couldn't hit an e. at this
distance LAST WORDS, 37

embalmer soft e. of the still
midnight SLEEP, 9

employee converted Eros into an
e. COMMERCIALISM, 3

every e. tends to rise WORK, 11

empty Bring on the e. horses
LANGUAGE, 6

E. vessels FOOLISHNESS, 4

end a beginning, a middle, and an
e. PLAYS, 1; CINEMA, 8

a beginning, a muddle, and an e.
NOVELS, 4

In my beginning is my e.
BEGINNING, 5

Keep Right on to the E. of the
Road PERSISTENCE, 4

my patience is now at an e.
PATIENCE, 8

of making many books there is no
e. BOOKS, 5

our minutes hasten to their e.
TIME, 26

what e. the gods have in store
DESTINY, 7

world without e. ETERNITY, 1

energy E. is Eternal Delight
EFFORT, 2

enfants Les e. terribles YOUTH, 6

engine of pollution DOGS, 8

England Common Law of E.
LAW, 9

don't say that in E....they will
surely tax it TAXATION, 8

E. a land of beauty ECOLOGY, 3

E. expects every man will do his
duty DUTY, 2

little ships of E. BOATS, 4

that is forever E. WAR, 13

think of E. SEX, 23

English cricket – it's so very E.
CRICKET, 2

...e f. that she keeps in a jar
COSMETICS, 3
...ur whole life shows in your f.
AGE, 4
...ils If thy heart f. thee
AMBITION, 5
...othing f. like success SUCCESS, 14
...ir all's f. in love and war
JUSTICE, 3
...rief has turned her f.
APPEARANCE, 16
...o foul and f. a day WEATHER, 8
...ort has nothing to do with f. play
SPORT AND GAMES, 1
...e Brave deserves the F.
COURAGE, 7
...lse beware of f. prophets
DECEPTION, 2
...he religions we call f. were once
...ue RELIGION, 17
...rue and F. are attributes of
...eech TRUTH, 16
...ain wisdom all, and f. philosophy
WISDOM, 5
...milies Murder, like talent,
...ems...to run in f. MURDER, 5
...e best-regulated f. ACCIDENTS, 3
...here are only two f. in the world
POVERTY AND WEALTH, 2
...natics when f. are on top
GOVERNMENT, 11
...ncy Ever let the f. roam
DISCONTENT, 3
... wit will come STUPIDITY, 9
...n the Spring a young man's f.
SEASONS, 6
...ittle of What You F. Does You
...ood PLEASURE, 8
...ntasy live in a f. world REALITY, 3
...rce Parliament is the longest
...nning f. GOVERNMENT, 18
...rt he can't f. and chew gum
STUPIDITY, 3
...scination a fight against...f.
PHILOSOPHY, 7
...ar...will always have its f. WAR, 60
...shions F. in sin change SIN, 8

fast f. till he is well GREED, 1
fat The opera isn't over till the f.
lady sings OPERA, 1
fate Each man the architect of his
own f. RESPONSIBILITY, 2
hostages given to f. FAMILY, 11
fault Condemn the f. and not the
actor of it PUNISHMENT, 10
worst f. of the working classes
CLASS, 16
favour enjoying his special f.
ROYALTY, 25
feathers Fine f. APPEARANCE, 1
feed The World CHARITY, 4
You cannot f. the hungry on
statistics STATISTICS, 5
feet better to die on your f.
COURAGE, 7
both f. firmly planted in the air
IDEALISM, 5
feigning truest poetry is the most f.
POETRY, 20
fellow f. of infinite jest
MOURNING, 4
fierce f. and bald and short of
breath WAR, 48
fight easier to f. for one's
principles PRINCIPLES, 1
I f. to win DETERMINATION, 7
we shall f. on the beaches
WORLD WAR II, 1
You cannot f. against the future
PROGRESS, 6
fighting not conquering but f. well
VICTORY, 5
You know I hate f. VIOLENCE, 1
fights He that f. and runs away
SELF-PRESERVATION, 2
final The f. solution FASCISM, 2
fine another f. mess ACCIDENTS, 4
pop art and f. art ART, 12
the f. print taketh BUSINESS, 15
finger Moving F. writes DESTINY, 3
The least pain in our little f.
SELF-INTEREST, 2
finite knowledge can only be f.
KNOWLEDGE, 16

girls

e truth shall make you f.
TRUTH, 6

uth that makes men f.
TRUTH, 3

eedoms four essential human f.
HUMAN RIGHTS, 1

ench F. governments more
elfish
GOVERNMENT, 6

do not say the F. cannot come
NAVY, 1

magine the Lord talking F.
LANGUAGE, 8

he F. are wiser than they seem
NATIONALITY, 1

eud F. is all nonsense
NEUROSIS, 4

iend A f. in power
POWER, 4

very time I paint a portrait I lose
f.
PAINTING, 8

ve me, from the candid f.
FRANKNESS, 6

ust ye not in a f.
TRUST, 1

ontier the edge of a new f.
BEGINNING, 7

cking all this cold-hearted f.
SEX, 28

o f. busy – or vice versa
SEX, 40

gitive a f. and a vagabond
PUNISHMENT, 1

hrer *Ein Reich, Ein Volk, Ein F.*
NAZISM, 1

n People must not do things for
f.
PLEASURE, 6

ting inside were making f. of our
ANIMALS, 7

e people have f.
PLEASURE, 9

ork is much more f. than f.
WORK, 4

nny Kings...are just as f.
ROYALTY, 6

ying to be f.
HUMOUR, 13

ry full of sound and f.
LIFE, 34

othing but beastly f.
FOOTBALL, 3

rength and f.
PATIENCE, 9

e F. of a Patient Man
PATIENCE, 7

ins no g. without pains
SUCCESS, 18

gallantry What men call g.
ADULTERY, 1

gamble Life is a g.
LIFE, 36

game given myself to the g.
CRICKET, 4

He no play-a da g.
CONTRACEPTION, 3

gamekeeper would you allow your
g. to read it
CENSORSHIP, 1

gangsters The great nations have
always acted like g.
DIPLOMACY, 10

general caviare to the g.
TASTE, 5

generation You are a lost g.
WAR, 56

gentleman a g....never inflicts pain
CHIVALRY, 4

g.....robbing the poor
CLASS, 20

God is a g.
GOD, 7

Not a g.; dresses too well
CLOTHES, 8

proved it not just a g.'s game
CRICKET, 5

geometry Poetry is as exact a
science as g.
POETRY, 11

There is no 'royal road' to g.
MATHEMATICS, 3

German I speak...G. to my horse
LANGUAGE, 4

Life is too short to learn G.
LANGUAGE, 11

Germany G. calling
TREASON, 3

In G., the Nazis came for the
Communists
NAZISM, 2

ghost the G. in the Machine
MIND, 1

gin Of all the g. joints
CHANCE, 1

girl a g. needs good parents
AGE, 38

Give me a g. at an impressionable
age
IMPRESSIONABILITY, 4

Sex and the Single G.
SEX, 7

girlfriend problem someone has
with his g.
CAPITALISM, 7

girls boys plan for what...g. plan
for whom
SEXES, 5

When you see what some g. marry
MARRIAGE, 45
glad A heart…too soon made g.
IMPRESSIONABILITY, 1
g. that part of my life is over
SEX, 19
glitters All that g. is not gold
APPEARANCES, 1
global the world in the image of a
g. village TECHNOLOGY, 6
gloria *g. mundi* GLORY, 1
godlike patient endurance is g.
ENDURANCE, 4
gods g. handing down new
commandments SCIENTISTS, 2
leave the rest to the G. DUTY, 1
Live with the g. CONTENTMENT, 1
Whom the g. love DEATH, 31
Whom the g. wish to destroy
TALENT, 1
gold A g. rush is what happens
when MATERIALISM, 13
Nothing melts a Woman's Heart
like g. WEALTH, 6
Silver threads among the g.
OLD AGE, 25
travell'd in the realms of g.
TRAVEL, 10
turn his g. into smoke SMOKING, 7
golden G. slumbers kiss your eyes
SLEEP, 5
the G. Road to Samarkand
KNOWLEDGE, 7
golf an earnest protest against g.
CRICKET, 1
Gomorrah Sodom and…G.
PUNISHMENT, 1
govern Every class is unfit to g.
GOVERNMENT, 1
Grammar, which can g. even kings
GRAMMAR, 3
He that would g. others
SELF-CONTROL, 5
No man is good enough to g.
another man DEMOCRACY, 6
Under socialism *all* will g.
SOCIALISM, 6

governing become accustomed to
no one g. SOCIALISM, 4
governors Our supreme g., the
mob PUBLIC, 1
grace but for the g. of God
LUCK,
Such g. had kings ROYALTY,
grain He reaps the bearded g. at a
breath DEATH, 2
grandeur g. is a dream WEALTH,
Many people have delusions of g.
DELUSION,
great Everything g. in the world is
done by neurotics NEUROSIS,
everything that is g.…done by
youth YOUTH,
ignominious getaways by the g.
COWARDICE,
the g. ones eat up the little ones
RUTHLESSNESS,
greater The g. the power POWER,
Greek it was G. to me
CONFUSION,
Greeks G. Had a Word
LANGUAGE,
I fear the G. even when they bring
gifts MISTRUST,
uncertainty: a state unknown to
the G. UNCERTAINTY,
green G. politics is not about
being far left CONSERVATION,
tree of life is g. THEORY,
green-ey'd g. monster
JEALOUSY,
grey soccer is a g. game
FOOTBALL,
theory is all g. THEORY,
grief G. has turned her fair
APPEARANCE,
in much wisdom is much g.
KNOWLEDGE,
grooves specialists…tend to think
in g. EXPERTS,
grow make two questions g. where
only one RESEARCH,
They shall g. not old MEMORIALS,

hear any of you at the back who do not h. me   DISABILITY, 1

ear begins to h.   IMPRISONMENT, 8

truth which men prefer not to h.   TRUTH, 7

heart Absence makes the h. grow fonder   ABSENCE, 2

A h....too soon made glad   IMPRESSIONABILITY, 1

a step away from the natural h. of man   WORRY, 3

A woman's h. always has a burned mark   SORROW, 3

Because my h. is pure   INTEGRITY, 3

cold untroubled h. of stone   SELFISHNESS, 2

h. and stomach of a King   ROYALTY, 15

look in thy h. and write   INSPIRATION, 2

My h. is a lonely hunter   LONELINESS, 5

strings...in the human h.   EMOTION, 2

Their h.'s in the right place   MANKIND, 14

The way to a man's h. is through his stomach   FOOD, 2

to lose your h.'s desire   DESIRE, 4

What comes from the h.   SINCERITY, 1

hearts Kind h. are more than coronets   ARISTOCRACY, 9

One equal temper of heroic h.   DETERMINATION, 6

those who have stout h. and sharp swords   RUTHLESSNESS, 4

heart-throbs We should count time by h.   TIME, 7

help our friends' h. that helps us   FRIENDSHIP, 7

The dead...look on and h.   DEATH, 26

the h. of too many physicians   DOCTORS, 1

what is past my h. is past my care   INDIFFERENCE, 1

with a little h. from my friends   FRIENDS, 5

hen A h. is only an egg's way   EVOLUTION, 1

Henry Hoorah H.   ARISTOCRACY, 8

herbs power of h.   MEDICINE, 18

heresies new truths...begin as h.   NOVELTY, 3

heritage grant youth's h.   AGE, 100

hero h. to his valet   FAMILIARITY, 1

herod It out-h.s H.   EXCESS, 7

heroes speed glum h....to death   WAR, 48

hidden Most good women are h. treasures   VIRTUE, 7

Nature is often h.   HUMAN NATURE, 2

hill beyond this h.   PROGRESS, 9

hills to be out on the h. alone   SOLITUDE, 4

hit if a man h. you   VIOLENCE, 2

h. the mark   AMBITION, 9

Hitler H. has only got one ball   WORLD WAR II, 1

hobgoblin the h. of little minds   CONSTANCY, 1

hold h. your tongue   SILENCE, 1

Now I h. creation in my foot   CREATION, 6

To have and to h.   MARRIAGE, 14

Hollywood H. – a place where people from Iowa   CINEMA, 4

H....the personality of a paper cup   PLACES, 6

In H., if you don't have happiness   CINEMA, 12

trend in H.   CINEMA, 1

holy everything that lives is h.   LIFE, 1

homely A h. face...aided many women heavenward   APPEARANCE, 2

be never so h.   HOME, 1

Homer even excellent H. nods   IMPERFECTION, 1

you must not call it H.   POETRY, 7

homos one of the stately h. of
England　　　HOMOSEXUALITY, 4

honest an h. man sent to lie abroad
　　　　　　　DIPLOMACY, 14

give me six lines...by the most h.
man　　　　EXECUTION, 8

It's better to be quotable than...h.
　　　　　　QUOTATIONS, 7

honey gather h. all the day
　　　　　　　WORK, 16

honi *H. soit qui mal y pense*　EVIL, 1

hopes to enter on far-reaching h.
　　　　　　MORTALITY, 1

horny-handed H. sons of toil
　　　　　　　WORK, 8

horror I have a h. of sunsets　SUN, 3

mere existence is swollen to a h.
　　　　　　IDEALISM, 3

horse Do not trust the h., Trojans
　　　　　　　MISTRUST, 5

Go together like a h. and carriage
　　　　LOVE AND MARRIAGE, 4

white h....could be a zebra
　　　　　　APPEARANCE, 9

You can lead a h. to the water
　　　　　　STUBBORNNESS, 1

hospital h. is the assumption
　　　　　　　MEDICINE, 10

the poor devils in the h.　CHARITY, 1

hostages h. given to fate
　　　　　　　FAMILY, 11

hour An h. in the morning　TIME, 1

One h.'s sleep　　　　SLEEP, 1

wage war until the last quarter of
an h.　　　　　　WAR, 15

housekeeping H. ain't no joke
　　　　　　HOUSEWORK, 1

human Adam was but h.
　　　　　　PERVERSITY, 2

as if a h. being sitting inside were
making fun　　　ANIMALS, 1

faith in h. beings　　FAITH, 3

H. beings are like timid
punctuation marks　MANKIND, 11

imagine a boot stamping on a h.
face　　　　　OPPRESSION, 5

No h. being...was ever so free as a
fish　　　　　FREEDOM, 21

To err is h., to forgive, divine
　　　　　　MISTAKES, 8

To kill a h. being　KILLING, 6

humiliating Corporal punishment
is...h.　　　　PUNISHMENT, 7

humiliation greatest h. is...when
the spirit is proudest　PRIDE, 2

hundred still be alive in a h. years'
time　　　　　MORTALITY, 5

Hungarian It's not enough to be H.
　　　　　　　TALENT, 4

hungry You cannot feed the h. on
statistics　　　STATISTICS, 5

hunter My heart is a lonely h.
　　　　　　LONELINESS, 1

husband My h. and I　ROYALTY, 17

Never trust a h. too far　TRUST, 3

husbandry He was into animal h.
　　　　　　　SEX, 30

hymn-book Cassock, band, and h.
too　　　　　　CLERGY, 5

hymns My poems are h. of praise
　　　　　　　POETRY, 21

hypocrite h. in his pleasures
　　　　　　PLEASURE, 7

hypothesis no need of that h.
　　　　　　　GOD, 9

slaying of a beautiful h.
　　　　　　SCIENCE, 19

to discard a pet h. every day
　　　　　　　THEORY, 7

hysteria comedy at the moment of
deepest h.　　　WRITING, 17

I in the infinite I AM
　　　　　IMAGINATION, 1

I would have done it differently
　　　　　　ARROGANCE, 3

ice skating over thin i.　HASTE, 4

id the care of the i. by the odd
　　　　　　PSYCHIATRY, 1

idea An i. does not pass from one
language　　　TRANSLATION, 4

constant repetition...imprinting an
i. PUBLIC, 7
Dying for an i. MARTYRDOM, 3
Retirement...is not a good i.
ROYALTY, 10
the i. of death as an individual
NUCLEAR WEAPONS, 7
idiot tale told by an i. LIFE, 34
idle Young people ought not to be
i. YOUTH, 16
if I. you can keep your head
SELF-CONTROL, 4
much virtue in I. POSSIBILITY, 3
ifs If i. and ans UNCERTAINTY, 1
ignorant Let no one i. of
mathematics enter here
MATHEMATICS, 8
the opinionated, the i., and the
boorish STUBBORNNESS, 3
illiterate Violence is the repartee
of the i. VIOLENCE, 4
illogical Faith...an i. belief
FAITH, 5
illusion The House of Lords, an i.
RESPONSIBILITY, 4
visible universe was an i.
UNIVERSE, 2
image A photograph is not only an
i. PHOTOGRAPHY, 3
imagining this world...with...my i.
BLINDNESS, 4
imitate never failed to i.
CHILDREN, 5
immoral i., illegal, or fattening
PLEASURE, 13
moral or an i. book BOOKS, 23
worse than i. MISTAKES, 2
immortal I have lost the i. part
REPUTATION, 4
make me i. with a kiss BEAUTY, 16
impossible I believe because it is i.
BELIEF, 7
something is i. SCIENCE, 3
inclination read just as i. leads him
READING, 3
income Annual i. twenty pounds
ECONOMICS, 4

hardest thing...to understand is i.
tax TAXATION, 2
private i. SELF-INTEREST, 1
incomplete A man in love is i.
MARRIAGE, 29
inconvenient No one wants the
truth if it is i. TRUTH, 19
indecency public i. SIN, 6
the more one likes i. AGE, 40
independent To be poor and i.
POVERTY, 4
India I. is a geographical term
PLACES, 5
Indian in a world of Gary Coopers
you are the I. RACISM, 1
indigestion Don't tell your friends
about your i. MANNERS, 1
I., n. A disease RELIGION, 6
indignation Moral i. MORALITY, 10
puritan pours righteous i.
PURITANISM, 1
the mists of righteous i. PRUDERY, 3
individual the idea of death as an i.
NUCLEAR WEAPONS, 7
The liberty of the i. FREEDOM, 17
industry Captains of i.
LEADERSHIP, 2
Life without i. is guilt ART, 16
inebriated i. with...his own
verbosity VERBOSITY, 1
inexactitude terminological i.
LYING, 1
inexperience I. is what makes a
young man AGE, 32
infallible an i. sign of the second-
rate INFERIORITY, 2
i. criterion of wisdom SUCCESS, 6
infanticide as indefensible as i.
CENSORSHIP, 7
inferiors I. revolt REVOLUTION, 1
infinitive When I split an i.
GRAMMAR, 1
infinity I. in the palm of your hand
WONDER, 1
infirmity last i. of noble mind
FAME, 8

inhumanity Man's i. to man
　　　　　　　　　　CRUELTY, 2
insolence i. is not invective
　　　　　　　　IMPERTINENCE, 1
institution Any i. which does not
suppose　　　　　　CORRUPTION, 6
insult i. his wife　　MARRIAGE, 54
Marriage is an i.　　MARRIAGE, 38
One does not i. the river god
　　　　　　　　　　PRUDENCE, 1
insured you cannot be i. for the
accidents　　　　　ACCIDENTS, 2
insurrection I. is an art
　　　　　　　　　REVOLUTION, 1
integrate I i. the current export
drive　　　　　　　　BUSINESS, 2
intellectual Beware of the artist
who's an i.　　　　　ARTISTS, 2
intelligent i. full of doubt DOUBT, 1
intent A truth that's told with bad
i.　　　　　　　　　　TRUTH, 1
prick the sides of my i.
　　　　　　　　　　AMBITION, 13
intermission i. of pain PLEASURE, 11
interval an opera without an i.
　　　　　　　　　　OPERA, 1
investment no finer i.　BABIES, 1
To bear many children is...an i.
　　　　　　　　　　CHILDREN, 14
invisible evil that walks I.
　　　　　　　　　HYPOCRISY, 6
iron An i. curtain　COLD WAR, 1
rule them with a rod of i.
　　　　　　　　　LEADERSHIP, 1
irony everyone gets i. nowadays
　　　　　　　　　　HUMOUR, 15
irretrievably marriage had i.
broken down　　　ROYALTY, 1
Islam In some remote regions of I.
　　　　　　　　　　MODESTY, 2
I. unashamedly came with a sword
　　　　　　　　　RELIGION, 34
women's rights in I.　FEMINISM, 2
island No man is an I.　SOCIETY, 5
isolation our splendid i.
　　　　　　　　　DIPLOMACY, 6

Israel When I. was in Egypt land
　　　　　　　　　OPPRESSION, 1
Italian I speak...I. to women
　　　　　　　　　LANGUAGE, 4
Jack Damn you, J. – I'm all right
　　　　　　　　　SELFISHNESS, 1
J. of all trades　OCCUPATIONS, 1
Japan not necessarily to J.'s
advantage　　WORLD WAR II, 12
jaw-jaw To j. is better than to
war-war　　　　DIPLOMACY, 3
jazz J. will endure
　　　　　　POPULAR MUSIC, 9
jealous Art is a j. mistress ART, 7
jelly Out vile j.　　　EYES, 4
Jesus If J. Christ were to come
　　　　　　　　　BELIEF, 4
J. loves me　　　RELIGION, 35
Jew I'm a coloured, one-eyed J.
　　　　　　　　　DISABILITY, 2
jewellery rattle your j. WEALTH, 13
job Being a husband is a whole-
time j.　　　　　MARRIAGE, 11
Giz a j.　　UNEMPLOYMENT, 1
joking My way of j. is to tell the
truth　　　　　　　TRUTH, 22
Joneses drag the J. down to my
level　　　ONE-UPMANSHIP, 1
journalists j. put theirs on the front
page　　　　OCCUPATIONS, 2
judge do not j. by appearances
　　　　　　　APPEARANCES, 17
justified No man is j. in doing evil
　　　　　　　EXPEDIENCY, 1
justifying interested in...j.
themselves　　　　MOTIVE, 1
Kaiser the kibosh on the K.
　　　　　　　WORLD WAR I, 1
keen a polished razor k. SATIRE, 2
out of a k. city　　MOON, 1
keep if they k. on saying it
　　　　　　　JOURNALISM, 1
K. up appearances APPEARANCES, 8
keeper am I my brother's k.
　　　　　　　MURDER, 1
k. stands up　　FOOTBALL, 4

kicks

334

kicks Get your k. on Route 66
TRAVEL, 23
kid Here's looking at you, k.
ADMIRATION, 1
kill explosive to k. a man WAR, 61
He would k. Himself
HUMAN CONDITION, 2
k. a wife with kindness KINDNESS, 7
When you have to k. a man
DIPLOMACY, 4
word for which you k.
REVOLUTION, 10
kills k. all its pupils TIME, 9
Who k. a man k. a reasonable
creature BOOKS, 17
kin knew no other k.
SELF-RELIANCE, 6
kind be cruel only to be k.
CRUELTY, 5
king the eternal k. TREASON, 4
The k. has been very good to me
MARTYRDOM, 1
kingdom my k. for a horse
HORSES, 1
kings Grammar, which can govern
even k. GRAMMAR, 3
'Twixt k. and tyrants TYRANNY, 6
knock Don't k. it SEX, 2
K. as you please STUPIDITY, 9
know all Ye k. on earth TRUTH, 17
feels what other men...
INTELLIGENCE, 4
I do not k. myself
SELF-KNOWLEDGE, 3
I k. what I like SUBJECTIVITY, 1
the only person...I should like to k.
EGOTISM, 5
What we k. of the past HISTORY, 10
What you don't k. IGNORANCE, 2
knowing misfortune of k. anything
WOMEN, 6
known the k. and the unknown
METAPHYSICS, 3
knows He that k. little
IGNORANCE, 1
He who k. only his own side
SUBJECTIVITY, 2

Only the nose k. SECRECY, 1
Kodak the great artist K.
PHOTOGRAPHY, 4
Kuwait democracy in K. WAR, 12
laboratory All the world is a l.
SCIENCE, 13
guinea pigs in the l. of God
MANKIND, 27
labours Children sweeten l.
CHILDREN, 4
land take place in No Man's L.
THEATRE, 1
There is a happy l. HEAVEN, 7
they have the l. and we have the
Bibles RACISM, 5
Unhappy the l. that has no heroes
HEROISM, 3
We are as near to heaven by sea as
by l. SEA, 2
last the l. territorial claim
WORLD WAR II, 13
late Better never than l.
PROMPTNESS, 2
Never too l. to learn AGE, 1
We have met too l. INFLUENCE, 3
Latin A silly remark can be made
in L. LANGUAGE, 3
Don't quote L. SPEECHES, 4
laudanum Whipping and abuse are
like l. PUNISHMENT, 12
laugh Make 'em l. WRITING, 18
old man who will not l. AGE, 33
laughed Few women care to be l.
at RIDICULE, 1
laughing Happiness is no l. matter
HAPPINESS, 15
One cannot be always l. at a man
MEN, 1
laws simplicity of its l.
FOOTBALL, 2
the l. of poetic truth POETRY, 2
Where l. end, tyranny begins
TYRANNY, 7
you do not make the l. WOMEN, 12
laxative sweet l. of Georgian
strains STATELY HOMES, 2

leap one giant l. for mankind   SPACE, 2

learn how to l.   EDUCATION, 1
l. to be brave   COURAGE, 8

leave I must l. thee   PARTING, 1
l. a thing alone   CONSERVATISM, 2

leaves before the l. have fallen   WORLD WAR I, 10

leper bathing a l.   MEDIA, 6

less found it l. exciting   COWARDICE, 3
more and more about l. and l.   EXPERTS, 3
the l. they have   CHARACTER, 7

liaison partly a l. man   BUSINESS, 2

liar honorable member was a l.   APOLOGIES, 4
I am the club L.   SUPERIORITY, 5
they called me a l.   WRITERS, 11

liberation war of l.   HUNGER, 6

liberté L.! Égalité! Fraternité!   HUMAN RIGHTS, 2

liberty constitutional l.   CORRUPTION, 1
defence of l.   EXCESS, 4
give me l.   FREEDOM, 9
l. cannot long exist   CORRUPTION, 1
l. for one person is constrained only   EQUALITY, 8
People contend for their L.   REBELLION, 3
why is my l. judged   CONSCIENCE, 1

lie L. follows by post   APOLOGIES, 1
The camera cannot l.   PHOTOGRAPHY, 1
The greater the l.   PROPAGANDA, 2
The old L.   PATRIOTISM, 10
you would l.   TRUTH, 7

lies, damned l. and statistics   STATISTICS, 1
no longer l.   TRUTH, 15
polite by telling l.   COURTESY, 1
The cruellest l.   SILENCE, 1

light l. a l. for a cigarette   GENEROSITY, 3
a l. form of premature baldness   AGE, 17

Empty space and points of l.   REALITY, 4
I can't stand a naked l. bulb   VULGARITY, 5
sweetness and l.   CULTURE, 1
the l. that led astray   DELUSION, 1

like I know what I l.   SUBJECTIVITY, 1
L. cures like   REMEDIES, 9
People who l. this sort of thing   CRITICISM, 7
To l....the same things   FRIENDSHIP, 10

liked He's l., but he's not well l.   POPULARITY, 6

limit draw a l. to thinking   THINKING, 8

line cancel half a L.   DESTINY, 2
l. in the sand   WAR, 11
thin red l.   WAR, 47
walks along a l.   GENIUS, 8

lines give me six l.   EXECUTION, 8

little He who knows only his own side...knows l.   SUBJECTIVITY, 2
L. things affect l. minds   TRIVIALITY, 3
L. things are...the most important   SMALLNESS, 2
So l. done, so much to do   LAST WORDS, 35
These l. grey cells   INTELLECT, 1

live anything but l. for it   RELIGION, 3
Come l. with me   LOVE, 22, 31
Do you want to l. for ever   WAR, 1
eat to l., not l. to eat   FOOD, 11
Houses are built to l. in   HOUSES, 1
If you l. long enough   LONGEVITY, 8
in Rome, l. as the Romans   CONFORMITY, 1
I was learning how to l.   DEATH, 48
L. among men   RIGHTEOUSNESS, 3
l. dangerously   DANGER, 3
Rascals, would you l. for ever   WAR, 23
than to l. up to them   PRINCIPLES, 2
We l. in stirring times   PRESENT, 4

You might as well l.   SUICIDE, 10

Liverpool L. is the pool of life
PLACES, 8

lives l. of quiet desperation
DESPAIR, 4

living Civilization is a method of l.
CIVILIZATION, 1

he who lives without tobacco isn't
worthy of l.   SMOKING, 12

History is…the wrong way of l.
HISTORY, 7

let the earth bring forth the l.
creature   ANIMALS, 3

two people l. together
MARRIAGE, 30

way to drink for a l.   ALCOHOL, 19

We owe respect to the l.
RESPECT, 3

Livingstone Dr L., I presume
EXPLORATION, 4

Lloyd George L. could not see a
belt   INSULTS, 2

loafed It is better to have l. and
lost   LAZINESS, 4

loitered I l. my life away
DISCONTENT, 2

Lolita L., light of my life   LUST, 4

London dominate a L. dinner-table
INFLUENCE, 5

Hell is a city much like L.   HELL, 4

lonely the l. sea and the sky   SEA, 5

looking Here's l. at you, kid
ADMIRATION, 1

somebody may be l.
CONSCIENCE, 5

Women have served…as l.-glasses
WOMEN, 42

looks A woman as old as she l.
AGE, 13

man who l. you…in the eye
INSINCERITY, 1

Lord Praise the L. and pass the
ammunition   WAR, 21

Lords Great l. have their pleasures
PLEASURE, 9

None ought to be l. or landlords
HUMAN RIGHTS, 4

The House of L., an illusion
RESPONSIBILITY, 8

lose A man who does not l. his
reason   REASON, 4

It doesn't hurt to l. my crown
FAILURE, 3

nothing to l. but their chains
MARXISM, 3

We Don't Want To L. You
DISMISSAL, 2

lost better to have fought and l.
DEFEAT, 1

better to have loafed and l.
LAZINESS, 4

better to have loved and l.   LOSS, 1

I look upon every day to be l.
FRIENDSHIP, 8

You are a l. generation   WAR, 56

lucky I wasn't l.   MERIT, 4

lunatic l. asylums STATELY HOMES, 5

lunch no such thing as a free l.
BUSINESS, 8

lyric modifying your l. content
CENSORSHIP, 8

machine One m. can do the work
TECHNOLOGY, 5

the Ghost in the M.   MIND, 11

machines m. will ever force
themselves   TECHNOLOGY, 8

mad Don't get m., get even
REVENGE, 2

Went m. and bit the man   DOGS, 3

maggot how to create a m.
RELIGION, 28

magic mistook m. for medicine
MEDICINE, 17

That old black m.
SUPERNATURAL, 4

maid the simple m.   WOMEN, 19

maidens M., like moths, are ever
caught by glare   WEALTH, 5

Majesty His M.'s Opposition
OPPOSITION, 1

sex to which Your M. belongs
MISOGYNY, 4

majors scarlet M.   WAR, 48

malady It is the m. of our age
YOUTH, 8

male especially the m. MEN, 6
m. can represent Christ
RELIGION, 12
more deadly than the m.
WOMEN, 24
the weapon of the m. SEXES, 2

malicious God is subtle but he is
not m. GOD, 6

malt M. does more than Milton
ALCOHOL, 17

man A m. is only as old as the
woman AGE, 25
A m. of straw WOMEN, 1
England expects every m. will do
his duty DUTY, 2
Every m. meets his Waterloo
DEFEAT, 6
Go West, young m.
EXPLORATION, 1
M....consumes CAPITALISM, 9
M. hands on misery to m.
CHILDREN, 24
M. is a dupable animal
GULLIBILITY, 2
M. is a history-making creature
HISTORY, 3
M. is an intellectual animal
INTELLECT, 4
m. is...a religious animal
RELIGION, 9
M. is a social animal SOCIETY, 10
m. is as old as he's feeling AGE, 13
M. is a tool-making animal
TECHNOLOGY, 4
M. is something that is to be
surpassed SUPERIORITY, 4
M. is the only animal HYPOCRISY, 3
M.'s inhumanity to man
CRUELTY, 2
M. was born free FREEDOM, 20
mean m. is always full of distress
SUPERIORITY, 1
most heavily m.-made habitats
CONSERVATION, 6

no m....hath lived better than I
ACHIEVEMENT, 7
No m. is a hero PSYCHIATRY, 4
No m. is an Island SOCIETY, 5
No m. is good enough
DEMOCRACY, 6
Nothing happens to any m.
ENDURANCE, 2
One m. shall have one vote
DEMOCRACY, 3
one small step for m.
MISQUOTATIONS, 1
Sex between a m. and a woman
SEX, 3
simple to keep a m. WOMEN, 22
Society, being codified by m.
SOCIETY, 3
The history of m. BIRTH, 2
The m. who makes no mistakes
MISTAKES, 6
When a woman behaves like a m.
WOMEN, 17
young m. not yet MARRIAGE, 8

Maradona the head of M.
FOOTBALL, 5

mark If you would hit the m.
AMBITION, 9
the m....of the beast DEVIL, 3

married don't sleep with m. men
ADULTERY, 1
Writing is like getting m.
WRITING, 16

marries a young person, who...m.
HUMAN NATURE, 1

Martini a dry M. ALCOHOL, 34

masses I will back the m. CLASS, 7

master m., is it I BETRAYAL, 1
m. of himself SELF-CONTROL, 5

masters good servants, but bad m.
PASSION, 2
people are the m. PUBLIC, 3
that the m. willingly concede to
slaves SLAVERY, 4

masturbation M. is the thinking
man's television SEX, 21
m. of war WAR, 42

materialistic Christianity is the most m. CHRISTIANITY, 12

matter Mind over m. MIND, 13
proverb is much m. decorated SAYINGS, 3

meaning language charged with m. LITERATURE, 12

means die beyond my m. EXTRAVAGANCE, 4
live within our m. BORROWING, 4

meat Some hae m. FOOD, 4

medicines Many m., few cures REMEDIES, 1

meditation M. is...the means and the end THINKING, 4

medium The m. is the message COMMUNICATION, 3
TV...is our latest m. TELEVISION, 5

megaphone M. diplomacy DIPLOMACY, 7

mental A m. stain can neither be blotted out PSYCHIATRY, 4
cause and effect as m. RELIGION, 15
unravel people's m. blocks PHILOSOPHY, 3

mercury Two years with m. SEX, 37

mercy To M., Pity, Peace, and Love PRAYER, 2

meritocracy The Rise of the M. MERIT, 5

mess another fine m. ACCIDENTS, 4

message The medium is the m. COMMUNICATION, 3

method madness, yet there is m. in't MADNESS, 17
You know my m. TRIVIALITY, 4

Methuselah all the days of M. AGE, 9

mice schemes o' m. an' men DISAPPOINTMENT, 2

Michelangelo If M. had been straight HOMOSEXUALITY, 10

microbes acquired a fear of m. FEAR, 1

middle M. age is when AGE, 20
move into the m. class CLASS, 22
no m. course MONARCHY, 4

mighty Another m. empire overthrown DEFEAT, 9

militarism m....bulwarks of capitalism CAPITALISM, 5

milk th' m. of human kindness KINDNESS, 6

millionaire I am a m. WEALTH, 18

Milton a Shakespeare or a M. WRITERS, 3
Malt does more than M. can ALCOHOL, 17

minds All things can corrupt perverted m. CORRUPTION, 5
Great m. think alike SIMILARITY, 2
M. are not ever craving BOOKS, 3
Superstition is the religion of feeble m. SUPERSTITION, 2
the hobgoblin of little m. CONSTANCY, 1
To be alone is the fate of all great m. GREATNESS, 5

ministers I don't mind how much my m. talk AUTHORITARIANISM, 6

minute M. Particulars GOOD, 2
no circumstance...is too m. PHILOSOPHERS, 2
not a m. on the day STRIKES, 2
sucker born every m. GULLIBILITY, 1

miracle a m. of rare device PLEASURE, 5

mirror A novel is a m. NOVELS, 3
Art is not a m. ART, 13

mirrors M. and fatherhood are abominable UNIVERSE, 2
Never believe in m. or newspapers NEWSPAPERS, 1

misery greatest m. is a battle gained VICTORY, 14
he Who finds himself, loses his m. SELF-KNOWLEDGE, 1
Man hands on m. to man HUMAN CONDITION, 4

misfortunes a share in their m. INJUSTICE, 3

mislead One to m. the public GOVERNMENT, 4

miss A m. is as good FAILURE, 1
to m. the one before it TRAVEL, 6

missiles guided m. and misguided
men WAR, 30

mistress Art is a jealous m. ART, 7

misunderstood To be great is to be
m. GREATNESS, 4

mob do what the m. do
MAJORITY, 3
Our supreme governors, the m.
PUBLIC, 11

modern m. art ART, 17
m. civilization DEVIL, 5

modest and is m. about it TALENT, 1

Mohamed M. wanted equality for
women EQUALITY, 3

moment A m. of time may make
us unhappy SORROW, 7
died at that m. ASSASSINATION, 4
Every m. one is born
LIFE AND DEATH, 10

Mona Lisa A lotta cats copy the M.
IMITATION, 1

monetarist she was a m.
ECONOMICS, 6

monkeys not only from m. but
from monks EVOLUTION, 7
pay peanuts...get m. BUSINESS, 9

monopoly m. over what is right
TOLERANCE, 2

moral Let us be m. EXISTENCE, 2
m. or an immoral book BOOKS, 23
more than a m. duty FRANKNESS, 3
one is unhappy one becomes m.
SORROW, 12
The highest possible stage in m.
culture SELF-CONTROL, 2
the m. law WONDER, 2
The worst government is the most
m. GOVERNMENT, 11

moralist no sterner m. than
Pleasure PLEASURE, 4

more m. and m. about less and less
EXPERTS, 3
M. will mean worse DECLINE, 1

the m. you get the m. you spend
MONEY, 3

morn He rose the morrow m.
WISDOM, 5
the opening eye-lids of the m.
DAY, 4

mortal men think all men m.
ARROGANCE, 4
we have been m. enemies
ENEMIES, 4

mother English girl hates...her m.
FAMILY, 16
I am...your m. AGE, 26
If poverty is the m. of crime
CRIME, 1
M. is far too clever to understand
PREJUDICE, 1
M. is the dead heart
MOTHERHOOD, 5
m. of battles WAR, 27
My m., drunk or sober
PATRIOTISM, 4
My m. said it was simple
WOMEN, 22
women become like their m.
SEXES, 14

mould If you cannot m. yourself
TOLERANCE, 8
Nature made him, and then broke
the m. INDIVIDUALITY, 1

mountain alone on a great m.
SOLITUDE, 4

Mozart when M. was my age
AGE, 22

muesli m.-belt malnutrition
FOOD, 10

mumble maunder and m.
PUBLIC, 4

mushroom a supramundane m.
NUCLEAR WEAPONS, 8

mystery Happiness is a m.
HAPPINESS, 4
Life itself is a m. LIFE, 29

mystic The m. sees the ineffable
PSYCHIATRY, 11

myth some magnificent m.
PROPAGANDA, 3

name crimes are committed in thy
n.   EXECUTION, 9
their n. liveth for evermore
      MEMORIALS, 1
they give it a n.   WORDS, 5
naming N. of Cats is a difficult
matter   CATS, 1
Today we have n. of parts
      WEAPONS, 4
Naples See N. and die   PLACES, 2
Napoleons worship the Caesars
and N.   TYRANNY, 5
nation America became top n.
      HISTORY, 16
An army is a n. within a n.   ARMY, 1
n....fall victim to a big lie   LYING, 7
N. shall speak peace   PEACE, 9
No n. was ever ruined by trade
      BUSINESS, 6
nationalism wind of n.   FREEDOM, 1
necessary a n. evil
      GOVERNMENT, 13
necessities n. of existence
      CIVILIZATION, 5
neck equipping us with a n.
      COURAGE, 9
people had but one n.
      RUTHLESSNESS, 1
necking Whoever named it n.
      SEX, 33
need All You N. Is Love   LOVE, 29
things that people don't n.
      ARTISTS, 1
needle the eye of a n.   WEALTH, 4
needs N. must   NECESSITY, 3
to each according to his n.
      MARXISM, 4
Your country n. YOU   WAR, 1
negotiate never fear to n.
      DIPLOMACY, 1
nervous winding up its n. and
intellectual system   SUICIDE, 8
neurotic expression of a n. impulse
      ACTING, 3
n. is the man who builds
      PSYCHIATRY, 17

never Better n. than late
      PROMPTNESS, 2
I n. talk about it   SEX, 42
news Literature is n.
      LITERATURE, 11
when a man bites a dog that is n.
      MEDIA, 1
night Morning in the Bowl of N.
      DAY, 1
real dark n. of the soul   SOUL, 3
The n. has a thousand eyes   SUN, 1
The n. was pain   SORROW, 1
nihilist a part-time n.
      COMMITMENT, 2
Nineveh Quinquireme of N.
      BOATS, 1
noise A loud n. at one end
      BABIES, 2
the more n. they make
      CHARACTER, 1
they...love the n. it makes   MUSIC, 3
nose hateful to the n.   SMOKING, 9
Only the n. knows   SECRECY, 1
nothingness the n. shows through
      CREATION, 10
notice no n. of their opinions
      LOYALTY, 3
nuisance exchange of one n. for
another n.   PROGRESS, 6
not composing...becomes a
positive n.   MUSIC, 11
nuisances a change of n.
      CHANGE, 11
nuns The n. who never take a bath
      MODESTY, 4
nurse Our foster n. of nature
      SLEEP, 7
nurseries n. of all vice
      EDUCATION, 6
oblivion alms for o.   TIME, 27
obscenely o. obvious COSMETICS, 2
observance the o. of trifles
      TRIVIALITY, 4
occupation apologizing for his o.
      BUSINESS, 11
ocean We mortals cross the o.
      HUMAN CONDITION, 1

whilst the great o. of truth
DISCOVERY, 5

odd the care of the id by the o.
PSYCHIATRY, 1

This world is very o. we see
CONFUSION, 4

Oedipuses a tense and peculiar
family, the O.
CLASSICS, 1

off he gets o. with women
SEX, 29

O. with his head
EXECUTION, 3

offence greatest o. against virtue
VIRTUE, 5

offensive You are extremely o.
IMPERTINENCE, 3

offer an o. he can't refuse
BUSINESS, 12

office in o. but not in power
GOVERNMENT, 8

o. sanctifies the holder
POWER, 3

old Better be an o. man's darling
MARRIAGE, 1

O. men forget
MEMORY, 10

O. sins
SIN, 1

O. men declare war
WAR, 26

to go on getting o.
SURVIVAL, 1

one All for o., and o. for all
UNITY, 5

O. Realm, O. People, O. Leader
NAZISM, 1

opinion a very good o. of himself
CONCEIT, 1

the o. of those we don't care for
CONCEIT, 3

opinionated the o., the ignorant,
and the boorish
STUBBORNNESS, 3

opium o. of the people
RELIGION, 26

oppressive Vatican is an o. regime
CHURCH, 1

oracular the use of my o. tongue
MALAPROPISMS, 3

oral story about o. contraception
CONTRACEPTION, 2

worst thing about o. sex
SEX, 31

orgy An o. looks particularly
alluring
PRUDERY, 3

you need an o., once in a while
DEBAUCHERY, 4

ourselves we convince o.
PERSUASION, 2

What isn't part of o. doesn't
disturb us
HATE, 3

out Mordre wol o.
MURDER, 3

outside I am just going o.
LAST WORDS, 29

overpaid They're o., overfed,
oversexed and over here
SOLDIERS, 7

overrated a highly o. performance
MARRIAGE, 26

overtakers It is the o. who
TRAVEL, 17

oyster bold man that first eat an o.
FOOD, 14

pacifism My p. is not...intellectual
theory
WAR AND PEACE, 4

pagan Christian glories in the
death of a p.
CHRISTIANITY, 1

pain a gentleman...never inflicts
p.
CHIVALRY, 4

I feel no p.
ALCOHOL, 4

momentary intoxication with p.
CRUELTY, 1

Neither shame nor physical p.
PUNISHMENT, 7

No p., no palm
SUCCESS, 16

owes its pleasures to another's p.
HUNTING, 2

Pleasure is...intermission of p.
PLEASURE, 11

Religion was my protection against
p.
RELIGION, 21

the art of avoiding p.
LIFE, 22

The least p. in our little finger
SELF-INTEREST, 2

The night was p.
SORROW, 1

pants p. were so thin
POVERTY, 21

parade the p. of riches
OSTENTATION, 3

paradise the p. of fools
HEAVEN, 2

Wilderness is P. enow
CONTENTMENT, 2

paradoxes P. are useful
IDEAS, 1

parallel we may not find a p.
SELF, 8
paranoid a p. can have enemies
ENEMIES, 3
Just because you're p.
PSYCHIATRY, 2
parent To lose one p.
LOSS, 3
parenthood p....feeding the mouth that bites you
FAMILY, 7
parliament no reference to fun in any Act of P.
PLEASURE, 4
P. is the longest running farce
GOVERNMENT, 18
parody devil's walking p.
ANIMALS, 9
party No p. has a monopoly over what is right
TOLERANCE, 2
the Conservative P. at prayer
CHURCH, 5
pass ideas simply p. through him
STUPIDITY, 1
p. the ammunition
WAR, 21
To p. away ere life hath lost its brightness
DEATH, 19
passions the two sweetest p.
LITERATURE, 10
pastime Art is not a p.
ART, 4
patent could you p. the sun
DISCOVERY, 6
patient a fool for a p.
DOCTORS, 12
disease which the p.
RELIGION, 6
Medicine is for the p.
MEDICINE, 13
p. endurance is godlike
ENDURANCE, 4
pays He who p. the piper
POWER, 2
peaches poetry in p.
POETRY, 14
peanuts pay p....get monkeys
BUSINESS, 9
pedigree languages are the p. of nations
LANGUAGE, 9
peerage When I want a p., I shall buy one
TITLES, 3
pennies P. do not come from heaven
WORK, 13
P. from Heaven
OPTIMISM, 8
penny A p. saved
THRIFT, 1
In for a p.
COMMITMENT, 1

Not a p. off the pay
STRIKES, 2
people always been interested in p.
MISANTHROPY, 1
Be nice to p. on your way up
PRUDENCE, 1
common-looking p.
APPEARANCE, 10
companions for grown p.
CHILDREN, 23
good of the p.
LAW, 3
government of the p., by the p., and for the p.
DEMOCRACY, 3
Hell is other p.
HELL, 3
my p. live in such awful conditions
POVERTY, 10
p....are attracted by God
RELIGION, 24
p. are the masters
PUBLIC, 5
p. as with...bottles
CHARACTER, 7
p. may be made to follow
UNDERSTANDING, 2
p.'s government
GOVERNMENT, 20
p....usually imitate
IMITATION, 3
P. who like this sort of thing
CRITICISM, 7
p. whose company is coveted
OSTENTATION, 1
Religion...is the opium of the p.
RELIGION, 26
show my head to the p.
EXECUTION, 1
there are no unimportant p.
IMPORTANCE, 4
perceptions limited by his P.
DESIRE, 2
perestroika essence of p.
SOCIALISM, 5
perfect a p. pleasure
SMOKING, 17
performance it takes away the p.
ALCOHOL, 3
perfumes All the p. of Arabia
GUILT, 1
perhaps grand P.
POSSIBILITY, 1
perish P. the Universe
REVENGE, 4
permissive The p. society
SOCIETY, 7

perspective What a delightful thing this p. is ART, 18

perversion that melancholy sexual p. ABSTINENCE, 3

War is...universal p. WAR, 42

pervert p. climbs into the minds CRUELTY, 1

twice: a p. DEBAUCHERY, 2

pessimist p....believes things couldn't possibly be worse OPTIMISM, 7

phallic the deterrent is a p. symbol NUCLEAR WEAPONS, 14

phone the most historic p. call COMMUNICATION, 4

physical a p. and metaphysical impossibility POETS, 2

physicists p. have known sin SCIENTISTS, 1

pianist do not shoot the p. EFFORT, 4

Picasso a bad P. INFERIORITY, 3

pick Whenever you fall, p. up something OPPORTUNITY, 5

pidgin-English I include p. LANGUAGE, 10

pie better than a fat p. KINDNESS, 2

p. in the sky when you die AFTERLIFE, 3

Promises and p.-crust PROMISES, 3

piece A p. of each of us died ASSASSINATION, 4

What a p. of work is a man MANKIND, 20

Pierian taste not the P. spring KNOWLEDGE, 15

Pilate P....washed his hands GUILT, 1

rather have blood on my hands... P. COMMITMENT, 4

pile P. it high, sell it cheap BUSINESS, 3

pillar a p. of the State LYING, 1

pilot Dropping the p. DISMISSAL, 5

Pimpernel That damned elusive P. ABSENCE, 1

pint a quart in a p. cup POSSIBILITY, 2

You spend half a p. WATER, 5

pissing inside my tent p. out PRUDENCE, 5

place A p. for everything ORDER, 2

firm p. to stand TECHNOLOGY, 1

plagues of all p. with which mankind are curst CHURCH, 3

plain Manners are...the need of the p. MANNERS, 4

planet it fell on the wrong p. WEAPONS, 1

the cancer of the p. MANKIND, 12

plans busy making other p. LIFE, 25

platitude A p. is simply a truth repeated SAYINGS, 1

platitudes Literature is the orchestration of p. LITERATURE, 14

Plato P. is dear to me TRUTH, 7

player poor P., That struts and frets his hour LIFE, 34

players men and women merely p. HUMAN CONDITION, 6

the fact that the p. cannot act ACTING, 1

pleasures greatest of life ILLNESS, 5

interfering with the p. of others ABSTINENCE, 5

Mid p. and palaces HOME, 8

One of the p. of middle age AGE, 31

plot the p. thickens INTRIGUE, 1

poems Anon, who wrote so many p. WOMEN, 41

pointless Making money is pretty p. MONEY, 9

poison bitter p. to others TASTE, 5

directions for using p. PSYCHOLOGY, 5

pole One step beyond the p. EXPLORATION, 2

policeman Ask a P. TIME, 22

The terrorist and the p. EQUALITY, 6

policemen sadists…become p.
                                        PUBLISHING, 3
pomp life more sweet Than that of
painted p.   COUNTRYSIDE, 4
poor great men have their p.
relations   FAMILY, 8
grind the faces of the p.
                                        CAPITALISM, 2
If a free society cannot help the…
p.   SOCIETY, 3
the p. person…thinks money
would help   MONEY, 13
population P. growth…environ-
mental damage   ENVIRONMENT, 3
p.…is to fill heaven   PURPOSE, 9
possession p. in another   UNITY, 7
P. is nine points   LAW, 2
powerful Guns will make us p.
                                  POWER POLITICS, 2
P. men…help of their wives
                                        SUCCESS, 11
The rich and p. know   GOD, 1
powers *hidden* and *forbidden* p.
                                        SCIENCE, 25
practice p. in excellent   THEORY, 1
P. makes perfect   EXPERIENCE, 2
P. should always be based
                                        THEORY, 6
practiced thirty-seven years I've p.
                                        GENIUS, 4
practise P. what you preach
                                        EXAMPLE, 1
preach but do not p.   MORALITY, 7
praises He who p. everybody
                                        INSINCERITY, 1
pregnancy avoid p. by…math-
ematics   CONTRACEPTION, 4
prejudices collection of p.
                                        POLITICS, 21
freedom to print…proprietor's p.
                                        MEDIA, 5
preservation the p. of property
                                        GOVERNMENT, 9
president nobody is strongminded
around a P.   SERVILITY, 3
sons…to become p.   POLITICS, 16
the P. is dead   ASSASSINATION, 2

press Facing the p.   MEDIA, 6
more sensible than politicians or
the p.   PUBLIC, 5
presume p. not God to scan
                                  SELF-KNOWLEDGE, 4
pretending p. to be wicked
                                        HYPOCRISY, 1
prevent not knowing how to p.
them   CONTRACEPTION, 6
prevention P. is better than cure
                                        PRUDENCE, 2
prevents Nothing p. us from being
natural   SPONTANEITY, 3
price Courage is the p.
                                        COURAGE, 6
The p.…for pursuing any
profession   DISILLUSION, 1
the p. of everything   CYNICISM, 4
those men have their p.
                                        CORRUPTION, 8
priest rid me of this turbulent p.
                                        ASSASSINATION, 1
principle most useful thing about a
p.   EXPEDIENCY, 3
the p. seems the same   WATER, 1
priorities The language of p.
                                        SOCIALISM, 1
prison at home in p.
                                        EDUCATION, 24
mind about going to p.
                                        PUNISHMENT, 6
The world…is but a large p.
                                        EXECUTION, 7
prisoner I object to your being
taken p.   ROYALTY, 20
p. sees the door of his dungeon
open   IMPETUOSITY, 6
prisoners p. of addiction and…p.
of envy   MATERIALISM, 8
process chaos is a science of p.
                                        SCIENCE, 15
prodigal P. of Ease
                                  WORLD-WEARINESS, 1
profession Politics is…the only p.
                                        POLITICS, 24
The price…for pursuing any p.
                                        DISILLUSION, 1

everybody wants to have r.
LITERATURE, 13

he had r. of the effects of smoking
SMOKING, 14

will bear to be r. twice WRITING, 20

real amount of r. estate they own
RELIGION, 39

Nothing ever becomes r. till it is
experienced EXPERIENCE, 7

realist idealist without being a true
r. IDEALISM, 1

realize I saw it, but I did not r. it
PERCEPTION, 4

reaper a R. whose name is Death
DEATH, 28

reasonable figure of 'The R. Man'
LAW, 9

It is his r. conversation MADNESS, 7

Who kills a man kills a r. creature
BOOKS, 17

reasoners most plausible r.
THINKING, 2

recession R. when...neighbour
loses his job UNEMPLOYMENT, 5

recovery Despair of all r.
LONGEVITY, 3

red Better r. than dead
NUCLEAR WEAPONS, 2

R. sky at night WEATHER, 2

thin r. line tipped with steel WAR, 47

reform Every r. movement
CHANGE, 14

refuse an offer he can't r.
BUSINESS, 12

related closely r. persons FAMILY, 12

relation No human r. gives one
possession UNITY, 7

relations Fate chooses your r.
FAMILY, 6

remember r. even these hardships
ENDURANCE, 8

We will r. them MEMORIALS, 2

remembrance R. is the secret
MEMORIALS, 5

repetition constant r. PUBLIC, 7

History is an endless r. HISTORY, 7

reporting not simply a r. device
LANGUAGE, 15

reprehend If I r. any thing
MALAPROPISMS, 5

republic An aristocracy in r.
ARISTOCRACY, 7

resist everything except
temptation TEMPTATION, 6

resources statistics, born to
consume r. STATISTICS, 3

revolutionary I would be a r. myself
POVERTY, 10

Patriotism...is a r. duty
PATRIOTISM, 13

revolver I reach for my r.
PHILISTINISM, 3

reward avoidance of taxes...
carries...r. TAXATION, 5

The r. of a thing well done
SATISFACTION, 2

Vice is its own r. VICE, 3

rewarded Men are r. and punished
MOTIVE, 3

rhetoric Out of the quarrel...we
make r. POETRY, 25

rich get r., get famous and get laid
FAME, 6

r. beyond the dreams of avarice
WEALTH, 15

The r. and powerful know GOD, 1

whether to be r. in things
MATERIALISM, 1

riches R. are for spending
EXTRAVAGANCE, 1

rid gladly...am I r. of it all SEX, 4

glad to get r. of it STUPIDITY, 6

rides He who r. a tiger
AMBITION, 1

rights dignity and r.
HUMAN RIGHTS, 1

Men...r. and nothing more
FEMINISM, 1

r. and interests of the laboring man
STRIKES, 1

The Sovereign has...three r.
MONARCHY, 1

riot A r. is at bottom REBELLION, 1

river can't step into the same r.
twice   CHANGE, 9
Fame is like a r.   FAME, 2
One does not insult the r. god
                                         PRUDENCE, 3
road All I seek...the r. below me
                                         TRAVEL, 20
a r....that does not go through the
intellect   EMOTION, 1
robbed We wuz r.   DEFEAT, 1
when you've r. a man of everything
                                         POWER, 12
robin A r. redbreast in a cage
                                         IMPRISONMENT, 3
rock R. and roll or Christianity
                                         POPULARITY, 5
R. Around the Clock
                                    POPULAR MUSIC, 6
R.'n'roll is part of a pest
                                    POPULAR MUSIC, 1
rod he that spareth his r. hateth his
son   PUNISHMENT, 3
rule them with a r. of iron
                                    LEADERSHIP, 1
rolling Like a r. stone   TRAVEL, 8
Rome R. has spoken
                              AUTHORITARIANISM, 1
R. was not built   PATIENCE, 4
When in R.   CONFORMITY, 3
room struggle for r. and food
                                    SURVIVAL, 4
There is always r. at the top
                                    AMBITION, 15
roses days of wine and r.
                                    TRANSIENCE, 2
hand that gives you r.
                                    GENEROSITY, 1
I will make thee beds of r.
                                    FLOWERS, 1
Nor does a...gardener scent his r.
                                    POETS, 5
rotten r. in the state of Denmark
                                    CORRUPTION, 7
rubs r. you up the wrong way
                                    SENTIMENTALITY, 3
rug you'll end up a r.
                                    SELF-CONFIDENCE, 6

ruled Art is r....imagination
                                    IMAGINATION, 2
ruling instrument...of the r. class
                                    STATE, 4
rum r., sodomy, and the lash
                                    NAVY, 2
rush R. hour   TRAVEL, 16
Russia in R. communism is a dead
dog   COMMUNISM, 9
Why will America not reach out...
to R.   DIPLOMACY, 5
Russians test the R., not the
bombs   NUCLEAR WEAPONS, 6
sack Either back us or s. us
                                    SUPPORT, 1
sadists repressed s....become
policemen   PUBLISHING, 4
safety s. is in our speed   HASTE, 4
said Nothing has yet been s.
                                 ORIGINALITY, 3
saint never a s. took pity
                                    SOLITUDE, 1
saints All are not s.   HYPOCRISY, 1
salvation There is no s. outside the
church   RELIGION, 3
Sam Play it, S.   MISQUOTATIONS, 6
Samaritan remembered the Good
S.   MONEY, 21
Samarkand the Golden Road to S.
                                 KNOWLEDGE, 7
same never been the s. since God
died   GOD, 10
principle seems the s.   WATER, 1
we're all made the s.   SIMILARITY, 3
sand line in the s.   WAR, 11
s. in their eyes   SLEEP, 7
World in a grain of s.   WONDER, 1
savage man who has not wept is a
s.   AGE, 33
soothe a s. breast   MUSIC, 1
saw I came, I s., God conquered
                                  VICTORY, 2
I came, I s., I conquered
                                  VICTORY, 1
I s. it, but I did not realize it
                                 PERCEPTION, 2

say cannot s. what you have to s.
SPEECHES, 1

I have nothing to s. POETRY, 6
s. what one thinks FRANKNESS, 2
When you have nothing to s.
SILENCE, 2

scarce S., sir. Mighty s.
WOMEN, 40

schemes best laid s. o' mice an'
men DISAPPOINTMENT, 2

school Example is the s. of
mankind EXAMPLE, 5
The world is but a s. of inquiry
CURIOSITY, 5

Scotland In S. there is no shadow
REPRESENTATION, 1

scum The rich are the s.
WEALTH, 7

second sign of the s.-rate
INFERIORITY, 2
first and s. class citizens CLASS, 26
put up with poets being s.-rate
POETS, 6
Would you buy a s.-hand car
TRUST, 4

secret s. of reaping the greatest
fruitfulness DANGER, 3
We have discovered the s. of life
DISCOVERY, 3

secrets Conversation…elicits s.
from us CONVERSATION, 5

sect sad-coloured s. RELIGION, 22

seek s….gainful employment
GOVERNMENT, 1
We s. him here, we s. him there
ABSENCE, 4

seize S. the day PRESENT, 3
S. today OPPORTUNITY, 8

sell S. a country WORLD, 3

sense Common s. is the collection
of prejudices PREJUDICE, 2
Let's talk s. to the American
people ENDURANCE, 6

sensible S. men are all of the same
religion RELIGION, 14

sentences Backward ran s.
JOURNALISM, 9

serious A joke's a very s. thing
HUMOUR, 4

servants Few men have been
admired by their s. ADMIRATION, 4
good s., but bad masters
PASSION, 4
he wouldn't have white s.
RACISM, 13

serve permit his ministers to s.
him ROYALTY, 27

set best plain s. VIRTUE, 1

sewage volumes of s. into the sea
ENVIRONMENT, 2

Shakespeare S….grammar school
kids EDUCATION, 4
the making up of a S. or a Milton
WRITERS, 3

shame Neither s. nor physical pain
PUNISHMENT, 7
Put off your s. with your clothes
MODESTY, 1

share a s. in their misfortunes
INJUSTICE, 3

sheep A s. in s.'s clothing
WEAKNESS, 3
false prophets…in s.'s clothing
DECEPTION, 3
like lost s. SIN, 1
the wolf in the s.'s clothing
APPEARANCES, 6

ships little s. of England BOATS, 4
the face that launch'd a thousand
s. BEAUTY, 16

shop All English s. assistants
SERVICE, 1
keep a little back s. SOLITUDE, 4

short Life is too s. WORK, 3

shortage a s. of coal and fish
INCOMPETENCE, 1

shorter s. by a head ROYALTY, 16

sick eats till he is s. GREED, 1
object if I'm s. SMOKING, 3
you usually find that you are s.
ILLNESS, 8

sides both s. of the paper
EXAMINATIONS, 2

everything has two s.
SUBJECTIVITY, 4

sighs over the Bridge of S.
DEATH, 25

S. are the natural language of the
heart SPEECH, 7

sight Out of s. ABSENCE, 1

sign Never s. a valentine
SIGNATURES, 1

S. language is the equal of speech
LANGUAGE, 12

the s. 'Members Only' SEX, 36

signifying S. nothing LIFE, 34

silent His thoughts...lay s.
THINKING, 8

simple as s. as possible SCIENCE, 11

Simpson Mrs S.'s pinched our
king ROYALTY, 8

sincerest Imitation...s. of flattery
IMITATION, 2

sink The s. is the great symbol
FAMILY, 13

sins atone for the s. of your fathers
INJUSTICE, 6

must not reheat his s.
FORGIVENESS, 3

sisters little s. to all the world
WOMEN, 14

situation s. excellent. I shall attack
WAR, 20

skeleton a s. in the cupboard
FAMILY, 7

sky pie in the s. when you die
AFTERLIFE, 3

Which prisoners call the s.
IMPRISONMENT, 6

Skye Over the sea to S. ROYALTY, 6

slack a man becomes s. and selfish
MARRIAGE, 49

slave came to America in s. ships
EQUALITY, 4

man...is Reason's s. PASSION, 1

In a consumer society there are...
two kinds of s. MATERIALISM, 8

sleeping Everybody is s. with
everybody else POPULAR MUSIC, 7

S. as quiet as death OLD AGE, 31

There will be s. enough DEATH, 5

we have only awakened a s. giant
WORLD WAR II, 20

small commonly thought s.
SMALLNESS, 4

From s. beginnings BEGINNING, 2

only s. countries EUROPE, 1

Popularity?...glory's s. change
POPULARITY, 3

S. is beautiful
BEAUTY, 4; SMALLNESS, 3

The best things come in s. parcels
SMALLNESS, 1

smaller these have s. fleas to bite
'em PARASITES, 2

smart you had better be too s. to
get ill ILLNESS, 2

smattering A s. of everything
KNOWLEDGE, 4

smell rose...would s. as sweet
NAMES, 3

Sweet S. of Success SUCCESS, 12

smells s. to heaven GUILT, 4

the only dead thing that's sweet
PAST, 5

snake There's a s. hidden in the
grass DANGER, 1

snare a s. in which the feet of
women WOMEN, 4

snow I used to be S. White
PURITY, 9

the wrong kind of s. WEATHER, 10

social a great s. and economic
experiment ALCOHOL, 16

Beauty is a s. necessity BEAUTY, 11

s. progress GOVERNMENT, 19

soldier Ben Battle was a s. bold
PUNS, 5

The summer s. and the sunshine
patriot COWARDICE, 5

solitary Life is for each man a s.
cell LIFE, 30

Man is not a s. animal
MANKIND, 17

solution difficulty for every s.
BUREAUCRACY, 3

Life itself is a mystery which defies
s. LIFE, 29
The final s. FASCISM, 2
son for every s. and daughter of
mankind HUMAN RIGHTS, 4
I've examined your s.'s head
STUPIDITY, 8
sons I have a wife, I have s.
FAMILY, 11
souls their s. dwell in the house of
tomorrow CHILDREN, 15
the s. of five hundred...Newtons
WRITERS, 3
Soviet as the S. press
NEWSPAPERS, 7
Communism is S. power
COMMUNISM, 6
ship follows S. custom CLASS, 23
spaceship s., Earth
ENVIRONMENT, 4
Spaniards the S. seem wiser
NATIONALITY, 1
to thrash the S.
SPORT AND GAMES, 5
Spanish I speak S. to God
LANGUAGE, 4
spare s. the rod PUNISHMENT, 4
Woodman, s. that tree TREES, 5
speak duty to s. one's mind
FRANKNESS, 3
I didn't s. up NAZISM, 2
Never s. ill of the dead DEATH, 3
province of knowledge to s.
KNOWLEDGE, 9
some...s....before they think
IMPETUOSITY, 1
S. softly and carry a big stick
POWER POLITICS, 4
s. to God RIGHTEOUSNESS, 3
S. up for yourself
SELF-CONFIDENCE, 6
spheres Fifty-five crystal s.
SCIENCE, 32
spice Variety's the very s. of life
CHANGE, 2
spies sorrows...come not single s.
MISFORTUNE, 6

spinning s. the thread of your
being DESTINY, 1
spiteful s. to me in the American
press NEWSPAPERS, 7
I like to write when I feel s.
WRITING, 13
splendid our s. isolation
DIPLOMACY, 6
split They s. the atom SCIENCE, 17
when I s. an infinitive GRAMMAR, 1
spoil Don't s. the ship
ECONOMICS, 1
s. the child PUNISHMENT, 4
spoke s. among your wheels
OBSTRUCTION, 1
spoons let us count our s.
MISTRUST, 3
spots or the leopard his s.
CHANGE, 1
spring can S. be far behind
SEASONS, 5
Drink deep, or taste not the
Pierian s. KNOWLEDGE, 15
In the S. a young man's fancy
SEASONS, 6
S. has returned SEASONS, 4
stage All the world's a s.
HUMAN CONDITION, 6
Don't put your daughter on the s.
THEATRE, 6
stages The four s. of man AGE, 24
stand a firm place to s.
TECHNOLOGY, 1
s. not upon the order of...going
DISMISSAL, 4
Stanislavsky All S. ever said
GENERALIZATIONS, 3
star Being a s. has made it possible
FAME, 4
Hitch your wagon to a s.
AMBITION, 4
s. treatment...as good when I was
poor WEALTH, 14
starry the s. heaven above me
WONDER, 2
stars some of us are looking at the
s. OPTIMISM, 16

strives to touch the s. AMBITION, 14
Tempt not the s. DESTINY, 4
the Stone that puts the S. to Flight
DAY, 1

Through endeavour to the s.
AMBITION, 2

starts make certain it never s.
NUCLEAR WEAPONS, 3

steals s. a common from a goose
THEFT, 1

stealth Do good by s. GOOD, 6

step a s. from the sublime to the
ridiculous DECLINE, 3
one small s. for man
MISQUOTATIONS, 3
only the first s....is difficult
BEGINNING, 4

stick kind of burr; I shall s.
PERSISTENCE, 6

Speak softly and carry a big s.
POWER POLITICS, 4

sticks S. and stones INSULTS, 1

stiff a s. upper lip COURAGE, 3

sting O death! where is thy s.
DEATH, 38

stomach a little wine for thy s.'s
sake ALCOHOL, 6

An army marches on its s.
FOOD, 12

my s. must just digest in its
waistcoat ALCOHOL, 30

The way to a man's heart is
through his s. FOOD, 6

stone Constant dripping hollows
out a s. PERSISTENCE, 5
if someone throws a s. at you
FORGIVENESS, 2

Virtue is like a rich s. VIRTUE, 1

stop s. everyone PERVERSITY, 1
S. the World WORLD-WEARINESS, 3

stops The buck's here
RESPONSIBILITY, 9

straight If Michelangelo had been
s. HOMOSEXUALITY, 10

strangeness s. in the proportion
BEAUTY, 5

stream Time is but the s. TIME, 29

street don't do it in the s. SEX, 9

strength My s. is as the s. of ten
INTEGRITY, 3
s. and fury PATIENCE, 9
We are not now that s.
DETERMINATION, 6

stretch clothes have s. marks
CLOTHES, 10

strike S. while the iron is hot
OPPORTUNITY, 4
themselves must s. the blow
FREEDOM, 4

strings 'There are s.', said Mr
Tappertit EMOTION, 2

strive I s. to be brief BREVITY, 2
needst not s....to keep alive
KILLING, 3

To s., to seek, to find
DETERMINATION, 6

strives s. to touch the stars
AMBITION, 14

strong Sorrow and silence are s.
ENDURANCE, 4
s. enough to bear the misfortunes
of others MISFORTUNE, 5
those who think they are s.
MISTAKES, 3
woe unto them that...follow s.
drink ALCOHOL, 5

struggles the history of class s.
CLASS, 12

stuff The future is made of the
same s. FUTURE, 6
the s. of which tyrants are made
TYRANNY, 1

stupid s. are cocksure DOUBT, 3
to get...money, one must be s.
MATERIALISM, 3

sublime the s. to the ridiculous
DECLINE, 3

succeed If at first you don't s.
PERSISTENCE, 3
It is not enough to s.
RUTHLESSNESS, 5
s. in the world ENVY, 5
those who ne'er s. SUCCESS, 7

temper I should lose my t.
ROYALTY, 22

temple in the very t. of delight
MELANCHOLY, 3

tennis Anyone for t.
SPORT AND GAMES, 1

terminological t. inexactitude
LYING, 5

terrorist The t. and the policeman
EQUALITY, 6

Thatcherism characteristic of T.
SOCIETY, 1

theologian This stranger is a t.
ATHEISM, 3

therapy I go to t.
ROYALTY, 34

thief Time, the subtle t. of youth
AGE, 27

think If you start to t.
ILLNESS, 4

I never t. of the future
FUTURE, 6

Mirrors should t. longer
APPEARANCE, 4

not so t. as you drunk
DRUNKENNESS, 4

t. too little...talk too much
VERBOSITY, 6

time to t. before I speak
SPEECH, 2

thought capable of original t.
IDEAS, 7

A t. is often original
ORIGINALITY, 7

exchange of t.
CONVERSATION, 4

ingenious device for avoiding t.
READING, 5

something between a thing and a t.
PAINTING, 6

was t. twice
WRITING, 20

thoughtless t. are rarely wordless
SPEECH, 5

thoughtlessness t. is the weapon of
the male
SEXES, 2

thoughts my t. remain below
WORDS, 11

To understand God's t.
STATISTICS, 7

we ought to control our t.
SELF-CONTROL, 2

your love but not your t.
CHILDREN, 15

thread the t. of your being
DESTINY, 1

threatened diversity are now
severely t.
ECOLOGY, 2

t. with a great injustice
INJUSTICE, 4

thriller bolt down a cheap t.
LITERATURE, 3

throat good talker with a sore t.
CONVERSATION, 8

throne a t. of bayonets
POWER POLITICS, 6

gave up a t. her
MARRIAGE, 58

no thorns, no t.
SUCCESS, 16

thyself Be so true to t.
INTEGRITY, 1

Know then t.
SELF-KNOWLEDGE, 4

ticky-tacky all made out of t.
HOUSES, 1

tiger The atom bomb is a paper t.
NUCLEAR WEAPONS, 9

T.! T.! burning bright
ANIMALS, 7

tigers ride to and fro upon t.
AUTHORITARIANISM, 3

tightrope to walk a t. safely
NUCLEAR WEAPONS, 12

Timbuctoo On the plains of T.
CLERGY, 5

times logic of our t.
DECLINE, 2

The good old t.
NOSTALGIA, 1

Timor T.'s petroleum smells better
OPPRESSION, 1

tinsel Strip the phoney t.
APPEARANCES, 11

toil blood, t., tears and sweat
EFFORT, 2

Horny-handed sons of t.
WORK, 8

tolerate learning to t. fools
LAW, 10

tomorrow Never put off till t.
PROCRASTINATION, 1

t. is another day
HOPE, 8

T. never comes
FUTURE, 1

tongue hold your t.
SILENCE, 4

One t. is sufficient for a woman
EDUCATION, 15

the use of my oracular t.
MALAPROPISMS, 5

tool Man is a t.-using animal
TECHNOLOGY, 2
time as a t., not as a couch TIME, 17
tourist t. class passengers' deck
CLASS, 15
vulgar…is the British t. TRAVEL, 11
town man made the t.
COUNTRYSIDE, 1
This t. was made to make money
in COMMERCIALISM, 2
towns in all the t. in all the world
CHANCE, 1
trade It is not your t. to make
tables CRITICISM, 5
tragedies There are two t. in life
DESIRE, 4
t. are finish'd by a death
THEATRE, 4
tragedy a t. and therefore not
worth reading PLAYS, 2
great t. of Science SCIENCE, 19
hero and I will write you a t.
HEROISM, 5
T. is if I cut my finger THEATRE, 3
we have conceived life as a t.
LIFE, 38
You *may* abuse a t. TRAVEL, 6
train The only way…of catching a
t. TRAVEL, 6
tranquillity a sense of t. CLOTHES, 3
T. comes with years OLD AGE, 8
trapeze on the flying t.
SPORT AND GAMES, 8
traveller from whose bourn no t.
returns AFTERLIFE, 6
travels A man t. the world over
HOME, 6
He t. fastest SELF, 3
tree as leaves to a t. POETRY, 16
I shall be like that t. DECLINE, 5
same t. that a wise man sees
WISDOM AND FOOLISHNESS, 3
t. of life is green THEORY, 3
triangles if t. invented a god
RELIGION, 30
triumph One more devils'-t.
DAMNATION, 1

We t. without glory VICTORY, 4
Trojans Do not trust the horse, T.
MISTRUST, 5
trouble a lot of t. in his life
WORRY, 1
it saves me the t. of liking them
NASTINESS, 2
true advantage for…philosophy to
be…t. PHILOSOPHY, 5
All one's inventions are t.
POETRY, 11
A thing is not necessarily t.
MARTYRDOM, 4
He said t. things WORDS, 1
if they keep on saying it…it will be
t. JOURNALISM, 4
One religion is as t. as another
RELIGION, 10
The religions we call false were
once t. RELIGION, 17
whatsoever things are t. VIRTUE, 2
truths All great t. begin as
blasphemies NOVELTY, 5
He was a man of two t. LYING, 9
new t.…begin as heresies
NOVELTY, 2
try everything once
EXPERIENCE, 3
T., t. again PERSISTENCE, 3
tunnel light at the end of the t.
PESSIMISM, 4
turbulent rid me of this t. priest
ASSASSINATION, 1
twelve I was born at the age of t.
CINEMA, 6
twice can't step into the same
river t. CHANGE, 3
t. as natural LIFE, 14
will bear to be read t.…was
thought t. WRITING, 20
two grant that twice t. be not four
PRAYER, 2
It takes t. ARGUMENTS, 1
typing That's not writing, that's t.
WRITING, 5
ugliest The u. of trades have their
moments OCCUPATIONS, 3

ugly Christian resolution to find the world u. RELIGION, 31

It's nothing to be born u. APPEARANCE, 5

knowledge of its u. side DISILLUSION, 1

There is nothing u. BEAUTY, 8

ulcer an u. is wonderful to a pathologist APPEARANCES, 12

unassisted Force, if u. by judgement JUDGMENT, 5

undiscovered ocean of truth lay all u. DISCOVERY, 1

undone Things hitherto u. ORIGINALITY, 1

uneducated government by the u. DEMOCRACY, 2

unendurable original thought would probably be u. IDEAS, 7

unequal Men are made by nature u. EQUALITY, 7

unfaithful original is u. to the translation TRANSLATION, 1

unhappy A moment of time may make us u. for ever SORROW, 7

each u. family is u. in its own way FAMILY, 17

U. the land that has no heroes HEROISM, 3

uniformity let use be preferred before u. HOUSES, 1

union To make a u. with Great Britain WORLD WAR II, 15

unite Workers of the world, u. MARXISM, 3

United States defence of the U. WORLD WAR II, 16

universities U. are the cathedrals EDUCATION, 13

unknown the known and the u. METAPHYSICS, 3

unsatisfied it leaves one u. SMOKING, 17

unwashed The great U. PUBLIC, 1

upper Like many of the u. class ARISTOCRACY, 2

the person that…has the u. hand CHARACTER, 6

the u. classes Have still the u. hand STATELY HOMES, 3

useless All Art is quite u. ART, 21

A u. life is an early death PURPOSE, 2

most beautiful things…are the most u. BEAUTY, 19

uses all the u. of this world WORLD-WEARINESS, 4

vacation as good as a v. CHANGE, 11

vaccination V. is the medical sacrament MEDICINE, 5

vacuum A v. can only exist SCIENCE, 14

v….better…stuff that nature replaces NATURE, 13

value All knowledge is of itself of some v. KNOWLEDGE, 1

the v. of nothing CYNICISM, 4

variety a sad v. of woe SORROW, 11

V.'s the very spice of life CHANGE, 2

vasectomy V. means not ever CONTRACEPTION, 1

Vatican V. is an oppressive regime CHURCH, 1

vegetables you must talk to your v. GARDENS, 3

veterinarian best doctor in the world is the V. DOCTORS, 15

viable I'm v. from ten o'clock till five BUSINESS, 2

vices small v. do appear APPEARANCES, 14

vicious can't expect a boy to be v. EDUCATION, 18

Victorian the V. Era PRUDERY, 1

V. values MORALITY, 12

victories Peace hath her v. WAR AND PEACE, 6

Vietnam To win in V. WAR, 5

village global v. TECHNOLOGY, 6

vivisect We v. the nightingale RESEARCH, 1

voice Conscience is the inner v.
CONSCIENCE, 5

The v. of the intellect INTELLECT, 3

v. of the people is the v. of God
PUBLIC, 1

vote One man shall have one v.
DEMOCRACY, 1

The v....means nothing to women
FEMINISM, 6

vulgar the most v....is the British tourist TRAVEL, 11

war...is looked upon as v. WAR, 60

vulture I eat like a v.
APPEARANCE, 11

wallpaper Either that w. goes, or I do LAST WORDS, 46

walls Stone w. do not a prison make IMPRISONMENT, 4

W. have ears GOSSIP, 5

walrus The W. and the Carpenter
SEASIDE, 2

wars as many...w. as the kingdom of Christ CHRISTIANITY, 10

Still war and lechery SEX, 48

wash Don't w. your dirty linen
GOSSIP, 2

washed Pilate...w. his hands
GUILT, 1

watchmaker I should have become a w. NUCLEAR WEAPONS, 5

Waterloo Every man meets his W.
DEFEAT, 6

waters as the w. cover the sea
PEACE, 2

waves the w. make towards the pebbled shore TIME, 26

way blow out your candle...to find your w. ATHEISM, 3

though hell should bar the w.
DETERMINATION, 5

w. of all flesh HUMAN NATURE, 8

woman has her w. SEXES, 6

weak admiration...of w. minds
BEAUTY, 17

The w. have one weapon
MISTAKES, 1

wealthy some people are very w.
GOVERNMENT, 3

weapon art is not a w. ART, 9

The weak have one w. MISTAKES, 1

thoughtlessness is the w. of the male SEXES, 2

weariness much study is a w. of the flesh BOOKS, 5

weep She must w. or she will die
MOURNING, 5

so that I do not w. LAUGHTER, 2

w. for her sins at the other
ADULTERY, 2

well as w. off as if he were rich
WEALTH, 3

eat wisely but not too w.
ETIQUETTE, 2

reward of a thing w. done
SATISFACTION, 2

The skilful doctor treats those who are w. DOCTORS, 7

We never do anything w.
ACHIEVEMENT, 5

West Go W., young man
EXPLORATION, 1

wheels A cruel story runs on w.
CRUELTY, 4

spoke among your w.
OBSTRUCTION, 2

whimper not with a bang but a w.
ENDING, 3

whipping W. and abuse
PUNISHMENT, 12

whisky A good gulp of hot w. at bedtime ALCOHOL, 12

whisperings Foul w. are abroad
CONSCIENCE, 7

whistle a shrimp learns to w.
COMMUNISM, 5

white I want to be the w. man's brother RACISM, 7

The w. man knows how to make everything CHARITY, 10

When the w. man came we had the land RACISM, 5

whites because the w. oppressed us POWER, 9

the w. of their eyes   WAR, 41

whitewash no w. at the White House   TRUTH, 20

wicked As long as war is regarded as w.   WAR, 60

no peace…unto the w.   PEACE, 7

wickedness capable of every w.   EVIL, 4

more to shape history than…w.   MISTAKES, 10

wife A man should not insult his w. publicly   MARRIAGE, 54

his w. is beautiful   TOLERANCE, 4

Whose w. shall it be   ADULTERY, 3

w. to tell him   LAZINESS, 2

wilderness the w. of this world   WORLD, 7

W. is Paradise   CONTENTMENT, 2

wimp think he is a w.   DRINKS, 4

win Heads I w.   VICTORY, 6

I fight to w.   DETERMINATION, 7

loses if it does not w.   WAR, 31

wind Gone With the W.   TRANSIENCE, 2

what w. is to fire   ABSENCE, 3

wine A Flask of W.   CONTENTMENT, 2

good w. needs no bush   PLAYS, 6

W. comes in at the mouth   AGE, 41

w. is a mocker   DRUNKENNESS, 2

wing on a W. and a Prayer   HOPE, 4

wings Fear lent w.   FEAR, 7

man with w.   FLYING, 3

wins Who dares, w.   COURAGE, 1

winter No one thinks of w.   SEASONS, 2

wise A w. man will make more opportunities   OPPORTUNITY, 1

The only wretched are the w.   IGNORANCE, 7

wiser Be w. than other people   WISDOM, 4

rubbed it into the young that they are w.   OLD AGE, 7

The French are w.   NATIONALITY, 1

wish Justice is the…perpetual w.   JUSTICE, 7

The w. to hurt   CRUELTY, 1

wit a w. out of two half-wits   FOOLISHNESS, 7

Brevity is the soul of w.   BREVITY, 6

fancy w. will come   STUPIDITY, 9

proverb is one man's w.   SAYINGS, 5

witch thou shalt not suffer a w. to live   SUPERNATURAL, 3

witchcraft All w. comes from carnal lust   LUST, 5

Medical science is…w.   MEDICINE, 15

witty a very w. prologue   MARRIAGE, 22

stumbling on something w.   MEN, 1

wives Bricklayers kick their w. to death   CLASS, 25

husbands and w.…belong to different sexes   SEXES, 3

husbands, love your w.   MARRIAGE, 12

through the help of their w.   SUCCESS, 11

you…are the w.   WOMEN, 21

wolf The boy cried 'W., w.!'   LYING, 2

the w. in the sheep's clothing   APPEARANCES, 6

woman As a w. I can't go to war   WAR, 43

A w. who is loved   SUCCESS, 4

body of a weak and feeble w.   ROYALTY, 15

educate a w.   EDUCATION, 14

Every w. knows   ACHIEVEMENT, 1

good w. if I had five thousand   MONEY, 20

If a w. like Eva Peron   IDEALISM, 6

In an uncorrupted w.   SEX, 15

No one ever speaks of 'a beautiful old w.'   OLD AGE, 7

nor w. neither   MANKIND, 20

No w. should ever be quite accurate about her age   AGE, 39

Old age is w.'s hell   OLD AGE, 19

one of w. born   BIRTH, 4

One tongue is sufficient for a w.
                          EDUCATION, 15
romance makes a w. look like a
ruin   MARRIAGE, 57
Sex between a man and a w.   SEX, 3
vengeance than a w.   REVENGE, 5
w. as old as she looks   AGE, 13
w. has her way   SEXES, 6
w.'s heart   SORROW, 9
W.'s virtue is man's greatest
invention   SEXES, 11
womanhood W. is the great fact in
her life   WOMEN, 37
womb mother's w. Untimely
ripp'd   BIRTH, 4
think with our w.   INTELLIGENCE, 2
wonders His w. to perform GOD, 5
workers W. of the world, unite
                           MARXISM, 3
working the w. classes   CLASS, 24
To the ordinary w. man
                         SOCIALISM, 8
worlds best of all possible w.
                          OPTIMISM, 8
destroyer of w.
                 NUCLEAR WEAPONS, 10
So many w.   ACTION, 8
wound Religion...the w.
                          RELIGION, 32
W. with a touch   SATIRE, 2
wreckage Literature is strewn
with the w. of men   WRITERS, 13
Wren Sir Christopher W. Said
                      ARCHITECTURE, 1
write look in thy heart and w.
                       INSPIRATION, 2
w. on both sides   EXAMINATIONS, 2
wrong History is...the w. way of
living   HISTORY, 7

Of course not...I may be w.
                      UNCERTAINTY, 3
Science is always w.   SCIENCE, 30
support me when I am...w.
                          SUPPORT, 2
The right divine of kings to govern
w.   MONARCHY, 5
wrongs the w. of another CLASS, 21
Two w. do not make a right
                         MISTAKES, 1
yacht sink my y.   PARTIES, 3
years how many y. can some
people exist   FREEDOM, 6
thousand y. more   MANKIND, 25
yellow Y. Brick Road   TRAVEL, 9
yesterday Y., all my troubles
                         NOSTALGIA, 4
yeti appeal to a Y. CIVILIZATION, 4
yield To strive, to seek...and not
to y.   DETERMINATION, 6
yoghurt more on a month-old
carton of y.   ROYALTY, 21
Yorick Alas, poor Y.   MOURNING, 4
you Your country needs Y.   WAR, 3
young about looking y.   AGE, 21
get y. at the age of sixty   YOUTH, 10
Grieve not that I die y.   DEATH, 19
to make me y. again   SURVIVAL, 1
y. men to die   DIPLOMACY, 1
Y. people ought not to be idle
                         IDLENESS, 6
yourself If you hate a person, you
hate...y.   HATE, 3
What you do not want done to y.
                         EXAMPLE, 3
zeal stir up the z. of women
                        FEMINISM, 4
zebra white horse...could be a z.
                       APPEARANCE, 9
zipless The z. fuck   SEX, 26

NAME INDEX

2; DISABILITY, 1; GOOD AND EVIL, 1; HISTORY, 3; HUNTING, 1; LOVE, 8; OPERA, 3; POETRY, 1; PROSE, 1; SCIENTISTS, 1; SIN, 2; TASTE, 1; WAR, 5; WRITING, 2

Augustine of Hippo, St
AUTHORITARIANISM, 1; PROCRASTINATION, 3; RELIGION, 3; VICE, 1

Austen, Jane
CONCEIT, 1; FLATTERY, 2; HUMAN NATURE, 1; MARRIAGE, 6, 7; MEN, 1; NASTINESS, 1; PARTIES, 1; PLAYS, 2; PLEASURE, 2; RIDICULE, 1; WEATHER, 3; WOMEN, 6

Austin, Warren
DIPLOMACY, 1; RELIGION, 4

Ayckbourn, Alan
RIDICULE, 2

Ayer, A. J. MORALITY, 1; PHILOSOPHY, 1; PUBLISHING, 2

Babbage, Charles
LIFE AND DEATH, 3

Bacall, Lauren AGE, 4

Bacon, Francis AGE, 5; ATHEISM, 2; BEAUTY, 5; BOOKS, 3; CERTAINTY, 1; CHARITY, 3; CHILDREN, 4; COURTESY, 2; DEATH, 8, 9; DISEASE, 4; EDUCATION, 2; EXTRAVAGANCE, 1; FAME, 2; FEAR, 2; HOUSES, 1; HUMAN NATURE, 2; INTEGRITY, 1; KNOWLEDGE, 3; LOVE, 5; MARRIAGE, 8; NATIONALITY, 1; OPPORTUNITY, 6; READING, 1; REMEDIES, 3; REVENGE, 2; TIME, 6; VIRTUE, 1

Bacon, Roger
MATHEMATICS, 1

Baez, Joan LIFE, 7

Baldwin, James
CHILDREN, 5; DISILLUSION, 1; MONEY, 4; RACISM, 1; SLAVERY, 1

Baldwin, Stanley
DIPLOMACY, 2; FREEDOM, 1; SAYINGS, 1; WAR, 6

Balfour, Arthur
ENTHUSIASM, 1; HISTORY, 4; JOURNALISM, 2; TRIVIALITY, 1

Balzac, Honoré de DETERMINATION, 2; EQUALITY, 4; MARRIAGE, 9

Bankhead, Tallulah
DIARIES, 1; PURITY, 1; SEX, 4; THEATRE, 2

Barker, Howard
SOCIETY, 1

Barker, Ronnie
HUMOUR, 2

Barnes, Julian AGE, 6; CERTAINTY, 2; HAPPINESS, 2; LOVE, 10; RELIGION, 5

Barnum, Phineas Taylor
GULLIBILITY, 1

Barrie, J. M.
ACHIEVEMENT, 1; CLASS, 3; DEATH, 10; FAIRIES, 1; MOTIVE, 1; SELF-CONFIDENCE, 1; SMOKING, 2; WRITING, 3

Baruch, Bernard
COLD WAR, 1; OLD AGE, 6

Bashkirtseff, Marie
INJUSTICE, 1

Baudelaire, Charles
BEGINNING, 2; SEX, 5

Beaumarchais
LAUGHTER, 2; MANKIND, 3

Beaumont, Francis
ACTION, 2; HURT, 1; INDIFFERENCE, 1; OBSTRUCTION, 1

Beauvoir, Simone de
AGE, 7; DISILLUSION, 2; HAPPINESS, 3; OLD AGE, 7; SOCIETY, 2; TRUTH, 13; WOMEN, 7, 8

Beaverbrook, Lord
JOURNALISM, 3; SELF-RELIANCE, 2; TYRANNY, 1

Beckett, Samuel
MADNESS, 1

Beecham, Thomas
MUSIC, 2, 3; SMOKING, 3; TRAVEL, 4

Beerbohm, Max ART, 2; CLASSICS, 1; COSMETICS, 1; CRICKET, 1; EXPERIENCE, 4; ORIGINALITY, 1; SUBJECTIVITY, 1

Beethoven, Ludwig van
MUSIC, 4

Behan, Brendan CHILDREN, 6; JUSTICE, 1; MARRIAGE, 10; POLICE, 1; VIOLENCE, 3

Behn, Aphra LOVE, 11

Bell, Alexander Graham
SUMMONS, 1

Belloc, Hilaire
ARISTOCRACY, 2; BOOKS, 6; CRITICISM, 1; DOCTORS, 4; DRINKS, 1; HEROISM, 2; POWER POLITICS, 1; PUNS, 1

Benn, Tony MARXISM, 1; PHOTOGRAPHY, 1

Bennett, Alan
CHILDREN, 7; LIFE, 8

Bennett, Arnold JOURNALISM, 4; PESSIMISM, 1; PREJUDICE, 1; PROGRESS, 1; TASTE, 2

Benny, Jack MERIT, 2

Bentham, Jeremy
LAWYERS, 2

Bentley, Edmund
ARCHITECTURE, 1

Bergerac, Cyrano de
REVENGE, 4

Bergman, Ingrid
ACTING, 2

Berlin, Irving
CHRISTMAS, 2; NAVY, 1;
POPULAR MUSIC, 2

Berlioz, Hector TIME, 9

Bernhardt, Sarah
ACTING, 4; CRICKET, 2

Berra, Yogi SPORT
AND GAMES, 2

Berry, Chuck
POPULAR MUSIC, 3

Bertolucci, Bernardo
CHILDREN, 8

Betjeman, John
BUSINESS, 2; POETRY, 5

Bevan, Aneurin
INCOMPETENCE, 1;
RIGHTEOUSNESS, 1;
SOCIALISM, 1

Bevin, Ernest
CONSERVATISM, 1;
MIXED METAPHORS, 1

Bierce, Ambrose ACCI-
DENTS, 1; DOCTORS, 5;
EGOTISM, 1; IGNOR-
ANCE, 3; LOGIC, 1;
LONGEVITY, 1; MAN-
KIND, 4; MEDICINE, 4;
MISFORTUNE, 2; PAINT-
ING, 2; PATIENCE, 6;
PHILOSOPHERS, 1;
PRAYER, 1; RELIGION, 6

Birt, John
JOURNALISM, 6

Bismarck CHILDREN,
11; POLITICS, 7; WAR, 7

Blackstone, William
JUSTICE, 2; SOCIETY, 2

Blade, Toledo MIND, 1

Blair, Tony
UNEMPLOYMENT, 1

Blake, Eubie MUSIC, 5

Blake, William
ACTION, 3; ANIMALS, 4;
BEAUTY, 6; CREATION, 1;
DESIRE, 1, 2; EFFORT, 2;
EXCESS, 3; GENERAL-
IZATIONS, 1; GOOD, 2;
HUMILITY, 1; HYPO-
CRISY, 1; IMPRISON-
MENT, 1; LIFE, 10; LOVE,
14; PRAYER, 2; SORROW,
2; SOUL, 2; TRUTH, 7;
WISDOM, 3; WONDER, 1

Blank, Joost de OP-
PRESSION, 3; RACISM, 3

Bleasdale, Alan
UNEMPLOYMENT, 2

Blixen, Karen
MANKIND, 5

Boccaccio, Giovanni
RIDICULE, 3

Bogart, Humphrey
ADMIRATION, 1;
CHANCE, 1;
MISQUOTATIONS, 6

Bohr, Niels EXPERTS,
1; SUPERSTITION, 1

Boileau, Nicolas
ADMIRATION, 2;
IDLENESS, 2; VICE, 2

Boleyn, Anne
MARTYRDOM, 1

Bonaparte, Lucien
TYRANNY, 2

Bono, Edward de
DISAPPOINTMENT, 1

Boone, Daniel
CONFUSION, 1

Boorstin, Daniel J.
BOOKS, 8; FAME, 3

Borge, Victor
REMEDIES, 4

Borges, Jorge Luis
MARTYRDOM, 1;
TRANSLATION, 1;

UNCERTAINTY, 2;
UNIVERSE, 2

Bowen, Elizabeth
ART, 3; INNOCENCE, 1;
JEALOUSY, 3; WOMEN, 9

Bowra, Maurice
FOOD, 2; MARRIAGE, 15

Boyle, Robert
SCIENCE, 1

Bradbury, Malcolm
COURTESY, 3; FRIEND-
SHIP, 3; LIBERALISM, 1;
MARRIAGE, 16;
NEWSPAPERS, 1; SEX, 6;
SYMPATHY, 1

Bragg, Melvyn
PATRIOTISM, 2

Brahms, Johannes
INSULTS, 2

Brand, Jo VIOLENCE, 2

Brando, Marlon
ACTING, 3; ACTORS, 1

Branson, Richard
LEADERSHIP, 2

Braun, Wernher von
WEAPONS, 2

Brecht, Bertolt FRIEND-
SHIP, 4; HEROISM, 3;
HUNGER, 2; INJUSTICE, 3;
PEACE, 5; SURVIVAL, 1;
VIRTUE, 3; WAR, 9

Brittain, Vera POLI-
TICS, 8; WRITERS, 2

Bronowski, Jacob
CRUELTY, 1; SCIENCE, 2

Brontë, Emily BELIEF,
3; IMPRISONMENT, 2

Brooke, Rupert WAR, 10

Brooks, Mel OSTEN-
TATION, 1; THEATRE, 1

Brown, Helen Gurley
SEX, 7; VIRTUE AND
VICE, 1

Browne, Thomas
CHARITY, 6; DEATH, 13;
INDIVIDUALITY, 2;

MANKIND, 6; SELF, 5; WORLD, 1

Browning, Robert
AGE, 10; AMBITION, 3; ANIMALS, 7; BETRAYAL, 2; DAMNATION, 1; FREEDOM, 2; HORSES, 2; HUMAN CONDITION, 1; NOVELS, 1; POSSIBILITY, 1; ROYALTY, 1; SUMMONS; WORDS, 3

Bruce, Lenny
RELIGION, 7

Bruno, Frank SUCCESS, 5

Buck, Pearl FAITH, 3; KILLING, 2; UNIVERSE, 3

Buddha RELIGION, 8; RIGHTEOUSNESS, 2

Bukovsky, Vladimir
OPTIMISM, 7

Bunyan, John
DESPAIR, 2; DREAMS, 1; WORLD, 2

Burgess, Anthony
CLEANNESS, 2; FUTURE, 2; SEX, 8; SLEEP, 4

Burke, Edmund
COMPROMISE, 1; CORRUPTION, 1; DANGER, 2; EXAMPLE, 2; FREEDOM, 3; POWER, 5; PUBLIC, 3; RELIGION, 9; ROYALTY, 8; SUCCESS, 6; SUPERSTITION, 2; THEORY, 1

Burns, George
GOVERNMENT, 5

Burns, Robert
ACTION, 4; ANIMALS, 6; CRUELTY, 2; DELUSION, 1; DEVIL, 4; DISAPPOINTMENT, 2; FOOD, 4; FRIENDSHIP, 5; LOVE, 15; MEN, 2; SATISFACTION, 1

Burton, Richard
ACTORS, 2

Burton, Robert
MELANCHOLY, 2;

RELIGION, 10; SMOKING, 4; WRITING, 4

Bush, George WAR, 11, 12

Bussy-Rabutin
ABSENCE, 1

Butler, Samuel AGE, 11; DOGS, 1; EVOLUTION, 1; FAMILY, 4; HATE, 1; HYPOCRISY, 3; ILLNESS, 5; LEARNING, 3; LIFE, 11, 12; LOSS, 1; LOVE, 16; MEDICINE, 5; MONEY, 6; PLEASURE, 3; PRAISE, 3; SPONTANEITY, 1; TRUTH, 9; VIRTUE AND VICE, 2; WOMEN, 10

Byatt, A. S.
MOTHERHOOD, 2

Byron, Lord
ADULTERY, 1; AGE, 12; ALCOHOL, 2; BEAUTY, 7; BOOKS, 6; BORES, 2; FREEDOM, 2; LONGEVITY, 3; NOSTALGIA, 1; PLEASURE, 4; THEATRE, 4; TRUTH, 10, 11; WEALTH, 5

Caesar, Julius IRREVOCABILITY, 1; VICTORY, 1

Cage, John POETRY, 6

Cagney, James
MISQUOTATIONS, 7

Cahn, Sammy LOVE AND MARRIAGE, 1

Caligula
RUTHLESSNESS, 1

Callaghan, James
LYING, 4; SUPPORT, 1

Calvin, John
RELIGION, 11

Campbell, Mrs Patrick
MARRIAGE, 17; SEX, 9

Campbell, Thomas
SELFISHNESS, 2; TREES, 2

Camus, Albert ARROGANCE, 1; COMMITMENT, 2; MANKIND, 7;

MONEY, 7; POLITICS, 10; REBELLION, 1; REVOLUTION, 2; SLAVERY, 4; SUICIDE, 3; WORK, 3

Canetti, Elias
ANIMALS, 7; SAYINGS, 2

Capone, Al MURDER, 2; PLACES, 3

Capote, Truman
WRITING, 5

Carey, George
CHURCH, 2; CLERGY, 6; COMMERCIALISM, 1; RELIGION, 13; SIN, 5

Carlyle, Thomas
BELIEF, 4; BOOKS, 7; ECONOMICS, 2; EDUCATION, 3; GENIUS, 1; GREATNESS, 1; LEADERSHIP, 3; POETS, 2; PUBLIC, 4; SLAVERY, 5; STATISTICS, 1; TECHNOLOGY, 2; UNIVERSE, 4

Carroll, Lewis CURIOSITY, 2; EXECUTION, 3; LIFE, 14; LOGIC, 2; OLD AGE, 10; SEASIDE, 2

Carson, Rachel
ECOLOGY, 1

Carter, Angela APPEARANCE, 3; COMPROMISE, 2; FICTION, 2; HUMOUR, 3; MARRIAGE, 18; OPTIMISM, 10; PAST, 2

Castro, Fidel
REVOLUTION, 3

Catherine the Great
ROYALTY, 9

Catullus LOVE AND HATE, 1; POETRY, 7

Cervantes, Miguel de
CHARACTER, 2; FEAR, 3; LANGUAGE, 3; MADNESS, 2; TACT, 1

Cézanne, Paul
PAINTING, 3

Chamberlain, Neville WORLD WAR II, 2

Chandler, Raymond GRAMMAR, 1; PLACES, 4

Chanel, Coco FASHION, 1; YOUTH, 2

Chaplin, Charlie LUXURY, 1

Charles V LANGUAGE, 4; VICTORY, 2

Charles, Prince of Wales ARCHITECTURE, 2; GARDENS, 3; MARRIAGE, 19; MONARCHY, 3; ROYALTY, 10, 11

Charlton, Jack MEDIA, 2

Chaucer, Geoffrey ALCOHOL, 4; APPEARANCES, 7; CREATION, 4; EDUCATION, 4; LIFE AND DEATH, 5; MATERIALISM, 3; MURDER, 3

Chekhov, Anton DOCTORS, 6

Chesterton, G. K. ANIMALS, 8; ARISTOCRACY, 4; CHARITY, 1; CHRISTIANITY, 8; CIVILIZATION, 2; COMPROMISE, 2; CONSERVATISM, 2; DEMOCRACY, 2; EDUCATION, 5; EMOTION, 1; HAPPINESS, 4; HOPE, 5; JOURNALISM, 7; LANGUAGE, 5; LOGIC, 3; MADNESS, 3; MATERIALISM, 4; NATURE, 2; OBESITY, 2; OPINIONS, 3; PATRIOTISM, 4; PROGRESS, 2; PSYCHOLOGY, 2; REASON, 1; TRAVEL, 5, 6; TRUTH, 12; WEALTH, 7

Chevalier, Maurice LOVE, 17; OLD AGE, 11

Chou En Lai DIPLOMACY, 11

Christie, Agatha

HABIT, 2; INTELLECT, 1; MARRIAGE, 20; MONEY, 8; PRINCIPLES, 3

Churchill, Jennie Jerome AMBITION, 4; LOVE AND MARRIAGE, 2

Churchill, Lord MATHEMATICS, 2

Churchill, Winston ALCOHOL, 9; AUTHORITARIANISM, 3; BETRAYAL, 3; CLASSICS, 2; COLD WAR, 2; DEATH, 14; DESTINY, 4; DETERMINATION, 4; DIPLOMACY, 3, 4; EFFORT, 3; GRAMMAR, 2; LAST WORDS, 7; LEARNING, 4; LYING, 3; NAVY, 2; NEWSPAPERS, 2; NOSTALGIA, 2; NUCLEAR WEAPONS, 4; PLACES, 5; POLITICS, 11; PROSE, 2; RESPONSIBILITY, 2; SPEECHES, 2; VICTORY, 3; WATER, 1; WORLD WAR II, 3, 4, 5, 6, 7, 8; WORRY, 3

Ciano, Count Galeazzo DEFEAT, 1

Cibber, Colley FASHION, 2; THEFT, 2

Cicero GOOD, 3; LAW, 3; PHILOSOPHERS, 2; PSYCHIATRY, 6

Clarke, Arthur C. SCIENCE, 3; TECHNOLOGY, 3

Clarke, Kenneth PUBLIC, 5

Clausewitz, Karl von WAR, 14

Clemenceau, Georges OFFICERS, 2; OLD AGE, 12; WAR, 15

Clinton, Hillary CONFUSION, 3

Cocteau, Jean

APPEARANCE, 4; ART, 4; POETRY, 8; POETS, 3; TACT, 2

Cohen, Leonard LOVE, 18

Coleridge, Samuel Taylor BIRTH, 2; BOATS, 1; CHRISTIANITY, 5; HUMOUR, 2; IMAGINATION, 1; MARRIAGE, 21; PLEASURE, 5; POETRY, 9; POETRY AND PROSE, 1; SINCERITY, 1; SOLITUDE, 1; WATER, 2; WISDOM, 5; WRITERS, 3

Colette APPEARANCE, 5; CLASS, 5; HUMOUR, 7; SMOKING, 5

Confucius ACHIEVEMENT, 3; CAUTION, 5; EXAMPLE, 3; FRIENDS, 3; HABIT, 3; IMPERFECTION, 2; KINDNESS, 3; PAST, 3; SERVILITY, 1; UNDERSTANDING, 2

Congreve, William AGREEMENT, 1; LOVE, 19; MARRIAGE, 22; MUSIC, 6; SECRECY, 4

Connolly, Billy COMMERCIALISM, 2; MARRIAGE, 23

Connolly, Cyril LONGEVITY, 4; OBESITY, 3, 4; PASSION, 3; PUBLISHING, 3; SELF, 6; SEXES, 2; SUICIDE, 6; TALENT, 2; WRITERS, 4; WRITING, 6

Constable, John BEAUTY, 8

Cook, James DISCOVERY, 2

Cook, Peter THEATRE, 5; UNIVERSE, 5

Cooke, Alistair POPULAR MUSIC, 4

Coolidge, Calvin

7; MONEY, 10; POVERTY, 8; WORDS, 6

Franklin, Benjamin AGE, 18; BUSINESS, 6, 7; DOCTORS, 8; HOPE, 6; NEGLECT, 1; PURPOSE, 1; SECRECY, 5; TAXATION, 3; TECHNOLOGY, 4; UNITY, 6; WAR AND PEACE, 5; WISDOM, 7

Frederick the Great ROYALTY, 19; WAR, 23

French, Marilyn MEN, 3

Freud, Clement ABSTINENCE, 2; PLACES, 6

Freud, Sigmund BELIEF, 6; DESTINY, 5; GOD, 7; INTELLECT, 3; MIND, 4; PSYCHIATRY, 7

Friedman, Milton ECONOMICS, 5

Frost, Robert CHANGE, 6; HOME, 5; SURVIVAL, 3; TRANSLATION, 3; WORK, 4; YOUTH, 5

Fry, Christopher NOSTALGIA, 1; POETRY, 13; SLEEP, 6

Fry, Elizabeth PUNISHMENT, 5

Fry, Stephen TRUTH, 15

Gabor, Zsa Zsa MARRIAGE, 29; MATERIALISM, 5; SEX, 18

Galen HOPE, 7; WORK, 6

Gallo, José SOCIALISM, 4

Galsworthy, John LAW, 6; SECRECY, 6; WEAKNESS, 2

Gandhi, Indira CHILDREN, 14; LAST WORDS, 14; RELIGION, 18

Gandhi, Mahatma MATERIALISM, 6; RELIGION, 19; VIOLENCE, 5

Garbo, Greta MISQUOTATIONS, 10; SEX, 19

Gardner, John W. HISTORY, 9; POVERTY, 9

Garfield, James A. ASSASSINATION, 2

Garfield, Leon APPEARANCES, 10

Garland, Judy CINEMA, 9

Gaskell, Elizabeth PATRIOTISM, 5

Gasset, José Ortega y VIOLENCE, 9

Gay, John ENVY, 3; SORROW, 7; WOMEN, 19

Geldof, Bob FAME, 6

Gell-Mann, Murray ECOLOGY, 2

George V FAMILY, 9; POVERTY, 10

Getty, J. Paul WEALTH, 10

Gibbon, Edward CORRUPTION, 2; PROGRESS, 5

Gibran, Kahlil CHILDREN, 15; CONSERVATION, 5; LOVE, 24; UNITY, 7

Gide, André KINDNESS, 4; OPPOSITES, 1; SORROW, 8; SPONTANEITY, 2

Gielgud, John CINEMA, 7; LITERATURE, 3

Gilbert, W. S. BOATS, 3; COWARDICE, 3; EVOLUTION, 5; INDIFFERENCE, 2; LAW, 7; PLACES, 7; POLICE, 2; POLITICIANS, 9; TITLES, 2

Gladstone, William CLASS, 7; PROGRESS, 6

Gleick, James NATURE, 5; SCIENCE, 15

Godard, Jean-Luc CINEMA, 8, 9

Goering, Hermann PHILISTINISM, 2; POWER POLITICS, 2; WORLD WAR II, 10

Goethe BEGINNING, 6; CHARACTER, 4; DISCOVERY, 4; ILLNESS, 8; LAST WORDS, 16; MORTALITY, 3; OLD AGE, 14; PURPOSE, 2; SCIENCE, 16; SUPERSTITION, 3; THEORY, 3

Golding, William EVOLUTION, 6; INNOCENCE, 2; REVOLUTION, 5

Goldsmith, James BEAUTY, 11; BUSINESS, 8

Goldsmith, Oliver ALCOHOL, 14; CONSCIENCE, 3; DEATH, 17, 18; DOGS, 3; GENIUS, 3; LAW, 8; PHILOSOPHERS, 3; SPEECH, 3

Goldwyn, Samuel CINEMA, 10; MIXED METAPHORS, 2; PSYCHIATRY, 8

Gorbachov, Mikhail DEMOCRACY, 5; SOCIALISM, 5; TOLERANCE, 2

Gordimer, Nadine CHANGE, 7

Gorky, Maxim GOOD AND EVIL, 3; WORK, 7; WRITING, 8

Grable, Betty SUCCESS, 9

Grace, W. G. CRICKET, 3

Grade, Lew PLAYS, 4

Graf, Steffi FAILURE, 4

Graham, Billy RELIGION, 20

Grahame, Kenneth

BOATS, 3; KNOWLEDGE, 8; VICE, 4

Graves, Robert LOVE, 25; POETS, 5

Greeley, Horace EXPLORATION, 1

Greene, Graham COMMITMENT, 4; FAME, 7; MADNESS, 8; SENTIMENTALITY, 1; WEALTH, 11

Greer, Germaine CHILDREN, 16; FEMINISM, 2, 3; MEN, 4; MOTHERHOOD, 5; PSYCHIATRY, 9; SEX, 20; WOMAN'S ROLE, 3

Greville, Fulke HUMAN CONDITION, 7

Grimké, Sarah Moore VIOLENCE, 6

Grisham, John WRITING, 9

Gropius, Walter ARCHITECTURE, 3

Guedalla, Philip BOATS, 4; PUNS, 4; WORLD WAR II, 11

Guevara, Che REVOLUTION, 4

Haig, Douglas WORLD WAR I, 5

Hailsham, Lord BOREDOM, 3; SINCERITY, 2

Haldane, J. B. S. ARISTOCRACY, 5; UNIVERSE, 7

Halifax, Lord POPULARITY, 2; REBELLION, 2; VIRTUE AND VICE, 3

Hall, Jerry WOMEN, 22

Hammarskjöld, Dag LONELINESS, 2; OLD AGE, 15; PRAYER, 3

Hammerstein, Oscar DAY, 2; LOVE, 26; MUSIC, 10; REASON, 2

Hampton, Christopher

Hancock, John SIGNATURES, 2

Hardy, Oliver ACCIDENTS, 4

Hardy, Thomas POETRY, 15

Hare, David NEWSPAPERS, 4; RELIGION, 21; WRITING, 10

Haw-Haw, Lord TREASON, 3

Hawthorne, Nathaniel AFTERLIFE, 2

Hay, Ian HUMOUR, 9

Hay, Will SCIENCE, 17

Hazlitt, William ACHIEVEMENT, 5; ANGER, 5; CLOTHES, 5; COUNTRYSIDE, 3; DISCONTENT, 2; FREEDOM, 8; INTELLECT, 4; LAST WORDS, 18; LIFE AND DEATH, 8; NAMES, 1; RULES, 2; SELF-INTEREST, 2; SOLITUDE, 3; THINKING, 2; VIRTUE, 5; YOUTH, 7

Hegel LAST WORDS, 19; UNDERSTANDING, 3

Heine, Heinrich CENSORSHIP, 3

Heinlein, Robert SPACE, 4

Heisenberg, Werner EXPERTS, 3

Heller, Joseph IMMORTALITY, 2; LITERATURE, 4; MEDIOCRITY, 3; SELF-MADE MEN, 2

Hemingway, Ernest DEFEAT, 4; MORALITY, 3; SEX, 22

Hendrix, Jimi DEATH, 20

Henri IV CONSCIENCE, 4

Henry II ASSASSINATION, 3; CORRUPTION, 3; GUILT, 2

Henry, O. WOMEN, 23

Henry, Patrick FREEDOM, 9

Heraclitus CHANGE, 8, 9

Herbert, A. P. BABIES, 3; LAW, 9; MARRIAGE, 30; PLEASURE, 6

Herbert, George DAY, 3; GUILT, 3

Herodotus WORLD-WEARINESS, 2

Hesiod MARRIAGE, 31

Hesse, Hermann HATE, 3

Hill, Aaron DECISION, 1

Hillary, Edmund ACHIEVEMENT, 6; CIVILIZATION, 4

Hillingdon, Lady Alice MISQUOTATIONS, 11

Hippocrates ALCOHOL, 15; DOCTORS, 9; MEDICINE, 8; OPINIONS, 3; REMEDIES, 10

Hirohito WORLD WAR II, 12

Hitchcock, Alfred ACTORS, 3; CINEMA, 11; POLITICS, 13

Hitler, Adolf AMBITION, 7; DESTINY, 6; FASCISM, 2; LYING, 7; PATIENCE, 8; POLITICS, 14; PROPAGANDA, 2; PUBLIC, 7; RACISM, 6; WAR, 25; WORLD WAR II, 13, 14

Hobbes, Thomas LAST WORDS, 20; OPINIONS, 4; TRUTH, 16

Hockney, David ART, 8

Hoffer, Eric IMITATION, 3; YOUTH, 8

Joad, Cyril ECOLOGY, 3; KNOWLEDGE, 11

Joel, Billy POPULAR MUSIC, 7

John Paul II MEN, 5; WAR, 28

Johnson, Amy FLYING, 1

Johnson, Hiram WAR, 29

Johnson, Lyndon B. AMBITION, 8; POVERTY, 13; PRUDENCE, 5; REASON, 3; STUPIDITY, 3

Johnson, Samuel CLERGY, 4; CLOTHES, 6; CONVERSATION, 2; CRITICISM, 5; CRITICS, 4; DEATH, 23; DECEPTION, 3; DETERMINATION, 3; DISILLUSION, 3; EDUCATION, 11; EXPECTATION, 1; FLATTERY, 3; FRIENDSHIP, 8; HUMOUR, 10; IDLENESS, 5; INSINCERITY, 2; INTEGRITY, 2; KNOWLEDGE, 12; LANGUAGE, 9; LONGEVITY, 5; LUST, 3; MARRIAGE, 32; MISTRUST, 3; MUSIC, 12; NUMBERS, 1; PATRIOTISM, 8; PLEASURE, 7; SEA, 3; TRUST, 2; WEATHER, 6; WRITERS, 3

Jong, Erica COSMETICS, 2; SEX, 26

Jonson, Ben CLASSICS, 3; FUNERALS, 2; INSULTS, 5; LOVE, 28; LUCK, 2; SPEECH, 4

Jowett, Benjamin FAITH, 4; RESEARCH, 2; SELFLESSNESS, 2

Joyce, James HISTORY, 12; INFLUENCE, 3; SCIENCE, 20; SEA, 4; TIME, 15

Jung, Carl Gustav EXISTENCE, 3; HUMAN NATURE, 5; INFERIORITY, 1; MADNESS, 10; MIND, 7; NEUROSIS, 1; PASSION, 3; PLACES, 8; PSYCHOLOGY, 4; SENTIMENTALITY, 2

Junius MEDIA, 4; PERSUASION, 2

Juvenal AUTHORITARIANISM, 4; CHILDREN, 19; DEBAUCHERY, 3; MISTRUST, 4; POVERTY, 14; REVENGE, 5; SATIRE, 1; THEFT, 3

Kafka, Franz DESPAIR, 3; FREEDOM, 10

Kant, Immanuel HAPPINESS, 7; HUMAN NATURE, 6; WONDER, 2

Kaufman, George S. EPITAPHS, 4

Keats, John ADMIRATION, 3; ALCOHOL, 18; ARGUMENTS, 4; BEAUTY, 14, 15; DISCONTENT, 3; EXPERIENCE, 7; HUMAN NATURE, 7; MELANCHOLY, 3; SLEEP, 9; TIME, 16; TRAVEL, 10; TRUTH, 17

Keith, Penelope SHYNESS, 3

Keller, Helen BLINDNESS, 4; CAPITALISM, 5; COURAGE, 8

Kennedy, J. F. ART, 9; BEGINNING, 4; DIPLOMACY, 9; HUNGER, 6; KNOWLEDGE, 13; MERIT, 3; OLD AGE, 13; PEACE, 7; POPULARITY, 4; SOCIETY, 8; TIME, 17

Kennedy, Joseph P. REVENGE, 6

Kennedy, Robert OPPOSITION, 2

Kerouac, Jack CONFUSION, 5

Kerr, Jean ALCOHOL, 19; CHILDREN, 20; FLYING, 2; HYPOCRISY, 5; MONEY, 13

Key, Ellen CHILDREN, 21; PUNISHMENT, 7

Keynes, John Maynard CONSERVATISM, 3; NUMBERS, 2; ORTHODOXY, 2; TAXATION, 5; TYRANNY, 6

Khomeini, Ayatollah CENSORSHIP, 7

Khrushchev, Nikita BUSINESS, 10; COMMUNISM, 4, 5; POLITICIANS, 17; VICTORY, 8

Kierkegaard, Søren DEATH, 25; ENDURANCE, 3

King, Benjamin Franklin PESSIMISM, 3

King, Martin Luther EQUALITY, 10; EVIL, 5; IDEALISM, 2; IGNORANCE, 5; RACISM, 7; REBELLION, 5; SCIENCE, 21; WAR, 30

Kingsley, Charles CHIVALRY, 2

Kinnock, Neil FOOLISHNESS, 7

Kipling, Rudyard ART, 10; OBITUARIES, 2; RESPONSIBILITY, 4; SEASONS, 2; SELF-CONTROL, 4; SOLDIERS, 1; SUPERIORITY, 2; WORLD WAR I, 6

Kissinger, Henry ENEMIES, 3; MODERATION, 3; POWER, 7; WAR, 31

Klerk, F. W. de PROGRESS, 4

Klinger, Friedrich LITERATURE, 6

Knox, Ronald BABIES, 4; DEVIL, 5; EXISTENCE, 4

Kollwitz, Käthe WAR, 32

Korda, Alexander TALENT, 4

Kostalenetz, André MUSICIANS, 3

Kubrick, Stanley DIPLOMACY, 10

La Bruyère, Jean de ALCOHOL, 21; CRIME, 1; CRITICISM, 6; ILLNESS, 4; LAUGHTER, 3; MEMORY, 3; SUCCESS, 10

Laing, R. D. BOOKS, 13; MADNESS, 11; PSYCHIATRY, 10; VIOLENCE, 8

Lamb, Charles BOOKS, 14; BORROWING, 6; CHILDREN, 23; MODERATION, 4; POSTERITY, 3; PUNS, 7; SPORT AND GAMES, 7

Lambert, Rex TELEVISION, 5

Lamont, Norman GOVERNMENT, 8

Landor, Walter Savage GOOD, 4; POETRY AND PROSE, 6; WRITING, 12

Landseer, Edwin PAINTING, 5

Laplace, Marquis de GOD, 9

Lara, Brian CRICKET, 4

Larkin, Philip BOOKS, 15; CHILDREN, 24; FAMILY, 10; HUMAN CONDITION, 4; MARRIAGE, 34; NOTHING, 2; NOVELS, 4; SEX, 27

Laski, H. HUMILITY, 4

Laurence, William L. NUCLEAR WEAPONS, 8

Lawrence, D. H. DEATH, 26; IDEALISM, 3; MEN, 4; MORALITY, 4; PROMISCUITY, 3; PUN-

ISHMENT, 8; PURITANISM, 2; SCIENCE, 22; SEX, 28; SIN, 9; WORLD WAR I, 7; WRITING, 13

Lawrence, T. E. LIFE AND DEATH, 9

Leacock, Stephen CLASSICS, 4; DEATH, 27; LOVE AND MARRIAGE, 4; LUCK, 3

Lebowitz, Fran BOOKS, 16; FOOD, 7; LIFE, 23

Le Corbusier HOUSES, 2

Lee-Potter, Linda SUCCESS, 11

Lehrer, Tom AGE, 22; LIFE, 24; SEX, 30

Le Mesurier, John LAST WORDS, 23

Lenin CAPITALISM, 6; CLASS, 9; COMMUNISM, 6; DEMOCRACY, 5; FREEDOM, 12; LIBERALISM, 2; SOCIALISM, 6; STATE, 1

Lennon, John AGE, 23; COSMETICS, 3; FRIENDS, 5; LIFE, 25; LONELINESS, 4; LOVE, 29; MONEY, 14; NOSTALGIA, 6; POPULARITY, 5; WEALTH, 13

Leonardo da Vinci DEATH, 48; FLYING, 3; THEORY, 6

Lessing, Doris CATS, 2; LAW, 10; LEARNING, 6; RACISM, 8

Lewis, C. Day DECLINE, 2

Lewis, C. S. FRIENDSHIP, 6; HUMOUR, 11; TIME, 18

Lewis, Sinclair LITERATURE, 6; UNDERSTANDING, 6

Lewis, Wyndham MARTYRDOM, 3

Lin, Maya ARCHITECTURE, 4

Lincoln, Abraham APPEARANCE, 10; CRITICISM, 7; DECEPTION, 4; DEMOCRACY, 6, 7, 8; FREEDOM, 13

Linklater, Eric STUPIDITY, 5

Linkletter, Art AGE, 24

Lin Yutang FOOD, 9

Livy DEFEAT, 5

Llosa, Mario Vargas POLITICS, 26

Lloyd, Marie PLEASURE, 8; TRAVEL, 12

Lloyd George, David ARISTOCRACY, 6; CHANGE, 11; POLITICIANS, 8; STATISTICS, 8; WAR, 34; WOMEN, 27

Locke, John GOVERNMENT, 9; NOVELTY, 3

Lodge, David CHILDREN, 25; EDUCATION, 13; LITERATURE, 8, 9; WRITERS, 7

Longfellow, Henry AMBITION, 9; CHANCE, 2; ENDURANCE, 4

Longford, Lord SEX, 32

Loos, Anita MATERIALISM, 9; WOMEN, 28

Lorenz, Konrad MANKIND, 13; THEORY, 7

Louis XIV LAST WORDS, 24; ROYALTY, 22

Lucretius NOTHING, 1; PERSISTENCE, 5; TASTE, 3

Luther, Martin RELIGION, 25

Macaulay, Lord BETRAYAL, 5; MORALITY, 5; POETRY, 17; POLITICS, 17

Macaulay, Rose FAMILY, 12; POETRY, 18; TRAVEL, 13

MacCarthy, Desmond OSTENTATION, 2

McCarthy, Joseph R. COMMUNISM, 7

McCarthy, Mary DECISION, 3; NEUROSIS, 3

McCartney, Paul PEACE, 8

MacDonald, Ramsey DIPLOMACY, 13

McGinley, Phyllis SIN, 10; SUCCESS, 14

Machiavelli CHURCH, 4

MacInnes, Colin ART, 12; RACISM, 9

McKellen, Ian HOMOSEXUALITY, 6

McLuhan, Marshall COMMUNICATION, 3; PSYCHIATRY, 12; TECHNOLOGY, 6; TRAVEL, 15

Macmillan, Harold CHANGE, 12; ECONOMICS, 6; POLITICIANS, 9; POLITICS, 18; PURPOSE, 4

Maeterlinck, Maurice LIFE, 26

Mailer, Norman FACTS, 4; MARRIAGE, 35

Mamet, David THEATRE, 7

Mandela, Nelson FREEDOM, 15; RACISM, 11

Manikan, Ruby EDUCATION, 14

Mansell, Nigel SPORT AND GAMES, 9

Mansfield, Katherine NAKEDNESS, 1; REGRET, 4; TRAVEL, 14

Mao Tse-Tung NUCLEAR WEAPONS, 9; READING, 4

Maradona, Diego FOOTBALL, 5; SPORT AND GAMES, 10

Marcuse, Herbert CAPITALISM, 7

Marguerite of Valois SCIENCE, 23

Marie-Antoinette HUNGER, 7

Marley, Bob FREEDOM, 16; MUSIC, 15; SATISFACTION, 4; WEALTH, 14

Marlowe, Christopher BEAUTY, 16; FLOWERS, 1; LOVE, 31

Marquis, Don IDEAS, 6; OPTIMISM, 14

Marvell, Andrew FLOWERS, 2; SHYNESS, 4

Marx, Groucho AGE, 25; APPEARANCE, 11; BED, 3; CHIVALRY, 3; CRITICISM, 8; DEATH, 29; DISMISSAL, 2; MEMORY, 4; NAMES, 2; POVERTY, 16; PUNS, 9; SEX, 33; SIMPLICITY, 3; STUPIDITY, 6; SUCCESS, 19; TIME, 19

Marx, Karl CAPITALISM, 8; CLASS, 12; HISTORY, 13; MARXISM, 3, 4, 5; PHILOSOPHERS, 4; RELIGION, 26

Maschwitz, Eric MEMORY, 5

Masefield, John BOATS, 6; SEA, 5

Maugham, W. Somerset ACTION, 6; ADULTERY, 4; CHARACTER, 6; CIVILIZATION, 5; CRITICISM, 9; DEATH, 30; DECISION, 2; ETIQUETTE, 2; EXPEDIENCY, 3; FUTURE, 9; HUMOUR, 12; IMPERTINENCE, 2; MANKIND, 14; MISANTHROPY, 1; OLD AGE, 20; PERFECTION, 2; PRUDERY, 1; PSYCHIATRY, 11; SENTIMENTALITY, 3; WOMEN, 29; WORK, 9; WRITING, 14

Maupin, Armistead HOMOSEXUALITY, 7

Mayakovsky, Vladimir ART, 13

Mead, Margaret CONSERVATION, 5; MEDIOCRITY, 4

Meir, Golda KILLING, 9; OLD AGE, 22

Melba, Nellie MUSIC, 16

Melbourne, Lord RELIGION, 27; ROYALTY, 24; SELF-CONFIDENCE, 2; SUPPORT, 2

Menander DEATH, 31

Mencken, H. L. ALCOHOL, 22; BUSINESS, 11; CONSCIENCE, 5; CONTRACEPTION, 4; CYNICISM, 2; FAITH, 5; GOVERNMENT, 11; IDEALISM, 4; IDEAS, 7; INTELLIGENCE, 3; MEDICINE, 12; POETRY, 19; PURITANISM, 3; RACISM, 12; SELF-RESPECT, 2; TOLERANCE, 4; WAR, 35

Mercer, Johnny EYES, 3; SUPERNATURAL, 2

Middleton, Thomas HONESTY, 2

Midler, Bette SEX, 34

Mill, John Stuart FEMINISM, 4; FREEDOM, 17; HAPPINESS, 8; STATE, 5; SUBJECTIVITY, 2

Mille, Cecil B. de CRITICS, 1

Miller, Arthur FUNERALS, 3; JOURNALISM, 2; MATERIALISM, 10; POPULARITY, 6; TRUTH, 19

Miller, Henry CLASSICS, 5; LIFE, 27

Milligan, Spike

Milne, A. A.

APPEARANCES, 12;
FAMILY, 14; WEALTH, 16
O'Neill, Eugene
LIFE, 30
Oppenheimer, J. Robert
NUCLEAR WEAPONS, 3;
SCIENTISTS, 3
Orczy, Baroness
ABSENCE, 4
Orton, Joe GOD, 12;
POLICE, 5; PROMIS-
CUITY, 4; TASTE, 4
Orwell, George AGE,
29; ATHEISM, 5;
AUTHORITARIANISM, 5;
CAPITALISM, 9; CLASS,
17; COWARDICE, 4; CRITI-
CISM, 10; EQUALITY, 13;
FREEDOM, 19; NOSTAL-
GIA, 6; OBESITY, 5; OP-
POSITES, 2; OPPRESSION,
5; PERFECTION, 3;
POWER, 10; SOCIALISM, 8;
WAR, 39; WEAPONS, 2
Osborne, John EDU-
CATION, 16; NEWS-
PAPERS, 6; NOSTALGIA, 7
Ouida CHRISTIANITY,
11; CRUELTY, 4
Ovid CORRUPTION, 5
Owen, Wilfred PATRI-
OTISM, 10; WORLD WAR I, 8
Palin, Michael
SUPERIORITY, 4
Palmer, Samuel
PAINTING, 6
Pankhurst, Christabel
PRIDE, 2; WOMEN, 34
Pankhurst, Emmeline
FEMINISM, 7
Parker, Charlie
MUSIC, 17
Parker, Dorothy AP-
PEARANCE, 12; BREVITY,
4; CONSERVATISM, 2;
DRINKS, 5; EXPECTA-
TION, 2; IGNORANCE, 6;

LOVE, 33; MONEY, 18;
PROMISCUITY, 5; PUNS,
12; QUOTATIONS, 5;
RACISM, 13; SEX, 40;
SUICIDE, 10; VIRTUE, 7
Parkinson, Cyril
MARRIAGE, 39; WORK, 10
Parris, Matthew
HOMOSEXUALITY, 9
Pascal, Blaise AP-
PEARANCE, 13; CREA-
TION, 7; MADNESS, 14;
PHILOSOPHERS, 5
Pavese, Cesare DEATH,
35; DISILLUSION, 4
Pavlova, Anna
SUCCESS, 15
Paz, Octavio
COMMERCIALISM, 3
Peabody, Elizabeth
PERCEPTION, 2
Peacock, Thomas Love
MARRIAGE, 40
Peel, Lord POLICE, 6
Penn, William FAMI-
LY, 15; GOVERNMENT, 14;
SUCCESS, 16
Pepys, Samuel BED, 4
Perelman, S. J.
DISEASE, 9; PUNS, 13
Pétain, Marshal
WORLD WAR II, 15
Peter, Laurence J.
INCOMPETENCE, 2;
PESSIMISM, 6; WORK, 11
Petronius Arbiter
DEATH, 8; DOGS, 6
Philip, Prince LAN-
GUAGE, 10; MARRIAGE,
41; MISTAKES, 7; ROY-
ALTY, 26; SELF-
RELIANCE, 5; WATER, 5
Phillips, Captain Mark
TITLES, 5
Picasso, Pablo ART,
15; INFERIORITY, 3; OLD

AGE, 23; PAINTING, 7;
WOMEN, 35; YOUTH, 10
Pindar REMEDIES, 12
Pinter, Harold CRICK-
ET, 6; METAPHYSICS, 3;
NOSTALGIA, 8
Pitt the Elder, William
POWER, 11; TYRANNY, 7
**Pitt the Younger,
William** NECESSITY, 4
Plath, Sylvia DEATH,
37; TIME, 20
Plato DEMOCRACY, 10;
GOOD, 5; ILLNESS, 12;
MATHEMATICS, 8; MIND,
9; PHILOSOPHERS, 5;
PROPAGANDA, 3; SEX, 41
Plautus YOUTH, 11
Pliny the Elder
ALCOHOL, 24; NOVELTY,
4; SUICIDE, 11
Polo, Marco LAST
WORDS, 31; PLACES, 9
Pope, Alexander AD-
MIRATION, 5; CHARAC-
TER, 7; CRITICISM, 11;
DEATH, 38; DOCTORS, 14;
DOGS, 7; EXPECTATION,
3; GOOD, 6; HOPE, 9;
KNOWLEDGE, 15; LOVE,
34; MISTAKES, 8;
MONARCHY, 7; ORDER, 1;
PRIDE, 3; SORROW, 11;
SUBJECTIVITY, 3
Popper, Karl DESTINY,
8; KNOWLEDGE, 16;
MYTHS, 1; SCIENCE, 26, 27
Porter, Cole LOVE, 35;
PARTIES, 3; TRAVEL, 18;
WEALTH, 17
Porter, George EN-
VIRONMENT, 5; WAR, 40
Potter, Dennis
RELIGION, 32
Potter, Stephen
ALCOHOL, 25; ONE-

DESIRE, 4; DOCTORS, 16;
DUTY, 4; ECONOMICS, 8;
EDUCATION, 20; FAMILY,
16; FASHION, 5; HAPPI-
NESS, 12; HEAVEN, 5;
LANGUAGE, 13; LON-
GEVITY, 7; MEDICINE, 15;
MONEY, 19; MORALITY,
8; NOVELS, 6; NOVELTY,
5; OLD AGE, 28; PARTIES,
4; PATRIOTISM, 12;
REPUTATION, 5; RULES,
3; SCIENCE, 30; SELF, 11;
SILENCE, 5; SOLDIERS, 4;
TASTE, 6; TEMPTATION,
5; TRUTH, 21, 22; VICE, 5;
VICTORY, 12; VIOLENCE,
10; WAR, 53; WAR AND
PEACE, 7; WEALTH, 18

Shelley, Percy Bysshe
CONVERSATION, 6;
DEATH, 43; DEVIL, 7;
HELL, 4; MARRIAGE, 47;
SEASONS, 5; WEATHER, 9

Sheridan, Richard AL-
COHOL, 30; APOLOGIES,
4; MALAPROPISMS, 3, 4, 5

Sibelius, Jean
CRITICS, 5

Simon, Neil
MEDICINE, 16

Sitwell, Edith APPEAR-
ANCE, 15; POETRY, 21

Sitwell, Osbert AR-
CHITECTURE, 9; TIME, 28

Smith, Adam BUSI-
NESS, 16; OSTENTATION,
3; SCIENCE, 31; TAX-
ATION, 7; WEALTH, 19

Smith, Delia FOOD, 13

Smith, Logan ADVICE,
4; BOOKS, 21; DEATH, 44;
READING, 5; WEALTH, 20

Smith, Stevie
PLEASURE, 12

Smith, Sydney DEATH,
45; MINORITY, 2

Snow, C. P.
NASTINESS, 4

Socrates GOOD, 8;
LAST WORDS, 38; LIFE,
35; LUXURY, 3;
NATIONALITY, 4

Solon LAW, 13; VICE, 6

Solzhenitsyn, Alexander
COMMUNISM, 9; FREE-
DOM, 23; HAPPINESS, 13;
LYING, 12; NEWSPAPERS,
5; POWER, 12

Sophocles SLEEP, 12;
THEATRE, 6; WORLD-
WEARINESS, 5

Spark, Muriel COM-
MITMENT, 5; COMMU-
NISM, 10; IMPORTANCE,
3; PSYCHIATRY, 14

Spielberg, Steven
CINEMA, 13, 14

Spinoza, Benedict
DESIRE, 5; SOCIETY, 10

Spock, Benjamin
CHILDREN, 26; WAR, 55

Stalin, Joseph REVO-
LUTION, 8; STATE, 4

Stanley, Henry Morton
EXPLORATION, 4

Stein, Gertrude FAM-
ILIARITY, 3; WAR, 56

Stendhal NOVELS, 6

Stevenson, Adlai EN-
DURANCE, 6; FLATTERY,
5; FREEDOM, 24; LYING,
13; NUCLEAR WEAPONS,
13; POWER, 13; SUCCESS,
18; WORDS, 12

Stevenson, Robert Louis
ALCOHOL, 31; BOOKS, 22;
CONCEIT, 5; MARRIAGE,
49; MORALITY, 11;
POLITICS, 24; SEXES, 12;
SILENCE, 8; TRAVEL, 20

Stoppard, Tom ART, 17;
ARTISTS, 4; DEMOC-
RACY, 12; ETERNITY, 2;

JUSTICE, 11; LIFE, 36;
SCIENCE, 32; THEATRE,
9; WAR, 57

Stravinsky, Igor
CRITICS, 6; HASTE, 7;
MUSIC, 19

Strindberg, August
DOGS, 9

Swift, Jonathan
COURAGE, 10; DECLINE,
5; FLATTERY, 6; FOOD,
14; GENIUS, 3; PARA-
SITES, 2; PROMISES, 3;
SATIRE, 3; TAXATION, 8

Szasz, Thomas HAPPI-
NESS, 14; MADNESS, 18;
MEDICINE, 17; MOTIVE,
3; PSYCHIATRY, 16; PSY-
CHOLOGY, 8; RIGHT, 2

Szent-Györgyi, Albert
DISCOVERY, 8

Tacitus WAR, 58

Taylor, A. J. P. COM-
MUNISM, 11

Taylor, Elizabeth PA-
TIENCE, 10; SHYNESS, 5

Tebbitt, Norman
UNEMPLOYMENT, 4

Tennyson, Alfred, Lord
ACTION, 8; ARISTOC-
RACY, 9; DETERMINA-
TION, 6; DREAMS, 4;
ENEMIES, 6; INTEGRITY,
3; IRREVOCABILITY, 3;
MOURNING, 5; PRAYER,
4; SLEEP, 13; SORROW, 15;
TRANSIENCE, 4

Terence COURAGE, 11;
ORIGINALITY, 3

Teresa, Mother MEDIA,
6; POVERTY, 20

Terry, Ellen DIARIES, 3

**Thackeray, William
Makepeace** LOVE, 45;
MARRIAGE, 50; MONEY,
20; SERVILITY, 4;
SNOBBERY, 3